Poetics of Influence

For Constance Old
with all best wishes

Harold Bloom

Poetics of Influence

Harold Bloom

New and selected criticism

edited and with an introduction by

John Hollander

HENRY · R · SCHWAB

This is a Doberman Book
Published by Henry R. Schwab, Inc.
290 York Street
New Haven, Connecticut 06511

Hardcover: ISBN 0-939681-00-5
Paper: ISBN 0-939681-01-3

Design: Michael Ross/NeoScribe International
Printed in the United States of America

Portions of the Introduction appeared in *Poetry*, and permission to reprint
is acknowledged.

To Angelo Bartlett Giamatti

Contents

Introduction
John Hollander

From his earliest writing on Shelley down to the essay on his most
recently formulated concept of "facticity," Harold Bloom has
always been an antithetical critic. Whether the primary system
against which he was writing was the New Criticism, that heuristic *DISCOVERING*
ideology of Anglo-American literary modernism in which most of
us were nursed, or, whether at the present point of his career, he
is melodramatizing (or so it would have to appear to a theologian
of any seriousness) the originality of the so-called "J" author of the
Hebrew bible, he has always written against his teachers. If he
does so more radically now, it may be because he has moved forward to revise the lessons of his own earliest days, those of the rabbinic exegetes. The *matere* (I use the Middle-English word to *EXEGETICS – SCIENCE OF*
encompass the senses of topic, question and realm, as they *EXPOSITION /*
applied to the central "matter" of medieval fiction) of the evening *CRITICAL EX- PLATON*
of romanticism led his work into that of America and the morn-
ing of its imagination that arose from the European afternoon,
and finally to the dawn of poetry in Scripture, and to the interestingly problematic way in which Judaic thought has altered the
notion of text as radically as did the Fathers of the Christian
Church. The stance he has taken toward critical and interpretive
institutions is the same one he has sought to distinguish in the
relation of "strong" (or major) poets toward literary institutions,
whether built in synchrony or diachrony. His writing has drawn
the rage of writers of ephemeral verse ("drasty rhymers" for
Chaucer, "Tom Piper" for Spenser) and of professors of literature
who have no taste for Bloom's way of honoring greatness by con-

fronting it, and of their student apprentices who would rather, as
Robert Frost once put it, vote than think. His name is taken in
vain – both held up in detraction and dropped, in whatever dis-
eased form of praise names are dropped – by many who have
never read him with any care or intensity. Nobody who has read
much of, and thought about, the horde of French theories loosely
called "post-structural" will see in Bloom's work anything but
those theories' most implacable (but hardly imperturbable)
enemy. Indeed, associating him with a "deconstructionist school,"
or even mentioning him and Paul de Man in the same taxonomic
breath would be as touchingly naive as some genially garrulous
Anglican clergyman, ca.1635, comfily squatting in the middle of
his *via media*, referring to "You know, Calvin and Loyola and that
crowd." One might add that although Bloom appeared to invite
this sort of thing by publishing the essay called "The Breaking of
Form" in a book called *Deconstruction and Criticism*, it should have
been clear to any reader of the other three essays, by post-structuralist colleagues, in that volume that the "Criticism" of the title
was taken by Bloom as applying to him, and the "and" of same to
be a disjunctive "and on the other hand."

In any event, his work has disposed itself in so many different books that a collection of essays from various points in its history now looks to be extremely useful. The present volume is the
only selection of his writings in existence. It covers the entire
range of his work and at the same time makes available essays
never previously gathered. The selections from larger works are
chronologically arranged in Parts I and II; the self-contained
essays which follow in III conclude with three unpublished ones
which reflect his most recent and urgent concerns. I have provided some preliminary remarks to this *cento* or conflation of chapters of his books; but it is difficult, even in a considerable space, to
do justice to all the phases of his œuvre, and in the pages which
follow I have tried only to guide the reader through some basic
problems that that œuvre raises but does not trivially solve.

I

Bloom's somewhat prodigious career as an academic literary critic has both traced and influenced the current revision of the critical theories and version of literary history ordained by modernism. He has never really been interested in poetic language or formal structures, but in mythologies and the larger created presences of the primary imagination – in poetry as a prophetic and visionary mode. Starting out at the height of the establishment of new critical practice in university departments of English, he produced a study of *Shelley's Mythmaking* in 1959; it treated a still unapproved poet with an intellectual and rhetorical intensity which many modernist critics, on the one hand, and more traditional scholars of romanticism, on the other, found outrageous. Most of them attacked him as much for his use of concepts derived from Martin Buber (actually, they were more of an expository device than central to his reading of romantic poetry) as for the celebration of the visionary mode of Shelley's longer poems to which they were put. *The Visionary Company* (its title, characteristically quoting a modern American romantic, Hart Crane) appeared two years later. It gave a comprehensive view of English romantic poetry from Blake through Beddoes, Clare and Darley. In the course of readings which were not so much explications as redirections of the reader's critical consciousness (presumably educated to think romantic poetry rather like failed exposition: diffuse, inauthentically uncolloquial and weakly ironic), Bloom introduced many of the concerns which were to occupy him subsequently. Among these were the dialectics of nature and consciousness, of selfhood and the imagination's created forms, and the major theme which in a later essay he called "the internalization of quest romance." This involved the mature and post-renaissance transformation of the simple heroics of combat and trial (the domain of what Kierkegaard named the esthetic hero) into a rich mythology of imaginative quests for non-trivial questings, of erotic visions reaching beyond the eternal cycles of hungering and being fed up, of moral hopes for the transcendence of self-negating categories, and of that central quest which Freud chronicled in his tale of the family romance, the rejection by the young man of his real father leading to a search for his true one.

All this seemed to parallel very compellingly the successive ecclesiastic and theological internalizations, in the historical unfolding of protestant traditions implied in the promise made to Milton's Adam of "A paradise within thee, happier far." It led Bloom to trace a whole phase of literary history descending from Milton to subsequent English and American poets. Comprehending the different ways, for example, by which Blake and Wordsworth constituted themselves as Milton's followers (and their different modes of acknowledgment of this), Bloom's map of romantic tradition led through the second generation of poets, Keats and Shelley, to their respective Victorian descendants, Tennyson and Browning. His marginal warnings that the reciprocal followers in the next generation, Tennyson's unwitting stepson Eliot and Browning's Childe Pound, were a bit off the map of central poetic tradition, that modernism was a blocked romanticism rather than an escape from it, did little to make Bloom popular with critics schooled in the tradition of the new.

Nor were his warnings gentle. Bloom's manner was polemical, and his joy in propounding the antithetical almost unbounded. Following his *Blake's Apocalypse* (1963), a study of Yeats (1970) and a wide range of essays (collected in *The Ringers in the Tower* in 1971) extended his view of an expanded romanticism into the twentieth century, where Yeats and Wallace Stevens were the major poets for him. But Bloom's Yeats is not the canonical hero of modernist sensibility who shed his earlier romantic garbs to walk naked in a forest of symbols. Instead, the later poetry is read through the primary corpus of poems like *The Wanderings of Oisin,* with which previous Yeats criticism had been less than absorbed.

In the opening chapters of *Yeats,* Bloom sketched out a theory of poetic influence in order to correct what he felt were misreadings, and to explain the ways in which Blake, Shelley, Browning, and Pater must be adduced in interpreting Yeats' poetry.

They were needed, he argued, rather than the hermetic materials about which Yeats and some of his critics continually carried on, to translate the symbolic systems of his later poetry into a more general vision of the timeless imagination's interpenetration with human history. But the context of that sketch was still the domain of the literary historian and of the interpretive critic.

Like magicians, poets and prophets can seem to be of two minds about the source of their powers. At one moment authenticating an effect by claiming its descent from Houdini or Merlin, the illusionist may at the next boast of the utter novelty and originality of what his audience is about to see. So too the poet; he is alternately a creative bee, preserving in his honey a transformed fragrance which would otherwise die when its flowers withered, and an original spider, spinning his tapestry of necessary gossamer out of his own guts. Tradition, a line of masters and predecessors, can be for the creator a line-current into which he is plugged. It can be a hill from whose top he sees beyond, and rules over, what is on the plain below. Or it can be a dead yesterday entombed in the night just past and grandly canceled by the creative sun that is the originality of his magic or his skill, making it new, darkening the past into mere History.

But accreditation and disclaimers are all part of what a magician calls his patter, a distraction from the dexterity of his art, and nevertheless part of it. So too the poet's assertion of *originality* – whether in the older sense of the word (i.e. being in touch with the origin of power in the past through the stream of tradition), or in the modern one (i.e. of being one's own fountain). What he may say about his creative processes and their relation to the past may very well be part of his own patter, his own literature.

"Milton was the poetical son of Spenser," said John Dryden, "for we have our lineal descents and clans as well as other families. Spenser more than once insinuates that the soul of Chaucer was transfused into his body; and that he was begotten by him two hundred years after his decease. Milton has acknowledged to me that Spenser was his original...." Dryden, although not at the moment claiming Ben Jonson to be his own father, was never more serious. But hungry generations of the family of modern literary criticism and scholarship have contrived, in their various ways, to make light of Dryden's confession. Older, philological schools studying great works by building up a structure of literary history would condescend to its generality, and turn to tracing Milton's debts to the minor French protestant Du Bartas. The revisionary, modernist tradition of the so-called "new criticism," denying that the remark had much content, would content itself with considering the relation between metaphor and rhetorical stance in Dryden's prose style. The post-new-critical study of analogues and genres, masterfully and influentially derived by Northrop Frye from his own study of Blake, would be more concerned with defining the genre of patter, with charting Dryden's way of coming clean with the reader as itself a fictional mode, than with the happiness or unhappiness of poetic families. Nor would a mild, belle-lettristic impressionism do more than draw from a major poet and his work anecdotes about his literary aunts.

Bloom's brilliant and difficult book on the poetic imagination announced its intention not only to take seriously the poetic family, but to treat with an analogue of psychoanalytic respect its role in shaping the creative lives of its children. I say "an analogue" because although *The Anxiety of Influence* is in many ways a profoundly Freudian meditation on how great poets can stand being what they are and knowing what they know, it is very far from representing the reductive method of what is usually considered psychoanalytic literary criticism. Brooding over its understanding of how poetic tradition is far more complex than ceremonialized ancestor-worship, it uses what Freud called the family romance, and the fantasies about fathers it generates in sons, as a model for a study of the creative psyche, rather than as a substrate to which the life of the imaginations of great visionaries, like the little dreams and mistakes we all create, shall be reduced. It is a book fraught with paradoxes – wildly comprehensive, and yet quite short; evolving its theme, and yet aphoristic; making the art of poetic creation into something rather like an ultimate, apocalyptic critical reading of an ancestor poem, and yet maintaining that true criticism must itself be poetry. Based on a profound study of the various degrees of warmth or chill cast by the shadow of Milton over his English followers (and by Emerson's, whom Bloom reads as a kind of transmogrified Milton, over his American ones), this tense, experimental book owes some of its rhetorical modes and para-arguments to Germans – Schopenhauer and Nietzsche in particular – as well as to Kierkegaard, Emerson himself and Talmudic parable. It seemed wild and extremely erratic at the time of its appearance. But like Leo Strauss' *Persecution and the Art of Writing*, its central notions have so completely dissolved in contemporary responsible discourse that Bloom's younger detractors frequently employ concepts and unargued premises which were originally advanced in it.

    The Anxiety of Influence is neither a contribution to the literary history of the romantic movement, like those of Meyer Abrams or W.J. Bate, nor a theory of texts and language. It provides a myth of poetic creativity at a point close to the sources of self-assertion and questioning. Bloom is not concerned with inherited, borrowed or stolen aspects of style, rhetoric, form, convention, genre or even, here, mytho-poetic modes. Should these matters be thought of as occupying the second through the sixth days of the Creation of a poetic world, then Bloom's theory would be obsessed with the first day, almost unbelievably asking of the Word itself, "Why?" – not "How?" – and perhaps too shockingly, "Who do you think you are?"

    His mode of doing so is far from reductive. The book starts out with a prose poem about creation, and concludes with another about criticism's own quest. In between, a synoptic introduction sets out the six "ratios," or relations between a major poet's work and that of his predecessors, each of which forms the basis for one of the book's six central essays. A reader will look in vain for such simple archetypal patterns as the killing of a priest-king by a rising poetic ephebe, or its anecdotal burlesques such as Norman Mailer, say, boxing with the shadow of Hemingway. (Bloom is not concerned with prose fiction, although his kind of relationship might be that of Cervantes to eighteenth-century English fiction, or Balzac to Proust, who flourished in his shadow). Some readers are still put off by Bloom's mythology – of a covering cherub, for example, as the angelic presence of a poetic predecessor working as a blocking-agent. His ratios include such concepts as a swerve away from a forerunner in a corrective reading of the prior poet, fulfilled by a rewriting of part of his work in the new poem. *Tessera,* or antithetical completion of a precursor poem, *kenosis,* or a reaction-formation of discontinuity with it, an *askesis* or working fiction of self-sufficiency and origination – these are among the relations, acted out in misreadings and rewritings, over which Bloom broods. Their names are drawn from such Greek sources as ritual patterns treated by E.R. Dodds in *The Greeks and the Irrational.*

A strange, aphoristic little "interchapter" operates like a set of critical Proverbs of Hell. Strategically placed between the third and fourth essays, they are witty and outrageous (where, out of context, they would be merely impossible). Thus, treating a poem not as an utterance in a language, a use or modulation of a formal convention, or an embodiment of a historical moment, but as *a state of anxiety about not having invented itself,* Bloom can say: "A poem is a poet's melancholy at his lack of priority. The failure to have begotten oneself is not the cause of the poem, for poems arise out of the illusion of freedom, out of a sense of priority being possible. But the poem – unlike the mind in creation – is a made thing, and as such is an achieved anxiety." For such a view, implying that the meaning of a poem can only be another poem, rhetorical criticism, even in the sophisticated form of the most modish structuralism, must remain not false, not exactly irrelevant, but profoundly uninteresting.

What Bloom had written, in fact, was an anatomy of critical melancholy, of criticism as itself a romantic creation in a state of Angst at its own secondariness to poetry. The dialectic of precursorship, if his poetic is to be believed, must not stop with poets themselves. *The Anxiety of Influence* is a melodramatically self-limiting book (in the mode of the last aphorisms of Wittgenstein's

Tractatus), exemplifying in extreme form its own remark that
"There are no interpretations but only misinterpretations, and so
all criticism is prose poetry." It exhibits its own revisionary ratios
with respect to its various precursors: *askesis* from the teaching of
its surprising dedicatee, the late W.K. Wimsatt, who may have felt
that his sleep of reason had produced a monster; a complex rereading and completion of Northrop Frye. Bloom's book can
probably be useful only through being mis-taken itself, although
not reductively so – industrious genealogists who try overly to
literalize the book's own heuristic myths will end up with dry
trees. Frye's *Anatomy of Criticism* was prone to dangerous misuses:
the perpetual calendar on which he mapped types and genres was
crudely rejected or, with equal ignorance, busily applied, as practical criticism, rather than being understood as providing an
enabling study of the deep nature of convention. Perhaps it was a
nervous swerve away from this lee shore which led Bloom to
adopt gnomic Greek names for his ratios, each of which,
undoubtedly, could be the subject of a discursive book.

Subsequent scholars may or may not attempt such projects,
but Bloom has in any case protected himself from betrayal by a
school of followers. It is not only the difficulty of the book (and
throughout, Bloom would rather be inaccessible than cheap).
The first two chapters would be most widely read and perhaps
applied. The others, full of allusion, echo, quotation and indirec-
tion, get progressively more difficult and look less and less like
critical theory. Finally, the last one, on the spooky way in which
parts of a great poetic *œuvre* can seem to have been written by
their progeny, may have had the greatest consequences for
Bloom's subsequent notion of transumption. One quickly heard
the outraged cries of poets denying that Bloom's domain of anxiety applies to their creativity – *they* don't feel anything like that! – at
which he might grimly observe that it is a wise poetic child that
knows its own father. While his field of forces and motions –
reaching, falling, turning, running, hiding, wrestling – is not to
be identified with the Freudian Unconscious, it might be added
that such protestations sounded like the righteous denials of its

unapplicability to *their* lives by early twentieth-century Viennese physicians.

Bloom's final chapter also extends a line of descent in American literature, from Emerson to Whitman to Stevens, down to our contemporaries A. R. Ammons and John Ashbery. Indeed, *The Anxiety of Influence* could have been read as a prolegomenon to a new study of America. Milton's Satan, whom Bloom invokes at the outset of his study as a type of the modern poet in his relation to a godlike predecessor and disavowed creator, might be made to stand as well for a type of Emersonian vision. In Book IX of *Paradise Lost*, struck with the beauty of the garden he is about to blast, Satan makes the shocking but touching mistake America has from its dawn of conscience made about itself: "O Earth, how like to Heaven," he says "if not preferred/More justly. Seat worthier of Gods, as built/With second thoughts, reforming what was old!/For what God after better worse would build?" (as if Eden, made after Heaven, were Mark II). The American Imagination has placed itself, in the intricacies of what Henry James called "the complex fate," in Bloomian ratios both to its European father and its aboriginal mother. The next major study of American literature, of the order of Perry Miller's and F. O. Matthiesson's, might well come from just such an understanding of post-Miltonic creativity, a poetic of secondariness.

II

In *The Anxiety of Influence*, Bloom sought to reinterpret the idea of poetic tradition as it has been most widely received. Going beyond Northrop Frye's introduction to the notion that the formation of literary canons is as much part of the res of literature as the composing of texts, Bloom believed tradition to be internalized in the psyche of each major (or, as he calls it, "strong") poet. Instead of a mere conscious acknowledgment of great formal or thematic predecessors, a profound and pervasive deliberateness, operating at many levels of consciousness and avowal, commits the poet to a total stance or attitude toward his precursors. The taxonomies of parental relationships have been mapped both by depth psychology and novelists and dramatists, all seeming to be on firmest ground when that ground has been shared. Bloom sought, in his offerings of six revisionary ratios, as he called them, to open up the question of the family romance of poetic influence; and while fleeing always such models and systems as those of taxonomy, he introduced a series of archetypal patterns to represent these ratios of continuing, completing, fulfilling, reconstituting, opposing, abstracting, spiritualizing, and so forth, the presences of creative forbears. The archetypes went far beyond those employed by Frye in his *Anatomy of Criticism* (which, in the long run, turned out to have been heuristic devices for presenting a kind of neo-Kantian theory of the naturalness of convention); they were at once text, poem, image and model, named and formulated powerfully but often enigmatically.

Even in the first of these, the *clinamen* or swerve which Bloom borrowed from Lucretius, can be seen as a type of the others. His text is *Paradise Lost,* Books I and II; his reading of Satan's fall is conditioned by the Lucretian swerve of atoms dropping through the void, which swerve constitutes the peculiar randomness which is all that, for the atomist, can lead out of the chaos of mere (and, in fact, ordered) dropping to eventual fortuitous concourses – to structures, in fact. Bloom's ratios are the varied positions of freedom; *Paradise Lost* is a central text for teaching the relation of true position to movingly, tragically false gesture; but it was not surprising that many writers with an innocence of dialectic were unable to read Bloom's analysis of the relations between the living and the dead as anything but a mechanistic and narrowed determinism.

If the previous book was mainly about freedom, its theory, practice, and illusory life, Bloom's new *A Map of Misreading* was, as I shall suggest later, profoundly about lying. Its central trope or image is that of *misreading,* a general figure for the way in which all the stances or ratios manifest themselves in textual practice, in the realm of reading, rewriting, interpreting, and reconstructing the texts of predecessors, rather than the previously expounded

realm of their presences as forces, and as total *œuvres*. Misreading
or poetic misprision is for Bloom's new book the central poetic
act. It becomes so powerful a notion that it must be considered
not merely as what one text does to a previous one, but as what
poetic texts do to "ordinary" language (thus engaging the whole
theory of rhetoric in its concern with literalness and transfer of
meaning) and as what linguistic tradition does to language itself.
In its way, this book is an introduction to a kind of diachronic
rhetoric which has not yet been studied. And yet its method is
itself so figurative, and its basic text so far removed from the ordinary reader's experience (as compared, say, with the fallen
Satan's relation to God as a type of the modern poet vis-à-vis the
romantic), that one may be put off in one of two ways. The reader
may either be confounded by the use to which Bloom at this stage
put concepts from the body of para-Rabbinic thought known generally as Kabbalah, or, at best, he may assume that they are being
used, like Frye's seasonal and other cyclical myths, as heuristic
devices. In addition, this new book's insistence on an essential
relation of revisionary ratios, the psychic defenses of Freudian psychology, and the tropes and figures of classical literary rhetoric,
may prove initially perplexing. It uses such a relation to map the
misprisionings of literary history, but there is no clear key in the
lower right-hand corner, as it were; the key is part of the map
itself.

This is all the more difficult since the later chapters of the
book are indeed examples of practical criticism of a strange but
palpable sort; taking Milton, for English poetry, and Emerson, for
American poetry, as continental divides, they trace the course of
rivers of influence with a precision and a force which *The Anxiety
of Influence* gave to its central thesis, and to assimilations of
Nietzsche and Emerson which bear fruit in the present volume.
Then, too, there is a fine chapter on the "Dialectics of Poetic
Tradition", connecting in a passionate way the common work of
poets, scholiasts, and teachers; quite independently of its role in
the book, it stands as a necessary manifesto for the present period
of the decline of the text and the rise of a new barbarism. The vol-

ume also makes clear, despite its greater surface difficulty, some of
the central notions of the earlier one. In this new context,
Bloom's notion of a "strong" poet emerges as in such a way as to
suggest more immediately that poetic greatness consists in the
ability to be influenced by great poets – to misconstrue them in a
way their greatness merits (not, therefore, a reductive diminish-
ing). Weaker poets have as ancestors styles and modes, rather
than powerful parental figures. The great anomaly here is probably Milton's magnificent contemporary Andrew Marvell, who
seems to exhibit all but ultimate strength, but who yet derived
from a seeming babble of contemporary French and English voices not quite like his own. In any event, Marvell's major subject of
retirement (*chez* Fairfax, perhaps, but shaded surely from the light
of Milton's sun to which he was more exposed than other contemporaries) might be seen by Bloom as an evasion, brilliant, systemat-
atic, and tactful, of greatness. (If, as Geoffrey Hartman has shown
us, *The Nymph Complaining* is a kind of misprision of a mode of
allegorizing and, as I believe, that strange poem, *The Unfortunate
Lover*, wryly personifies English Petrarchism, surely *Upon Appleton
House,* a substitute for a major poem, anticipates in some way the
quest for successful failure which Bloom delineates in the second
of his readings of *Childe Roland to the Dark Tower Came* of
Browning, a touchstone for his method in this book. Another
problematic pre-Miltonic figure for Bloom must be Spenser. The
patron knights of *The Faerie Queene,* each one dreaming the region
of the poem for which his moral condition is the pattern, are all
types of the strong poet, emanating from greatness (Arthur) and
serving an absented Gloriana, or the muse of light. It is significant
that, for a theory of genres like Frye's, Spenser's *Epithalamion* is a
central poem in the history of lyric: it imports other genres
(masque-like processional, etc.), adapts and transfers verse form,
and makes the bridegroom the singer of the song "made in lieu of
many ornaments". For Bloom in this book, the problematic
Spenserian poem is the somewhat neglected *Prothalamion,* in
which the poetic intentions of the more conventionally external
singer of the "spousall verse" are connected with the flow of elo-

quence, patronage, power, fame and the course of ambition. For
Bloom's antithetical criticism – which in one sense completes
Kenneth Burke by being both a dialectic, and a diachronic, of
motives – it is the later, shorter poem which is the true precursor
of *Lycidas*.

A word should be said here about the use of Kabbalah in *A
Map of Misreading*. In a lucid and powerful essay on Gershom
Scholem's *Kabbalah* (which became the first chapter of *Kabbalah
and Criticism*, but which should, I feel, have appeared as an
appendix, or even attached to a preface to *A Map*), Bloom outlined some elements of Kabbalistic tradition which he felt might
have some relevance for his theories of creativity and its relation
to literary history. These included such matters as the essential
secondariness or belatedness of Kabbalistic thought and, particularly of the thirteenth-century book called the *Zohar*, the internal
structure of Kabbalistic tradition, with its – for him – characteristic secondary phase of Lurianic doctrine (sixteenth-century
Palestinian, rather than medieval Spanish in place of origin); the
exemplary character of the body of Kabbalah itself as a model for
a neoteric, or "modern," literary work (in some ways, a revision
of the objectification by Curtius of Latin tradition in medieval
Europe); and, finally, the reinterpretation of Creative Process in
the Kabbalistic reading of the book of Genesis. This last is most
important for Bloom. Milton had interpreted poetic creativity at
its most ambitious as being given energy by a force which – as he
invoked it – "with mighty wings outspread / Dove-like satst brooding on the vast Abyss / And mad'st it pregnant." For the post-Miltonic realm of belated or modern poetry, Bloom also turns to an
association of Creation with creativity, but the account he chooses
is the complex and dialectical one of Kabbalah, which might most
generally be described as comprising three phases: a kind of withdrawal or contraction (an ultimate spiritual *reculer pour mieux
sauter*), a phase of destruction or smashing of elements objectified
during the process itself, and a final stage of restriction.

To most readers, "Kabbalah" suggests magical numerology,
dusty theosophy, forbidden mysteries and the shelves of second-
hand bookstores that used to be labeled "Occult." The history of
this alternative, counter- and antithetical-Tradition, from before

thirteenth-century Spain and the book called the *Zohar*, through its reinterpretation in sixteenth-century Palestine by Moses Cordovero and Isaac Luria, has been profoundly and elegantly explored by Gershom Scholem throughout his works. Bloom's penetrating review of Scholem's book suggested that some of the strange concepts of Kabbalistic theology (such as the relations of emanations of divinity to the Godhead itself) could be useful for a totally naturalistic theory of figurative truth. Then, in a provocative little book which appeared shortly after *A Map of Misreading*, he explored this connection much further. But because this exploration is the evident tip of a submerged textual iceberg, it might be useful to consider the importance of Kabbalah for the author's entire critical theory. Controversial, somewhat misshapen and only partly understood, it has nevertheless contributed significantly to discussions of the ways in which reading what we might think of as our secular Scriptures can become more than academic, scholastic exercises.

Such a scheme would have been problematic enough, and provided sufficient material for discussion of how to apply it to the reading of – or rather *through* – major English poetry, for years to come. But Bloom went dangerously further, and sought to map his series of basic poetic devices in a more general domain of the human psyche. This last stage of relation for him was between tropes and Freudian defenses, which he systematically connected. Put very simply, this is like saying that fictions *are*, after all, like lies (the kind we tell ourselves, for example), that non-literal assertions are like the equivocations by and with which we live and keep sane (even though they must often needs be broken down in the care of illness). The title of his subsequent *Poetry and Repression*, which studied instances of poetic revisionism from Blake to Wallace Stevens, put this association with an almost polemical clarity.

The peculiar function of Bloom's little book on Kabbalah was to reinforce this connection between trope and psychic defense. By analyzing the violent and grotesque phases of Creation as poetically treated in the *Zohar* and, with important

HAMITO - SEMITIC
SEMITIC   ASSYRIAN
  AKKADIAN - BABYLONIAN   HAMITIC
  CANAANITE - HEBREW   EGYPTIAN - EGYPT   CHAD
  ARAMAIC - BIBLICAL - PALESTINIAN   COPTIC   HAUSA
  ARABIC · CLASSICAL ARABIC   BERBER - LIBYA   ANGUS
    ETHIOPIC · ABYSSINIAN   CUSHITIC · SOMALI

revisions, centuries afterward by the Safed Kabbalists, he found a
basic rhythm of contraction, filling and breaking, and restitution,
which he rushed to diagram into his prior schemata as areas of
what he termed limitation, substitution and representation.
Kabbalah and Criticism provides a genetic link between the exemplary phenomenon of Kabbalah as a *model* for all neoteric, or
modern (as opposed to classical) literatures, and a theory of the
poetic imagination which employs Kabbalah's own concepts of
withdrawing from linguistic signification (or, indeed from truth),
filling it with meaning (as an effusion of will, of intending to
utter) to overflowing, and a final restitution of meaning in a transformed significance.

   Bloom's concerns with belatedness, with the struggle with
prior greatness as the only mode of approaching greatness, gave
such a text as the *Zohar* a heavy explanatory value for him, had he
cared to use it to explain. A view of literary history which implicitly embraces a model of prophecy and fulfillment (*e.g.* classical
antiquity and then the Renaissance), also can be implicitly said to
depend upon a bi-Testamentary model (the New redeeming and
giving full meaning to the Old). The *Zohar,* written in medieval
Spain, in Aramaic (rather than in Hebrew, Spanish or even
Arabic), is obsessed with its own *modernity,* coming after Scripture,
after rabbinic tradition, even after Christianity. For Bloom, this
essential Kabbalistic work is a better figure for all modernisms of
various sorts throughout Western literary history than the bi-
Testamentary one (which he might – although perhaps I assume
too much – associate with the rhetorical criticism of Northrop
Frye).

   But the *Zohar* is in good part a violently anti-traditional
interpretation of the Creation sections of *Genesis.* Bloom, who
knows how central a figure for major poetry's sense of its own origins was the Great Creating Word of *Genesis* (*e.g.* Milton's association of Creation with creating poems) was quick to observe that a
belated version of the Origin would revise the traditional account
by starting out with a Divine presence that filled everything, and
therefore had to contract, withdraw, make room for Something,

by providing a Nothing to be filled. The relation between this mythology, as it were, and the psychology of composition – the sense of originality (which has changed, in the last century, to one of being one's own source, rather than close to The Source), to the actual manifestation of these matters in the ways in which poems say one thing and mean another – was becoming the subject of his work.

Kabbalah and Criticism contains three essays. The first is an account of the work of Gershom Scholem; it was in some ways the most lucid thing Bloom had written in years, in that it does not eschew explanation. Properly speaking, it cannot be considered part of his œuvre, which the final essay, "The Necessity of Misreading," maintains quite baldly what he has said elsewhere in his writings: "A theory *of* poetry must belong *to* poetry, must *be* poetry, before it can be of any use in interpreting poems." This is so palpably not what people who interpret poems believe, that some other sense must be made of "interpreting." That this sense is deeply Freudian, rather than, as it were, novelistic, created difficulties for Bloom's theory, and more than one sympathetic reader of his works observed that Bloom's "Necessity of Misreading" (the title of his third essay), itself calls for a kind of misreading if it is to be used in "interpreting" (in the usual sense) poems at all. Bloom himself hints at this. The condensed, often wild, frequently humorous and good natured tone of this little book (particularly at moments when he is acknowledging the manifest outrageousness of one of his own statements) helped to make some of its difficulties easier to get by. Bloomian "misreading" was indeed creative interpreting, and this book an excellent introduction to what it can and cannot do (I would cite, for example, the brilliant page and a half on Wallace Stevens's "Anecdote of the Jar" in the book, *Kabbalah and Criticism*.) Despite the eccentricity of the material of Kabbalah itself, the book's misprision of it lines it up with the central concerns of the intersecting studies of Tradition and Creation Anew, within which every important poem creates a new wonder.

The theoretical sections of *A Map of Misreading*, then, adduce this Kabbalistic sequence of phases to generate a compli-

cated paradigm, in which stances of the poetic psyche, the poetic
intention, and the poetic language are juxtaposed and connected.
The historical use of the Kabbalistic model might have been high-
lighted more had Bloom chosen to discuss even briefly some of
the implicit models he was replacing. Thus, traditional literary
history has always understood how the *Aeneid* was a quintessential
literary poem, flourishing its Homeric predecessors (*arma
virumque* taken as "*Iliad* and *Odyssey*"): in *The Anxiety of Influence* he
suggested that such flourishing – perhaps even brandishing –
might possibly be a reaction-formation. Contemporary writers of
verse, who objected that Bloom was condemning an inherent
weakness in all great poetry, could not see that he was also anato-
mizing the sinews of its strength. Another implicit model for the
old and the new in tradition is that of the two testaments. The
Hebrew Bible is complete in itself, and its life is sustained and
watered by ongoing commentary; the Old Testament is the New
Testament's misprision, or mode of persuasively reading, the
Hebrew Bible. The Old Testament is completed and fulfilled by
the neoteric text, but the modern work has, in fact, invented its
predecessor. So, perhaps, with the Antiquity of Renaissance
humanism. And so forth.

But Bloom thrusts into the midst of things, and presents us
with some of his ultimate concerns even as he explores the phenomena which lead him to them. He is devoted – like, indeed, a
number of other modern literary theoreticians with whom he is
in deep disagreement on other matters – to the central problem
of the formation of secular canons throughout history. He is also
interested, as I have mentioned before, in truth-telling. Other
writers of very different sorts have touched on some of his area of
interest here (Leo Strauss in *Persecution and the Art of Writing*, perhaps, and certainly Stanley Cavell, in his observations on knowing
the truth and being afraid to tell it, in connection with Wittgenstein's way of writing). He constantly raises the question, too,
about the continuity of human discourse. The very difficulty –
some of it maddening – of his own method of presentation and its
tendency to eschew explanation makes us wonder whether a system of discourse (poetry, criticism) which finds strength in eva-

sion is not doomed to some kind of total human failure. Or, perhaps, assured of a certain success, in being the authentic record
of that failure and thereby a model of authenticity. For an orthodox Christian like John Donne, the evasions of the truth found in
figure or trope were a breaking of the husk of letter to release the
seeds of light; he could joke in passages in his sermons about how
God's loving joke with the world was, in a way, one vast trope. Not
so for his more evasively protestant ephebe George Herbert, for
whom the sense of displacement in figurative language was always
there, and who wrestled against metaphor with metaphors, the
only arms he could command.

There is no doubt that Bloom's study of evasion is itself evasive; but I do not wish myself to map his own evasions here, nor to
expound the paradigms and schemata of his relations between
psychology and rhetoric. Instead, I should like to consider for a
moment his idea of misprision, and then to explore in greater
detail the consequences of Bloom's theories of poetic language,
particularly his concern with trope, for the critical and creative
processes both.

III

Misprision: the term can refer to anything from treason, malfea-
sance in office, wrongful capture, through mistake to scorn or
misprizing. These all mean being wrong. The larger sense is mis-
taking. While we know poetry to be making, Bloom reminds us of
the rhyming processes which are needed to expand the concept –
where the potter's wheel is too trivial a model to account for more
than work habits in the production of manuscript – of *breaking*
and *taking.* By this he does not mean merely taking-away-from (viz.
the relative triviality of Eliot's notion that great writers steal, for
only paradigms like "plots" can be taken in that sense); there are
also taking in, taking out (e.g. an opposing lineman), taking on,
up, over, down, to; there are under- and over-taking, and, ultimately, the sum of these in mistaking itself: the misprision of the
prior body of text leads to the operation of all these processes in

the generation of a new one. The use of "misprision" which most significantly anticipates Bloom's is, strangely enough, to be found in Scott Fitzgerald, in the last sentence of the opening paragraph of "The Rich Boy" (I quote the entire passage; it seems more and more to read like a Bloomian paradigm of the writing not of novels, but of criticism):

> Begin with an individual, and before you know it you find that you have created a type; begin with a type, and you find that you have created – nothing. That is because we are all queer fish, queerer behind our faces and voices than we want any one to know or than we know ourselves. When I hear a man proclaiming himself an "average, honest, open fellow," I feel pretty sure that he has some definite and perhaps terrible abnormality which he has agreed to conceal – and his protestation of being average and honest and open is his way of reminding himself of his misprision.

In this last sentence an aspect of self is treated as if it were a text, the purer dialectic of Freud's reaction-formation is interestingly revised, and that most authorial of moves invoked by the phrase "he has agreed to conceal" ("agreed"? and with whom?) slips casually but resonantly by. For a novelist, the ways in which persons make representations of, and to, themselves are a matter of great importance. Similarly for Bloom, mis-taking is central to the workings of the imagination: it is almost as if it alone were the correct, because non-literal, translation of *poesis*. Poetic theories which would as it were rhyme *making* with *shaking, faking* or *waking* would for Bloom only correctly represent the creation of false poetry, or falsely represent the generation of the true.

At the textual level, and thus framed by the view of literary history, misprision is represented by misreading, and Bloom's interest in the family romance of poetic authority and authorship in *The Anxiety of Influence,* manifested in a study of stances, or turns of position toward a predecessor, shifts in the new book to a study of alterations of another sort. Tropes, or turns that occur between the meanings of intention and the significances of linguistic utterances, are twisted through the plane of truth while yet all the more strongly connecting the will and the text which it flies like a flag "as it fitfully gleams, half-conceals, half-discloses" the impulses which raise it. Whereas formalist criticisms have concerned themselves with the trope in the text alone, Bloom's sees this kind of study as two-dimensional and paradigmatic at best. For him, a trope is a twisted strand of transformational process, anchored deep in a rock of expressive need, and stretched upward, taut, to a connection at the surface with a flat sheet of text. Formalist and structuralist readings would be like more or less detailed plans of the textual surface, affording a view of the end-section only of the tropical rope. Bloom is concerned with the length of the rope, the layers of whatever it is through which it passes, the ways in which, at any particular level, the strands may seem in their twisting to be pointing away from the determined direction upward, the relative degrees of tension and slackness and so forth. His is the most recent manifestation in a strange history of troping the concept of trope itself.

This might be said to start with the classical rhetoricians' presently unhelpful distinctions between figures of thought and of speech, such a distinction itself being, after all, figurative; the very notion of the non-literal that they implicitly employed contains the seeds of subsequent metaphor. Bloom himself observes Vico's concern for the atomic quality of four basic figures – irony, metaphor, synecdoche, metonymy – and although he does not choose to expound their relation for Vico, he sees their identification as a precursor of Kenneth Burke's rather astonishing essay on "Four Master Tropes," where metaphor is seen in terms of perspective, metonymy of reduction, synecdoche as representation, and irony as dialectic or dramatic. For Bloom a trope is not a figure of speech, nor of thought; it is not a mode of not being literal. In his concern for the schematic and deep connections between stances toward a predecessor, stances taken by utterance itself against what one means to say, stances taken by what one means to say against what the unconscious means for one to mean, and so forth, he has undertaken to deal with a concept of trope far more general than that of the rhetorician. Operating in the realm in which the relation between realities and superstructures (Freudian, Marxian), between source and manifestation usually seeks to reduce the latter to the former, he has propounded a kind of opening unscientific preface to a quest in these dialectical regions. Seeing the war for authenticity and finality between surface (text) and depths (intentions variously clear and dark) as a true struggle of contraries, Bloom has to regard reductive (and thereby traditional) uses of the concept of trope as part of, rather than interpretive of, the struggle. In short, for Bloom *trope is a figure of will.* And whether the will is an intention avowed, avowable, knowable, bearable, or not, is itself a matter, for him, of trope; for these terms (manifest vs. latent, conscious or unconscious, superficial or deep, etc.) are themselves all figures for the different kinds of responsibility we take, verbally, for our acts of awareness and of utterance.

Bloom's own major misprision in this branch of his critical theory may perhaps be an intricate mis-taking not only of rhetorical concepts, but of the use to which they were naively or sentimentally put by his formalist predecessors. For example, the late R. P. Blackmur would aften argue from trope to ontology: thus, not content with the easy truism that in an oxymoron, say, self-contradiction to the point of meaninglessness, is avoided by the non-literalness of either or both of the terms, (or at a minimum, by a transfer of meaning to a level at which they are not, in fact, opposites) he must in one essay inflate a commonplace device into a figure of *enantiosis.* Blackmur describes this, with a kind of pseudo-philosophic melodrama, as "that shocked condition in which a thing becomes its own opposite." Some of the difficulties readers may have with Bloom's theory of trope may result from their not being able to distinguish its strangeness from this sort of nonsense.

Or, again: John Crowe Ransom cared primarily to distinguish between metaphor and simile, associating the former with his kind of strong poetry (metaphysical and modern), and the latter with what he felt to be the tonal (and moral?) weakness of romantic diction. Yet, from the Bloomian position, irony is the basic trope both of modernist poetic and the critical theories which clustered about it. In its ambiance, for example, there flourishes the modernist mock-heroic so supremely manifested in *The Waste Land,* where the essential relation "past:present" is eternal bathos. For Bloom, at any rate, all this would account for the successes of formalist reading being limited to the domain of *tone.* – Except, of course, when applied to the parental nineteenth-century: two essential dogmas of modernist poetry are the primary authenticity of the speaking voice over the mediations of the written (Catullus over Horace; Donne over Milton) and the peculiar inability or refusal to confront the sexuality of romantic tradition (the inability to contemplate parental sex?). These merge in a preference for the ironies of wit to the ironies of dialectical vision.

Of course, irony can be seen in a reductive reading of trope itself. For by what process is troping revealed? The plangent and useful synecdoches of euphemism need the debunking that only irony raised to its height, sharpened to its finest point in satire, can give. Thus Mercutio the mocker denounces in essence the evasions of the major Petrarchan synecdoches, or the trope of the heart for the hole.

Bloom implicitly reminds us that political boundaries drawn among the "natural" configurations of trope can reveal some meta-rhetorical purpose (indeed, his strategy is somewhat like Nietzsche's insistence that even logical and metaphysical systems are produced from deep, if unavowed, moral intentions). We might casually observe that the structuralists, following Roman Jakobson, assimilate metonymy and synecdoche (as allotropic forms, as it were) and contrast them with metaphor. The latter is a figure of absence, in that the transfer of meaning occasions a removal; the combined metonymy-synecdoche clutches on to, keeps hold of, the hand or even the coattail of the literal. Both Vico and Burke clearly differentiate between metonymy and synecdoche although in the latter case there seems to be a considerable area of overlap. But it is revealing that in Bloom's mapping of tropes, images in the poem, revisionary ratios describing the stances of influence, and, ultimately, the psychic defenses of depth psychology, new relations among the tropes occur. In his mapping, irony and synecdoche are associated, metonymy and hyperbole (and its opposite mode, litotes), and metaphor and metalepsis: but the connections are dynamic ones and not merely paradigmatic. In the unfolding of creative process derived from Kabbalah, Bloom charts three stages of limitation, substitution, and representation, and the pairs of tropes start and end the sequence of stages.

Perhaps the animation of paradigms into processes will be more clearly invoked by an example. Metamorphosis may be taken as animated trope: "x-into-y" is a heuristic dramatization, among other things, of the x-y ratio or analogy. Thus, consider: girl-into-bird; coach-back-into-pumpkin; now-into-then; jovial-god-into-bull, into-gold; beauty-into-hag; even, stones-*not*-into-bread. Select one, say Ulysses-into-fox, and ask, "Is this the unfolding of a metaphor? Of a metonymy? Or even of a synecdoche?" (Ulysses being the man of many tropes, perhaps the foxiness inhered and the mechanism was simply Ulysses' foxiness-into-itself). . . . The question, as Alexander Bryan Johnson remarked when asking whether the sound was part of the thunder, only embarrasses.

The Dantean ratio, in *Hell,* of punishment to crime is another case which, like that of metamorphosis, puzzles the taxonomist of trope. One might also consider in this connection the juxtaposition of any thing or event with (a) its "essence"; (b) any schema or representation of it; even, (c) its cause or effect. All these relations become tropes for a theory like Bloom's; perhaps his consignment of scientific propositions and the philosophical speculation surrounding and protecting them to the realm of reduction is itself a reductive act. But science admits of no reductions, and thus would and could not defend itself from such a charge. Or again, this extended theory of trope might go so far as to imply that all statements of identity (as opposed to those of predication, some of which might be considered literal) are figurative, *that all is trope save in games.* Science would thus be a game in which, the rules being followed, one can predict what will satisfy the players in the way of truth. In life, and therefore in life as represented tropically, there are no rules, and few satisfactions. Truth is, like life, always in process of yielding up her nakedness, nay, even her insides.

For truth is, here, of the essence. One can begin to see the relation between rhetoric and psychology in Bloom's model (and, by the way, its own rhetoric purports to deny, like an eighteenth-century fiction, that it *is* a model – but further deconstruction seems unnecessary) by considering such processes as a simple Freudian reaction-formation or a manifestation of behavior or even a report of a feeling as a sarcasm of the will. (Complexes might then be thought of as the spirit's ironies, worked in the letter of feeling, belief, and action.) Bloom adds to the basic repertory of tropes hyperbole. For the rhetorician, uninterested in Truth and Falsehood, the old Over-reacher, the too-much-of-a muchness, is rather trivial in the power it gains from its alteration. But it is crucial when hyperbole is taken as an assertion of will: for the rhetorician, hyperbole's kind of lying seems overblown; for the revisionist rhetoric, its kind of lying involves a reaching *beyond,* rather than in excess (as the "over-" might too easily imply).

Or yet again: consider the central figure of oxymoron in love poetry. Sappho's freezing and burning at once, her invention of words like *glykypikrin* ("bitter-sweet") with which to represent ambiguous proprioceptions, leads to Catullus's even more wildly interpretive *odi et amo*. But what the erotic oxymoron reflects is not indecision, not "conflicting sensations" in the former case, "conflicting feelings" in the latter as it manifestly purports to do. And perhaps "desire" and "fear" in the oxymoron of love are, after all, merely readings of the condition of trembling. And perhaps the inner state of being in love is such that the only truths told about it that can satisfy it are a kind of lie.

A kind of lie . . . And here is where the revision of the theory of tropes may demand a revision of a theory of fictions as well. For Bloom's predecessors (Northrop Frye being a prime example here), Sir Philip Sidney's "Now for the poet, he nothing affirms, and therefore never lieth" is a central doctrine for an idealizing theory which would treat fictions as part of nature, rather than as a description of it, and thus as a candidate for possible ve-rification. For Bloom's theory, Sidney's statement becomes a lie. A major, necessary and, indeed, an enabling lie, but a central lie of all texts and the impulse to produce them.

This major, central lie is the lie against time, and the capabil-ity it occasions is that of the Imagination itself. If we suppose, with Nietzsche, that Truth be a woman, then Lie may be the strong poet in his quest for unshared, unmediated perpetuation. (It might amuse Bloom vastly, with his post-Miltonic habit of romanc-ing the etymon, to learn that the Germanic reconstruction, *liu-gan* – from which, "lie" as "falsehood" – derives directly from an Indo-European base with no transfer of meaning in its history: our word for lie has never meant anything else; it is unshaded by a history of trope.) The minor psychological modes of imaginative failure – "lying to oneself," for example – can be considered as counterproductive simulacra of the central fiction-as-lie. The con-sequences for revisionist theology are interesting as well, in sug-gesting a mapping of forms of belief that must flourish in the tomb of faith. Indeed, this taking of all the alterations – of poetic figure, of psychological defense, of revisionary ratio – with an ulti-mate seriousness leaves vast amounts unsaid, great territories unexplored, and much work for others to do in the spaces it illu-minates. It is this fruitfulness which, in the long run, more than compensates for some of the arcana of the theory and, particular-ly, of the mode of representing it.

One level at which this process of expanding trope seems to stop is that of form; the theory leaves everything to be said about that. This is not surprising: one has always felt that Bloom's way of reading texts would be perfectly content to consider, say, *Paradise Lost* as if it were printed without line breaks on a kind of continu-ous tape, with perhaps some rubric or scholia to the effect that the poem had been planned in a blank verse deriving both from Italian traditions and that of the Shakespearean and Jacobean hero-villains, a verse in which Milton could expand the mighty Elizabethan line beyond the closets of wit into roomy periods, and

could also have a Satan produce public declamations that were at
the same time asides. In other words, a *representation of a formal
intention* would always seem to be sufficient for his theory;
unaware of landscape in nature, he has always read (but not seen)
through the landscape and still life of the chambered text.

But there are great possibilities for a study of the fundamental evasions of form itself. Consider for a moment – which Bloom
does not do but which, curiously enough, Kierkegaard himself
does – repetition as trope manifested formally as *refrain*. The basic
question is: "Does repeating something at regular textual intervals
make it less important? Or more?" Does the formalist interpretation apply, correlating predictability inversely with significance,
and thus do all refrains approach the pure condition of *fa la la la
la*? Or does meaning, not signification, prevail: is strength of
intention manifested in reiteration, and thus do all refrains move
toward the condition of title or thematic rubric or closed termi-
nus? The whole matter opens up when the formalist theory is confronted by the antithetical one.

And as with refrain, so with other formal elements: structures, emblematic proclamations of genre, echoic and allusive
ryhthms, transfer of function in generic form (e.g. the *literariness*
of Theocritus's use of heroic hexameter not merely for a new
form of poem, but a new literary and social mode), and so forth.
"The trope of form" is itself an ambiguous phrase: does it refer to
the trope or strategic strangeness of a particular form or mode or
element or to the underlying trope of structural strangeness
itself? For the formalist (e.g. Jakobson's famous concept of poetic
structure as committing "organized violence" upon those of ordinary language), the strangeness is a matter of rhetorical health
and strength. In an antithetical theory, one would have to consider poetic formal structure possibly as a disease, certainly as a
suspicious oddity, and at best as either something like the graceful
awkwardness of a balletic phrase or the pained bending of a bow
in order that its snap of return to minimal tension may discharge
its shaft of meaning. In any event, purposeful, wanton distortion
of the ordinary cannot, for such a theory, be written off as well-

wrought urns; in this realm of truth and falsehood all poetic measures are somehow Draconian.

Or again, from a more linguistic point of view, a shadowy
domain of half-truths, half-meanings, and pregnant ambiguities
can be newly illuminated. Consider for example the previous
quoted phrase, "the trope of form." The general case in English:
"the x of y" can be either a genitive or a partitive construction. In
the first instance it may or may not be plain (e.g. "the middle of
the night" but "the hand of God"); in the second, it is metonymic
or synecdochic, doing the work of a compound in Greek or
German. Historically, the decision of the Jacobean Bible transla-
tors to use "the x of – " for the Hebrew construct state may have
had great rhetorical consequences for English. Such a rendering,
for example, would give for *beth ha-sefer* ("school", or literally
"bookhouse") the full Romance phrase, "house of the book." And
thus with a resonant phrase like "stagger-wine" of the Psalmist,
alluding to its intoxicating strength; in the King James Bible it
becomes "the wine of astonishment," and the necessary
metonymy then works to personify Astonishment (a witch who
lives on the shady side of the mountains? Is her wine dark? How is
she related to Desire? to Repose? to Violence? Where do *they* live
and what colors are their draughts?). This kind of construction
inhabits a domain where trope lives as secret an existence under
the legitimate cover of the literal as it does in the land of
Etymology. Christine Brooke-Rose gives a masterful taxonomic
analysis of what she calls this "genitive link" in *A Grammar of
Metaphor* (1958), 146-205.

Bloom's lack of concern for the higher surfaces through
which troping passes misses some central questions for rhetorical
theory. But it is very likely that attempts to explain, or revise, or
even reject the use of his conception of trope may water the arid
plains of transformation. Certainly his ellipses and incompletions
throughout are as stimulating as they are often exasperatingly
unsatisfying. Even when he seems to be monstrously *méchant*,
there is more than madness in the method: thus to characterize
perspectivism, or indeed, anything else, as "as self-contradictory as

a tautology is" is infuriating. Certainly no self-descriptive joke is at work, and we are forced to read "self-contradictory" tropically as "lying to us, and itself, that it is predicating anything, yet impelled into having been uttered by the impulse to predicate." But this is one of the more impossible sentences in *A Map of Misreading.* It is more useful to consider how, if one wants something more out of exemplification than Bloom gives one, readers have, as in reading a poem, themselves to supply further instances. One is moved to continue some of the chains of transumptive allusion which Bloom maps out: the "belated peasant" at the end of *Paradise Lost,* Book I who "sees,/Or dreams he sees" elfin revels to remind us of the illusory nature of Pandemonic grandeur has his reflex in Sir Bedivere at the end of "The Passing of Arthur" from *Idylls of the King:*

> Thereat once more he moved about, and clomb
> Even to the highest he could climb, and saw,
> Straining his eyes beneath an arch of hand,
> Or thought he saw, the speck that bare the King,
> Down that long water opening on the deep
> Somewhere far off, pass on and on . . .

where the interposed participial phrase only points up the echo of the enjambed qualifier from Milton. But these are matters of heightened critical attention which will be most easily assimilated (as, indeed, with the final revisionary ratio of *The Anxiety of Influence,* whose easy and by no means totally trivial critical application will show the ghost of the future text in the predecessor – today even graduate students can see the ghost of Emily Dickinson in:

> It cannot vault, or dance, or play;
> It never was in France or Spain;
> Nor can it entertain the day
> With a great stable or domain . . .

of Herbert).

IV

Bloom cites Vico's association of tropes with "poetic monsters and metamorphoses" (the latter meaning, I assume, the residues or end-products of the process rather than the change itself). The Renaissance mythographers, too, made this connection: the composite Chimera slain by Bellerophon with the aid of Pegasus' poetic flight was held to signify falsehood. But Nietzsche warns us moderns: "Whoever fights monsters should beware lest he thereby become a monster"; and so with the troper of tropes: gazing too long into the abyss of meaning you will see the abyss gazing back into you. This needs to happen, if I read this part of Bloom's theory correctly, to the critical process itself, which is why the rhetorician's trope of metalepsis or transumption, whose modern use probably traces back to a brilliant footnote in Angus Fletcher's *Allegory*, interests him so.

I have written extensively on the history of this trope as discussed by rhetoricians in another place, where I myself employ the concept as a figure operating diachronically. (See my *The Figure of Echo*, 113-14, 133-149.) Bloom's use of it varies and develops throughout his work. Indeed, his own phrase, "the trope of a trope" can be, and is, construed in several ways. It can simply mean catachresis – a trope added to another one, like Milton's "blind mouths," a metaphor of blindness operating on a synecdoche of "mouths" for preachers. Or it can describe a new trope which turns not – synchronically – on a literal designation of an element of non-textual experience (e.g., "A quartz contentment like a stone"), but rather – diachronically – on a prior trope. (An example is the phrase "Leaves of Grass," where the trope of leaf as human life, as it evolves from Homer and Virgil through Dante, Milton, Shelley, etc. and that of grass as human body, from Psalms and Isaiah, together with Wordsworth's "barren leaves" of books, are both re-figured in the profound syntactic ambiguity – "of" as designating formal, material, efficient, final, cause? possessive? – of the title.)

But the phrase, "trope of a trope," and its name, "metalepsis" or "transumption" come to mean more than that for Bloom.

In the first place, he engages recent theorizing about the history of rhetoric – rhetoric itself considered, as it were, rhetorically: what had been an art of purportedly potent political persuasion in classical times, the rhetorical art of the senator and the lawyer, became first the art of religious persuasion and then, in the Renaissance, the art of poetic persuasion (at least in that part of rhetoric known as *elocutio.*) Schemes and tropes were not used to manipulate other people's decisive actions (or at least, active decisions), but rather, in Renaissance and later rhetoric, to invade their workaday epistemologies through the arts of minute and even momentary fictions. For Bloom (as very differently for, say, Paul de Man), the literary study of rhetoric today is itself a trope of classical rhetoric – the whole system is a figure of the former one, in that the persuasion is internalized. The writer is using figuration to persuade part of the reader's consciousness of the authority of the fiction (instead of using, as in classical rhetoric, the authority of the speaker, it is the authority of writing as truth-telling which enables the kind of lying that these minute fictions entail. On top of that, as we have seen, modern rhetorical theorists are constantly redefining either the range or ground of various master-tropes, so that Bloom himself is continually troping tropes whenever he uses a technical rhetorical term in a persuasively redefined way. If we look at his earliest work, we can find the same thing happening in the personal, but not explicitly redefined, use of psychological and moral terms, such as "selfhood" in his early writing on Blake and Wordsworth. But Bloom clearly uses "transumption," particularly later on, to mean both the essence of poesis – in that each trope microcosmically embodies his notion of all true vision as re-vision, and the essence of his own poetic criticism – in that it is a troping of troping.

Bloom slips from one meaning of the phrase and of the word to another one, but this is, for better or worse, central to his writing, and may constitute one of its central difficulties. He not only uses terms in a special sense, but revises that sense in the same ways that poetry, rather than exposition, philosophy or, particularly political or moral polemic does. He not only tropes, but transumes, his own concepts (perhaps, in accord with his most

recent and problematic concept of "facticity," in order to keep
them his own, but that might be only the way a poet might think.)
Yet what might appear to be an evasively Protean quality of these
concepts is actually, I think, the result of Bloom's working
through (in a somewhat Freudian sense) the rhetorical consequences of a phrase (as they would occur to a poet, rather than to
a pseudo-philosopher), of his discovery of its meaning in the
course of using it. His term "misprision" which I discussed earlier
may very likely have come to him from its use in Shakespeare's
Sonnet 87 ("Farewell, thou art too dear for my possessing"),
which he had probably read at one point or another as a gesture
in the relation *not between writer/lover and object, but between text and
interpreter.* And thus

> And so my patent back again is swerving,
> Thyself thou gavest, thy own worth not yet knowing;
> Or me, to whom thou gavest it, else mistaking:
> So thy great gift, upon misprision growing,
> Comes home again on better judgement making.

The "swerve" of the first of these quoted lines, when taken by
Bloom, (or mis-taken, probably unconsciously) as his own *clinamen* or ratio of "swerving" in *The Anxiety of Influence,* seems to have
led him to allegorize these lines as a parable of reading and urging a reading on a text in an almost erotic way, with the effect of
having the text become what is misread in it. But although this
instance may underlie his first choice of the term, it cannot
explain all of the directions it takes: in "weak misreading," or
reductive or trivial interpretation, it has what for most of us would
be a literal sense of "misread"; in "strong misreading," or what in
fact Bloom means by what poetry and criticism have in common
in relation to precursor texts, it has a figurative sense of an appro-
priateness beyond correctness.

Any exhaustive treatment of Bloomian terminology would
lie beyond the scope of these remarks. But it might be helpful to
consider two words which emerge in his more recent writing. The
essay on "Poetic Crossing" is most remarkable, I think, for its reading of Steven's "Domination of Black." But it plunges the reader
into the cold-war with deconstruction which I mentioned before,

and, particularly, into a forest of "crossings," of suspended meanings of a term he makes central to the argument (and, as always
with Bloom, "argument" must mean "poetic argument," or story,
rather than logical, philosophical or even expository argument).
The notion of "crossing" he may, for all one can tell, have taken
from Paul de Man's allegorizing, in his own critical vocabulary, of
rhetorical terms for schemes, in which "chiasmus" or cross-pat-
tern, no longer simply designates a schematic patterning – ABBA
– of two elements (be they grammatical categories, vowel
phonemes, syntactic patterns, taxonomic categories of what in
nature names name, etc.) but a paradigm operating on other levels as well. When in the essay he says of his discovered "crossings"
that each "seems to me to have three characteristic marks in nearly every poem in which they occur," he goes on to list among
them a dialectical movement of the senses in the fiction or tropol-
ogy of a poem (sight giving way to sound, etc.); a moment of oscillation between the mimetic and expressive theories of poetic representation which the text itself seems to maintain at one point or
another, and so forth. In other words (and there are always other
words), *transitions*. It would be far less confusing to call them so;
and yet it would be to invoke in a privileged way a particular system of discourse about writing – a surface schematics of expository style, or narrative, or even language about painting. Rather
than deconstructing the tropes of these sorts entailed by "transition," Bloom uses the ambiguous "crossing," which implies a wholly different set of figures. They are tropes of romance, of a reader-
quester crossing over a river, a threshold, into another terrain
which is also, in romance, another condition of consciousness; of
a writer-quester moving into another relation to what he has
already written, and to what he will write once on the other side
of whatever boundary has been crossed, etc. The systematic ambiguity which makes the term hard to grasp results from its own
oscillation between designating a *process* of knowing and imagining, an element of textual structure or point of nexus (as in the
architectural term, the "crossing" in a cruciform ground-plan), or,
once again, a process of "discovering" or "reading" that nexus and

its own generative process. But it is essential, I think, that this intensely allegorical term not be read reductively in any instance; and yet, in order to avoid so doing, the reader must be precisely aware of just what the confusions are.

Bloom's most recent puzzling term is "facticity." It is of some, but only some limited, help to regard it as referring to a species of literalism. A communicant of the deconstructive orthodoxy, who daily consumes the wafer-trace of unreal presence, would want to deny that any literature could be much more literal-minded than any other. Bloom, who writes about poetry but not about the rest of literature, is deeply committed to that discrimination. Somewhere in the dialectical relation of a number of ordinary uses there must have lurked for him the spirit of a term. "Factitious" – meaning "made up," "contrived" and thereby "fake," "inauthentic" etc. – edges onto the terrain of "fictitious"; and yet "fiction" and "fact" are necessarily opposed, and embrace only in paradox. "Fiction," for a poetic theorist, has an authenticity and genuineness which mere "fact" does not possess (unless, as Oscar Wilde's great essay on fiction called "The Decay of Lying" implies, it has been recently created from the stuff of fiction). The etymon of "fiction," the Latin *"fingere,"* comes from an Indo-European base meaning kneading or shaping by molding. In a sense, then, the original creation of the human, in Genesis, is a poetic act of *fiction,* rather than a mere *factification* or *doing,* and such a notion undoubtedly hovered over the word for Bloom. The result is a concept of factitious or fake factuality, the hardening of trope into rigid, untwisted designation and, more importantly, the condition of consciousness and of utterance which is imprisoned in its rigidities. But "facticity" involves one in a host of difficulties. Tropes, whole fictions or fables even, can be kept alive through transumption by subsequent poems. But their lives can be threatened, even as the Snark's could be by a railway-share, by the very historical processes which Wilde observed to be at work when factuality eventually crept up on art: poets can imagine things in figures which are literally unthinkable and practically inconceivable, only to have technology eventually come around to feign them (Wordsworth never knew of the possibility of overlaid photographic transparencies when he wrote the opening lines of *Tintern Abbey*, nor did Shelley in *The Triumph of Life*, etc.). Objects can be tropes of tropes, as Kenneth Burke pointed out in "Language as Symbolic Action," in a sense that "things would be the signs of words." The famous opening paragraphs of Marx's *Eighteenth Brumaire of Napoleon III* suggest a parallel to Bloomian facticity in its notion of the farce into which all *literalized* historical replay must always collapse. The low-comic fixation of nineteenth-century British spiritualism on a substance like ectoplasm, or Wilhelm Reich's tragi-comic recapitulation of this in his factitious reduction of Freud, are merely glaring instances. Truly glowing instances, for Bloom, reside in the impulses of interpreters to read reductively without that saving grace of irony which makes reductive reading a kind of joke about itself, the greatest reduction of all being to an easy notion of experience. It is hardly that Bloom's theory slights the real, the life of the body, of the polis, of present nature; and yet I can think of no stronger moral argument for poetry than this one (from the essay on "Poetic Crossing"): "We believe the lies we want to believe because they help us to survive. Similarly, we read (reread) the poems that keep our discourse with our selves going. Strong poems strengthen us by teaching us *how to talk to ourselves,* rather than how to talk to others." It is not only that to read a poem as a manifesto is a sin of facticity: to read it as an ethical treatise, or as the projection of a theological, psychological or legal system is surely not a violent act, but it is as deadening as holding up to the gaze of poetry – and, alas, with the best intentions in the world, *e.g.,* to cast light on it – the severed, but still petrifying, head of the interpretive Gorgon.

I would not hold for a moment that the difficulties in reading Bloom are to be resolved at the level of terminology. His high allusiveness, higher humor (so different from the labored, solemn, punning to which many contemporary theorists are addicted), ellipsis of the kind of rhetorical analysis which all too frequently has never been done – as in the case of his book on

Wallace Stevens, which presupposed four or five volumes of the kind of reading given by Helen Vendler, but of greater intellectual sophistication and moral imagination, which even as yet do not, indeed, exist – all can be considered distracting. I do not feel that his contention with fashionable "post-structuralist" writing has yielded him the same kind of rebound which his earlier revision of modernism, or of its scholastic form in New Criticism, or his fight against what he considers the factitious church of Freud (as opposed to the greatness of the writer himself), or against normative rabbinic authority over the text of the Pentateuch, have afforded. In the long run, his quarrel with the ephebes of Derrida and de Man may come to sound like so much static noise. In any case, to read Bloom you have at some point or other to surrender yourself to his unique mode of writing – I am afraid that the writer most like him in this regard is one whom he may most dislike, namely, Heidegger.

But in any case, it is not Bloom's rhetorical struggle with his reader, but his ultimate will to power over texts, that is at issue. It is that will to power which makes him respect true originality so deeply, and thereby continue so relentlessly to work his visionary restoration on over-read texts, working down through layers of the varnish of facticity to the original image. This is perhaps why the so-called Yahvist of the biblical higher criticism – the putative author of the oldest parts of Genesis – has most recently occupied his concern, and why he may eventually write about Shakespeare, upon whom it has hitherto been inconvenient for him to reflect. But even though readers may find themselves overwhelmed at times, "stopped in the dooryard," in Wallace Stevens's words, by their own "capacious bloom," they must conclude, inevitably, with those equally proleptic lines of Dickinson, that "When the Winds of Will are stirred/Excellent is Bloom."

Poetics of Influence

1 Prometheus Rising: The Backgrounds of Romantic Poetry

The political background of English Romantic poetry is darkened by European revolution and English reaction against that revolution. The England in which Blake and Wordsworth grew up was a country one hundred years removed from its one great revolution, the Puritan movement. The most important political event in early-nineteenth-century England was one that failed to take place: the repetition among Londoners of the revolution carried through by Parisians. Out of the ferment that failed to produce a national renewal there came instead the major English contribution to world literature since the Renaissance, the startling phenomenon of six major poets appearing in just two generations.

No intelligent, thoroughgoing Marxist critic has yet studied all of English Romantic literature in any detail, and I shudder to contemplate a reading of Blake's epics or Byron's *Don Juan* in the light of economic determinism alone. Still, such a study would reveal much that now is only a matter for speculation, for the Romantic age saw the end of an older, pastoral England and the beginning of the England that may be dying now. When Blake was born, in 1757, and even as late as 1770, when Wordsworth was born, England was still fundamentally an agricultural society. When Blake died, in 1827, England was largely an industrial nation, and by 1850, when Wordsworth died, England was in every sense the proper subject for Marxist economic analysis that it became in *Das Kapital.* The power of England had passed from an established aristocracy holding huge estates, and an upper middle class of London merchants, to a much more amorphous grouping that combined both of these with a new class of industrial employers. And the common people of England were no longer just a peasantry and city artisans, but now a huge and tormented industrial working class as well. In the last quarter of the eighteenth century that emerging class was troubled by two foreign revolutions, neither like any known previously in modern Europe. The American Revolution looks tame enough to us today, but to Blake it was the first voice of the morning, and in his symbolism it assumed an importance greater even than that taken on by the French Revolution. The French Revolution, much more genuinely a modern social upheaval, is the single most important external factor that conditions Romantic poetry, as in Blake's *The Marriage of Heaven and Hell,* Wordsworth's *The Prelude,* and Shelley's *Prometheus Unbound.*

The English government under which Blake and Wordsworth lived was engaged either in continental warfare or in suppressing internal dissent, or both together, for most of their lives. The London of the last decade of the eighteenth century and the first of the nineteenth is the London shown in Blake's poem of that title in *Songs of Experience:* a city in which the traditional English liberties of free press, free speech, and the rights of petition and assembly were frequently denied. A country already shaken by war and anarchic economic cycles was beginning to experience the social unrest that had overthrown the French social order, and the British ruling class responded to this challenge by a vicious and largely effective repression.

Voices raised against this repression included Tom Paine, who had to flee for his life to France, where he then nearly lost it again, and a much more significant figure, the philosophical anarchist William Godwin, who was the major English theorist of social revolution. Godwin subsided into a timid silence during the English counterterror, but his philosophic materialism was crucial for the early Wordsworth and the young Shelley alike, though both poets were to break from Godwin in their mature works.

Behind the materialist vision of Godwin was a consciousness that older modes of thought were dying with the society that had informed them. When Blake was eight years old, the steam engine was perfected, and what were to be the images of prophetic labor in Blake's poetry, the hammer and the forge, had their antagonist images prepared for them in the furnaces and mills of another England. In the year of Wordsworth's birth, we have the ironical juxtaposition of Goldsmith's poem *The Deserted Village,* a sad celebration of an open, pastoral England vanishing into the isolated farm holdings, and wandering laborers resulting from enclosure. "Nature," insofar as it had an outward, phenomenal meaning for Pope, was a relaxed word, betokening the gift of God that lay all about him. Wordsworthian nature, the hard, phenomenal otherness that opposes itself to all we have made and marred, takes part of its complex origin from this vast social dislocation.

The real misery in England brought about through these economic and social developments was on a scale unparalleled since the Black Death in the fourteenth century. The French wars, against which all of Blake's prophetic poetry protests with Biblical passion, were typical of all modern wars fought by capitalistic countries. Enormous profits for the manufacturing classes were accompanied by inflation and food shortages for the mass of people, and victory over Napoleon brought on all the woes endemic to a capitalist society when peace breaks out – an enormous economic depression, unemployment, hunger, and more class unrest.

This unrest, which there was no means of channeling into organization or a protest vote, led to giant public meetings, riots, and what was called frame-breaking, a direct attempt to end technological unemployment by the destruction of machines. The government reacted by decreeing that frame-breaking was punishable by death. The climax of popular agitation and government brutality came in August 1819, in the Peterloo Massacre at Manchester, where mounted troops charged a large, orderly group that was meeting to demand parliamentary reform, killing and maiming many of the unarmed protesters. For a moment, England stood at the verge of revolution, but no popular leaders of sufficient force and initiative came forward to organize the indignation of the mass of people, and the moment passed. A similar moment was to come in 1832, at the start of another age, but then revolution was to be averted by the backing-down of parliament, and its passage of the first Reform Act that helped to establish the Victorian compromise. So the political energies of the age were not without issue, even in England, but to idealists of any sort living in England during the first three decades of the nineteenth century it seemed that a new energy had been born into the world and then had died in its infancy. The great English writers of the period reacted to a stagnant situation by withdrawal, either internal or external. In Blake and Wordsworth this internal movement helped create a new kind of poetry; it created modern poetry as we know it.

The useful term "Romantic," describing the literary period that was contemporary with the French Revolution, the Napoleonic wars, and the age of Castlereagh and Metternich afterward, was not employed until the later Victorian literary historians looked back at the early years of the nineteenth century. Since that time, the word has meant not only that cultural period, in England and on the Continent, but a kind of art that is timeless and recurrent as well, usually viewed as being in some kind of opposition to an art called classical or neoclassical. The word goes back to a literary form, the romance, the marvelous story suspended part way between myth and naturalistic representation. By the middle of the eighteenth century in England, "romantic" had become an adjective meaning wild or strange or picturesque, and was applied more to painting and to scenery than to poetry. The critical terms by which mid-eighteenth-century literature named itself, in direct opposition to the classicism of Pope, Swift, and Dr. Johnson, were "the Sublime" and "sensibility." No poet of the Romantic period ever characterized his own poetry or that of any of his contemporaries as "Romantic." All that the six major poets thought they shared was what William Hazlitt called "The Spirit of the Age." In the semi-apocalyptic dawn of the French Revolution, it really did seem that a renovated universe was possible – that life could never again be what it had been. It is not very easy now for any of us to summon up the fervor of that moment, through whatever leap of historical imagination. We have no real analogue to it as a universal psychic shock that at first promised liberation from everything bad in the past. The Russian Revolution, even if it were not now almost as historically remote from us as the French, would not be an adequate analogue, for it took place in a world already suffering through a war. The French Revolution was, in its day, a new kind of ideological revolution – hence the terror it aroused in its opponents, and the hope in its sympathizers.

To understand fully the link between the Revolution and English Romantic literature, it is perhaps most immediately illuminating to consider the case, not of one of the great poets, but of the critic William Hazlitt, who kept his faith in the Revolution and even in Napoleon long after every other literary figure of the time had turned reactionary or indifferent,or had died young. Hazlitt not only lived and died a Jacobin, but his entire background and career are archetypal of English Romanticism, and his personality and psychology are representative of English Romanticism, as those of Rousseau perfectly incarnate the French variety.

Like that of all the English Romantic poets, Hazlitt's religious background was in the tradition of Protestant dissent, the kind of nonconformist vision that descended from the Left Wing of England's Puritan movement. There is no more important point to be made about English Romantic poetry than this one, or indeed about English poetry in general, particularly since it has been deliberately obscured by most modern criticism. Though it is a displaced Protestantism, or a Protestantism astonishingly transformed by different kinds of humanism or naturalism, the poetry of the English Romantics is a kind of religious poetry, and the religion is in the Protestant line, though Calvin or Luther would have been horrified to contemplate it. Indeed, the entire continuity of English poetry that T. S. Eliot and his followers attacked is a radical Protestant or displaced Protestant tradition. It is no accident that the poets deprecated by the New Criticism were Puritans, or Protestant individualists, or men of that sort breaking away from Christianity and attempting to formulate personal religions in their poetry. This Protestant grouping begins with aspects of Spenser and Milton, passes through the major Romantics and Victorians, and is clearly represented by Hardy and Lawrence in our century. It is also no accident that the poets brought into favor by the New Criticism were Catholics or High Church Anglicans – Donne, Herbert, Dryden, Pope, Dr. Johnson, Hopkins in the Victorian period, Eliot and Auden in our own time. Not that literary critics have been engaged in a cultural-religious conspiracy, but there are at least two main traditions of English poetry, and what distinguishes them are not only aesthetic considerations but conscious differences in religion and politics. One line, and it is the central one, is Protestant, radical, and Miltonic-Romantic; the other is Catholic, conservative, and by its claims, classical. French culture has been divided between those who have accepted the French Revolution and its consequences and those who have sought to deny and resist them. Similarly, but more subtly, English culture has been divided between those who have accepted the Puritan religious revolution of the late sixteenth and seventeenth century and those who have fought against it. Though I oversimplify, the conflict I seek to expose is most certainly there; it runs all through the criticism of T. S. Eliot, in many concealments, and it accounts finally for *all* of Eliot's judgments on English poetry. Hazlitt's criticism, which by any standards remains at least as vital as Eliot's, illustrates the same dialectical point in reverse – the sensibility involved is that of a Protestant dissenter, and the judgments are shaped accordingly.

The main characteristic of English religious dissent was its insistence on intellectual and spiritual independence, on the right of private judgment in questions of morality, on the inner light within each soul, by which alone Scripture was to be read – and most of all, on allowing no barrier or intermediary to come between a man and his God. Academic criticism of literature in our time became almost an affair of church wardens; too many students for instance learned to read Milton by the dubious light of C. S. Lewis's *Preface to Paradise Lost,* in which the major Protestant poem in the language becomes an Anglo-Catholic document. The best preparation for reading Romantic poetry always will be a close rereading of Book I of Spenser's *Faerie Queene* and of Milton's *Paradise Lost* which judges the spiritual content of these poems wholly and maturely. Milton begins his poem with an invocation to the Muse, an epic device that he transforms into the summoning of the Holy Spirit of God, which "before all temples dost prefer/the upright heart and pure." He means just that; he is repudiating the temples, all of them, and offering instead his own arrogantly pure and upright heart as the true dwelling place of the creative Word of God. The spirit that moved over the face of the waters and brought forth our world is identical with the shaping spirit dwelling within the soul of the inspired Protestant poet. Spenser is not so forthright, but Book I of his poem offers a Calvinist-oriented allegory that is scarcely less iconoclastic in juxtaposing a Puritan knight-errant to a corrupt machinery of salvation. The spirit of Hazlitt, of Blake, of the younger Wordsworth, of Shelley and Keats, is a direct descendant of the Spenserian and Miltonic spirit – the autonomous soul seeking its own salvation outside of and beyond the hierarchy of grace. The spiritual nakedness of Hazlitt, Blake, and the others is a more extreme version of that English nonconformist temper which had so triumphed in Milton that it made him a church with one believer, even at last a nation unto himself.

It was not until 1828 that Dissenters gained legal equality in matters of religion and education in England. Hazlitt, in 1818, wrote the following eloquent praise of his coreligionists, the sectaries – the men and women who embodied what Edmond Burke had called "the dissidence of dissent and the Protestantism of the Protestant religion." The nonconformists, Hazlitt wrote, "are the steadiest supporters of [England's] liberties and laws, they are checks and barriers against the insidious or avowed encroachments of arbitrary power: and they are depositaries of the love of truth." Dissent or religious individualism was always more a state of mind than a doctrine, and it was opposed to the Establishment steadily from the Restoration, in 1660, down to the repeal of the Test Acts, in 1828. From then on dissent, in the form of the evangelical revival, attempted to take over the Church of England itself, and secured enough of a hold to engender the counterreaction of the Oxford movement of Newman and his friends and followers.

Dissent had begun as a protest against ecclesiastical authority, but it grew into an affirmation of both civil and religious freedom. Milton's prose works utilize as their central concept the Protestant doctrine of "Christian Liberty," which holds that it is the prerogative of every regenerated man under the New Law of the Gospel to be free of every ecclesiastical constraint. After the Stuart Restoration, Milton turned his energies to exploring the Paradise within each man, for Christian Liberty could still offer this. The outward energies of Protestant individualism, balked by the Restoration, tended to go into the fight for the natural liberties of Englishmen. The inward energies largely died out of poetry after Milton, and did not appear again until the Miltonic revival of the 1740's, of which Collins's *Ode on the Poetical Character* is one of the great monuments. In the meantime they were partly secularized by the more radical wing of the Whig party, led by Charles James Fox in the later eighteenth century. In religion proper they became incarnated in George Fox and the Quakers, and more significantly for Romanticism, in the two great nonconformist theologians of the late eighteenth century – Richard Price and Joseph Priestley. Price and Priestley led the radical Unitarian agitation for reform of church and state that enlisted the young Coleridge and Wordsworth as supporters and helped stir them to an early discontent with eighteenth-century culture and its institutions.

When the Bastille fell, the Dissenters hailed the events in France with elation. Richard Price preached a sermon on November 4, 1789, that greeted the Revolution in the name of English nonconformist tradition from Cromwell and Milton on, a sermon that provoked Edmund Burke into the eloquent counterattack of his *Reflections on the Revolution in France*. In their later lives, when both had turned into Tories, Coleridge and Wordsworth became disciples of Burke. But when they were

young men, they followed Priestley and Godwin in attacking
Burke and in defending the French Revolution. When the
Anglican Bishop Watson published his sermon against the
Revolution, charmingly entitled *The Wisdom and Goodness of God* √
in Having Made Both Rich and Poor, Wordsworth replied with his
angry pamphlet, *A Letter to the Bishop of Llandaff,* in which the
Bishop and Burke are invited to contemplate the daily terrors
afflicting the English working class – "the scourge of labour, of
cold, of hunger," as Wordsworth phrased it. Even more ironic was
Coleridge's role in these times, for the older Coleridge was to
make the ideological foundations for English conservatism and
established Anglicanism in the Victorian period. But the young
Coleridge followed Priestley to the extent of imitating his famous
sermon of 1794, in which the French Revolution is interpreted as
being the time of troubles preceding the millennium that is the
first stage of the apocalypse, the last judgment prophesied in the
Revelation of St. John the Divine. In his long poem *Religious
Musings,* written in 1794-1796, Coleridge also wrote of the
Revolution as a necessarily violent threshold to a thousand years
of peace, after which Christ would come again to judge the
nations of the earth. The same apocalyptic language appears also
in Wordsworth's *Recluse* and *Prelude* and in Blake's *Marriage of
Heaven and Hell* and in his poems on the French and American
Revolutions. A generation later, the apocalyptic impulse abandons
the contemporary world, which belongs to Metternich and his
colleagues, and enters the purely ideal world explored so magnificently by Shelley in his lyrical drama *Prometheus Unbound.*

   It is these apocalyptic longings, themselves expressions of a
radically Protestant temperament, that most clearly distinguish
Romantic poetry from most of the English poetry that had been
written since the Renaissance. It is not a deprecation of
Restoration and Augustan poets to generalize that they treated
man as a distinctly limited being, set in a context of reason,
nature, and society, that ordered his horizons and denied any possibility of a radical alteration in his mundane hopes. Indeed, it is
the strength and even the glory of such poets that they so power-

fully attacked man's vain pride and his dangerous longings to escape the harsh realities of a reasonable existence. One can call this a glory, even if one has not a conservative or classical or Catholic temperament, if one takes a little history into account. Restoration literature and its Augustan successors – the whole line of neoclassicists from Dryden through Addison, Pope, and Swift down to its rear-guard fighter, Samuel Johnson – were in reaction against the most disordered age of England's history, a time of civil warfare, religious struggle, and a complete change in the philosophical and scientific world view. The age of Cromwell and Milton is from one standpoint the glorious culmination of the Elizabethan age of Renaissance and Reformation, but from a more traditional standpoint it was a brutal and anarchic collapse of a settled society into a chaos of rebellion and sectarianism, brought about through overweening spiritual pride and the original sin of civil and ecclesiastical arrogance and disobedience. Pope and Swift, and Johnson afterward, set themselves against every innovation, every mark of dissent, every extreme position in ethics, politics, metaphysics, or art. The Augustan fear of madness, so strong in Swift and Johnson, plays a considerable part in this opposition, which goes so far as to attack what Johnson calls "the dangerous prevalence of the imagination." Swift, in his later years, went mad; Johnson came dangerously close to it. The poets of the age of sensibility – say 1740 through 1770 – reacted against Pope and Johnson and sought to return to the intellectual and aesthetic daring of Milton, with results in their lives, at least, which bore out Johnson's melancholy warnings. Chatterton killed himself at seventeen; Cowper, Collins, Christopher Smart, and others spent years in asylums for the insane, as the Romantic poet John Clare was to do after them; while poets like Gray and Burns ended in deep melancholy or profound social alienation. The spectre haunting these generations was the fear of psychic energy, and the conviction that death-in-life awaited any poet who indulged his imagination.

As a phenomenon, this mid-eighteenth-century prevalence and fear of creative madness, of "perilous imbalance" as one critic has called it, has still not been solved, and what we cannot understand we need not attempt to judge. But we need to keep this phenomenon in mind if we are to understand William Blake, the sanest of all poets, who by the dubious irony of literary history was considered mad by some of his contemporaries, and is still considered so by some of ours, who have no excuse for not knowing better. In Blake the satirical theme of a willful intellectual madness becoming an involuntary spiritual disorder is sounded as early as the youthful *Mad Song* in *Poetical Sketches.* In *The Book of Urizen,* Blake gives his definitive analysis of the phenomenon of eighteenth-century imaginative madness, one that I suspect we are not likely to improve upon, even if we wince at the rigor of the intellectual satire by which it is presented. The contrary to the Johnsonian fear of imagination is the Romantic apocalyptic hope to be achieved through and in imagination. It is here, in the astonishingly fecund and bewilderingly varied concept of imagination, that Romantic poetic theory finds its center.

The neoclassic theory of poetry was a refined and coherent version of the ancient mimetic theory, in which poetry is regarded as an imitation of human actions. In Romantic poetic theory, this is not so. We find it today the merest commonplace to speak of the "creative" power of the artist or poet, forgetting that the very considerable metaphor involved in the word "creative" in this context is a great departure from the more primary notion of art as imitation. A colorless or dead metaphor or stock term is, as M. H. Abrams says, the residue of a figure of speech "which only four centuries ago was new, vital, and – because it equated the poet with God in his unique and most characteristic function – on the verge, perhaps, of blasphemy." The ancient history of this aesthetic metaphor, one should add, contains no consciousness that blasphemy could ever be involved. The metaphor appears in premonitory hints in first-century Christian writings and second-century Greek aestheticians. In the third century, the metaphor emerges clearly in the founder of Neoplatonism, Plotinus. In the Italian Renaissance, the Neoplatonists of the Florentine Academy expand the metaphor into a theory, until it reaches the bald statement of the critic Scaliger, for whom the poet is one who "maketh a new Nature and so maketh himself as it were a new God." Scaliger is the source for Sir Philip Sidney's similar declaration in his *Apologie for Poetrie.* We reach the end of this account with Sidney's contemporary George Puttenham, who joined to the idea he found in Sidney's *Apologie* the crucial word "create," based on the ecclesiastical Latin common word that connoted the orthodox concept that God made the world out of nothing. If poets, said Puttenham, "be able to devise and make all these things of themselves, without any subject or veritie," then "they be (by manner of speech) as creating gods."

This nutshell history, if taken too literally, would make it sound as if Sidney and his contemporaries already had a Romantic theory of imagination, but this is one of the curious illusions that the relative flatness of intellectual history is liable to give us. Sidney states the aesthetic metaphor of creation, and then instantly abandons it for a definition of poetry as imitation, "that the truth" of the poet's role, as he says, "may be the more palpable." Sidney's rapid passage from the theological to the more traditional metaphor of art as a mirror held up to nature is the precise point at which Romanticism both derives from and separates itself from its Renaissance forebear.

Before the Romantics, literature and the arts had somewhat the same educational and cultural status that they now possess, but they were generally judged to be dependent for their meanings on theology, philosophy, and history; that is, they allegorically were reduced to truths that were held to be stated more plainly in more privileged fields of learning. If a poem possessed truth, it was an elaborated or ornamented truth that could be met more directly in a religious or moral context. When the Romantics, from Blake on to Shelley and Keats, talk about the relation of poetry to other areas of culture, they make the direct claim that poetry is prior to theology or moral philosophy, and by "prior" they mean both more original and more intellectually powerful.

As an assertion, this Romantic self-exaltation can be viewed as mere megalomania of course, and it has been so viewed by a

series of modern critics from Irving Babbitt and T. E. Hulme
through T. S. Eliot down to the American academic critics called
"New" in the decades just past. But the Romantic assertion is not
just an assertion; it is a metaphysic, a theory of history, and much
more important than either of these, it is what all of the Romantics – but Blake in particular – called a vision, a way of seeing, and
of living, a more human life. Northrop Frye notes that even in the
dissenting Protestant vision, all the traditions of civilization that
were held worthy of preservation were believed to have been instituted by God himself. But by the early nineteenth century, as Frye
adds, the idea that much of civilization was of human institution
had begun to appear, however uncertainly, in radical Protestant
writing. It is present, for example, in the Unitarians Price and
Priestley, and it plays a central role in the thought of William
Godwin, who began as a Dissenter and then converted himself
into a curious blend of idealistic anarchist and materialistic
humanist. In Blake it appears as a new myth, that is, a new and
comprehensive story of how man got to be what he is now, and
how he is again to become what once he was. If all deities, as
Blake said, reside in the human breast, then all traditions of
knowledge are human also, and it followed that the most human
and complete knowledge was that of poetry.

Milton is the fountainhead of this kind of belief, and yet
would have rejected it, in the conviction that it led to a Satanic
idolatry of self. It is one of the great characteristics of the
Romantic period that each major poet in turn sought to rival and
surpass Milton, while also renewing his vision. To surpass Milton
in this context could only mean to correct his vision by humanizing it, which is a secular analogue to the entire process by which
Calvinist Protestantism became the radical dissent of the later
eighteenth century. The immense hope of Blake and of the early
Wordsworth, of Shelley and of Keats, was that poetry, by expressing the whole man, could either liberate him from his fallen condition or, more compellingly, make him see that condition as
unnecessary, as an unimaginative fiction that an awakened spirit
could slough off. So Blake's Milton, in the brief epic of which he

is the hero, comes to cast off the rags of decayed conceptions, to strip himself of the nonhuman. And so, in the poetry of our own time which is the direct legacy of Romanticism, Yeats cries out:

> Thought is a garment, and the soul's a bride
> That cannot in that trash and tinsel hide.

So also with the vision of Wordsworth, in which we are to be saved by words which speak of nothing more than what we are, a vision that finds its highest honorific words in "simple" and "common," and human felicity in the moving line "the simple produce of the common day," in which we are told our lives are perpetually renewed by that ordinary process of hallowing the commonplace that Wordsworth had first described in poetry. This vision is renewed for us in the poetry of Wallace Stevens, the most authentic and relevant I think of our time. Romanticism opposed to supernatural religion the natural passion that Wallace Stevens has so eloquently expressed:

> The greatest poverty is not to live
> In a physical world, to feel that one's desire
> Is too difficult to tell from despair.

The central desire of Blake and Wordsworth, and of Keats and Shelley, was to find a final good in human existence itself. It is these poets who came closest to answering the question that Wallace Stevens, following after them, propounds:

> And out of what one sees and hears and out
> Of what one feels, who could have thought to make
> So many selves, so many sensuous worlds,
> As if the air, the mid-day air, was swarming
> With the metaphysical changes that occur,
> Merely in living as and where we live.

2   The Internalization of Quest Romance

Freud, in an essay written sixty years ago on the relation of the
poet to daydreaming, made the surmise that all aesthetic pleasure
is forepleasure, an "incitement premium" or narcissistic fantasy.
The deepest satisfactions of literature, on this view, come from a
release of tensions in the psyche. That Freud had found, as almost
always, either part of the truth or at least a way to it, is clear
enough, even if a student of Blake or Wordsworth finds, as probably he must, this Freudian view to be partial, reductive, and a kind
of mirror-image of the imagination's truth. The deepest satisfactions of reading Blake or Wordsworth come from the realization
of new ranges of tensions in the mind, but Blake and Wordsworth
both believed, in different ways, that the pleasures of poetry were
only forepleasures, in the sense that poems, finally, were scaffold-
ings for a more imaginative vision, and not ends in themselves. I
think that what Blake and Wordsworth do for their readers, or can
do, is closely related to what Freud does or can do for his, which is
to provide both a map of the mind and a profound faith that the
map can be put to a saving use. Not that the uses agree, or that
the maps quite agree either, but the enterprise is a humanizing
one in all three of these discoverers. The humanisms do not agree
either; Blake's is apocalyptic, Freud's is naturalistic, and
Wordsworth's is – sometimes sublimely, sometimes uneasily –
blended of elements that dominate the other two.

Freud thought that even romance, with its element of play,
probably commenced in some actual experience whose "strong
impression on the writer had stirred up a memory of an earlier

experience, generally belonging to childhood, which then arouses a wish that finds fulfillment in the work in question, and in which elements of the recent event and the old memory should be discernible." Though this is a brilliant and comprehensive thought, it seems inadequate to the complexity of romance, particularly in the period during which romance as a genre, however displaced, became again the dominant form, which is to say the age of Romanticism. For English-speaking readers, this age may be defined as extending from the childhood of Blake and Wordsworth to the present moment. Convenience dictates that we distinguish the High Romantic period proper, during which a half-dozen major English poets did their work, from the generations that have come after them, but the distinction is difficult to justify critically.

Freud's embryonic theory of romance contains within it the potential for an adequate account of Romanticism, particularly if we interpret his "memory of an earlier experience" to mean also the recall of an earlier insight, or yearning, that may not have been experiential. The immortal longings of the child, rather variously interpreted by Freud, Blake, and Wordsworth, may not be at the roots of romance, historically speaking, since those roots go back to a psychology very different from ours, but they do seem to be at the sources of the mid-eighteenth-century revival of a romance consciousness, out of which nineteenth-century Romanticism largely came.

J. H. Van den Berg, whose introduction to a historical psychology I find crucial to an understanding of Romanticism, thinks that Rousseau "was the first to view the child as a child, and to stop treating the child as an adult." Van den Berg, as a doctor, does not think this was necessarily an advance: "Ever since Rousseau the child has been keeping its distance. This process of the child and adult growing away from each other began in the eighteenth century. It was then that the period of adolescence came into existence." Granting that Van den Berg is broadly correct (he at least attempts to explain an apparent historical modulation in consciousness that few historians of culture care to confront), then we are presented with another in a series of phenomena, clustering around Rousseau and his age, in which the major change from the Enlightenment to Romanticism manifested itself. Changes in consciousness are of course very rare, and no major synthesizer has come forth as yet, from any discipline, to demonstrate to us whether Romanticism marks a genuine change in consciousness or not. From the Freudian viewpoint, Romanticism is an "illusory therapy" (I take the phrase from Philip Rieff), or what Freud himself specifically termed an "erotic illusion." The dialectics of Romanticism, to the Freudians, are mistaken or inadequate, because the dialectics are sought in Schiller or Heine or in German Romantic philosophy down to Nietzsche, rather than in Blake or the English Romantics after him. Blake and Coleridge do not set intellect and passion against one another, any more than they arrive at the Freudian simplicity of the endless conflict between Eros and Thanatos. Possibly because of the clear associations between Jung and German Romanticism, it has been too easy for Freudian intellectuals to confound Romanticism with various modes of irrationalism. Though much contemporary scholarship attempts to study English and Continental Romanticism as a unified phenomenon, it can be argued that the English Romantics tend to lose more than they gain by such study.

Behind Continental Romanticism there lay very little in the way of a congenial native tradition of major poets writing in an ancestral mode, particularly when compared to the English Romantic heritage of Spenser, Shakespeare, and Milton. What allies Blake and Wordsworth, Shelley and Keats, is their strong mutual conviction that they are reviving the true English tradition of poetry, which they thought had vanished after the death of Milton, and had reappeared in diminished form, mostly after the death of Pope, in admirable but doomed poets like Chatterton, Cowper, and Collins, victims of circumstance and of their own false dawn of Sensibility. It is in this highly individual sense that English Romanticism legitimately can be called, as traditionally it has been, a revival of romance. More than a revival, it is an internalization of romance, particularly of the quest variety, an internalization made for more than therapeutic purposes, because made in the name of a humanizing hope that approaches apocalyptic intensity. The poet takes the patterns of quest-romance and transposes them into his own imaginative life, so that the entire rhythm of the quest is heard again in the movement of the poet himself from poem to poem. M. H. Abrams brilliantly traces these patterns of what he calls "the apocalypse of imagination." As he shows, historically they all directly stem from English reactions to the French Revolution, or to the intellectual currents that had flowed into the Revolution. Psychologically, they stem from the child's vision of a more titanic universe that the English Romantics were so reluctant to abandon. If adolescence was a Romantic or Rousseauistic phenomenon of consciousness, its concomitant was the very secular sense of being twice-born that is first discussed in the fourth chapter of *Émile*, and then beautifully developed by Shelley in his visionary account of Rousseau's second birth, in the concluding movement of *The Triumph of Life*. The pains of psychic maturation become, for Shelley, the potentially saving though usually destructive crisis when the imagination confronts its choice of either sustaining its own integrity or yielding to the illusive beauty of nature.

The movement of quest-romance, before its internalization by the High Romantics, was from nature to redeemed nature, the sanction of redemption being the gift of some external spiritual authority, sometimes magical. The Romantic movement is from nature to the imagination's freedom (sometimes a reluctant freedom), and the imagination's freedom is frequently purgatorial, redemptive in direction but destructive of the social self. The high cost of Romantic internalization, that is, of finding paradises within a renovated man, tends to manifest itself in the arena of self-consciousness. The quest is to widen consciousness as well as intensify it, but the quest is shadowed by a spirit that tends to narrow consciousness to an acute preoccupation with self. This shadow of imagination is solipsism, what Shelley calls the Spirit of Solitude or *Alastor*, the avenging daimon who is a baffled residue of the self, determined to be compensated for its loss of natural assurance, for having been awakened from the merely given condition that to Shelley, as to Blake, was but the sleep of death-in-

life. Blake calls this spirit of solitude a Spectre, or the genuine
Satan, the Thanatos or death-impulse in every natural man.
Modernist poetry in English organized itself, to an excessive
extent, as a supposed revolt against Romanticism, in the mistaken
hope of escaping this inwardness (though it was unconscious that
this was its prime motive). Modernist poetry learned better, as its
best work, the last phases of W. B. Yeats and Wallace Stevens,
abundantly shows, but criticism until recently was tardy in catching up, and lingering misapprehensions about the Romantics still
abide. Thus, Irving Howe, in an otherwise acute essay on literary
Modernism, says of the Romantic poets that "they do not surrender the wish to discover in the universe a network of spiritual
meaning which, however precariously, can enclose their selves."
This is simply not true of Blake or Wordsworth or Shelley or
Keats, nor is the statement of Marius Bewley's that Howe quotes
approvingly, that the Romantics' central desire is "to merge oneself with what is greater than oneself." Indeed, both statements
are excellent guides to what the major Romantics regarded as
human defeat or a living death, as the despairing surrender of the
imagination's autonomy. Since neither Howe nor Bewley is writing as an enemy of the Romantics, it is evident that we still need
to clear our mind of Eliotic cant on this subject.

Paul De Man terms this phenomenon the post-Romantic
dilemma, observing that every fresh attempt of Modernism to go
beyond Romanticism ends in the gradual realization of the
Romantics' continued priority. Modern poetry, in English, is the
invention of Blake and of Wordsworth, and I do not know of a
long poem written in English since then that is either as legitimately difficult or as rewardingly profound as *Jerusalem* or *The
Prelude*. Nor can I find a modern lyric, however happily ignorant
its writer, that develops beyond or surmounts its debt to
Wordsworth's great trinity of *Tintern Abbey, Resolution and
Independence,* and the *Intimations of Immortality* Ode. The dreadful
paradox of Wordsworth's greatness is that his uncanny originality,
still the most astonishing break with tradition in the language, has
been so influential that we have lost sight of its audacity and its
arbitrariness. In this, Wordsworth strongly resembles Freud, who

rightly compared his own intellectual revolution to those of Copernicus and Darwin. Van den Berg quietly sees "Freud, in the desperation of the moment, turning away from the present, where the cause of his patients' illnesses was located, to the past; and thus making them suffer from the past and making our existence akin to their suffering. It was not necessary." Is Van den Berg right? The question is as crucial for Wordsworth and Romanticism as it is for Freud and psychoanalysis. The most searching critique of Romanticism that I know is Van den Berg's critique of Freud, particularly the description of "The Subject and his Landscape":

> Ultimately the enigma of grief is the libido's inclination toward exterior things. What prompts the libido to leave the inner self? In 1914 Freud asked himself this question – the essential question of his psychology, and the essential question of the psychology of the twentieth century. His answer ended the process of interiorization. It is: the libido leaves the inner self when the inner self has become too full. In order to prevent it from being torn, the I has to aim itself on objects outside the self; ". . . ultimately man must begin to love in order not to get ill." So that is what it is. Objects are of importance only in an extreme urgency. Human beings, too. The grief over their death is the sighing of a too-far-distended covering, the groaning of an overfilled inner self.

Wordsworth is a crisis-poet, Freud a crisis-analyst; the saving movement in each is backward into lost time. But what is the movement of loss, in poet and in analyst? Van den Berg's suggestion is that Freud unnecessarily sacrificed the present moment, because he came at the end of a tradition of intellectual error that began with the extreme Cartesian dualism, and that progressively learned to devalue contact between the self and others, the self and the outer world, the self and the body. Wordsworth's prophecy, and Blake's, was overtly against dualism; they came, each said, to heal the division within man, and between man and the world, if never quite between man and man. But Wordsworth, the more influential because more apparently accessible of the two (I myself would argue that he is the more difficult because the more problematic poet), no more overcame a fundamental dualism than Freud did. Essentially this was Blake's complaint against him; it is certainly no basis for us to complain. Wordsworth made his kind of poetry out of an extreme urgency, and out of an overfilled inner self, a Blakean Prolific that nearly choked in an excess of its own delights. This is the Egotistical Sublime of which Keats complained, but Keats knew his debt to Wordsworth, as most poets since do not.

Wordsworth's Copernican revolution in poetry is marked by the evanescence of any subject but subjectivity, the loss of what a poem is "about." If, like the late Yvor Winters, one rejects a poetry that is not "about" something, one has little use for (or understanding of) Wordsworth. But, like Van den Berg on Freud, one can understand and love Wordsworth, and still ask of his radical subjectivity: was it necessary? Without hoping to find an answer, one can explore the question so as to come again to the central problem of Romantic (and post-Romantic) poetry: what, for men without belief and even without credulity, is the spiritual form of romance? How can a poet's (or any man's) life be one of continuous allegory (as Keats thought Shakespeare's must have been) in a reductive universe of death, a separated realm of atomized meanings, each discrete from the next? Though all men are questers, even the least, what is the relevance of quest in a gray world of continuities and homogenized enterprises? Or, in Wordsworth's own terms, which are valid for every major Romantic, what knowledge might yet be purchased except by the loss of power?

Frye, in his theory of myths, explores the analogue between quest-romance and the dream: "Translated into dream terms, the quest-romance is the search of the libido or desiring self for a fulfillment that will deliver it from the anxieties of reality but will still contain that reality." Internalized romance, and *The Prelude* and *Jerusalem* can be taken as the greatest examples of this kind, traces a Promethean and revolutionary quest, and cannot be translated into dream terms, for in it the libido turns inward into the self. Shelley's *Prometheus Unbound* is the most drastic High Romantic version of internalized quest, but there are more drastic versions still in our own age, though they present themselves as parodistic, as in the series of marvelous interior quests by Stevens, that go from *The Comedian As the Letter C* to the climactic *Notes Toward a*

Supreme Fiction. The hero of internalized quest is the poet himself, the antagonists of quest are everything in the self that blocks imaginative work, and the fulfillment is never the poem itself but the poem beyond that is made possible by the apocalypse of imagination. "A timely utterance gave that thought relief" is the Wordsworthian formula for the momentary redemption of the poet's sanity by the poem already written, and might stand as a motto for the history of the modern lyric from Wordsworth to Hart Crane.

The Romantics tended to take Milton's Satan as the archetype of the heroically defeated Promethean quester, a choice in which modern criticism has not followed them. But they had a genuine insight into the affinity between an element in their selves and an element in Milton that he would externalize only in a demonic form. What *is* heroic about Milton's Satan is a real Prometheanism and a thoroughly internalized one; he can steal only his own fire in the poem, since God can appear as fire, again in the poem, only when he directs it against Satan. In Romantic quest the Promethean hero stands finally, quite alone, upon a tower that is only himself, and his stance is all the fire there is. This realization leads neither to nihilism nor to solipsism, though Byron plays with the former and all fear the latter.

The dangers of idealizing the libido are of course constant in the life of the individual, and such idealizations are dreadful for whole societies, but the internalization of quest-romance had to accept these dangers. The creative process is the hero of Romantic poetry, and imaginative inhibitions, of every kind, necessarily must be the antagonists of the poetic quest. The special puzzle of Romanticism is the dialectical role that nature had to take in the revival of the mode of romance. Most simply, Romantic nature poetry, despite a long critical history of misrepresentation, was an antinature poetry, even in Wordsworth who sought a reciprocity or even a dialogue with nature, but found it only in flashes. Wordsworthian nature, thanks to Arnold and the critical tradition he fostered, has been misunderstood, though the insights of recent critics have begun to develop a better interpretive tradition, founded on A. C. Bradley's opposition to Arnold's view. Bradley stressed the strong side of Wordsworth's imagination, its Miltonic sublimity, which Arnold evidently never noticed, but which accounts for everything that is major in *The Prelude* and in the central crisis lyrics associated with it. Though Wordsworth came as a healer, and Shelley attacked him, in *Mont Blanc,* for attempting to reconcile man with nature, there is no such reconciliation in Wordsworth's poetry, and the healing function is performed only when the poetry shows the power of the mind over outward sense. The strength of renovation in Wordsworth resides only in the spirit's splendor, in what he beautifully calls "possible sublimity" or "something evermore about to be," the potential of an imagination too fierce to be contained by nature. This is the force that Coleridge sensed and feared in Wordsworth, and is remarkably akin to that strength in Milton that Marvell urbanely says he feared, in his introductory verses to *Paradise Lost.* As Milton curbed his own Promethianism, partly by showing its dangers through Satan's version of the heroic quest, so Wordsworth learned to restrain his, partly through making his own quest-romance, in *The Prelude,* an account of learning both the enormous strength of nature and nature's wise and benevolent reining-in of its own force. In the covenant between Wordsworth and nature, two powers that are totally separate from each other, and potentially destructive of the other, try to meet in a dialectic of love. "Meet" is too hopeful, and "blend" would express Wordsworth's ideal and not his achievement, but the try itself is definitive of Wordsworth's strangeness and continued relevance as a poet.

If Wordsworth, so frequently and absurdly called a pantheist, was not questing for unity with nature, still less were Blake, Shelley, and Keats, or their darker followers in later generations, from Beddoes, Darley, and Wade down to Yeats and Lawrence in our time. Coleridge and Byron, in their very different ways, were oddly closer both to orthodox Christian myth and to pantheism or some form of nature-worship, but even their major poems hardly approximate nature poetry. Romantic or internalized romance, especially in its purest version of the quest form, the poems of symbolic voyaging that move in a continuous tradition from Shelley's *Alastor* to Yeats's *The Wanderings of Oisin,* tends to see the context of nature as a trap for the mature imagination. This point requires much laboring, as the influence of older views of Romanticism is very hard to slough off. Even Northrop Frye, the leading romance theorist we have had at least since Ruskin, Pater, and Yeats, says that "in Romanticism the main direction of the quest of identity tends increasingly to be downward and inward, toward a hidden basis or ground of identity between man and nature." The directional part of this statement is true, but the stated goal I think is not. Frye still speaks of the Romantics as seeking a final unity between man and his nature, but Blake and Shelley do not accept such a unity as a goal, unless a total transformation of man and nature can precede unity, while Wordsworth's visions of "first and last and midst and without end" preserve the unyielding forms both of nature and of man. Keats's closest approach to an apocalyptic vision comes when he studies Moneta's face, at the climax of *The Fall of Hyperion*, but even that vision is essentially Wordsworthian, seeing as it does a perpetual change that cannot be ended by change, a human countenance made only more solitary in its growing alienation from nature, and a kind of naturalistic entropy that has gone beyond natural contraries, past "the lily and the snow." Probably only Joyce and Stevens, in later Romantic tradition, can be termed unreconstructed naturalists, or naturalistic humanists. Late Romantics as various as Eliot, Proust, and Shaw all break through uneasy natural contexts, as though sexuality was antithetical to the imagination, while Yeats, the very last of the High Romantics, worked out an elaborate sub-myth of the poet as antithetical quester, very much in the mode of Shelley's poetry. If the goal of Romantic internalization of the quest was a wider consciousness that would be free of the excesses of self-consciousness, a consideration of the rigors of experiential psychology will show, quite rapidly, why nature could not provide adequate context. The program of Romanticism, and not just in Blake, demands something more than a natural man to carry it through. Enlarged and more numerous senses are necessary, an enormous virtue of Romantic poetry clearly being that it not only demands such expansion but begins to make it possible, or at least attempts to do so.

The internalization of romance brought the concept of nature, and poetic consciousness itself, into a relationship they had never had before the advent of Romanticism in the later eighteenth century. Implicit in all the Romantics, and very explicit in Blake, is a difficult distinction between two modes of energy, organic and creative (Orc and Los in Blake, Prometheus bound and unbound in Shelley, Hyperion and Apollo in Keats, the Child and the Man, though with subtle misgivings, in Wordsworth). For convenience, the first mode can be called Prometheus and the second "the Real Man, the Imagination" (Blake's phrase, in a triumphant letter written when he expected death). Generally, Prometheus is the poet-as-hero in the first stage of his quest, marked by a deep involvement in political, social, and literary revolution, and a direct, even satirical attack on the institutional orthodoxies of European and English society, including historically oriented Christianity, and the neoclassic literary and intellectual tradition, particularly in its Enlightenment phase. The Real Man, the Imagination, emerges after terrible crises in the major stage of the Romantic quest, which is typified by a relative disengagement from revolutionary activism, and a standing-aside from polemic and satire, so as to re-center the arena of search within the self and its ambiguities. In the Prometheus stage, the quest is allied to the libido's struggle against repressiveness, and nature is an ally, though always a wounded and sometimes a withdrawn one. In the Real Man, the Imagination, stage, nature is the immediate though not the ultimate antagonist. The final enemy to be overcome is a recalcitrance in the self, what Blake calls the Spectre of Urthona, Shelley the unwilling dross that checks the spirit's flight, Wordsworth the sad perplexity or fear that kills or, best of all, the hope that is unwilling to be fed, and Keats, most simply and perhaps most powerfully, the Identity. Coleridge calls the antagonist by a bewildering variety of names since, of all these poets, he is the most hagridden by anxieties, and the most humanly vulnerable. Byron and Beddoes do not so much name the antagonist as they mock it, so as to cast it out by continuous satire and demonic farce. The best single name for the antagonist is Keats's Identity, but the most traditional is the Selfhood, and so I shall use it here.

Only the Selfhood, for the Romantics as for such Christian visionaries as Eckhart before them, burns in Hell. The Selfhood is not the erotic principle, but precisely that part of the erotic that cannot be released in the dialectic of love, whether between man and man, or man and nature. Here the Romantics, all of them, I think, even Keats, part company with Freud's dialectics of human nature. Freud's beautiful sentence on marriage is a formula against which the Romantic Eros can be tested: "A man shall leave father and mother – according to the Biblical precept – and cleave to his wife; then are tenderness and sensuality united." By the canons of internalized romance, that translates: a poet shall leave his Great Original (Milton, for the Romantics) and nature – according to the precept of Poetic Genius – and cleave to his Muse or Imagination; then are the generous and solitary halves united. But, so translated, the formula has ceased to be Freudian and has become High Romantic. In Freud, part of the ego's own self-love is projected onto an outward object, but part always remains in the ego, and even the projected portion can find its way back again. Somewhere Freud has a splendid sentence that anyone unhappy in love can take to heart: "Object-libido was at first ego-libido and can again be transformed into ego-libido," which is to say that a certain degree of narcissistic mobility is rather a good thing. Somewhere else Freud remarks that all romance is really a form of what he calls "Family-romance"; one could as justly say, in his terms, that all romance is necessarily a mode of ego-romance. This may be true, and in its humane gloom it echoes a great line of realists who culminate in Freud, but the popular notion that High Romanticism takes a very different view of love is a sounder insight into the Romantics than most scholarly critics ever achieve (or at least state). All romance, literary and human, is founded upon enchantment; Freud and the Romantics differ principally in their judgment as to what it is in us that resists enchantment, and what the value of that resistance is. For Freud it is the reality-principle, working through the great disenchanter, reason, the scientific attitude, and without it no civilized values are possible. For the Romantics, this is again a dialectical matter, as two principles intertwine in the resistance to enchantment, one "organic," an anxiety-principle masquerading as a reality-principle and identical to the ego's self-love that never ventures out to others, and the other "creative," which resists enchantment in the name of a higher mode than the sympathetic imagination. This doubling is clearest in Blake's mythology, where there are two egos, the Spectre of Urthona and Los, who suffer the enchantments, real *and* deceptive, of nature and the female, and who resist, when and where they can, on these very different grounds. But, though less schematically, the same doubling of the ego, into passive and active components, is present in the other poets wherever they attempt their highest flights and so spurn the earth. The most intense effort of the Romantic quest is made when the Promethean stage of quest is renounced and the purgatorial crisis that follows moves near to resolution. Romantic purgatory, by an extraordinary displacement of earlier mythology, is found just beyond the earthly paradise, rather than just before it, so that the imagination is tried by nature's best aspect. Instances of the interweaving of purgatory and paradise include nearly everything Blake says about the state of being he calls Beulah, and the whole development of Keats, from *Endymion* with its den or cave of Quietude on to the structure of *The Fall of Hyperion* where the poet enjoys the fruit and drink of paradise just before he has had his confrontation with Moneta, whose shrine must be reached by mounting purgatorial stairs.

Nothing in Romantic poetry is more difficult to comprehend, for me anyway, than the process that begins after each poet's renunciation of Prometheus; for the incarnation of the Real Man, the Imagination, is not like psychic maturation in poets before the Romantics. The love that transcends the Selfhood has its analogues in the renunciatory love of many traditions, including some within Christianity, but the creative Eros of the Romantics is not renunciatory though it is self-transcendent. It is, to use Shelley's phrasing, a total going-out from our own natures, total because the force moving out is not only the Promethean libido but rather a fusion between the libido and the active or imaginative element in the ego; or simply, desire wholly taken up into the imagination. "Shelley's love poetry," as a phrase, is almost a redundancy, Shelley having written little else, but his specifically erotic poems, a series of great lyrics and the dazzling *Epipsychidion*, have been undervalued because they are so very difficult, the difficulty being in the Shelleyan and Romantic vision of love.

Blake distinguished between Beulah and Eden as states of being, the first being the realm of family-romance and the second of apocalyptic romance, in which the objects of love altogether lose their object-dimension. In family-romance or Beulah, loved ones are not confined to their objective aspect (that would make them denizens of Blake's state of Generation or mere Experience), but they retain it nevertheless. The movement to the reality of Eden is one of recreation or better, of knowledge not purchased by the loss of power, and so of power and freedom gained *through* a going-out of our nature, in which that last phrase takes on its full range of meanings. Though Romantic love, particularly in Wordsworth and Shelley, has been compared to what Charles Williams calls the Romantic theology of Dante, the figure of Beatrice is not an accurate analogue to the various Romantic visions of the beloved, for sublimation is not an element in the movement from Prometheus to Man. There is no useful analogue to Romantic or imaginative love, but there is a useful contrary, in the melancholy wisdom of Freud on natural love, and the contrary has the helpful clarity one always finds in Freud. If Romantic love is the sublime, then Freudian love is the pathetic, and truer of course to the phenomenon insofar as it is merely natural. To Freud, love begins as ego-libido, and necessarily is ever after a history of sorrow, a picaresque chronicle in which the ever-vulnerable ego stumbles from delusion to frustration, to expire at last (if lucky) in the compromising arms of the ugliest of Muses, the reality-principle. But the saving dialectic of this picaresque is that it is better thus, as there is no satisfaction in satisfaction anyway, since in the Freudian view all erotic partners are somewhat inadequate replacements for the initial sexual objects, parents. Romantic love, to Freud, is a particularly intense version of the longing for the mother, a love in which the imago is loved, rather than the replacement. And Romantic love, on this account, is anything but a dialectic of transformation, since it is as doomed to overvalue the surrogate as it compulsively overvalues the mother. Our age begins to abound in late Romantic "completions" of Freud, but the Romantic critiques of him, by Jung and Lawrence in particular, have not touched the strength of his erotic pessimism. There is a subtly defiant attempt to make the imago do the work of the imagination by Stevens, particularly in the very Wordsworthian *The Auroras of Autumn,* and it is beautifully subversive of Freud, but of course it is highly indirect. Yet a direct Romantic counter-critique of Freud's critique of Romantic love emerges from any prolonged, central study of Romantic poetry. For Freud, there is an ironic loss of energy, perhaps even of spirit, with every outward movement of love away from the ego. Only pure self-love has a perfection to it, a stasis without loss, and one remembers again Van den Berg's mordant observation on Freud: "Ultimately the enigma of grief is the libido's inclination toward exterior things." All outward movement, in the Freudian psychodynamics, is a fall that results from "an overfilled inner self," which would sicken within if it did not fall outward, and downward, into the world of objects and of other selves. One longs for Blake to come again and rewrite *The Book of Urizen* as a satire on this cosmogony of love. The poem would not require that much rewriting, for it now can be read as a prophetic satire on Freud, Urizen being a superego certainly overfilled with itself, and sickening into a false creation or creation-fall. If Romantic love can be castigated as "erotic illusion," Freudian love can be judged as "erotic reduction," and the prophets of the reality-principle are in danger always of the Urizenic boast:

> I have sought for a joy without pain,
> For a solid without fluctuation
> Why will you die O Eternals?
> Why live in unquenchable burnings?

The answer is the Romantic dialectic of Eros and Imagination, unfair as it is to attribute to the Freudians a censorious repressiveness. But, to Blake and the Romantics, all available accounts of right reason, even those that had risen to liberate men, had the disconcerting tendency to turn into censorious moralities. Freud painfully walked a middle way, not unfriendly to the poetic imagination, and moderately friendly to Eros. If his myth of love is so sparse, rather less than a creative Word, it is still open both to analytic modification and to a full acceptance of everything that can come out of the psyche. Yet it is not quite what Philip Rieff claims for it, as it does not erase "the gap between therapeutic rationalism and self-assertive romanticism." That last is only the first stage of the Romantic quest, the one this discussion calls Prometheus. There remains a considerable gap between the subtle perfection to which Freud brought therapeutic rationalism and the mature Romanticism that is self-transcendent in its major poets.

There is no better way to explore the Real Man, the Imagination, than to study his monuments: *The Four Zoas, Milton,* and *Jerusalem; The Prelude* and the *Recluse* fragment; *The Ancient Mariner* and *Christabel; Prometheus Unbound, Adonais,* and *The Triumph of Life;* the two *Hyperions; Don Juan; Death's Jest-Book;* these are the definitive Romantic achievements, the words that were and will be, day and night. What follows is only an epitome, a rapid sketch of the major phase of this erotic quest. The sketch, like any that attempts to trace the visionary company of love, is likely to end in listening to the wind, hoping to hear an instant of a fleeting voice.

The internalization of quest-romance made the poet-hero not a seeker after nature but after his own mature powers, and so the Romantic poet turned away, not from society to nature, but from nature to what was more integral than nature, within himself. The widened consciousness of the poet did not give him intimations of a former union with nature or the Divine, but rather of his former selfless self. One thinks of Yeats's Blakean declaration: "I'm looking for the face I had/Before the world was made." Different as the major Romantics were in their attitudes toward religion, they were united (except for Coleridge) in *not* striving for unity with anything but what might be called their Tharmas or id component, Tharmas being the Zoa or Giant Form in Blake's mythology who was the unfallen human potential for realizing instinctual desires, and so was the regent of Innocence. Tharmas is a shepherd-figure, his equivalent in Wordsworth being a num-

ber of visions of man against the sky, of actual shepherds Wordsworth had seen in his boyhood. This Romantic pastoral vision (its
pictorial aspect can be studied in the woodcuts of Blake's Virgil
series, and in the work done by Palmer, Calvert, and Richmond
while under Blake's influence) is biblical pastoralism, but not at
all of a traditional kind. Blake's Tharmas is inchoate when fallen,
as the id or appetite is inchoate, desperately starved, and uneasily
allied to the Spectre of Urthona, the passive ego he has projected
outward to meet an object-world from which he has been severed
so unwillingly. Wordsworth's Tharmas, besides being the shep-
herd image of human divinity, is present in the poet himself as a
desperate desire for continuity in the self, a desperation that at its
worst sacrifices the living moment, but at its best produces a saving urgency that protects the imagination from the strong
enchantments of nature.

In Freud the ego mediates between id and superego, and
Freud had no particular interest in further dividing the ego itself.
In Romantic psychic mythology, Prometheus rises from the id,
and can best be thought of as the force of libido, doomed to
undergo a merely cyclic movement from appetite to repression,
and then back again; any quest within nature is thus at last irrelevant to the mediating ego, though the quest goes back and forth
through it. It is within the ego itself that the quest must turn, to
engage the antagonist proper, and to clarify the imaginative component in the ego by its strife of contraries with its dark brother.
Frye, writing on Keats, calls the imaginative ego *identity-with* and
the selfhood ego *identity-as,* which clarifies Keats's ambiguous use
of "identity" in this context. Geoffrey Hartman, writing on
Wordsworth, points to the radical Protestant analogue to the
Romantic quest: "The terror of discontinuity or separation enters,
in fact, as soon as the imagination truly enters. In its restraint of
vision, as well as its peculiar nakedness before the moment, this
resembles an extreme Protestantism, and Wordsworth seems to
quest for 'evidences' in the form of intimations of continuity."
Wordsworth's greatness was in his feeling the terror of discontinuity as acutely as any poet could, yet overcoming this terror nevertheless, by opening himself to vision. With Shelley, the analogue

of the search for evidences drops out, and an Orphic strain takes its place, as no other English poet gives so continuous an impression of relying on almost literal inspiration. Where Keats knew the Selfhood as an attractive strength of distinct identity that had to be set aside, and Wordsworth as a continuity he longed for yet learned to resist, and Blake as a temptation to prophetic wrath and withdrawal that had to be withstood, Shelley frequently gives the impression of encountering no enchantment he does not embrace, since every enchantment is an authentic inspiration. Yet this is a false impression, though Yeats sometimes received it, as in his insistence that Shelley, great poet as he certainly was, lacked a Vision of Evil. The contrary view to Yeats is that of C. S. Lewis, who held that Shelley, more than any other "heathen" poet (the word is from Lewis), drove home the truth of Original Sin. Both views are mistaken. For Shelley, the Selfhood's strong enchantment, stronger even than it is for the other Romantics, is one that would keep him from ever concluding the Prometheus phase of the quest. The Selfhood allies itself with Prometheus against the repressive force Shelley calls Jupiter, his version of Blake's Urizen or Freud's superego. This temptation calls the poet to perpetual revolution, and Shelley, though longing desperately to see the tyrannies of his time overturned, renounces it at the opening of *Prometheus Unbound,* in the Imagination's name. Through his renunciation, he moves to overturn the tyranny of time itself.

There are thus two main elements in the major phase of Romantic quest, the first being the inward overcoming of the Selfhood's temptation, and the second the outward turning of the triumphant Imagination, free of further internalizations, though "outward" and "inward" become cloven fictions or false conceptual distinctions in this triumph, which must complete a dialectic of love by uniting the Imagination with its bride, a transformed, ongoing creation of the Imagination rather than a redeemed nature. Blake and Wordsworth had long lives, and each completed his version of this dialectic. Coleridge gave up the quest, and became only an occasional poet, while Byron's quest, even had he lived into middle age, would have become increasingly ironic. Keats died at twenty-five, and Shelley at twenty-nine; despite their fecundity, they did not complete their development, but their death-fragments, *The Fall of Hyperion* and *The Triumph of Life*, prophesy the final phase of the quest in them. Each work breaks off with the Selfhood subdued, and there is profound despair in each, particularly in Shelley's, but there are still hints of what the Imagination's triumph would have been in Keats. In Shelley, the final despair may be total, but a man who had believed so fervently that the good time would come, had already given a vision of imaginative completion in the closing act of *Prometheus Unbound*, and we can go back to it and see what is deliberately lacking in *The Triumph of Life*. What follows is a rapid attempt to trace the major phase of quest in the four poets, taking as texts *Jerusalem* and *The Prelude*, and the *Fall* and *Triumph*, these two last with supplementary reference to crucial earlier erotic poems of Keats and Shelley.

Of Blake's long poems the first, *The Four Zoas*, is essentially a poem of Prometheus, devoting itself to the cyclic strife between the Promethean Orc and the moral censor, Urizen, in which the endless cycle between the two is fully exposed. The poem ends in an apocalypse, the explosive and Promethean *Night the Ninth, Being The Last Judgment*, which in itself is one of Blake's greatest works, yet from which he turned when he renounced the entire poem (by declining to engrave it). But not before he attempted to move the entire poem from the Prometheus stage to the Imagination, for Blake's own process of creative maturation came to its climax while he worked on *The Four Zoas*. The entrance into the mature stage of the quest is clearly shown by the different versions of *Night the Seventh*, for the later one introduces the doubling of the ego into Spectre of Urthona and Los, Selfhood or *Identity-As*, and Imagination or *Identity-With*. Though skillfully handled, it was not fully clarified by Blake, even to himself, and so he refused to regard the poem as definitive vision. Its place in his canon was filled, more or less, by the double-romance *Milton* and *Jerusalem*. The first is more palpably in a displaced romance mode, involving as it does symbolic journeys downward to our world by Milton and his emanation or bride of creation, Ololon, who descend from an orthodox Eternity in a mutual search for one

another, the characteristic irony being that they could never find
one another in a traditional heaven. There is very little in the
poem of the Prometheus phase, Blake having already devoted to
that a series of prophetic poems, from *America* and *Europe* through
The Book of Urizen and on to the magnificent if unsatisfactory (to
him, not to us) *The Four Zoas*. The two major stages of the mature
phase of quest dominate the structure of *Milton*. The struggle
with the Selfhood moves from the quarrel between Palamabron
(Blake) and Satan (Hayley) in the introductory Bard's Song on to
Milton's heroic wrestling match with Urizen, and climaxes in the
direct confrontation between Milton and Satan on the Felpham
shore, in which Milton recognizes Satan as his own Selfhood. The
recognition compels Satan to a full epiphany, and a subsequent
defeat. Milton then confronts Ololon, the poem ending in an
epiphany contrary to Satan's, in what Blake specifically terms a
preparation for a going-forth to the great harvest and vintage of
the nations. But even this could not be Blake's final Word; the
quest in *Milton* is primarily Milton's and not Blake's, and the
quest's antagonist is still somewhat externalized. In *Jerusalem, The
Prelude's* only rival as the finest long poem of the nineteenth century, Blake gives us the most comprehensive single version of
Romantic quest. Here there is an alternation between vision
sweeping outward into the nightmare world of the reality-principle, and a wholly inward vision of conflict in Blake's ego, between
the Spectre and Los. The poet's antagonist is himself, the poem's
first part being the most harrowing and tormented account of
genius tempted to the madness of self-righteousness, frustrate
anger, and solipsistic withdrawal, in the Romantic period. Blake-
Los struggles on, against this enchantment of despair, until the
poem quietly, almost without warning, begins to move into the
light of a Last Judgment, of a kind passed by every man upon himself. In the poem's final plates (Blake's canonical poems being a
series of engraved plates), the reconciliation of Los and his ema-
native portion, Enitharmon, begins, and we approach the completion of quest.

Though Blake, particularly in *Jerusalem,* attempts a continuity based on thematic juxtaposition and simultaneity, rather than

on consecutiveness, he is in such sure control of his own procedure that his work is less difficult to summarize than *The Prelude*, a
contrast that tends to startle inexperienced readers of Blake and
of Wordsworth. *The Prelude* follows a rough, naturalistic chronology through Wordsworth's life down to the middle of the journey,
where it, like any modern reader, leaves him, in his state of preparation for a further greatness that never came. What is there
already, besides the invention of the modern lyric, is a long poem
so rich and strange it has defied almost all description.

 The Prelude is an autobiographical romance that frequently
seeks expression in the sublime mode, which is really an invitation
to aesthetic disaster. *The Excursion* is an aesthetic disaster, as
Hazlitt, Byron, and many since happily have noted, yet there
Wordsworth works within rational limits. *The Prelude* ought to be
an outrageous poem, but its peculiar mixture of displaced genre
and inappropriate style *works*, because its internalization of quest
is the inevitable story for its age. Wordsworth did not have the
Promethean temperament, yet he had absolute insight into it, as
The Borderers already showed. In *The Prelude,* the initial quest phase
of the poet-as-Prometheus is diffuse but omnipresent. It determines every movement in the growth of the child's consciousness,
always seen as a violation of the established natural order, and it
achieves great power in Book VI, when the onset of the French
Revolution is associated with the poet's own hidden desires to sur-
mount nature, desires that emerge in the great passages clustered
around the Simplon Pass. The Promethean quest fails, in one way
in the Alps when chastened by nature, and in another with the
series of shocks to the poet's moral being when England wars
against the Revolution, and the Revolution betrays itself. The
more direct Promethean failure, the poet's actual abandonment
of Annette Vallon, is presented only indirectly in the 1805
Prelude, and drops out completely from the revised, posthumously
published *Prelude* of 1850, the version most readers encounter. In
his crisis, Wordsworth learns the supernatural and superhuman
strength of his own imagination, and is able to begin a passage to
the mature phase of his quest. But his anxiety for continuity is too
strong for him, and he yields to its dark enchantment. The

Imagination phase of his quest does not witness the surrender of
his Selfhood and the subsequent inauguration of a new dialectic
of love, purged of the natural heart, as it is in Blake. Yet he wins a
provisional triumph over himself, in Book XII of *The Prelude,* and
in the closing stanzas of *Resolution and Independence* and the Great
Ode. And the final vision of *The Prelude* is not of a redeeming
nature, but of a liberated creativity transforming its creation into
the beloved:

> Prophets of Nature, we to them will speak
> A lasting inspiration, sanctified
> By reason, blest by faith: what we have loved
> Others will love, and we will teach them how;
> Instruct them how the mind of man becomes
> A thousand times more beautiful than the earth
> On which he dwells, above this frame of things . . .

Coleridge, addressed here as the other Prophet of Nature,
renounced his own demonic version of the Romantic quest (clearest in the famous triad of *Kubla Khan, Christabel,* and *The Ancient
Mariner*), his wavering Prometheanism early defeated not so much
by his Selfhood as by his Urizenic fear of his own imaginative
energy. It was a high price for the release he had achieved in his
brief phase of exploring the romance of the marvelous, but the
loss itself produced a few poems of unique value, the *Dejection*
Ode in particular. These poems show how Coleridge preceded
Wordsworth in the invention of a new kind of poetry that shows
the mind in a dialogue with itself. The motto of this poetry might
well be its descendant Stevens's "The mind is the terriblest force
in the world, father,/Because, in chief, it, only, can defend/
Against itself. At its mercy, we depend/Upon it." Coleridge
emphasizes the mercy, Wordsworth the saving terror of the force.
Keats and Shelley began with a passion closer to the Prometheus
phase of Blake than of Wordsworth or Coleridge. The fullest
development of Romantic quest, after Blake's mythology and
Wordsworth's exemplary refusal of mythology, is in Keats's
Endymion and Shelley's *Prometheus Unbound.* In this second generation of Romantic questers the same first phase of Prometheanism

appears, as does the second phase of crisis, renounced quest, overcoming of the Selfhood, and final movement toward imaginative love, but the relation of the quest to the world of the reality-principle has changed. In Blake, dream with its ambiguities centers in Beulah, the purgatorial lower paradise of sexuality and benevolent nature. In Wordsworth, dream is rare, and betokens either a prolepsis of the imagination abolishing nature or a state the poet calls "visionary dreariness," in which the immediate power of the mind over outward sense is so great that the ordinary forms of nature seem to have withdrawn. But in Keats and Shelley, a polemical Romanticism matures, and the argument of the dream with reality becomes an equivocal one. Romanticism guessed at a truth our doctors begin to measure; as infants we dream for half the time we are asleep, and as we age we dream less and less, while we sleep. The doctors have not yet told us that utterly dreamless sleep directly prophesies or equals death, but it is a familiar Romantic conceit, and may prove to be true. We are our imaginations, and die with them.

Dreams, to Shelley and Keats, are not wish-fulfillments. It is not Keats but Moneta, the passionate and wrong-headed Muse in *The Fall of Hyperion,* who first confounds poets and dreamers as one tribe, and then overreacts by insisting they are totally distinct, and even sheer opposites, antipodes. Freud is again a clear-headed guide; the manifest and latent content of the dream can be distinct, even opposite, but in the poem they come together. The younger Romantics do not seek to render life a dream, but to recover the dream for the health of life. What is called real is too often an exhausted phantasmagoria, and the reality-principle can too easily be debased into a principle of surrender, an accommodation with death-in-life. We return to the observation of Van den Berg, cited earlier; Rousseau and the Romantics discovered not only the alienation between child and adult, but the second birth of psychic maturation or adolescence. Eliot thought that the poet of *Adonais* and *The Triumph of Life* had never "progressed" beyond the ideas and ideals of adolescence, or at least of what Eliot had believed in his *own* adolescence. Every reader can be left to his own judgment of the relative maturity of *Ash Wednesday* and *The Witch of Atlas,* or *The Cocktail Party* and *The Cenci,* and is free to formulate his own dialectics of progression.

The Promethean quest, in Shelley and in Keats, is from the start uneasy about its equivocal ally, nature, and places a deeper trust in dream, for at least the dream itself is not reductive, however we reduce it in our dissections. Perhaps the most remarkable element in the preternatural rapidity of maturation in Keats and Shelley is their early renunciation of the Prometheus phase of the quest, or rather, their dialectical complexity in simultaneously presenting the necessity and the inherent limitation of this phase. In *Alastor,* the poem's entire thrust is at one with the poet-hero's self-destruction; this is the cause of the poem's radical unity, which C. S. Lewis rightly observed as giving a marvelous sense of the poet's being at one with his subject. Yet the poem is also a daimonic shadow in motion; it shows us nature's revenge upon the imagination, and the excessive price of the quest in the poet's alienation from other selves. On a cosmic scale, this is part of the burden of *Prometheus Unbound,* where the hero, who massively represents the bound prophetic power of all men, rises from his icy crucifixion by refusing to continue the cycles of revolution and repression that form an ironic continuity between himself and Jupiter. Demogorgon, the dialectic of history, rises from the abyss and stops history, thus completing in the macrocosmic shadow what Prometheus, by his renunciation, inaugurates in the microcosm of the individual imagination, or the liberating dream taken up into the self. Shelley's poetry after this does not maintain the celebratory strain of Act IV of his lyrical drama. The way again is down and out, to a purgatorial encounter with the Selfhood, but the Selfhood's temptations, for Shelley, are subtle and wavering, and mask themselves in the forms of the ideal. So fused become the ideal and these masks that Shelley, in the last lines he wrote, is in despair of any victory, though it is Shelley's Rousseau and not Shelley himself who actually chants:

. . . thus on the way
Mask after mask fell from the countenance
And form of all; and long before the day

Was old, the joy which waked like heaven's glance
The sleepers in the oblivious valley, died;
And some grew weary of the ghastly dance,

And fell, as I have fallen, by the wayside –

For Shelley, Rousseau was not a failed poet, but rather the poet whose influence had resulted in an imaginative revolution, and nearly ended time's bondage. So, Rousseau speaks here not for himself alone, but for his tradition, and necessarily for Coleridge, Wordsworth, and the Promethean Shelley as well, indeed for poetry itself. Yet, rightly or wrongly, the image Shelley leaves with us, at his end, is not this falling-away from quest but the image of the poet forever wakeful amidst the cone of night, illuminating it as the star Lucifer does, fading as the star, becoming more intense as it narrows into the light.

The mazes of romance, in *Endymion,* are so winding that they suggest the contrary to vision, a labyrinthine nature in which all quest must be forlorn. In this realm, nothing narrows to an intensity, and every passionate impulse widens out to a diffuseness, the fate of Endymion's own search for his goddess. In reaction, Keats chastens his own Prometheanism, and attempts the objective epic in *Hyperion.* Hyperion's self-identity is strong but waning fast, and the fragment of the poem's Book III introduces an Apollo whose self-identity is in the act of being born. The temptation to go on with the poem must have been very great, after its magnificent beginnings, but Keats's letters are firm in renouncing it. Keats turns from the enchantments of Identity to the romance-fragment, *The Fall of Hyperion,* and engages instead the demon of subjectivity, his own poetic ambitions, as Wordsworth had done before him. Confronted by Moneta, he meets the danger of her challenge not by asserting his own Identity, but by finding his true form in the merged identity of the poethood, in the high function and responsibilities of a Wordsworthian humanism. Though the poem breaks off before it attempts the dialectic of love, it has achieved the quest, for the Muse herself has been transformed by the poet's persistence and integrity. We wish for more, necessarily, but only now begin to understand how much we had received, even in this broken   monument.

I have scanted the dialectic of love, in all of these poets. Romantic love, past its own Promethean adolescence, is not the possessive love of the natural heart, which is the quest of Freudian Eros, moving always in a tragic rhythm out from and back to the isolate ego. That is the love Blake explicitly rejected:

> Let us agree to give up Love
> And root up the Infernal Grove
> Then shall we return and see
> The worlds of happy Eternity
>
> Throughout all Eternity
> I forgive you you forgive me . . .

The Infernal Grove grows thick with virtues, but these are the selfish virtues of the natural heart. Desire for what one lacks becomes a habit of possession, and the Selfhood's jealousy murders the Real Man, the Imagination. All such love is an entropy, and as such Freud understood and accepted it. We become aware of others only as we learn our separation from them, and our ecstasy is a reduction. Is this the human condition, and love its only mitigation?

> To cast off the idiot Questioner who is always questioning,
> But never capable of answering . . .

Whatever else the love that the full Romantic quest aims at may be, it cannot be a therapy. It must make all things new, and then marry what it has made. Less urgently, it seeks to define itself through the analogue of each man's creative potential. But it learns, through its poets, that it cannot define what it is, but only what it will be. The man prophesied by the Romantics is a central man who is always in the process of becoming his own begetter, and though his major poems perhaps have been written, he as yet has not fleshed out his prophecy, nor proved the final form of his love.

3   Yeats and the Romantics

Yeats remarks in his *Autobiographies* that we are never satisfied with the maturity of those whom we have admired in boyhood, and that insight is the ironic undersong of this essay. I commence though with another kind of irony. There is a bad paradox in the relationship between the poetry of our time and what was the most influential of our critical schools, the rhetorical or formalistic New Criticism. The best of our modern poets, in Britain and America alike, were Romantics, akin in creative procedure and in theme to a main tradition in English poetry, the line that runs from aspects of Spenser and of Milton, through Blake and Wordsworth, Coleridge, Shelley and Keats on to Tennyson, Browning, Swinburne and William Morris. Yeats and D. H. Lawrence in Great Britain, Wallace Stevens and Hart Crane in this country, are the legitimate inheritors of this Spenserian or Romantic line of poets, whose theme is the saving transformation that attends some form of humanism, and whose creative mode is the heterocosm, or the poem as an alternative world to that of nature. These opening remarks are polemical, and yet are intended as mere description. That they should be polemical is the consequence of a considerable body of critical misrepresentation that has been applied to Yeats and to Lawrence, to Stevens and to Crane. The rhetorical critics who have admired these poets have justified such admiration, where they could, by distorting the nature of the work they read. R. P. Blackmur gave us Wallace Stevens, that most Wordsworthian of poets, as another Alexander

Pope, elegantly troping a Late Augustan idea of order into the essential gaudiness of what we were asked to believe was a deliberately minor poetry. Allen Tate, with the pugnacity of strong-minded mis-information, assured us that Yeats's Romanticism would be invented by his critics. With Lawrence and Hart Crane, the New Criticism sought safer grounds, and judged those fierce Romantics as splendid failures, as men who did not know enough, and who ostentatiously lacked the inner check, the saving Eliotic balance of the only true tradition.

One hopes to seek only the pure purposes of the pure critic – plainly to propound a poet – and yet so many extra-critical cultural preferences have become critical principle among the followers of Eliot, and their students, and now *their* students' students, that one is compelled to affirm again the continuity of the best modern poetry with nineteenth-century poetic tradition. With Yeats, one begins with mere external fact. He edited Spenser and Blake, Blake on a very large scale, and edited very badly indeed. He wrote extensive commentaries on Blake, again very bad indeed, as well as the best critical essay yet written on Shelley's poetry, balanced later in life by one of the worst. He called William Morris his "chief of men," and said of Morris's romances that they were works he read very slowly, unable to bear the notion of ever being finished. He began, as he said, in all things Pre-Raphaelite, and passed to the companionship of the Tragic Generation, the Rhymers' Club of the Nineties, two of whom, Ernest Dowson and Lionel Johnson, haunted him to the end of his own life.

All these are only antecedents. They do not refute the barren but still prevalent critical commonplace that Yeats's greatness is in the utter contrast between his earlier manner, pejoratively called Romantic, and his late style, so curiously called "Metaphysical" by many of the New Critics. Against this false commonplace I urge the contrary statement: Yeats began as a mock or decadent Romantic, and matured into a true one, a genuine inheritor of the fulfilled renown of Blake and of Shelley, the apocalyptic myth-makers among the Romantics. To chronicle the attitudes of Yeats towards Blake and Shelley, and toward Shelley in particular, is to chronicle also the stages by which Yeats found at last his true self as a poet.

No poet, I suppose, has ever assumed as many deliberate masks as Yeats did, or been so adept at self-dramatization. At such necromancy of the self perhaps Byron was Yeats's peer, but Byron was all that Yeats merely hoped to be, a nobleman, an adventurer and a genuinely tormented quester, who could seek to become that single one in his own age whose search after his own self might prove to be authentic. The mask-seeking quests of Yeats were searches for a voice or voices, rather than a self or selves. Yeats lusted after communal voices, that the authority of many might strengthen the speech of his own tongue. His search took him first to the voice of the folk, next to spirit voices, and at last to the voices of the dead. In the dank morasses of occult and arcane traditions, he sought a tone rather than a language, a stance rather than a doctrine.

When a poet, or I suppose any man, wishes to speak with the voice of many men, and yet despises the multitude of mankind, as Yeats most assuredly did, he risks an error that manifests itself as flatulence in the world of the imagination, and Fascism in the world of events. This error Yeats did not avoid, and a certain silliness throughout his work is the sad consequence. The Yeats who wrote eccentric essays about eugenics, who composed marching songs for an Irish Fascist brigade, and who loved to go about his house brandishing a Japanese ceremonial sword – this Yeats can safely be ignored, for he scarcely is to be encountered in the important poems and plays. It is the occult Yeats who is not so easily ignored, though he was only a little less absurd. This is the Yeats who was an intimate of MacGregor Mathers and of Madame Blavatsky; the Yeats whose chief emotion at the outbreak of World War I was annoyance that he was thus prevented from pursuing a particularly promising poltergeist in Transylvania; the Yeats, who on learning that his true daimon or dark opposite was the dead sage, Leo Africanus, proceeded not only to write letters to that great personage, but judiciously composed the replies also. Of this Yeats we have heard rather too much and are likely to hear rather too much more in the future, for a school of Yeatsian occult enthusiasts has risen among us, in this country and in Britain, as eager to drown the poems and plays in a mass of arcane commentary, as their friends have already all but drowned the poetry of Spenser, Blake, and Shelley. We are now given a neo-platonized and cabbalized Yeats, whom to understand we must first master an august company that ranges from Cornelius Agrippa to Madame Blavatsky, from the astral wanderings of Swedenborg to the secret speculations of the Rosicrucians.

With Yeats – as opposed to Blake and Shelley – the scholarly and pseudo-scholarly researchers into esoterica appear at first to be on safe ground, for the subject of their investigations really did share their preternatural interests. But Yeats the poet was much wiser than Yeats the man, and the occultizers are welcome to the man. The vulgar error of the occultizers in Yeats's verse is only a local instance of a widespread malady in modern scholarly criticism, one whose final cause is the influence of the history-of-ideas, that most pernicious of anti-poetic disciplines. From this source has come the confused notion that the sources of a poet's thought, and the meaning of his verbal figures, are to be found in philosophy or in other discursive modes of organized knowledge, such as history, theology and psychology. But the argument of poetry is not a philosophical one, or frequently a discursive argument of any sort. Poems, as Milton said, really are more passionate and more sensuous than philosophic ideas are, but if they are simpler, as Milton added, it is a simplicity that opposes itself to complication, rather than to complexity. There is, as Blake theorized, a contrary logic of the imagination, in which the possibility of coherence counts for more than the iron law of non-contradiction. What matters to a poet, or perhaps one ought to say to the poet in a poet, is only that element in any notion that can help him to write his poem, and that element is already a form of poetry, for only poetry can be made into poems, as Wallace Stevens wittily surmised. That is why poets, in their poems, are more likely to be influenced by other poets than by discursive writers of any kind whatsoever. In speaking of poetic influences, we stumble now-a-days upon another confusion that inhibits our apprehension of poetry, for even when we speak of one poet influencing another, we so rarely know just what we mean, or else perversely we seek a verbal echoing as the full substance of what such influencing can mean. To study the relation of Yeats's poetry to Blake's or to Shelley's might teach us not only something of value about Yeats, but might clarify the whole problem of how and why one poem helps to form another.

I begin however, with the more conventional gestures of chronology, with the young Yeats first learning his craft. Yeats says that he had a relatively late sexual awakening, when nearly seventeen, and that his first sexual reveries took their images from Shelley's poems *Alastor* and *Prince Athanase,* and from Byron's *Manfred* – all to be expected from a boy who was seventeen in 1882. Yeats's first poetry was an attempt at a Spenserian epic on the story of Roland, which was abandoned for the Spenserian and Shelleyan blend that was to develop into Yeats's first published poetry, not to be found in his *Collected Poems,* but printed in the *Dublin University Revue* when Yeats was twenty, and now available in the appendices to the Variorum Edition of his poetry.

The longest and most ambitious of these works is an allegorical verse-drama, *The Island of Statues,* subtitled by Yeats *An Arcadian Faery Tale* – in *Two Acts,* which I shall briefly summarize. Two Arcadian shepherds, timid but clamorous creatures, love a proud shepherdess who scorns them for their lack of courage. A hunter, to win her love, goes forth on a quest to the enchanted Island of Statues, seeking a mysterious Flower, which is guarded by a dread enchantress. The choice of the wrong flower on this Island has turned many a quester into stone, and the hunter suffers a similar fate. He is then sought in turn by his shepherdess, who pauses long enough in her wanderings to provoke her two timid pastoral suitors into a mutually destructive dual for the favors she does not intend to grant. Reaching the enchanted Island of Statues in the disguise of a boy, she entices the enchantress into falling in love with her, and so gains the enchanted flower, with which she restores the statues into breathing flesh, and thus destroys the poor enchantress, as earlier she had destroyed her shepherd-suitors. This frightening little Arcadian drama ends with the shepherdess, her hunter-lover and the other restored statues resolving to remain forever on the Island. The closing touch, befitting the play's theme, is that the rising moon casts the shadows of the hunter and the other restored creatures far across the grass, but the destructively successful quester, the shepherdess, stands shadowless in the moonlight, symbolizing the loss of her soul. Yeats, in later life, writing about Shelley, said that a man's mind at twenty contains everything of importance it will ever possess. Whatever we think of this as a general principle, it does seem relevant to Yeats himself. *The Island of Statues* takes its Circe-like enchantress from Spenser, and most of its verse-texture from Shelley, yet its decadent and savage theme is curiously Yeats's own, holding in embryo much that is to come. The shepherdess's desire to convert her Arcadian lovers into murderous men-of-action; the equivocal Enchantress longing for the embrace of ordinary flesh; the frozen sculpture that ensues from a defeated naturalistic quest; the mocking and embittering moonlight that exposes an occult victory as a human defeat – all these, despite their Pre-Raphaelite colorings, are emblems that Yeats was never to abandon. But the verse-drama, and most of its companion-pieces written up through 1885, he certainly did abandon. One of these pieces, a dramatic poem called *The Seeker,* introduces an Old Knight who has devoted sixty years to a dream-led wandering in search of his beloved enchantress. Her vision had made him a coward on the field of battle; now at last he has found her and craves a single glance at her face before he dies. A sudden light burst over her, and he sees her as what she is – a bearded witch, called Infamy by men. The witch raises a mirror, in which the

Knight sees his own shadowed face and form, and he dies. This grim phantasy is rather clearly blended out of Shelley's *Alastor* and Spenser's Fradubio discovering that his beloved is the Whore of Infamy, Duessa; but Yeats's allegory is charactistically more savage and more destructively self-directed. The quest that reduces a man-of-action to a coward is truly only a lust after infamy, and ends with a mirrored image of the faded self. Though Yeats rejected *The Seeker* as he had *The Island of Statues,* he chose long afterwards to open his *Collected Poems* with a Song originally printed as an Epilogue to both *The Island of Statues* and *The Seeker.* A satyr enters, carring a sea-shell, emblem of poetic prophecy in Wordsworth and in Shelley. He chants:

> The woods of Arcady are dead,
> And over is their antique joy,
> Of old the world on dreaming fed –
> Grey truth is now her painted toy –
> But O, sick children of the world,
> Of all the many changing things
> In dreary dancing past us whirled,
> To the old cracked tune that Chronos sings,
> Words alone are certain good.

The chant goes on to offer the hypothesis that our world may be only a sudden flaming word, soon to be silenced. The reader is therefore urged not to seek action or truth, but only whatever story a murmuring sea-shell will give to him, after which the satyr closes by insisting on the value of mere dreaming as its own end. As an epilogue to works that have given us a vision of the dream as self-destruction, this is very curious, and even the young poet's faith in a verbal universe is rather disconcertingly allied to the Shelleyan image of a self-consuming flame. What Yeats had attained to in 1885 was precisely that dead-end of vision that Shelley had come to in *Alastor* some seventy years before, and moreover at about the same age at which Shelley also had come to the crossways of life and art. That this parallel between the two poets was altogether deliberate on Yeats's part, one has not the slightest doubt. His Arcadian plays were followed in 1886 by the dramatic poem *Mosada* and the much more powerful *The Two Titans*, both of them overwhelmingly Shelleyan poems. In *Mosada* a Moorish maiden is martyred by the Inquisition because she practices magic in order to recover a vision of her lost Christian lover, who by a characteristic Yeatsian touch enters the poem as his own anti-self, no less than the Grand Inquisitor. *The Two Titans* is rather mis-leadingly subtitled *A Political Poem* and therefore has been read subtly but reductively by Richard Ellmann as an allegory of Ireland's bondage to England. Yet here, though with a rhetoric so Shelleyan as to be scarcely his own at all, Yeats wrote the most imaginatively impressive poem of his youth before *The Wanderings of Usheen*, though it perhaps has its preposterous aspects if it is read as political allegory alone. Gerard Manley Hopkins, resident in Dublin during 1886, read *The Two Titans*, called its allegory "strained and unworkable" yet found the poem to contain fine lines and vivid imagery. *The Two Titans* is a mixture of the archetypal situations presented by Shelley in two very different poems, the baffled quest-romance *Alastor*, and the darkly triumphant lyrical drama, *Prometheus Unbound*. One of Yeats's Titans is "a grey-haired youth" like the doomed poet in Shelley's *Alastor*; like Prometheus he is imprisoned on a rock, but this is a wave-beaten promontory, where he is chained to a fiercely dreaming Sibyl of a Titaness. The poem is thus either an anticipation of Blake's influence on Yeats, as it reproduces the situation most powerfully set forth by Blake at the opening of his ballad, *The Mental Traveller*, or more likely, it is the first of the many times that the influences of Blake and Shelley will mingle in Yeats's poetry, until their confluence will help produce such masterpieces as *The Second Coming* and the Byzantium poems. All that happens in Yeats's *The Two Titans* is that the enchained poet makes yet another heroic attempt to get free of the Titaness and fails, receiving as his reward a sadistic kiss from his tyrannical captor, who is yet as bound as he is. On the Shelleyan and Blakean analogues, the poem has a clear and impressive meaning – the poet, if he relies on a naturalistic Muse, participates in the bondage of nature, and is devoured by his own Muse, destroyed by the cyclic rhythms of a running-down natural world. With *The*

Two Titans we come to the end of Yeats's first poetic period – he is now twenty-one years old; a considerable poet rather desperately struggling with an overwhelming influence, Shelley's, that he must somehow modify if he is to achieve his own individuality, and just beginning to undergo the kindred influence of Blake – more liberating for being free of the very personal elements in Yeats's early Shelley-obsession.

Some poets, as we know, never recover from the immortal wound of the poetry they first come to love, though they learn to mask their relationship to their own earlier selves. In 1914, when he was nearly fifty, Yeats wrote the very beautiful section of his *Autobiographies* entitled *Reveries over Childhood and Youth*. He was past the mid-point of his poetic career, and already well into that middle style in which he is furthest from Romantic tradition, the style of the volumes *The Green Helmet* and *Responsibilities*, a bitter, restrained style, relying on the themes of self-correction, disillusionment, a new control. His poetic models for a time will be Landor and Donne and what he has to say in 1914 of his own earlier feelings for Shelley is therefore not likely to be colored by a strong positive emotion, and is all the more valuable for our present purpose, which is to trace how a poetic influence can apparently be repudiated, and yet go underground, like Coleridge's Sacred River, until it emerges finally with a turbulence of creation and destruction, in a form more powerful than before.

The seventeen-year-old Yeats, experiencing the awakening of sexuality, slept out among the rocks in the wilds around Howth Castle, where later he would walk with Maud Gonne in that most desperately unsuccessful and yet poetically fruitful of courtships. "As I climbed along the narrow ledge," he reminisced, "I was now Manfred on his glacier, and now Prince Athanase with his solitary lamp, but I soon chose Alastor for my chief of men and longed to share his melancholy, and maybe at last to disappear from everybody's sight as he disappeared, drifting in a boat somewhere along some slow-moving river between great trees. When I thought of women they were modelled on those in my favorite poets and loved in brief tragedy, or like the girl in *The Revolt of*

Islam, accompanied their lovers through all manner of wild places, lawless women without homes and without children."

The avenging daimon or Alastor in Shelley's poem is the dark double of the melancholy poet, the spirit of solitude that will haunt him and drive him on to destruction. As such he is probably Yeats's first literary encounter with the notion of an anti-self, to be so richly developed later in Yeats's writing. Prince Athanase, the young magus in his literary tower, we will meet many times again in Yeats's work, while the lawless heroine, Cyntha, of Shelley's *Revolt of Islam,* will inform Yeats's heroic conception of Maud Gonne as a rebel against all established order.

The antithetical solitude of the young Shelley, with his gentleness and humanitarian character, who yet creates as the heroes of his early poetry the isolated figures of sage, magician, violent revolutionary, and proudly solitary noble and poet, is very clearly the ultimate origin of Yeats's later theories of the mask and the antithetical self. The young Yeats elaborated a not very convincing autobiographical parallel between himself and the young Shelley – since Shelley was persecuted at Eton as "Shelley the atheist" so Yeats was made miserable at school in London as "the Mad Irishman." John Butler Yeats, the poet's father, occupies the role of Shelley's Dr. Lind, nursing the imagination of the young poet. Yeats noted also the adolescent Shelley's interest in the occult, though he either ignored or condemned the mature Shelley's dismissal of such interests.

Later in the *Reveries over Childhood and Youth* Yeats tells us that he made Shelley's *Prometheus Unbound* the first of his sacred books or poetic scriptures. In *Four Years,* the next of his *Autobiographies,* the influence of Shelley is cited as having given him his two prime images. "In later years," he writes, "my mind gave itself to gregarious Shelley's dream of a young man, his hair blanched with sorrow, studying philosophy in some lonely tower, or of his old man, master of all human knowledge, hidden from human sight in some shell-strewn cavern on the Mediterranean shore." The young man is Prince Athanase:

His soul had wedded Wisdom, and her dower
Is love and justice, clothed in which he sate
Apart from men, as in a lonely tower,

Pitying the tumult of their dark estate.

The image of the old man was to haunt Yeats's poetry even
more decisively. In *Four Years* he calls it the passage of poetry that
"above all ran perpetually in my ears." It is the dialogue from
Hellas concerning the sage Ahasuerus, the Wandering Jew who
will become the Old Rocky Face of *The Gyres,* that daimonic intelli-
gence we must urge to look out at our world from his secret
home, "where he dwells in a sea-cavern/Mid the Demonesi," less
accessible than the Sultan or God:

Some feign that he is Enoch; others dream
He was pre-Amadite, and has survived
Cycles of generation and of ruin.

These two images are the *personae* of Yeats in the first and in
the final phases of his career as a poet – the prematurely old
young man seeking the secret wisdom, and the ageless old magus
who has conquered age by long possessing such wisdom. Between
is the bitter phase of the middle-Yeats, anti-Romantic against his
own grain, lamenting that traditional sanctity and loveliness have
vanished, and that Romantic Ireland is dead and gone.

Both these images, as Yeats himself said, are always opposite
to the natural self or the natural world, an insight as to the poetic
role arrived at by Shelley and by Blake alike. We can see Yeats
demonstrating an astonishing critical power as he ascertains this
truth in the magnificent essay on Shelley written in 1900, and
curiously mis-entitled *The Philosophy of Shelley's Poetry,* for it is a
study of Shelley's imagery, and even more of the emotional dialectic of Shelley's poetry, and finally one of the earliest studies of
poetry as myth-making that we have. For Yeats it was more than
just an essay on Shelley – the erstwhile disciple was now thirty-five,
at the mid-point of his life, and consciously determined to throw
off the embroidered coat of his earlier poetry – to demonstrate,
for a while, that there's more enterprise in walking naked. In that
coat there were prominently displayed what Yeats called the reds

and yellows that Shelley had gathered in Italy. The poet of *The Rose* and *The Wind Among the Reeds* now sought what his father had called "unity of being" – to write in perfect tune with the tension of his own lyre. At least one aim of Yeats's essay on Shelley is to demonstrate that the poet of *Prometheus Unbound* lacked this Unity of Being, and so could not realize his full gifts as a poet.

The clue to Yeats's dissatisfaction with Shelley is given by Yeats throughout this otherwise model essay. Shelley – we know – was the most heroic of agnostics, humanistically convinced that "the deep truth is imageless," as Demogorgon puts it in *Prometheus Unbound*. But Yeats, who hungered after belief, could not accept this. He in effect blames Shelley for not being Yeats – for not seeking the support of a popular mythology, or of magic and occult tradition – indeed he closes his essay by denouncing Shelley for having been "content merely to write verses," when he possessed and should have realized the religion-making faculty. He cannot then forgive Shelley for not having founded a new faith, and he contrasts Shelley to Blake, for he believes that this is precisely what Blake attempted to do. Critically speaking, this is both fascinatingly perverse and yet of the utmost importance. Yeats has read Shelley with great accuracy and insight, but will not abide in that reading, for if Shelley's way as a poet is right, then indeed Yeats's developing way is wrong. In compensation, Yeats has read Blake with great inaccuracy and deliberately befuddled insight, so as to produce an antithetical poetic father to take Shelley's place.

Before moving on to Blake and Yeats, a closer inspection of Yeats's first essay on Shelley should serve to test these generalizations. Yeats begins by stating his early belief about the relation between poetry and philosophy. "I thought," he writes, "that whatever of philosophy has been made poetry is alone permanent, and that one should begin to arrange it in some regular order, rejecting nothing as the make-believe of the poets." From this early principle he goes on to state his mature belief at thirty-five – "I am now certain" he affirms, "that the imagination has some way of lighting on the truth that the reason has not," and he offers as evidence for his certainty that he has just reread *Prometheus Unbound,* and it seems to him to have an even more certain place than he had thought among the sacred books of the world. He then proceeds to show that Shelley's *Prometheus* is an apocalyptic work, and he brilliantly parallels Shelley and Blake by way of Shelley's most Blakean poem, *The Witch of Atlas.* It is the calculating faculty or reason that creates ugliness, and the freed faculty of imagination that alone creates the exuberance that is beauty, and so becomes the supreme agency of what a poet can consider as moral good. In the poet's infinite desire to break through natural barriers and so uncover an altogether human universe Yeats magnificently locates the common ground held by Blake and by Shelley. As Yeats quotes and describes passage after passage from Shelley to support his characterization of that great Promethean poet as the poet of infinite desire, he reveals also to the student of his own later poetry just those passages that will be transformed into crucial moments in such poems as *Leda and the Swan, Nineteen Hundred and Nineteen, The Second Coming, Sailing to Byzantium,* and *Byzantium, Two Songs from a Play, The Gyres* and the death-poem, *Under Ben Bulben.* All these poems have quite direct verbal echoes of or allusions to the Shelleyan passages that Yeats quotes. Yet this is of only secondary importance in a consideration of Yeats's Romanticism, or even in seeking to understand the complexity of Shelley's abiding influence on Yeats's poetry. More vital is the argument that Yeats proceeds to conduct with Shelley, once he has demonstrated the religious intensity of Shelley's unappeasable and apocalyptic desires, those infinite aspirations towards a world where subject and object, thought and passion, lover and beloved, shall be joined in perfect wholeness.

Inevitably Yeats concentrates on Shelley's speculations upon death and survival, for the single great theme uniting all of Yeats's poetry from the very start, as he himself proclaimed, is a passion against old age, and the insistence that man has somehow invented death. Shelley died at twenty-nine and Blake was too great a humanist to regard the fear of death as more than a failure of the imagination, but Yeats lived into his seventy-fourth year, and surrendered his imaginative humanism to a rage for survival in some form, however desperately unimaginative. The seeds of this surrender can be found in the most astonishing moment in Yeats's first Shelley essay, when he suddenly passes from quoting the nobly agnostic quatrains that conclude *The Sensitive Plant* to the incredible deduction that those quatrains show Shelley's belief in the *Anima Mundi* or Great Memory in which all our smaller selves survive. It is an intellectual comedy of dismal intensity to first read Shelley's last quatrain and then Yeats's comment upon it. Here is Shelley:

> For love, and beauty, and delight
> There is no death nor change; their might
> Exceeds our organs, which endure
> No light, being themselves obscure.

What these lines clearly say is that our senses are inadequate to the full humanity of our desire; Blake says precisely the same in *The Marriage of Heaven and Hell* when he proclaims that "if the doors of perception were cleansed everything would appear to man as it is, infinite. For man has closed himself up, till he sees all things thro' narrow chinks of his cavern." But in Yeats's reading Shelley's lines are a reference to a palpable spirit-world, a universe of squeaking phantasms that can be invoked by a Soho medium or a self-induced trance. Having so mis-read, Yeats goes on to condemn Shelley for having no roots in Irish folklore, Hindu theosophy, and cabbalistic magic. It is Shelley's freedom from this witch's cauldron, we are asked to believe, that gives some of his poetry that air of rootless fantasy the anti-Shelleyans breathe and condemn. Shelley, Yeats goes on to say, had reawakened in himself the age of faith, but failed to understand that the content of such faith now rested in peasant superstitions and the arcane doctrines of the Rosicrucians. Shelley, we know, was an urbane and gracious man, and a visionary with profound though limited respect for human reason. In his spirit, we can shrug off Yeats at his silliest, and marvel at a great poet's wilfulness. We will return to Yeats on Shelley but only after considering Yeats on Blake, an interpretive mare's nest whose perversities are not to be shrugged off quite so easily.

Of the three volumes of the Yeats-Ellis edition of Blake, the *Text,* the *System,* the *Meaning* – it is a little difficult to decide just which now appears the most outrageous. The *Text* is the preposterous consequence of the editorial tradition of re-writing Blake that the Rossettis and Swinburne had so grandly begun. The *System* is not Blake's at all, but a lovely mixture of Blavatsky and bluster, and the *Meaning,* as Northrop Frye rightly remarked, is considerably more difficult to grasp than Blake's own. Yeats is much more enlightening, both on Blake and his own relation to Blake, in the two essays first published with "The Philosophy of Shelley's Poetry" in the critical volume, *Ideas of Good and Evil.* These essays – the brief "William Blake and the Imagination" and the more ambitious "Blake and his Illustrations to the Divine Comedy" – were written four years after the Yeats-Ellis edition of Blake appeared and three years before the Shelley essay was written, and clearly prepare the way in Yeats's attempt to substitute Blake for Shelley as his archetype of the poet. Already, in the Yeats-Ellis edition, a personal identification had been suggested by Yeats's happy and altogether original discovery that William Blake had really been an Irishman, whose true name was O'Neill. Though Yeats, after a bombardment by Swinburne, gave up this startling notion, he did become more and more convinced that he was a new incarnation of the earlier William.

We understand today that Blake was an epic poet consciously in the Protestant tradition of Spenser and Milton, and not any sortof a mystic, a word he never uses. Blake's divine vision is of a more human man, and not of God at all, and the mystic's way of union with a supernatural reality that exists outside of himself is the negation of everything that Blake believed. We have also progressed to a point where we see that Blake had a genial contempt for all occultists; that he repudiated Swedenborg, and sought the mental companionship of the poets, and not the theosophists. But Yeats simply did not want to know this, and his writings on Blake had a good deal to do with the misconceptions of Blake-as-mystic and Blake-as-arcane-speculator that somehow managed to drift on in the popular and even the learnèd consciousness. Yeats took from Swedenborg and from occult tradition in general, the doctrine of correspondence, the belief that everything visible has an invisible counterpart in the spiritual world. The ultimate origin of this doctrine is the brief Hermetic text called the Smaragdine Tablet, mentioned approvingly by Yeats both in his prose and poetry. But Blake, in a crucial moment in his major poem, the epic *Jerusalem*, condemns the Smaragdine Tablet and all theosophy with it, calling it an attempt on the part of the Spectre, or abstract intellect, to destroy imagination by drawing Los, the Poetic Genius of man, down into the Indefinite, where no one can believe without demonstration, and where the living form of poetry is darkened by the mathematic form of abstract speculation. Coming to this passage in his commentary in the Yeats-Ellis edition, Yeats chose to ignore Blake's emphatic rejection of this central occult text. When one is done blinking at such high-handedness, one accepts it as another moment of involuntary revelation on Yeats's part. He needed magic, he had to have the occult support of mystery, yet he needed also the authority of Romantic poetic tradition, and he was perfectly willing to distort that tradition to satisfy what he considered his imaginative need. With this as background, we can now consider Yeats's essays on Blake, where he tries to assert the essential affinity between Blake and himself, while indicating his own advantages over Blake in having a national mythology still to be exploited.

The brief essay on "Blake and the Imagination" begins by praising Blake as having been the first to announce the religion of art. It is not clear that Yeats is not confounding Blake with Oscar Wilde, until he goes on to say that Blake believed the imaginative arts to be the greatest of Divine revelations, which is true. But soon we see where Yeats is taking us: Blake, we are told, was a symbolist who had to invent his symbols, a man crying out for a mythology, and trying to make one because he could not find one to his hands. This is sublimely to misunderstand Blake, who would have made his own mythology in any case, for he believed that this is the function of poets, to speak an individual Word so clearly and coherently that it would necessarily be the Word of God, that is, the Imagination in man. Yeats closes his essay with the wish that

Blake had taken his myths from Ancient Norway or Ancient Wales or, best of all, Ancient Ireland, for then he would have been less arbitrary and less obscure. Yeats is of course rationalizing his own use of Irish mythology, and so did not mind contradicting his own description of Blake's belief in art as the only source of divine revelation.

In the long essay on "Blake's Illustrations to Dante" Yeats is refreshingly improved as a critic; he understands the apocalyptic aim of Blake as a corrector-by-illustrations of other men's visions, and he seems warier of chiding Blake for not having had the good fortune to have read Lady Gregory on the Irish mythological cycles. He sets forth expertly Blake's quarrel with Dante, based on Blake's insistence that "God took always a human shape," and on Blake's conviction that Dante mixed with his genuinely imaginative visions those symbols that were enemies to the imagination because drawn from an idolatry of nature or, at the other extreme, from the abstract diagramming of the theologians. As though he foresees his own writing of *A Vision* decades later, Yeats is nervous about this disagreement, and refuses to commit himself as between Blake and Dante.

Yeats's own poetry during the painful years of his transition, let us say, from the turn of the century through the Easter Rebellion in 1916, has little to do with the myth-making of either Blake or Shelley, little to do that is with either a complex attempt at creating a new mythology, like Blake's, or with the affirmation of the possibilities of mythical relationship, like Shelley's. For Yeats, the turning-point as poet and man came in October 1917, at the age of fifty-two, with his marriage, and with the revelation made to him by the spirits (as he asks us to believe) through the mediumship of his wife. The origins of Yeats's systematic mythology, as set forth in *A Vision,* are in this curious moment of elemental breakthrough, though it took Yeats twenty years of revision before the dictation of spirits had properly flowered into what Ellman calls esoteric Yeatsianism.

The complications of *A Vision* do not concern the subject I am discussing, except to note that the book is more thoroughly quarried out of Blake than either Yeats or his critics have realized, though I would add that the result is a parody of Blake rather than a work in his tradition. What does concern the present subject is the character-analysis carried out upon Blake and Shelley by Yeats in the exposition of the Great Wheel, or human incarnations founded upon the phases of the moon. Blake, we are told, is a man of phase 16 – his will is the Positive Man, his true Mask illusion, his true creative mind dominated by vehemence. He is classified with the apocalyptic satirist Rabelais, with the brutally comic Aretino, and even with that witty cosmic charlatan, Paracelsus. For all these, Yeats says, "discover symbolism to express the overflowing and bursting of the mind." In them Yeats finds "always an element of frenzy, and almost always a delight in certain glowing or shining images of concentrated force: in the smith's forge; in the heart; in the human form in its most vigorous development." Yet, according to Yeats, this is a phase haunted by the false Mask of delusion, and the false creative mind of opiniated will, and doomed finally to the deterministic body of fate Yeats calls Enforced Illusion, for this is the last phase of those who suffer rather than do violence. It is just short of the ideal phase for a poet, for it is followed by phase 17, named for its will as "The Daimonic Man" and here we find Dante, Shelley of course and Landor, and though he does not explicitly say so in *A Vision*, Yeats himself, as he made clear to his family and friends, and in his unpublished work. The man of phase 17, Yeats says, "is called the *Daimonic* man because Unity of Being, and consequent expression of *Daimonic* thought, is now more easy than at any other phase." What Yeats for a while believed Shelley to lack, Shelley now seems to posses in abundance. The reason for this reversal is simply that Yeats is beginning to recognize again what he was ruefully to admit in a late essay on *Prometheus Unbound*, written in 1932, that Shelley had shaped his imaginative career to a greater extent than any other poet. The Daimonic Man has a true mask of simplification through Intensity and a creative mind which reaches creative imagination through *antithetical emotion*. His false mask is dispersal, and his false creative mind manifests itself through what Yeats eloquently called "enforced self-realization." The tragic

Body of Fate of the Daimonic Man has the terrible loneliness about it that Yeats expresses in a single word: "Loss." Though he strains to fit Dante into this characterization and briefly mentions Landor, it is perfectly clear that all of Yeats's description of this – his own phase – is founded on a deeply passionate and indeed emotionally self-contradictory account of Shelley. This is – Yeats says – the phase where all mental images flow, change, flutter, cry out, or mix into something else, but without, as at phase 16, Blake's phase, breaking and bruising one another, for the phase of Shelley and Yeats is without frenzy.

The Will is falling asunder, but without explosion and noise, and the poet's intellect finds, Yeats says, not the impassioned myth that Blake found, but a mask of simplicity that is also intensity, the mask of Prince Athanase in his lonely tower, or ageless Ahasuerus in his caverns measureless to man. Every object of desire selected by the intellect for a representation of the mask as Image, usually a Woman, is always snatched away by the Body of Fate. So Yeats assimilates Maud Gonne to that pathetically intense sequence of Shelleyan epipsyches – Harriet, Mary Godwin, Claire Clairmont, Emilia Viviani, Jane Williams; those morning stars who always faded in the experiential dawn. The result is nightmare, a phantasm world in which every object becomes an emblem of loss, of the world's separation from the self. As a reading of the central dialectic of Shelley's poetry I do not think that this is likely ever to be bettered. But Yeats, alas, does not stop there – he must go further, must break from the prison of his own earlier self. Shelley, he goes on to say, "lacked the Vision of Evil, could not conceive of the world as a continual conflict, so, though great poet he certainly was, he was not of the greatest kind." Because he lacked this Yeatsian Vision of Evil, Shelley fell into an *automatonism*, as Yeats calls it, evading hatred by giving himself up to fantastic, constricted images. It is from this Shelleyan fate that Yeats believes he has saved himself, for to the daimonic intensity of a Shelley he has added Blake's conception of the contraries, a vision of evil in which all things are seen as living one another's death, dying one another's life, progressing always through the continual conflict of creative strife.

That Yeats knew better about Shelley we know from his earlier essay on that poet, where he correctly understands the great myth of Demogorgon in *Prometheus Unbound* as the principle of continual conflict that turns over the cycle in the universe from Jupiter to Prometheus, and that threatens destruction again in a world that cannot by its nature be finally redeemed. But Yeats *needed* his myth of Shelley as an embryonic Yeats who had fallen short of the Vision of Evil. Hence the late essay on *Prometheus* of 1932, in which Demogorgon is re-interpreted as being uninterpretable, as making the whole poem incoherent, for now Yeats must see him as the most monstrous of all Shelley's nightmare images of the negation of desire. Yet even here, in an essay clearly intended as a critical palinode, as an anti-Shelleyan document, the full force of Shelley's power upon Yeats breaks through. He has attacked Shelley for not being a mystic, unlike Yeats himself and Blake. The attack is weak – none of the three poets was in fact anything of a mystic – but Yeats throws the strength of his considerable rhetoric into the attack: Shelley's "system of thought" – he says – "was constructed by his logical faculty to satisfy desire, not a symbolical revelation received after the suspension of all desire." In the zeal of his rejecting passion Yeats makes his strongest indictment of Shelley, asserting: "He was the tyrant of his own being." After all that, one would expect a declaration of Yeatsian freedom from this mistaken being, but what follows is one of those moments of total self-revelation in which the paradoxical greatness of the mask-seeking Yeats consists. I quote it in full, so as to preserve its weight and complexity:

> When I was in my early twenties Shelley was much talked about. London had its important "Shelley Society," *The Cenci* had been performed and forbidden, provincial sketching clubs displayed pictures by young women of the burning of Shelley's body. The orthodox religion, as our mothers had taught it, was no longer credible; those who could not substitute connoisseurship, or some humanitarian or scientific pursuit, found a substitute in Shelley. He had shared our curiosities, our political problems, our conviction that, despite all experience to the contrary, love is enough; and unlike Blake, isolated by an arbitrary symbolism, he seemed to sum up all that was metaphysical in English poetry. When in middle life I looked back I found that he and not Blake, whom I had studied more and with

more approval, had shaped my life, and when I thought of the
tumultuous and often tragic lives of friends or acquaintance, I
attributed to his direct or indirect influence their Jacobin frenzies,
their brown demons.

Rather than analyze this confession of influence, I want only
to note it, and to pass on to characterize Yeats's later poems by
way of a rather large generalization about *all* English poetry since
the very early nineteenth century. Modern poetry in English
begins with the difficult greatness of Blake and of Wordsworth,
and the different modes each invented have been the only
significant kinds of poetry written during the past hundred and
fifty years. Blake restored myth-making to poetry; Wordsworth
inagurated that heroic nakedness of direct confrontation between
the self and nature in which so many poets since Shelley and
Keats have followed him, down to Stevens and Lawrence in our
own time. However much Yeats tried to be like Blake, he did not
succeed; *A Vision* remains one of the curiosities of literature, and
the poems written out of it usually succeed through their powerful independence of its not always very imaginative categories.
Yeats, despite himself, became a great poet of the Wordsworthian
kind, a poet of autobiographical self-recognition, whose theme
had less and less to do with the content of the poetic vision, and
more and more to do with the relationship of the poet to his own
vision. Yet Yeats never learned to like or understand Wordsworth,
and so he took the central model for his typical lyric of confrontation from those almost involuntary Wordsworthian disciples,
Shelley and Keats, and more clearly from Shelley, even in the
Byzantium poems, which have so clear a relationship to Keats's
Urn and *Nightingale* odes.

At the beginning of this essay I spoke of how little we understand the process by which one poet influences another, and I
want to return to that mysterious process now as I close. In old-
fashioned terms one can demonstrate that more lines of Yeats
allude to or repeat more lines of Shelley than of any other poet,
but all this would show us is that the memory does not easily lose
the stores it has gathered up by a poet's twentieth year.
Stylistically, late Yeats and Shelley have a great deal in common,

though that must sound odd in the ears of anyone who is still much under the influence of recent aberrations in the history of taste. I cannot read the final stanzas of *The Witch of Atlas* without thinking of the *Byzantium* poems, and this is more than my own eccentricity. Yet the deepest influence of Shelley on Yeats is not in style but in something far more fundamental – Shelley's most characteristic poetry has the same relation to the lyrics of *The Tower* and *The Winding Stair* that the Japanese Noh drama has to Yeats's plays – the very idea of the act that is the Yeatsian poem is Shelley's. In Shelley when he is most himself – in the *Ode to the West Wind, Adonais, The Triumph of Life* – one feels the entire weight of a poet's vocation and life veering on the destiny of the relational event that is the poem. When the poem breaks, as in Shelley it so frequently does out of sheer agnostic honesty, as in Yeats it sometimes does out of an extraordinary mixture of self-dramatization and heroic desperation – then the very concept of a poet breaks with it, in a fitting imaginative gesture for a daimonic man, that man whose role it is to hold himself open to unity of being. The Yeats of poems like *A Dialogue of Self and Soul, Vacillation* and the haunting *The Man and the Echo* is a very human, very Romantic and very Shelleyan Yeats, existing in the perilous dialectic that witnesses every object of desire disappearing into another experiential loss, that dares the true Romantic agony in which dialogue collapses towards monologue, and the confrontation of love expires into the crippling loneliness of enforced self-realization. Yeats strove mightily to overcome the Shelleyan identity of his own youth, but I think it fortunate that he failed in that striving. We would have lost the poet who finally cast his own mythologies aside, to cry aloud in the perfect moment of agnostic confrontation in the poetry of our time, the very humanistic and Shelleyan cry of almost his last poem:

> O Rocky Voice
> Shall we in that great night rejoice?
> What do we know but that we face
> One another in this place?

4   Toward *A Vision:*
Per Amica Silentia Lunae

Anima Hominis

Yeats first intended to call this "little philosophical book" of 1917 *An Alphabet*, as though he meant it to be a key to the rudiments of his imaginative work, or to the convictions upon which that work was founded. Starting with the poem *Ego Dominus Tuus* (1915) as extended motto, the book divides itself into two reveries, *Anima Hominis* and *Anima Mundi*, the first dealing with the Mask and the second with the relation of the Mask to the spiritual world, realm of *daimons* and the dead. In the total structure of Yeats's work, *Per Amica Silentia Lunae* serves as introduction to the visionary center, to the later poems in *The Wild Swans at Coole*, and to *Michael Robartes and the Dancer, Four Plays for Dancers*, and *A Vision* itself.

The cover design for *Per Amica Silentia Lunae*, done by Sturge Moore at Yeats's suggestion, is the Rose, now a symbol of the Mask, and thus a mark of deliberate continuity between the earlier and later Yeats. In this surpassingly beautiful little book, Pater and the Cambridge Platonist Henry More are made to join hands, as though the creator of Marius had his true affinities not with the second Renaissance of Romanticism but with the *Theologica Germanica* and related works. *Per Amica Silentia Lunae* is a masterpiece in the tradition of the marmoreal reverie, worthy to stand beside Browne's *Urn Burial* and *Garden of Cyrus* or most of Pater. Except for the *Autobiographies*, it is Yeats's great achievement in prose, a book to be read and reread, unlike *A Vision*, which we are compelled to study, but so frequently with regret.

The book begins with a brief, charming Prologue addressed to "Maurice," Iseult Gonne, with whom Yeats was, perhaps, half-in-love. Tone dominates here; the book, Iseult is told, completes a conversation her Persian cat interrupted the previous summer. There follows *Ego Dominus Tuus*, a poem on the image of desire or Mask, the starting point for *Anima Hominis* even as the essay, *Swedenborg, Mediums, and the Desolate Places* is the starting point of *Anima Mundi*. The poem ends with a reference to a secret doctrine, which "the mysterious one," the double and anti-self, will read in the subtler language of the Shelleyan characters written on the wet sand by the water's edge, and which he fears to communicate to "blasphemous men." This suggestion of the hieratic is taken up in the opening sentence of *Anima Hominus*, where Yeats comes home "after meeting men who are strange to me." He fears to have caricatured himself, being unfit to move among what he calls, in Blakean language, "images of good and evil, crude allegories."

What follows is an eloquent prophecy of what Yeats was to call "The First Principle" of his aesthetic, written years later as part of a general introduction for a projected edition of his complete works. A poet always writes out of the tragedy of his personal life, but never directly to the reader, for "there is always a phantasmagoria." It may be mythology, history, or romance, but even poets as personal as Shelley or Byron never write as what they and we are, bundles of accident and incoherence. They have been "reborn as an idea, something intended, complete." But note, in this age of Eliot, Auden, and the New Criticism, that there is *no* escape from or evasion of personality in this phantasmagoria, which is indeed precisely what Blake and Pater called "vision" and the other major Romantics the Secondary or creative Imagination. The artist becomes "part of his own phantasmagoria and we adore him because nature has grown intelligible." Nature is a power separated from our creative power, until the poet makes nature intelligible to us, "and by so doing a part of our creative power." There follows the most powerful and self-confident proclamation of the High Romantic imagination made in our time, and surely one that the host of anti-Romantic Yeats critics ought to have pondered. Yeats's Romanticism, Tate asserted, would be invented by his critics. Yeats has forestalled us, grandly: "The world knows nothing because it has made nothing, we know everything because we have made everything." So much for nature and God, and their merely Primary worlds.

Twenty years earlier, in *Anima Hominus,* Yeats was no less confident, but he was then a little warier at identifying himself with his anti-self, of being made one with his own phantasmagoria. Yet the wariness, even then, was poetic strategy, a crucial element in the vacillation necessary for Paterian style. The phantasmagoria is there as "an heroic condition," vision, justly compared to Dante's *Vita Nuova* where the "Lord of Terrible Aspect" says to Dante: *ego dominus tuus,* or to the landscape of the Lower Paradise in Boehme. Yeats makes a hieratic withdrawal from life, and finds himself as the poet-visionary proper, enjoying a heroic condition. He calls this a "compensating dream," but he means compensation in a Coleridgean rather than a psychoanalytic sense, judging by the major instances he gives, beyond himself. He admits cases of compensation, like that of Synge, who in ill-health delights in physical life, but his interest is in art as "an opposing virtue" rather than a therapy. Most profoundly, this idea of the "opposing virtue" creates a pattern of heroic desperation, which may be the most moving design in the mature Yeats. Though the pattern exhibits familiar elements – a withdrawal from experience into the *antithetical* quest, identified with Shelleyan poethood, the occult way, the war between men and women – a new clarity defines itself also. Against whatever he knew of Freud and what he knew of the Pre-Socratics, whose view that character is fate Freud shared, Yeats implicitly urges the contrary view that personality is fate, the *daimon* is our destiny. The purpose of this exaltation of self over soul is not to evade the tragic reality of the Freudian and Pre-Socratic view, but to oppose it with another conception of freedom, one necessarily not available to more than a handful of artists, men whose work is a flight from their horoscopes, their "blind struggle in the network of the stars." On the simplest level of his deliberate illustrations of the "opposing virtue," Yeats is hardly convincing; he gives us the "irascible" William Morris as following "an indolent muse," the genuinely violent Landor pursuing calm nobility, and Keats, "ignorant, poor, and in poor health" thirsting for luxury. Not only are all of these quasi-mechanical compensations, but the Yeatsian notion of Keats is too absurd to be interesting. But in passing to Dante, who with Shelley is to dominate the description of Yeats's own phase 17 in *A Vision*, Yeats returns to the true depths of his own *antithetical* conception. Thinking back to Simeon Solomon, painter and broken monument of the prelude to the Tragic Generation, Yeats remembers a Shelleyan phrase of Solomon's: "a hollow image of fulfilled desire." In Book iii, *Hodos Chameliontos*, of *The Trembling of the Veil*, Yeats distinguishes between the Mask or Image that is fated, because it comes from life, and the Mask that is chosen. Though in *Anima Hominis* he says that all happy art is but Solomon's hollow image, he means by this that tragic art is happy, yet expresses also the "poverty" of its creator, this use of "poverty" being strikingly similar to Stevens's use of it to mean "imaginative need," or a need that compels the imagination to come into full activity. Dante, like Shelley, fights a double war, with the world and with himself. Yeats touches the heights of his true visionary argument, truer than any he makes in *A Vision*, when he praises an ideal poet for choosing the Mask as an opposing virtue, and so attaining the "last knowledge." When the poet has seen *and foreseen* the image of all he dreads, while still seeking the image of desire to redress his essential poverty, then he will have his reward:

> I shall find the dark grow luminous, the void frutiful when I understand I have nothing, that the ringers in the tower have appointed for the hymen of the soul a passing bell.

The enormous plangency of this magnificent (and Paterian) sentence gains terrible poignance when set in the context of its genesis, February 1917, when Yeats was moving toward his fifty-second birthday, still unmarried, and not knowing he was to be married before the year was out.

Having attained to this "last knowledge," Yeats is free to explore the hollow image or *antithetical* self, and find there (with

Plutarch's help) the figure of the *daemon,* who whispers in the dark with the poet's beloved, as Yeats's own daemon (hardly Leo Africanus, but the Spirit that Denies) whispered in the dark with Maud Gonne. Hence, "the desire that is satisfied is not a great desire," a harsh judgment that goes back to the values of *Alastor,* and to Blake's early engraved tracts. There rises from this the doctrine that Yeats insists the true poet shares with saint, hero, martyr: that only the *antithetical* man is not deceived, and so finds reality, "a contemplation in a single instant perpetually renewed," a privileged moment or pulsation of the artery, a time of inherent excellence, epiphany not of the Divine shining out of a natural babe, but of the mind's own power over everything that is merely given.

When Yeats has reached this point, at the close of the ninth section of *Anima Hominis,* his reverie would appear to be accomplished, his warfare done. But in four more sections, the subtlest in the book, the subltest indeed that he wrote in prose, he passes inevitably to the probem of poetic originality, which is the problem of poetic influence.

Poet or sculptor, Yeats says, cannot seek originality; he will sing or mould after a new fashion anyway if he expresses *antithetical* emotion. This is infortunately an evasion, and Yeats does not rescue himself from it by bitter wit, when he finely insists that "no disaster is like another." So it seems to the lover, but hardly to the reader. Yeats is firmer when he implies that no originality can be sought deliberately, since the *daemon* is our enemy, and is interested only in our disaster, and not in what he can make of it. The *daemon* must be held off (he cannot be overcome) through the poet's true originality, which is the strong poet's creative misinterpretation of his strongest precursor. This is the burden of Section XI, which follows, and finds an image for Yeats's freedom by a *clinamen* that uses Blake as point-of-departure. Mentioning Balzac and "the Christian Kabbalah" as sources, but not Blake, the section transforms a Blakean image of apocalypse from Plates 97-98 of *Jerusalem.* The dialectic of the transformation was sketched in Section VI of *Anima Hominis,* which itself develops convictions that dominated *Adam's Curse,* and emerged again in *Ego Dominus Tuus.* The anti-self, which leads the poet to at least the possibility of his fuller self, leads also to an uncovering that promises release from time's burden, including the embarrassment of poetic tradition. So Section VI associates St. Francis and Caesar Borgia (a delightful conjunction) with the old nonchalance whose decay is lamented in *Adam's Curse.* Saint and man-of-power alike make their creativity by turning from a lesser to a greater mode of imitation, "from mirror to meditation upon a mask," the *daimonic* Will they meet in *antithetical* reverie. In Section XI the mirror is "the winding movement of nature" or "path of the serpent," and the meditation upon the mask is the straight line of an arrow shot into the heavens, aimed at the sun. The winding path is associated with Blake's vision of Milton's Shadow, the Covering Cherub, the burden of time including the sinister beauty not only of the historical churches but of Milton's own poetry, and of the beauty of all cultural traditions, Scripture included, when Scripture is used to help cover our creativity, to block the path to paradise. The arrow shot at the sun is the Cherub's uncovering, the originality of each strong, new poet, and in Yeats's view is fired only by the poet who meditates upon a mask.

On Plate 97 of *Jerusalem* a revived Albion stretches his hand into Infinitude and recovers his Bow. His fourfold flaming Arrow finds its target in "A sun of blood red wrath surrounding heaven on all sides around," a Sun composed of "the unnumerable Chariots of the Almighty," of the contraries reconciled, "Bacon & Newton & Locke, & Milton & Shakespeare & Chaucer," the empiricists and the visionaries at last together. In Section XI of *Anima Hominis* Yeats speaks "we who are poets and artists," unable to reach into Infinitude, "not being permitted to shoot beyond the tangible," and who are therefore subject to the endless cycle of desire and weariness, while living only for the sudden epiphany, the vision that comes "like terrible lightning." Prophesying the mystical geometry of *A Vision* (before the revelation made through Mrs. Yeats by ghostly Instructors), Yeats speaks of the winding mathematical arcs that prick upon the calendar the life-span of even the greatest men. Beneath these Urizenic heavens we are condemned to "seek reality with the slow toil of our weakness and are smitten with the boundless and unforeseen." Our efforts, in feeling or in thought, are doomed unless we learn to meditate upon the Mask, which means we must renounce mere *primary* experience, even with its saving epiphanies, "leave the sudden lightning," give up nature or "the path of the serpent" and thus take on the state of Blake's apocalyptic Man: we must "become the bowman who aims his arrow at the centre of the sun."

We confront here Yeats's *clinamen* in regard to his precursor, Blake; a creative misinterpretation overcomes poetic influence. In Blake's vision, to meditate upon a mask is only to be a Spectre vainly pursuing an elusive Emanation; this is natural religion,the worship of each day's unfulfilled desire. Here Blake is close to Freud, and Yeats opposed to both, even as Jung is opposed. Yeats begins Section XII of *Anima Mundi* by granting that the doctors are right in regard to certain dreams; unfulfilled desires and cen-soriousness can end in mere dream and nightmare, if they do not undergo the "purifying discouragement" that allows passion to become vision. But (whether we wake or sleep, in explicit echo of Keats) vision sustains itself by rhythm and pattern, and makes of our lives what it will. *Anima Hominis* ends, after this defiance of analytic reduction, with the poet's warning to himself. The imagi-nation can wither, as in Wordsworth, most terrible of instances; rhythm and pattern, once found, are not enough. There must be fresh experience: "new bitterness, new disappointment," for the nding of a true mask, and prolonged meditation upon it, does not make suffering less necessary. It is Yeats's highly individual contribution to the Romantic Sublime, this insistence that contin-ued loss is crucial. Without fresh loss, the Sublime becomes the Grotesque, and the poet only a pretender to the Mask.

Anima Mundi

Anima Hominis succeeds where Book I, *The Great Wheel,* of *A Vision* will fail, in giving a persuasive account of the necessity for finding a mask. Similarly *Anima Mundi* is more coherent and appealing than the later books of *A Vision* are, in showing us how the *antithetical* self can be related to the world of the dead. Partly, this superiority of *Per Amica Silentia Lunae* over *A Vision* is due to the extravagant over-elaborations of the later work, as contrasted with the simplistic reveries of a poet closer to his earlier thought. But I judge the larger difference to be that Yeats was a better literary theorist than he was an occultist. *A Vision* can be translated into aesthetic metaphors, as Mrs. Vendler shows, but a good deal of it obdurately resists such translation, or translates only by severe reduction. *Per Anima Silentia Lunae*, even in its more spectral second book, is closer to an aesthetic treatise, with poetic influence a more major concern in it than the vagaries of ghosts. Or rather, its ghosts are poetic ghosts, imprisoned imaginations and influences, like Shelley's, that linger and haunt and will not permit themselves to be lost.

Near the close of Section XII of *Anima Hominis,* Yeats says of his "vision" that "it compels us to cover all it cannot incorporate," and he means, to cover all of his life that seems merely accidental, and so irrelevant to meditation upon the Mask. Whether overtly or not, he is remembering the Shadow of Milton or Covering Cherub he had encountered in Blake. In my introductory chapter I sketched a theory of poetic influence (partly derived by me from Blake and Yeats) in which influence is seen both as blessing and as curse. The first comes about through the later poet's swerve away from his Great Original, by a revisionary act of misinterpretation, and such a process is illustrated by *Anima Hominis,* as I have tried to show. The second process, that of accepting the curse of the Original's (and traditions's) too-great achievement, is handled differently by Yeats than by any poet I know, for perhaps no other major poet is so much of a Gnostic in his mature vision. In *Anima Mundi,* Yeats takes on the curse of poetic influence as a Gnostic adept would; he enters the Shadow of the Cherub not to redeem it (as Blake's Milton did) nor even to redeem himself, but to attain what he will come to call justice, a passionate fullness, not of experience or of being, but of an instantaneous knowing. There are triumphs of this momentary knowing throughout the later lyrics, and a prolonged defense of it in those books of *A*

Vision that deal with history and the dead. The lyric triumphs and
the defense (and the application of the attained Gnosis in some
of the later plays) are more disputable than they would be if Yeats
had been able to keep to the mood of *Anima Mundi,* but bitterness kept breaking in, and the eloquence of reverie was abandoned. In May 1917, Yeats had much cause for embitterment, yet
a beautiful kind of slow wonder dominates *Anima Mundi,* and
induces even the contrary reader to set aside his wariness. In temperament, Yeats has little in common with the Cambridge
Platonist Henry More, who is so evident here, but he finds the art
(as Pater did) to assume a mood he rarely sustained elsewhere. It
is the mood of the beautiful sentence of Browne that Yeats quotes
in his 1914 treatise, *Swedenborg, Mediums, and the Desolate Places,* a
prelude to *Anima Mundi:*

> I do think that many mysteries ascribed to our own invention have
> been the courteous revelations of spirits; for those noble essences in
> heaven bear a friendly regard unto their fellow creatures on earth.

In this spirit, *Anima Mundi* begins, with Yeats genially
immersing his mind in "the general mind" of Eastern poets,
Connaught old women, and mediums in Soho. From this, it is an
easy step to the suspension of will and intellect, that images may
pass before him. But these images, throughout the treatise, are
not particularly random, and generally turn themselves into the
central images of Romantic poetry. So, this first evocation attains
its climax in the "immortal sea" of Wordsworth's *Intimations* Ode,
and subsequent sections will end with references to Coleridge,
Blake, Spenser, and Shelley. The *anima mundi,* though Yeats
quotes from "More and the Platonists," not surprisingly turns out
to be the general mind of Romantic poetic tradition, as Yeats has
fused it together. The explorers who perhaps knew all the shores
where Wordsworth's children sport appear to be the poets who
found their first seminary in Spenser's Garden of Adonis, from
which Yeats quotes two instructive passages. The women of
Connaught and Soho are more than amiable fiction, but something less than Yeats's Muses. And though we hear the vocabulary
of the spiritual Alchemists in Section III, the table of elements
given is Blake's, down to the bird born out of the simplifying,

reductive fire, from which Mystery rises again at the close of "Night VIII" of *The Four Zoas*. Yeats goes on, in Section IV, to desire contact with "those minds that I could divine," but chooses to quote Coleridge's fine lyric, *Phantom*, so as to give coherence to those minds.

In so occultizing Romantic tradition Yeats merely gave birth to the bad line of pseudo-scholars who have been reducing Blake, Shelley, Keats, Spenser, and of course Yeats himself to esoteric doctrine in recent times. But his motive was more honorable than what animates these literary Rosicrucians. His *anima mundi* as a poet is not in itself at all original, and something in his creativity feared the Covering Cherub, the negative strength of Romantic tradition. Thus, in Section VI, he goes to Henry More and anonymous mediums for speculation upon the after-life, yet his pragmatic finding is the staple of Romantic poetry. Beauty, he tells us, is "but bodily life in some ideal condition," and he ends the section by quoting *The Marriage of Heaven and Hell:* "God only acts or is in existing beings or men." In between, he gives us the kernel of the after life as the soul's "plastic power" which can mould whatever "to any shape it will by an act of imagination." When, in his next section, he needs to image forth the *anima mundi* he resorts to the opinions of Shelley and to the central image of all English Romanticism, Spenser's Garden of Adonis:

> There is the first seminary
> Of all things that are born to live and die
> According to their kynds.

Though he holds that coherence is provided by the occult image, he can show us only a coherence made by the poets themselves. The dead, like the spiritists who study them, become metaphors for Romantic art, rather than principles who inform that art. So the freedom of the dead, or Condition of Fire, itself is able to illustrate nothing, but is clarified for us when Yeats quotes his own lyric, *The Moods*, from *The Wind Among the Reeds*, immensely more coherent than Section X, and enabling us to see what these "fire-born moods" are.

Yeats was rarely a self-deceiver, and I think plainly attempts to deceive us here, presenting us with rhetoric, by his

own definition. He tells us that the dead are the source of everything we call instinct, and so of our passions, but what he means is
that our passions imitate art, and that tradition has taken the
place of instinct. Similarly, he wishes us to believe that we communicate with *anima mundi* through the famous and passionate dead,
but what he means is precisely what the fiercely skeptical Shelley
meant by the survival of Keats in *Adonais,* and he not only needs
Shelley to explain his thought, but he must both distort the context and misquote when he cites *Adonais.* Shelley writes of the crisis of young poets:

> The splendours of the firmament of time
> May be eclipsed, but are extinguished not;
> Like stars to their appointed height they climb,
> And death is a low mist which cannot blot
> The brightness it may veil. When lofty thought
> Lifts a young heart above its mortal lair,
> And love and life contend in it, for what
> Shall be its earthly doom, the dead live there
> And move like winds of light on dark and stormy air.

This intricate stanza firmly holds to the Shelleyan attitude
that is best described as a visionary skepticism, longing for imaginative survival yet remembering always: "All that we have a right
to infer from our ignorance of the cause of any event is that we do
not know it. . . ." Yeats, despite his own temperamental skepticism, adopted always the contrary attitude, inferring from his
ignorance a range of occult causes. In Section XIII of *Anima
Mundi* he deals with "the most wise dead," who "certainly" return
from the grave, and he remembers a doctrine of Henry More, on
the music of the shades, that he had quoted in *Swedenborg,
Mediums, and the Desolate Places.* He applies it here, saying that men
have affirmed always "that when the soul is troubled, those that
are a shade and a song: 'live there, /And live like winds of light on
dark or stormy air.'" Shelley's context, the "there" of what Yeats
quotes, is the uplifted heart of the young poet, and not the haunted state Yeats makes of it, while the misquotation of "live" for
"move," whether deliberate or not, is immensely illuminating, as
another instance of the happily perverse workings of poetic
influence. One remembers Shelley's brief, pungent essay, *On a*

Future State, where he remarks of the assertions made by those of "the secret persuasion" of an occult survival: "They persuade, indeed, only those who desire to be persuaded."

Shelley, as elsewhere in *Anima Mundi,* provides the key to Yeats's discourse: the "passionate dead" live only in our imagination, and their dream is only of our life. Alas that they do wear our colors there, though Yeats exultantly cries of them that they are rammed with life (itself a tag from another poet, Jonson). Though in *A Vision,* Yeats will depart from his uneasiness, and will postulate a world of the dead quite unlike the world of the living, here in *Per Amica Silentia Lunae* he is more of a poet and less of a necromancer, and he profits by his uneasiness, as do we. The Condition of Fire, with its purifying simplification through intensity, is precisely the Romantic Imagination, the burning fountain of *Adonais,* and the apparently mysterious Sections XV through XXI of *Anima Mundi* are an extended commentary upon *Adonais,* its stanza LIV in particular. The climax to this commentary, in Section XXI, is also the height of Yeats's visionary argument in *Per Amica Silentia Lunae.* Remembering that Shelley calls our minds "mirrors of fire for which all thirst" Yeats asks the inevitable question, for Gnostic or naturalist alike, "What or who has cracked the mirror?" And, for answer, he turns to study his own self again, finding in the Paterian privileged moment his only true access to the *anima mundi,* and so presenting his genuine defense of poetry. What he describes is the basis of the poem *Demon and Beast,* but his description here is more in the Romantic tradition. If, in the pulsation of an artery or displaced epiphany, he finds himself "in the place where the daemon is," this is still no victory, until the *daemon* "is with me," a work the poet must perform for himself.

5 *The Covering Cherub* or Poetic Influence

Shelley speculated that poets of all ages contributed to one Great Poem perpetually in process. Borges remarks that poets create their precursors. If the dead poets, as Eliot insisted, constituted their successors' particular advantage in knowledge, that knowledge is still their successors' creation, made by the living for the needs of the living.

But poets, or at least the strongest among them, do not read necessarily as even the strongest of critics read. Poets are neither ideal nor common readers. They tend not to think, as they read: "This is dead, this is living, in the poetry of X." Poets, by the time they have grown strong, do not read the poetry of X, for really strong poets can read only themselves. For them, to be judicious is to be weak, and to compare, exactly and fairly, is to be not elect. Milton's Satan, absurdly denigrated by the mass of modern critics (with the great and honorable exception of Empson) is the archetype of all modern poets, as Milton obscurely knew and feared. Milton's successors, Blake and Shelley, knew this more precisely, for they knew Milton, necessarily, better than he knew himself, and so *they* created Milton's Satan.

Let us try the apparently frivolous experiment of reading *Paradise Lost* as an allegory of the dilemma of the modern poet, at his strongest. Satan is that modern poet, while God is his dead but still embarrassingly potent and present ancestor, or rather, ancestral poet. Adam is the modern poet, potentially strong, but at his weakest moment, when he has yet to find his own voice. God has no muse, and needs none, since he is dead, and his creativity is all in the past time of the poem. Of the living poets in the poem, Satan has Sin, Adam has Eve, and Milton has only his Interior Paramour, an Emanation far within that weeps incessantly for his sin, but that is bewilderingly and magnificently invoked at least four times in the poem. Milton has no name for her, though he invokes her under several but, as he says, "the meaning, not the Name I call." It remained for Blake to name her in his poem *Milton,* a poem in which Milton descends from Heaven to find her, and she descends also from Heaven to find him, since Blake implicitly defines the orthodox Heaven as a state where no one finds, or is found. Blake creates Milton's Muse, and he names her Ololon, perhaps because she is a host yet ironically is all alone, and perhaps in memory of the Greek root of our word "ululate," the lamentation of women, their outcry to the gods.

What kind of poet is Satan? Why call him modern? Because he resembles something at the core of Milton and of Pope, something that becomes isolated in Collins and Gray, in Smart and in Cowper, and which emerges fully to stand clear in Wordsworth, who is the exemplary Modern Poet, the Poet proper. The incarnation of the Poetic Character in Satan begins when Milton's story proper begins, with the Incarnation of God's Son and Satan's rejection of *that* Incarnation. Modern poetry begins in two declarations of Satan: "We know no time when we were not as now" and "To be weak is miserable, doing or suffering."

To avoid excessive unfairness to Milton, let us adopt his own sequence in the poem. Poetry begins with our awareness, not of a Fall, but that *we are falling.* The poet is our *exemplum,* our chosen, and his consciousness of election comes as a curse; again, not "I am a fallen man," but "I am Man, and I am falling" or better still, "I *was* God, I *was* Man (for to a poet they were the same) and I *am* falling, from myself." When this consciousness of self is raised to an absolute pitch, *then* the poet hits the floor of Hell, or rather, comes to the bottom of the abyss, and by his impact there creates Hell. He says, "I seem to have stopped falling; now I *am fallen,* consequently, I lie here in Hell."

There and then, in this bad, he finds his good; he chooses the heroic, to know damnation and to explore the limits of the possible within it. The alternative is to repent, to accept a God altogether other than the self, wholly external to the possible. This God is cultural history, the dead poets, the embarrassments of a tradition grown too wealthy to need anything more. But we need to go further still, back into the poise before the consciousness of falling came.

When Satan or the poet looks around him on the floor of fire his falling self had kindled, he sees first a face he only just recognizes, his best friend, Beelzebub or, the talented poet who never quite made it, and now never shall. And, like the truly strong poet he is, Satan is interested in the face of his best friend only to the extent that it reveals to him the condition of his own countenance. I say this neither to mock the poets that we know, nor the truly heroic Satan. If Beelzebub is that scarred, if he looks that unlike the true form he left behind on the happy fields of light, then Satan himself is hideously bereft of beauty, doomed, like Walter Pater, to be a Caliban of Letters, trapped in essential poverty, in imaginative need, where once he was all but the wealthiest, and needed next to nothing. But Satan, in the accursed strength of the poet, refuses to brood upon this, and turns instead to his task, which is to rally everything that remains.

This is a heroism that is exactly on the border of solipsism, neither within nor without it. Satan's decline in the poem, as engineered by the malevolence of Milton, is that he retreats from this border *into* solipsism, and so is degraded; ceases, during his soliliquy on Mt. Niphates, to be a poet and, by intoning "Evil be thou my good," becomes a mere rebel, a childish inverter of convential moral categories, another wearisome ancestor of student non-students, the perpetual New Left. For the modern poet, in the gladness of his sorrowing strength, stands always on the verge of solipsism, having just emerged from it. His difficult balance, from Wordsworth to Wallace Stevens, is to maintain a stance just there, where by his very presence he says "What I see and hear come not but from myself" and yet also "I have not but I am and what I am I am." The first, by itself, is perhaps the fine defiance of an overt solipsism, leading back to an equivalent of "I know no time when I was not as now." Yet the second is the modification that makes for poetry instead of idiocy: "There are no objects outside of me because I see into their life, which is one with my own, and so 'I am that I am,' which is to say, 'I will be present wherever and whenever I choose to be present.' I am so much in process, that all possible movement is indeed possible, and if at present I explore only my own dens, at least I *explore.*" Or, as Satan might have said: "In doing and in suffering, I shall be happy, for even in suffering I shall be strong."

It is sad to observe most modern critics observing Satan, because they never do observe him. The catalog of unseeing could hardly be more distinguished, from Eliot who speaks of "Milton's curly haired Byronic hero" (one wants to reply, looking from side to side: "Who?") to the astonishing backsliding of Northrop Frye, who invokes, in urbane ridicule, a Wagnerian context (one wants to lament: "A true critic, and of God's party without knowing it"). Fortunately we have had Empson, with his apt rallying-cry: "Back to Shelley!" Whereto I go.

Contemplating Milton's meanness towards Satan, Shelley spoke of the "pernicious casuistry" set up in the mind of Milton's reader, who would be tempted to weigh Satan's flaws against God's malice towards him, and to excuse Satan because God had been malicious beyond all measure. Shelley's point has been twisted by the C. S. Lewis or Angelic School of Milton Criticism, who proceed to weigh up the flaws and God's wrongs, and find Satan wanting in the balance. This pernicious casuistry, Shelley would have agreed, would not be less pernicious if we were to find (as we do) Milton's God wanting. It would still be casuistry, and as discourse upon poetry it would still be moralizing, which is to say, pernicious.

Even the strong poets were at first weak, for they started as prospective Adams, not as retrospective Satans. Blake names one state of being Adam, and calls it the Limit of Contraction, and another state, Satan, and calls it the Limit of Opacity. Adam is given or natural man, beyond which our imaginations will not contract. Satan is the thwarted or restrained desire of natural man, or rather the shadow or Spectre of that desire. Beyond this Spectre, we will not harden against vision, but the Spectre is prevalent, and we are hardened enough, as we are contracted enough. Enough, that is, not to live our lives, enough to be frightened out of our still creative potential by the Covering Cherub, Blake's emblem (out of Milton, and Ezekiel, and Genesis) for that part of creativity in us that has gone over to constriction and hardness. Blake precisely named this renegade part of Man. Before the Fall (which for Blake is before the Creation, the two events being one and the same) the Covering Cherub was the pastoral figure Tharmas, a unifying process making for undivided consciousness; the innocence, pre-reflective, of a state without subjects and objects, yet in no danger of solipsism, for it lacked also a consciousness of self. Tharmas is a poet's (or any man's) power of realization, even as the Covering Cherub is the power that blocks realization.

No poet, not even so single-minded as Milton or Wordsworth, is a Tharmas, this late in history, and no poet is a Covering Cherub, though Coleridge and Hopkins both allowed themselves, at last, to be dominated by him, as perhaps Eliot did also. Poets this late in tradition are both Adams and Satans. They begin as natural men, affirming that they will contract no further, and they end as thwarted desires, frustrated perhaps only that they cannot harden apocalyptically. But, in between, the greatest of them are very strong, and they progress through a natural intensification that marks Adam in his brief prime and an heroic self-realization that marks Satan in his brief and more-than-natural glory. The dialectic of this movement remains to be traced, as this is still theme but little heard of among men. It is a dialectic that begins when a potential poet discovers poetry as being both external and internal to himself and ends when he has no more poetry within him, long after he has the power (or desire) to discover it outside himself again. This dialectic has always governed the *relation between poets as poets,* the actual ways in which poems by one poet *help to form* poems by another. And, while I do not think it governs the stages of a poet's growth and decay *as a poet,* it may help us to understand why some poets escape such decay, and some do not.

Poetic influence, as I understand it, is part of the larger phenomenon of intellectual revisionism, a phenomenon not peculiar to our century but probably more endemic among us than it has been before. And revisionism, whether in political theory, psychoanalysis, theology, poetics or whatever, has changed its nature in our time. The ancestor of revisionism is heresy, but heresy tended to change received doctrine by an alteration of balances, rather than by what could be called creative correction, the more particular mark of modern revisionism. Heresy resulted, generally, from a change in emphasis, while revisionism follows received doctrine along to a certain point, and then deviates, insisting that a wrong direction was taken at just that point, and no other. Blake was not a heretic but a revisionist, and he was also, I think, the most profound and original theorist of revisionism to appear since the Enlightenment. If poetic influence is itself a mode of revisionism, and I am urging the view that it is, then Blake is an inevitable theorist to apply towards the development of a new theory of poetic influence. And *Paradise Lost*, which served Blake as a second and less remote Bible, becomes an inevitable text against which a theory of poetic influence must be tested.

But what is poetic influence? Blake distinguished between States and Individuals. Individuals passed through States of Being, and remained Individuals, but States were always in process, always shifting. And only States were culpable, Individuals never. Poetic Influence is a passing of Individuals or Particulars through States. Like all revisionism, poetic influence is a gift of the spirit that comes to us only through what could be called, dispassionately, the perversity of the spirit, or what Blake more accurately judged the perversity of States.

It happens frequently that one poet influences another, or more precisely, that one poet's poems influence the poems of the other, through a generosity of the spirit, even a shared generosity. But, after much observation, I propose the following formula:

where generosity is involved, the poets influenced are minor or weaker; the more generosity, and the more mutual it is, the poorer the poets involved. And here also, the influencing moves by way of misapprehension, though this tends to be indeliberate and almost unconscious. But I need to state this argument's central principle now, and in the plainest form possible:

Poetic Influence, – when it involves two strong, authentic poets, – always proceeds by a misreading of the prior poet, an act of creative correction that is actually and necessarily a misinterpretation. The history of fruitful poetic influencing, which is to say the main tradition of Western poetry since the Renaissance, is a history of caricature, of distortion, of perverse, wilful revisionism without which modern poetry as such could not exist.

What is the use of such a principle, whether the argument it informs be true or not? Is it useful to be told that poets are not common readers, and particularly are not critics, in the true sense of critics, common readers raised to the highest power? And what *is* poetic influence anyway? Is it really anything more than the wearisome industry of source-hunting, of allusion-counting, an industry that will soon reach its apotheosis anyway when it passes from scholars to computers? Is there not the shibboleth bequeathed us by Eliot, that the good poet steals while the poor poet betrays an influence, borrows a voice?

The answer to such questions, at this point, can be in counter-questions. How much, or better, how little do we know about poems anyway? Do we know always whether a given work is a poem or not? Is there a poetic logic, rather than just a jumble of conceptual images and imagistic concepts? Can we ever interpret poems without reducing them to prose? Is Blake writing poetry in *Jerusalem?* Is Stevens writing poetry in *An Ordinary Evening in New Haven?* What happens when poets, particularly two connected by poetic influence, are read comparatively, are placed side-by-side? Is it reduction to read one poet in terms of another, and if it isn't, then why isn't it? What governs a poet's beginnings, what makes him choose one earlier poet rather than another as somehow being the voice of poetry itself? Why does it take so long to recognize a period style as such, and what determines whether an individual goes beyond it or not? These questions, and many others, can be answered more justly, if an adequate theory of poetic influence can be established. The one I have stated above, in its most reductive form, may be "the accomplishment of an extremist in an exercise," but so is poetry itself.

Romantic love is an analogue of poetic influence, another splendid perversity of the spirit, though it moves precisely in the opposite direction. The poet confronting his great original must find the fault that is not there, and at the heart of all but the highest imaginative virtue. The lover is beguiled to the heart of loss, but is found, as he finds, within mutual illusion, the poem that is not there. "When two people fall in love," wrote Kierkegaard, "and begin to feel that they are made for one another, then it is time for them to break off, for by going on they have everything to lose and nothing to gain." When the ephebe, or figure of the youth as virile poet, is found by his Great Original, then it is time to go on, for he has everything to gain, and his predecessor nothing to lose, if the fully written poets are indeed beyond loss.

But there is the state called Satan, and in that hardness poets must appropriate for themselves. For Satan is a pure or absolute consciousness of self compelled to have admitted its intimate alliance with opacity. The state of Satan is therefore a constant consciousness of dualism, of being trapped in the finite, not just in space (in the body) but in clock-time as well. To be pure spirit, yet to know in oneself the limit of opacity; to assert that one goes back before the Creation-Fall, yet be forced always to yield to number, weight and measure; this is the situation of the strong poet, the capable imagination, when he confronts the universe of poetry, the words that were and will be, the terrible splendor of cultural heritage.

Let us nominate a list of the Great Originals, of poets who have influenced strongly their stronger contemporaries or vital successors, since the Renaissance. They are not so many as one might expect: Spenser, Shakespeare, Jonson, Donne, Milton,

Pope, Blake, Wordsworth, Shelley, Keats, Tennyson, Browning, Whitman, before this century. Perhaps Cowley needs to be added; perhaps Marlowe, perhaps Hopkins; perhaps Poe. Such major poets as Sidney, Herbert, Marvell, Dryden, Coleridge, Byron, Arnold, Dickinson need not. Emerson would, but not primarily as a poet. In our century, one needs to add Yeats, and probably Pound and Eliot, though in the belief that the last two will resemble Cowley and Cleveland in their after-glow, rather than Jonson and Donne. Who else? Perhaps Hardy, perhaps Auden or even Graves or Dylan Thomas. Among the Americans, perhaps Williams, though the progeny remains disputable. But probably not the major figures beyond Yeats and Hardy, not Stevens or Frost or Lawrence, or even Crane or Owen. In our time, the problem of poetic influence grows more desperate even than it had become in the Milton-haunted eighteenth century, or the Wordsworth-haunted nineteenth, and our current and future poets are probably fortunate that no certain Titanic figure rose beyond Milton and Wordsworth, not even in Yeats or in Stevens.

If one examines the dozen or so major poetic influencers, before this century's, one discovers quickly who among them ranks as the Great Inhibitor, the Sphinx who murders even strong imaginations in their cradles: Milton. The motto to English poetry since Milton was stated by Keats: "Life to him would be Death to me." This deathly vitality in Milton is the state of Satan in him, and is shown us not so much by the character of Satan in *Paradise Lost*, as by Milton's editorializing relation to his own Satan, and by his relation to all the stronger poets of the eighteenth century, and to most of those in the nineteenth.

Milton is the central problem in any theory and history of poetic influence in English; perhaps he is also the most problematic poet in the language, more so even than Wordsworth, who is closer to us as he was to Keats, and who confronts us with everything that is most problematic in modern poetry, which is to say in ourselves. For Milton and Wordsworth are the most profoundly contemplative poets in the language, and as such were the principal influences upon Keats. The central British and American

poets appear to fall into four groups: dramatists, satirists and iro-
nists, visionaries and prophets, and contemplatives, with all of
their meditative, philosophical and devotional cross-categories,
but including a group that might best be called simply ruminative, explorers primarily of their own consciousnesses in relation
to outside pressures of reality. What unites this ruminative line, –
of which Milton is the ancestor; Wordsworth the great revisionist;
Keats and Wallace Stevens, among others, the heirs – is an honest
acceptance of an actual dualism as opposed to the fierce desire to
overcome all dualisms, a desire that dominates the visionary and
prophetic line from the relative mildness of Spenser's temperament down through the various fiercenesses of Blake, Shelley,
Browning, Whitman and Yeats.

   This is the authentic voice of the ruminative line, the poetry
of loss:

> Farewell happy Fields
> Where Joy forever dwells: Hail horrours, hail
> Infernal world, and thou profoundest Hell
> Receive thy new Possessor: One who brings
> A mind not to be chang'd by Place or Time,
> The mind is its own place, and in it self
> Can make a Heav'n of Hell, a Hell of Heav'n,
> What matter where, if I be still the same . . . ?

   These lines, to the C. S. Lewis or Angelic School, represent
moral idiocy, and are to be met with laughter, if we have remembered to start the day with our Good Morning's Hatred of Satan.
If, however, we are not so morally sophisticated, we are likely to be
very much moved by these lines. Not that Satan is not mistaken;
of course he is. There is terrible pathos in his "if I be still the
same," since he is not the same, and never will be again. But he
knows it. He is adopting an heroic dualism, in this conscious
farewell to Joy, a dualism upon which almost all post-Miltonic
poetic influence in the language founds itself.

   To Milton, all fallen experience had its inevitable foundation in loss, and paradise could be regained only by One Greater
Man, and not by any poet whatsoever. The quarrel, or better yet,

wrestling-match with Milton, is perhaps the crucial defining element during the major phase of English Romantic poetry, from Blake to Keats. We have a triad of matches: Jacob and Jehovah, Milton and Urizen (in Blake's poem *Milton*), and the Romantic poet and Milton. Jacob seeks a blessing (a name) and becomes Israel. Milton (Blake's) seeks to bless Urizen, by making Urizen-Jehovah over again in a more human image; the reversal of the blessing is an unnaming, or what Stevens might have called "a naming and unnaming in the eye." The major Romantics (each in turn) – Blake, Wordsworth, Shelley, Keats – seek to bless Milton, by humanizing him, and to re-name him – not Blake, Wordsworth, Shelley, Keats – but Man.

No modern poet is unitary, whatever his stated beliefs. They are necessarily miserable dualists, because this misery, this poverty is the starting-point of their art – Stevens speaks appropriately of the "profound poetry of the poor and of the dead." Poetry may or may not work out its own salvation in a man, but it comes only to those who are Reprobate, in Blake's sense. The Elect or Angelic cannot be touched by poetry, and the Redeemed exist not to be redeemed by it, but only to read it. The Reprobate *are* born or become poets, but the Elect *are* born, chosen from the womb by a Gnome who burrows home to them and whispers: "Live to a hundred and the Promise yet holds, for no poem will ever find you." Without the Elect, we could have poetry but not poems, for poems need context. The Elect are the frame for the Tyger's picture, the horizon against which he moves; the bound that circumscribes, not the Tyger, but the poem that renders him.

For Collins, for Cowper, for many a Bard of Sensibility, Milton was the Tyger; the Covering Cherub blocking a new voice from entering Paradise. The emblem of this discussion is the Covering Cherub. In Genesis he is God's Angel; in Ezekiel he is the Prince of Tyre; in Blake he is fallen Tharmas; in this discussion he is a Gnome, a poor demon of many names, but I summon him first namelessly, as a final name is not yet devised by men. He is something that makes men victims and not poets, a demon of discursiveness, the Gnome of exegesis who makes writings into Scriptures. He cannot strangle the Imagination, for nothing can do that, and he in any case is too weak to strangle anything. The Covering Cherub may masquerade as the Sphinx (as Milton masqueraded) but the Sphinx must be a female, or at least a female male. The Cherub is male, or at least a male female (my terms are Blake's, not Norman Brown's Roheimish variants upon Blake). The Sphinx riddles and strangles and is self-shattered at last, but the Cherub only covers, he only appears to block the way, he cannot do more than conceal. But the Sphinx *is* in the way, and must be dislodged. The unriddler is in every poet when he begins his quest. It is the high irony of poetic vocation that the strong poets can accomplish the greater yet fail the lesser task. They push aside the Sphinx (else they could not be poets, nor for more than one volume) but they cannot uncover the Cherub. Ordinary men (and sometimes weaker poets) can uncover enough of the Cherub so as to live (if not quite to choose Perfection of the Life) but approach the Sphinx only at the risk of the throttled death.

For the Sphinx is natural, but the Cherub is closer to the human. The Sphinx is sexual anxiety, but the Cherub is creative anxiety. The Sphinx is met upon the road back to origins, but the Cherub upon the road forward to possibility, if not to fulfillment. Good poets are powerful striders upon the way back – hence their profound joy as elegists – but only a few have opened themselves to vision. Whitman's road, despite his assertions, is back; retrospective; closed, not open. He would not be a better poet if he truly sang the Song of the Open Road, but he would have entered his own prophecy, and found himself there, more truly and more strange.

The Sphinx is a Siren, the Cherub is not, for the Cherub's voice is only a sobbing, the sound of ocean, but never a song rising above the waves. "I do not say myself like that in poems," the poet says, and proceeds to slay his Sphinx, and then drown anyway:

> He who the Syren's hair would win
> Is mostly strangled by the tide.

Yet the alternative is the dialectical victory that prophecy wins over itself. Do we prefer the fulfillment of Wordsworth (forty years, at the end, of bad poetry) or of Blake (twenty years, at the end, of no poetry), a poethood that does not know it is concluded, or a poethood that declared itself concluded? We prefer what Hermann Broch called the Style of Old Age, the style perhaps of Homer, the style perhaps of the aged Yeats or the even more aged Stevens. We desire the spirit's *alchemicana* – will it not come to us again, if we can weather a poet, again, long enough?

If the spirit must wither, at last, we desire it to wither gloriously, as it does in the air of monologue. The fine raptures of solipsism are the dying falls of our poetic tradition, for who but a solipsist (an unwilling, an anguished solipsist) could seek and find the art that allows yet one more poet? How little this art has changed or can change and in so many centuries:

[John Clare on William Cowper:]

Who travels o'er these sweet fields now
    And brings not Cowper to his mind?
Birds sing his name in every bough,
    Nature repeats it in the wind.

And every place the poet trod
    And every place the poet sung
Are like the Holy Land of God,
    In every mouth, on every tongue.

[Matthew Arnold on Wordsworth:]

And Wordsworth! – Ah, pale ghosts, rejoice!
For never has such a soothing voice
Been to your shadowy world convey'd
Since erst, at morn, some wandering shade
Heard the clear song of Orpheus come
Through Hades, and the mournful gloom.

[John Wheelwright on Hart Crane:]

Lie still. Your rage is gone on a bright flood away;
as, when a bad friend held out his hand you said,
"Do not talk any more. I know you meant no harm."
What was the soil whence your anger sprang, who are deaf as the

stones to the whispering flight of the Mississippi's rivers?
What did you see as you fell? What did you hear as you sank?
Did it not make you drunken with hearing?
I will not ask any more. You saw or heard no evil.

– the more deeply the reader moves into any poet's elegy for a prior poet who influenced the elegist strongly, the more surely the reader meets the one, the same, the inevitable poem. The lost poet has sanctified; he has hallowed Nature, Hades, the Great Deep itself. And he has done this more, better, other even than he could have intended to do it, and he has done this finally, by his death. Clare is infinitely gentle and loving; Arnold is genuinely admiring, and grateful; Wheelwright is movingly honest, and direct; but all have been freed, knowingly and unknowingly, by being left alone for their quest. They raise the song of thanks, even as they mourn the greatness without which they could not recognize their own.

The greatest case in point is Milton himself, in his major elegy for God, *Paradise Lost*. Milton, after all, chooses God over Satan because the vital element in Satan, the poetic imagination, is *even in its Satanic form stronger in God Himself*. Milton finds in Moses, peculiarly enough, *one* achievement that is definitive; the *writing-out* of the words and the Word. Marvell feared that Milton's powers of invention were too strong to allow Moses his role as Covering Cherub. But Milton, like every true poet, yielded to the Power of Invention (proclaimed by Pope and Dr. Johnson to be the essence of poetry). Moses had told the story of Jehovah's inventiveness, of a power to create, greater in kind than an allied power to destroy. But Moses had left Milton more than enough still to do, and Book VII of *Paradise Lost* is almost the mark of Milton's aesthetic debt to his own Hebraic theism.

The only way to uncover the Cherub is to burn him up, to cast him, as Ezekiel says, into the midst of the stones of the fire. But, alas, it is more like burning our own bodies than igniting our old clothes, or so it seems to be anyway. And we become very fond of our cherubim, generally. In the *Jubilate* Smart sang out: "For the Cherub Cat is a Term of the Angel Tyger," and most cherubim do end up looking like house-cats, as cheerfully domesticated as everything else by which poets evade their own vision. Poets despair once, and after that first despair there is no other. Everything survives in a poet after despair except persistence, the quality that would enable him to follow out his vision to its inherent climax. Frye rightly praises Stevens for persistence, thus giving him the Blakean accolade, for it is a quality in which Blake surpassed all other poets, except for Milton.

Persistence is an uncommon virtue in post-Romantic poets, because it is so hard to distinguish from its obsessive and demonic parody, the complusiveness that attends a poetry whose central theme is the poet's relation to his own work. Was Yeats persistent? or obsessed? Or is it his strength that we cannot know? Milton, as a poet, never despaired, and no poet was more persistent throughout every stage of his career. The vision that reached to the Son of *Paradise Regained,* and the hero of *Samson Agonistes,* is necessarily a total one. What was there left for Milton to have made? What the later poets fought through to, is surely one valid answer. Past Samson and the Son of Man are the mythic ego of *The Prelude,* the Solitary of *The Excursion,* the strenuous tongue of the poet-quester in *The Fall of Hyperion.*

But what is there in the imagination itself that makes for persistence? If the difference between the poet and most men comes in unriddling the Sphinx, we may expect poetic persistence to shine forth in that encounter:

POET:
What avails it, when shipwreck'd, that error appears?
Are the crimes we commit wash'd away by our tears?
(Crabbe)

SPHINX:
When Lazarus left his charnel-cave,
  And home to Mary's house return'd
  Was this demanded – if he yearn'd
To hear her weeping by his grave?
(Tennyson)

POET:
When sinews o'er the skeletons are spread,
Those clothed with flesh, and life inspires the dead

The sacred poets first shall hear the sound,
   And foremost from the tomb shall bound,
For they are cover'd with the lightest ground;
(Dryden)

SPHINX:
Be silent in that solitude,
   Which is not loneliness – for then
The spirits of the dead, who stood
   In life before thee, are again
In death around thee, and their will
Shall overshadow thee; be still.
(Poe)

POET:
Because of thee, the land of dreams
Becomes a gathering-place of fears:
Until tormented slumber seems
One vehemence of useless tears.
(Lionel Johnson)

SPHINX:
   Hark how they groan that died despairing!
               Oh, take heed, then!
   Hark how they howl for over-daring!
             All these were men.
      They that be fools, and die for fame,
         They lose their name;
          And they that bleed,
           Hark how they speed!
   Now in cold frosts, now scorching fires
   They sit, and curse their lost desires;
Now shall these souls be free from pains and fears,
Till women waft them over in their tears.
(John Fletcher)

POET:
Content you, let them burn:
It is not your concern;
   Sleep on, sleep sound.
(Housman)

But the "stony sleep" of Blake's Urizen and Yeats's Sphinx is always a vexed one. The monsters in poetry are childlike, and are troubled as children are troubled. Poets – strong ones – are truly demonic, and frighten sphinxes. The archetypal poet's nightmare is one in which the night world flees in terror from the poet. Blake knew this, and in his *Milton* nothing is so terrible as Milton himself, who re-enters our world as a Luciferic comet, frightening all who behold it. Blake's Urizen, who is both Jehovah and Satan, is no match for the courage and efficacy of Blake's Milton:

> Urizen emerged from his Rocky Form & from his Snows,
> And he also darkened his brows: freezing dark rocks between
> The footsteps, and infixing deep the feet in marble beds:
> That Milton labourd with his journey, & his feet bled sore
> Upon the clay now changed to marble; also Urizen rose,
> And met him on the shores of Arnon; & by the streams of the brooks
> Silent they met, and silent strove among the streams, of Arnon
> Even to Mahanaim, when with cold hand Urizen stoop'd down
> And took up water from the river Jordan: pouring on
> To Miltons brain the icy fluid from his broad cold palm.
> But Milton took of the red clay of Succoth, moulding it with care
> Between his palms; and filling up the furrows of many years
> Beginning at the feet of Urizen, and on the bones
> Creating new flesh on the Demon cold, and building him,
> As with new clay a Human form in the Valley of Beth Peor.

This is William Blake's Milton, the Poetic Father that a very powerful poet has begotten upon the Muse. What is the Primal Scene, for a poet *qua* poet? It is his Poetic Father's coitus with the Muse. There he was begotten? No – there they failed to beget him. He must be self-begotten, he must engender himself upon the Muse his mother. But the Muse is a phallic girl, as pernicious as Sphinx or Covering Cherub. Most poets' relations with her are sado-masochistic, and nothing is begotten. And most verse-writers never embrace her anyway, though as Rahab, Mother of Harlots, she is available to all.

The poet begets his Poetic Father upon the Muse. This is his triumph. But he fails to beget himself – he must wait for his Son. But to beget here means to usurp, and to usurp by castration. And castration, which the Sphinx fails to inflict upon poets, is the work of the Cherub. We enter here into the center of our contest, and must look clearly at the Cherub. Poetic Influence must deal with the Sphinx first of all, since no one overcomes the Poetic Father without first encountering the Sphinx. But the Sphinx is only a forerunner, matter for psychoanalysts but not for critics. The Sphinx has a serpent's tail, but is not a serpent – the Covering Cherub *is a Serpent,* a human serpent, a terrible dragon of God, as Blake calls him.

What does the Cherub cover in Genesis? in Ezekiel? in Blake? Genesis 3:24 – "So He drove out the man; and He placed at the east of the garden of Eden the cherubim, and the flaming sword which turned every which way, to keep the way to the tree of life." The rabbis took the cherubim here to symbolize the terror of God's *presence;* to Rashi they were "Angels of destruction." Ezekiel 28:14-16 gives us an even fiercer text: "Thou wast the far-covering [mimshach = 'far-extending,' according to Rashi] cherub; and I set thee so that thou wast upon the holy mountain of God; thou hast walked up and down in the midst of the stones of fire. Thou wast perfect in thy ways from the day that thou wast created, till unrighteousness was found in thee. By the multitude of thy traffic they filled the midst of thee with violence, and thou has sinned; therefore have I cast thee as profane out of the mountain of God; and I have destroyed thee, O covering cherub, from the midst of the stones of the fire."

Here God denounces the Prince of Tyre, who is a cherub because the cherubim in the Tabernacle and in Solomon's Temple spread their wings over the ark, and so protected it, even as the Prince of Tyre once protected Eden, the garden of God. Blake is a still fiercer prophet against the Covering Cherub. To Blake, Voltaire and Rousseau were Vala's Covering Cherubim, Vala being the illusory beauty of the natural world, and the prophets of naturalistic enlightenment being her servitors. In Blake's *Milton,* the Covering Cherub stands between the achieved Man who is at once Milton, Blake and Los, and the emanation Ololon. In *Jerusalem* the Cherub stands between Blake-Los and Jesus. The answer to what the Cherub covers is therefore: in Blake, everything that nature itself covers; in Ezekiel, the richness of the earth, but by the Blakean paradox of *appearing to be* those riches; in Genesis, the Eastern Gate, the Way to the Tree of Life.

Because he knew that Way to be blocked, Blake tried the Western Path, *through the body,* [domain of Tharmas.] The Eastern Gate is the gate of origins; the poet moving towards it meets the Sphinx, triumphs, and intoxicated by illusion loses afterwards to the Covering Cherub. Tharmas, before he became the Cherub, was the impulse towards a double realization:

1) To be fulfilled *in the act of desiring.*

2) To taste *by* touching; to touch *by* tasting.

But the Covering Cherub, the only form in which *we* know Tharmas, is the repressive force making for a double dissolving:

1) To block *by* desiring.

2) To deaden or dry the tongue *in the act of touching;* to numb the fingers, the toes, the limbs, the phallus *in the act of tasting.*

The Covering Cherub separates then? No – he has no power to do so. Tharmas is not an agent of the Fall; he is its victim. Luvah and Urizen separate, but they are the agents of the Fall; thus they form the content of poetic vision, but not the relation of a poet to his vision. It is the movement between Tharmas and Urthona that is the dialectic of a poet's life, *qua* poet. Poetic Influence is not a separation but a victimization – it is a destruction of desire. The emblem of Poetic Influence is the Covering Cherub because the Cherub symbolizes what came to be the Cartesian category of *extensiveness* – hence it is described as *mimshach* – "far-extending." It is not accidental that Descartes and his fellows and disciples are the ultimate enemies of poetic vision in the Romantic tradition, for the Cartesian *extensiveness* is the root-category of modern (as opposed to Pauline) dualism. Descartes saw objects as localized space; the irony of Romantic vision is that it rebelled against Descartes, but except in Blake did not go far enough – Wordsworth and Freud alike remain Cartesian dualists, for whom the present is a precipitated past, and nature a continuum of localized spaces.

The Covering Cherub is a demon of continuity; his baleful charm imprisons the present in the past, and reduces a world of differences into a grayness of uniformity. The identity of past and present is at one with the essential identity of all objects. This is Milton's "universe of death" and with it poetry cannot live, for poetry must leap, it must locate itself in a discontinuous universe, and it must make that universe (as Blake did) if it cannot find one. Discontinuity is freedom, a revolt against homogeneity. Prophets proclaim discontinuity; here Shelley and the phenomenologists are in agreement: "To predict, to really foretell, is still a gift of those who own the future in the full unrestricted sense of the word, the sense of what is coming toward us, and not of what is the result of the past." That is J. H. Van den Berg in *Metabletica* (p. 58). In Shelley's *A Defense of Poetry*, which Yeats considered the most profound discourse upon poetry in the language, the prophetic voice trumpets the same freedom: "Poets are the hierophants of an unapprehended inspiration; the mirrors of the gigantic shadows which futurity casts upon the present."

"He proves God by exhaustion" is Beckett's own note on a crucial passage in his *Whoroscope*, a dramatic monologue spoken by Descartes:

> No Matter, let it pass.
> I'm a bold boy I know
> so I'm not my son
> (even if I were a concierge)
> nor Joachim my father's
> but the chip of a perfect block that's neither old nor new,
> the lonely petal of a great high bright rose.

Any poet would want to claim at least as much for himself, despite Descartes. The triumph of Descartes came in a vision, not necessarily friendly to imaginations other than his own. The protests against Cartesian reductiveness never cease, in constant tribute to him. Beckett's fine handful of poems are too subtle to protest overtly, but they are strong prayers for discontinuity.

> what would I do without this world faceless incurious
> where to be lasts but an instant where every instant
> spills in the void the ignorance of having been
> without this wave where in the end
> body and shadow together are engulfed
> what would I do without this silence where the murmurs die

There is no Cartesian prejudice against poets, no analogue to the Platonic polemic against their authority. Descartes, in his *Private Thoughts,* could write: "It might seem strange that opinions of weight are found in the works of poets rather than philosophers. The reason is that poets wrote through enthusiasm and imagination; there are in us seeds of knowledge, as of fire in a flint; philosophers extract them by way of reason, but poets strike them out by imagination, and then they shine more bright." The Cartesian myth or abyss of consciousness nevertheless took the fire from the flint, and trapped poets in what Blake grimly called a "cloven fiction," with the alternatives, both anti-poetic, of Idealism and Materialism. Philosophy, in cleansing itself, has rinsed away this great dualism, but the whole of the giant line from Milton down to Yeats and Stevens had only their own tradition, Poetic Influence, to tell them that "both Idealism and Materialism are answers to an improper question." And the telling, (even in Stevens), is very different from the philosophic dismissal of the myth that Ryle gives:

> The 'reduction' of the material world to mental states and process-es, as well as the 'reduction' of mental states and processes to physical states and processes, presuppose the legitimacy of the disjunction 'Either there exist minds or there exist bodies (but not both).' It would be like saying, 'Either she bought a left-hand and a right-hand glove or she bought a a pair of gloves (but not both).'

Poets have purchased pairs consisting of left-hand or right-hand, but rarely both. Stevens, asked to sum up his life's work, replied with the fine desperation to which a majestic tradition had been reduced: "The author's work suggests the possibility of a supreme fiction, recognized as a fiction, in which men could propose to themselves a fulfilment." To feel the care of that pronouncement! Stevens, as much as Descartes (or Wordsworth), labored to see with the mind and not with the bodily eye alone. Blake, the genuine anti-Cartesian, found that too a Cloven Fiction, and satirized the Cartesian Dioptrics by opposing his Vortex to that of the Mechanist. That the Mechanism had its nobility we grant now; Descartes wished to save the phenomena by his myth of *extensiveness*. A body took definite shape, moved within a fixed area, and was divided within that area; and thus maintained an integrity in this strictly limited becoming. This established the world or manifold of sensation *given* to the poets, and from it the Wordsworthian vision could begin, rising from this confinement to the enforced ecstasy of the further reduction Wordsworth called Imagination. The manifold of sensation in *Tintern Abbey* initially is further isolated, and then dissolved into a fluid continuum, with the edges of things, the fixities and definites, fading out into a "higher" apprehension. Blake's protest against Wordsworth, the more effective for its praise of Wordsworth, is founded on his horror of this enforced illusion, this ecstasy that is a reduction. In the Cartesian theory of vortices all motion had to be circular (there being no vacuum for matter to move through) and all matter had to be capable of further reduction (there were thus no atoms). These, to Blake, were the circlings of the Mills of Satan, grinding on vainly in their impossible task of reducing the Minute Particulars, the Atoms of Vision that will not further divide. In the Blakean theory of vortices, circular motion is a self-contradiction; when the poet stands at the apex of his own Vortex the Cartesian-Newtonian circles resolve into the flat plane of Vision, and the Particulars stand forth, each as itself, and not another thing. For Blake does not wish to save the phenomena, anymore than he joins the long program of those who seek "to save the appearances," in the sense that Owen Barfield (taking the phrase from Milton) has traced. Blake is the theorist of the saving or revisionary aspect of Poetic Influence, of the impulse that attempts to cast out the Covering Cherub into the midst of the stones of the fire.

French visionaries, because so close to the spell of Descartes, to the Cartesian Siren, have worked in a different spirit, in the high and serious humor, the apocalyptic irony, that culminates in the *Pataphysics* of Jarry and his disciples. The study of Poetic Influence is necessarily a branch of *Pataphysics,* and gladly confesses its indebtedness to ". . . *the* Science, of Imaginary Solutions." As Blake's Urizen, his master Cartesian, comes crashing down in our

Creation-Fall, he *swerves,* and this parody of the Lucretian *clinamen* is, with final irony, *all* the individuality of Urizenic creation, of Cartesian vision as such. The *clinamen* or swerve, which is the Urizenic equivalent of the errors of re-creation made by the Platonic demiurge, is necessarily the central working concept of the theory of Poetic Influence, for what divides each poet from his Poetic Father (and so saves, by division) is an instance of creative revisionism. This *clinamen* is made by the whole being of the latter poet, and the true history of Modern Poetry would be the accurate recording of these revisionary swerves. To the pure *Pataphysician,* the swerve is marvelously gratuitous; Jarry, after all, was capable of considering the Passion as a three-day uphill bicycle race. The student of Poetic Influence is compelled to be an impure *Pataphysician;* he must understand that the *clinamen* always must be considered as though it were simultaneously intentional and involuntary, the Spiritual Form of each poet and the gratuitous gesture each poet makes as his falling body hits the floor of the abyss. Poetic Influence is the passing of Individuals through States, in Blake's language, but the passing is done ill when it is not a swerving. The strong poet indeed says "I seem to have stopped falling; now I *am fallen,* consequently, I lie here in Hell," but he is thinking, as he says this, "As I fell, *I swerved,* consequently I lie here in a Hell improved by my own making."

6   Six Revisionary Ratios

1. *Clinamen,* which is poetic misreading or misprision proper; I take the word from Lucretius, where it means a "swerve" of the atoms so as to make change possible in the universe. A poet swerves away from his precursor, by so reading his precursor's poem as to execute a *clinamen* in relation to it. This appears as a corrective movement in his own poem, which implies that the precursor poem went accurately up to a certain point, but then should have swerved, precisely in the direction that the new poem moves.

2. *Tessera,* which is completion and antithesis; I take the word not from mosaic-making, where it is still used, but from the ancient mystery cults, where it meant a token of recognition, the fragment say of a small pot which with the other fragments would reconstitute the vessel. A poet antithetically "completes" his precursor, by so reading the parent-poem as to retain its terms but to mean them in another sense, as though the precursor had failed to go far enough.

3. *Kenosis,* which is a breaking-device similar to the defense mechanisms our psyches employ against repetition compulsions; *kenosis* then is a movement towards discontinuity with the precursor. I take the word from St. Paul, where it means the humbling or emptying-out of Jesus by himself, when he accepts reduction from divine to human status. The later poet, apparently emptying him-

self of his own afflatus, his imaginative godhood, seems to humble himself as though he were ceasing to be a poet, but this ebbing is so performed in relation to a precursor's poem-of-ebbing that the precursor is emptied out also, and so the later poem of deflation is not as absolute as it seems.

4. *Daemonization,* or a movement towards a personalized Counter-Sublime, in reaction to the precursor's Sublime; I take the term from general Neo-Platonic usage, where an intermediary being, neither divine nor human, enters into the adept to aid him. The later poet opens himself to what he believes to be a power in the parent-poem that does not belong to the parent proper, but to a range of being just beyond that precursor. He does this, in his poem, by so stationing its relation to the parent-poem as to generalize away the uniqueness of the earlier work.

5. *Askesis,* or a movement of self-purgation which intends the attainment of a state of solitude; I take the term, general as it is, particularly from the practice of pre-Socratic shamans like Empedocles. The later poet does not, as in *kenosis,* undergo a revisionary movement of emptying, but of curtailing; he yields up part of his own human and imaginative endowment, so as to separate himself from others, including the precursor, and he does this in his poem by so stationing it in regard to the parent-poem as to make that poem undergo an *askesis* too; the precursor's endowment is also truncated.

6. *Apophrades,* or the return of the dead; I take the word from the Athenian dismal or unlucky days upon which the dead returned to reinhabit the houses in which they had lived. The later poet, in his own final phase, already burdened by an imaginative solitude that is almost a solipsism, holds his own poem so open again to the precursor's work that at first we might believe the wheel has come full circle, and that we are back in the later poet's flooded apprenticeship, before his strength began to assert itself in the revisionary ratios. But the poem is now *held* open to the precursor,

where once it *was* open, and the uncanny effect is that the new poem's achievement makes it seem to us, not as though the precursor were writing it, but as though the later poet himself had written the precursor's characteristic work.

7 The Dialectics of Poetic Tradition

Emerson chose three mottos for his most influential essay, "Self-Reliance." The first, from the *Satires* of Persius: "Do not seek yourself outside yourself." The second, from Beaumont and Fletcher:

> Man is his own star; and the soul that can
> Render an honest and a perfect man,
> Commands all light, all influence, all fate;
> Nothing to him falls early or too late. . . .

The third, one of Emerson's own gnomic verses, is prophetic of much contemporary shamanism:

> Cast the bantling on the rocks,
> Suckle him with the she-wolf's teat,
> Wintered with the hawk and fox,
> Power and speed be hands and feet.

Like the fierce, rhapsodic essay they precede, these mottos are addressed to young Americans, men and women of 1840, who badly needed to be told that they were not latecomers. But we, in fact, *are* latecomers (as indeed they were), and we are better off for consciously knowing it, at least right now. Emerson's single aim was to awaken his auditors to a sense of their own potential *power of making*. To serve his tradition now, we need to counsel a *power of conserving*.

"The hint of the dialectic is more valuable than the dialectic itself," Emerson once remarked, but I intend to contradict him on that also, and to sketch some aspects of the dialectics of literary tradition. Modernism in literature has not passed; rather, it has been exposed as never having been there. Gossip grows old and becomes myth; myth grows older, and becomes dogma. Wyndham Lewis, Eliot and Pound gossiped with one another; the New Criticism aged them into a myth of Modernism; now the antiquarian Hugh Kenner has dogmatized this myth into the Pound Era, a canon of accepted titans. Pretenders to godhood Kenner roughly reduces to their mortality; the grand triumph of Kenner is his judgment that Wallace Stevens represented the culmination of the poetics of Edward Lear.

Yet this is already dogma grown antique: Post-Modernism also has its canons and its canonizers; and I find myself surrounded by living classics, in recently dead poets of strong ambition and hysterical intensity, and in hyperactive novelist non-novelists, who are I suppose the proper seers for their armies of student non-students. I discover it does little good these days to remind literary students that Cowley, Cleveland, Denham and Waller were for generations considered great poets, or that much of the best contemporary opinion preferred Campbell, Moore and Rogers to John Keats. And I would fear to tell students that while I judge Ruskin to have been the best critic of the nineteenth century, he did proclaim *Aurora Leigh* by Mrs. Browning to be the best long poem of that century. Great critics nod, and entire generations go wrong in judging their own achievements. Without what Shelley called a being washed in the blood of the Great Redeemer, Time, literary tradition appears powerless to justify its own selectiveness. Yet if tradition cannot establish its own centrality, it becomes something other than the liberation from time's chaos it implicitly promised to be. Like all convention, it moves from an idealized function to a stifling or blocking tendency.

I intend here to reverse Emerson (though I revere him) and to assert for literary tradition its currently pragmatic as opposed to idealized function: it is now valuable precisely because it partly blocks, because it stifles the weak, because it represses even the strong. To study literary tradition today is to achieve a dangerous but enabling act of the mind that works against all ease in fresh "creation." Kierkegaard could afford to believe that he became great in proportion to striven-with greatness, but we come later. Nietzsche insisted that nothing was more pernicious than the sense of being a latecomer, but I want to insist upon the contrary: nothing is now more salutary than such a sense. Without it, we cannot distinguish between the energy of humanistic performance and merely organic energy, which never alas needs to be saved from itself.

I remember, as a young man setting out to be a university teacher, how afflicted I was by my sense of uselessness, my not exactly vitalizing fear that my chosen profession reduced to an incoherent blend of antiquarianism and culture-mongering. I recall also that I would solace myself by thinking that while a scholar-teacher of literature could do no good, at least he could do no harm, or anyway not to others, whatever he did to himself. But that was at the very start of the decade of the fifties, and after more than twenty years I have come to understand that I underrated my profession, as much in its capacity for doing harm as in its potential for good works. Even our treasons, our betrayals of our implicit trusts, are treasons of something more than of the intellectuals, and most directly damage our immediate students, our Oedipal sons and daughters. Our profession is not genuinely akin any longer to that of the historians or the philosophers. Without willing the change, our theoretical critics have become negative theologians, our practical critics are close to being Agaddic commentators, and all of our teachers, of whatever generation, teach how to live, what to do, in order to avoid the damnation of death-in-life. I do not believe that I am talking about an ideology, nor am I acknowledging any shade whatsoever of the recent Marxist critiques of our profession. Whatever the academic profession of letters now is on the Continent (shall we say an anthropology half-Marxist, half-Buddhist?) or in Britain (shall we say a middle-class amateurism displacing an aristocratic amateurism?), it is currently in America a wholly Emersonian phenomenon. Emerson abandoned his church to become a secular orator, rightly trusting that the lecture, rather than the sermon, was the proper and luminous melody for Americans. We have institutionalized Emerson's procedures, while abandoning (understandably) his aims, for the burden of his prophecy is already carried by our auditors.

Northrop Frye, who increasingly looks like the Proclus or Iamblichus of our day, has Platonized the dialectics of tradition, its relation to fresh creation, into what he calls the Myth of Concern, which turns out to be a Low Church version of T. S. Eliot's Anglo-Catholic myth of Tradition and the Individual Talent. In Frye's reduction, the student discovers that he becomes something, and thus uncovers or demystifies himself, by first being persuaded that tradition is inclusive rather than exclusive, and so makes a place for him. The student is a cultural assimilator who *thinks* because he has *joined* a larger body of thought. Freedom, for Frye as for Eliot, is the change, however slight, that any genuine single consciousness brings about in the order of literature simply by joining the simultaneity of such order. I confess that I no longer understand this simultaneity, except as a fiction that Frye, like Eliot, passes upon himself. This fiction is a noble idealization, and as a lie against time will go the way of every noble idealization. Such positive thinking served many purposes during the sixties, when continuities, of any kind, badly required to be summoned, even if they did not come to our call. Wherever we are bound, our dialectical development now seems invested in the interplay of repetition and discontinuity, and needs a very different sense of what our stance is in regard to literary tradition.

All of us now have been pre-empted, as I think we are all quite uneasily aware. We are rueful that we are asked ("compelled" might be more accurate) to pay for the discontents not only of the civilization we enjoy, but of the civilization of all previous generations from whom we have inherited. Literary tradition, once we even contemplate entering its academies, now insists upon being our "family history," and inducts us into its "family romance" in the unfortunate role prefigured by Browning's Childe Roland, a candidate for heroism who aspired only to fail at least as miserably as his precursors failed. There are no longer any archetypes to displace; we have been ejected from the imperial palace whence we came, and any attempt to find a substitute for it will not be a benign displacement but only another culpable trespass, neither more nor less desperate than any Oedipal return to origins. For us, creative emulation of literary tradition leads to images of inversion, incest, sado-masochistic parody, of which the great, gloriously self-defeating master is Pynchon, whose *Gravity's Rainbow* is a perfect text for the sixties, Age of Frye and Borges, but already deliberately belated for the seventies. Substitute-gratifications and myths-of-displacement turn out to be an identity in Pynchon's book.

Gershom Scholem has an essay on "Tradition and New Creation in the Ritual of the Kabbalists" that reads like a prescription for Pynchon's novel, and I suspect Pynchon found another source in it. The magical formula of the Kabbalistic view of ritual, according to Scholem, is as follows: "everything not only *is in* everything else but also *acts upon* everything else." Remind yourself that Kabbalah literally means "tradition," that which has been received, and reflect on the extraordinary over-determination and stupefying over-organization that a Kabbalistic book like *Gravity's Rainbow* is condemned to manifest. I will mention Kabbalism and its over-relevances again later in this chapter, but need first to de-mythologize and de-esotericize my own view of literary tradition. The proper starting point for any de-mystification has to be a return to the commonal. Let me ask then: what is literary tradition? What is a classic? What is a canonical view of tradition? How are canons of accepted classics formed, and how are they unformed? I think that all these quite traditional questions can take one simplistic but still dialectical question as their summing-up: do we choose a tradition or does it choose us, and why is it necessary that a choosing take place, or a being chosen? What happens if one tries to write, or to teach, or to think, or even to read without the sense of a tradition?

Why, nothing at all happens, just nothing. You cannot write or teach or think or even read without imitation, and what you imitate is what another person has done, that person's writing or teaching or thinking or reading. Your relation to what informs that person *is* tradition, for tradition is influence that extends past one generation, a carrying-over of influence. Tradition, the Latin *traditio*, is etymologically a handing-over or a giving-over, a delivery, a giving-up and so even a surrender or a betrayal. *Traditio* in our sense is Latin only in language; the concept deeply derives from the Hebraic *Mishnah*, an oral handing-over, or transmission of oral precedents, of what has been found to work, of what has been instructed successfully. Tradition is good teaching, where "good" means pragmatic, instrumental, fecund. But how primal is teaching, in comparison to writing? Necessarily, the question is rhetorical; whether or not the psychic Primal Scene is the one where we were begotten, and whether or not the societal Primal Scene is the murder of a Sacred Father by rival sons, I would venture that the artistic Primal Scene *is* the trespass of teaching. What Jacques Derrida calls the Scene of Writing itself depends upon a Scene of Teaching, and poetry is crucially pedagogical in its origins and function. Literary tradition begins when a fresh author is simultaneously cognizant not only of his own struggle against the forms and presence of a precursor, but is compelled also to a sense of the Precursor's place in regard to what came before *him*.

Ernst Robert Curtius, in the best study of literary tradition I have ever read, his definitive *European Literature and the Latin Middle Ages* (1948), concluded that "like all life, tradition is a vast passing away and renewal." But even Curtius, who could accept his own wisdom, cautioned us that Western literary tradition could be apprehended clearly "only" for the twenty-five centuries from Homer to Goethe; for the two centuries after Goethe we still could not know what was canonical or not. The later Enlightenment, Romanticism, Modernism, Post-Modernism; all these, by implication, are one phenomenon and we still cannot know precisely whether or not that phenomenon possesses continuity rather than primarily discontinuity in regard to the tradition between Homer and Goethe. Nor are there Muses, nymphs who *know*, still available to tell us the secrets of continuity, for the nymphs certainly are now departing. I prophesy though that the first true break with literary continuity will be brought about in generations to come, if the burgeoning religion of Liberated Woman spreads from its clusters of enthusiasts to dominate the West. Homer will cease to be the inevitable precursor, and the rhetoric and forms of our literature then may break at last from tradition.

It remains not arbitrary nor even accidental to say that everyone who now reads and writes in the West, of whatever racial background, sex, or ideological camp, is still a son or daughter of Homer. As a teacher of literature who prefers the morality of the Hebrew Bible to that of Homer, indeed who prefers the Bible aesthetically to Homer, I am no happier about this dark truth than you are, if you happen to agree with William Blake when he passionately cries aloud that it is Homer and Virgil, the Classics, and not the Goths and Vandals that fill Europe with wars. But how did this truth, whether dark or not, impose itself upon us?

All continuities possess the paradox of being absolutely arbitrary in their origins, and absolutely inescapable in their teleologies. We know this so vividly from what we all of us oxymoronically call our love lives that its literary counterparts need little demonstration. Though each generation of critics rightly re-affirms the aesthetic supremacy of Homer, he is so much part of the aesthetic *given* for them (and us) that the re-affirmation is a redundancy. What we call "literature" is inescapably connected to education by a continuity of twenty-five hundred years, a continuity that began in the sixth century B. C. when Homer first became a schoolbook for the Greeks, or as Curtius says simply and definitively: "Homer, for them was the 'tradition.'" When Homer became a schoolbook, literature became a school subject quite permanently. Again, Curtius makes the central formulation: "Education becomes the medium of the literary tradition: a fact which is characteristic of Europe, but which is not necessarily so in the nature of things."

This formulation is worth considerable dialectical investigation, particularly in a time as educationally confused as ours recently has been. Nothing in the literary world even sounds quite so silly to me as the passionate declarations that poetry must be liberated from the academy, declarations that would be absurd at any time, but peculiarly so some twenty-five hundred years after Homer and the academy first became indistinguishable. For the answer to the question "What is literature?" must begin with the word "literature," based on Quintilian's word *litteratura* which was his translation of the Greek *grammatike,* the art of reading and writing conceived as a dual enterprise. Literature, and the study of literature, were in their origin a single, unified concept. When Hesiod and Pindar invoke the Muses, they do so *as students,* so as to enable themselves *to teach their readers.* When the first literary scholars wholly distinct from poets created their philology in Alexandria, they began by classifying and then selecting authors, canonizing according to secular principles clearly ancestral in relation to our own. The question we go on asking – "What is a classic?" – they first answered for us by reducing the tragedians initially to five, and later to three. Curtius informs us that the name *classicus* first appears very late, under the Antonine emperors, meaning literary citizens of the first class, but the concept of classification was itself Alexandrian. We are Alexandrians still, and we may as well be proud of it, for it is central to our profession. Even "Modernism," a shibboleth many of us think we may have invented, is necessarily an Alexandrian inheritance also. The scholar Aristarchus, working at the Museion in Alexandria, first contrasted the *neoteroi* or "moderns" with Homer, in defense of a latecomer poet like Callimachus. *Modernus,* based on the word *modo,* for "now," first came into use in the sixth century A.D., and it is worth remembering that "Modernism" always means "For Now."

Alexandria, which thus founded our scholarship, permanently set the literary tradition of the school, and introduced the secularized notion of the canon, though the actual term of canon for "catalogue" of authors was not used until the eighteenth century. Curtius, in his wonderfully comprehensive researches, ascribes the first canon-formation in a modern vernacular, secular literature to the sixteenth-century Italians. The French in the seventeenth century followed, establishing their permanent version of classicism, a version that the English Augustans bravely but vainly tried to emulate before they were flooded out by that great English renaissance of the English Renaissance we now call the Age of Sensibility or the Sublime, and date fairly confidently from the mid-1740's. This renaissance of the Renaissance was and is Romanticism, which is of course *the* tradition of the last two centuries. Canon-formation, for us, has become a part of Romantic tradition, and our still-current educational crisis in the West is rather clearly only another Romantic epicycle, part ot the continuity of upheaval that began with revolution in the West Indies and America, spread to France and through her to the Continent, and thence to Russia, Asia and Africa in our time. Just as Romanticism and Revolution became one composite form, so the dialectic of fresh canon-formation joining itself to a gradual ideological reversal endures into this current decade.

But Romantic tradition differs vitally from earlier forms of tradition, and I think this difference can be reduced to a useful formula. Romantic tradition is *consciously late,* and Romantic literary psychology is therefore necessarily a *psychology of belatedness.* The romance-of-trespass, of violating a sacred or daemonic ground, is a central form in modern literature, from Coleridge and Wordsworth to the present. Whitman follows Emerson by insisting that he strikes up for a new world, yet the guilt of belatedness haunts him and all of his American literary descendants. Yeats was early driven into Gnostic evasions of nature by a parallel guilt, and even the apocalyptic Lawrence is most persuasive when he follows his own analyses of Melville and Whitman to trumpet the doom of what he calls our white race with its hideously belated aversion from what he oddly insisted upon calling blood-consciousness. Romanticism, more than any other tradition, is appalled by its own overt continuities, and vainly but perpetually fantasizes some end to repetitions.

This Romantic psychology of belatedness, from which Emerson failed to save us, his American descendants, is the cause, in my judgment, of the excessively volatile senses-of-tradition that have made canon-formation so uncertain a process during the last two centuries, and particularly during the last twenty years. Take some contemporary examples. A quick way to start a quarrel with any current group of critics would be to express my conviction that Robert Lowell is anything but a permanent poet, that he has been mostly a maker of period-pieces from his origins until now. Similarly, as violent a quarrel would ensue if I expressed my judgment that Norman Mailer is so flawed a writer that his current enshrinement among academics is the largest single index to our current sense of belatedness. Lowell and Mailer, however I rate them, are at least conspicuous literary energies. It would lead to something more intense than quarrels if I expressed my judgment upon "black poetry" or the "literature of Women's Liberation." But quarrels, or even abuse, is all such *obiter dicta* could lead to, for our mutual sense of canonical standards has undergone a remarkable dimming, a fading into the light of a common garishness. Revisionism, always a Romantic energizer, has become so much a norm that even rhetorical standards seem to have lost their efficacy. Literary tradition has become the captive of the revisionary impulse, and I think we must go past viewing-with-alarm if we are to understand this quite inescapable phenomenon, the subsuming of tradition by belatedness.

The revisionary impulse, in writing and in reading, has a directly inverse relationship to our psychological confidence in what I am calling the Scene of Instruction. Milton's Satan, who remains the greatest really Modern or Post-Enlightenment poet in the language, can give us a paradigm of this inverse relationship. The ultimate Scene of Instruction is described by Raphael in Book V of *Paradise Lost*, where God proclaims to the Angels that "This day I have begot whom I declare/My only son" and provocatively warns that "him who disobeys/Mee disobeys . . . /and . . . falls/Into utter darkness." We can describe this as an imposition of the psychology of belatedness, and Satan, like any strong poet, declines to be merely a latecomer. His way of returning to origins, of making the Oedipal trespass, is to become a rival creator to God-as-creator. He embraces Sin as his Muse, and begets upon her the highly original poem of Death, the only poem that God will permit him to write.

Let me reduce my own allegory, or my allegorical interpretation of Satan, by invoking a wonderful poem of Emily Dickinson's, "The Bible is an antique Volume – " (no. 1545), in which she calls Eden "the ancient Homestead," Satan "the Brigadier," and Sin "a distinguished Precipice/Others must resist." As a heretic whose orthodoxy was Emersonian, Dickinson recognized in Satan a distinguished precursor gallantly battling against the psychology of belatedness. But then, Dickinson and Emerson wrote in an America that needed, for a while, to battle against the European exhaustions of history. I am temperamentally a natural revisionist, and I respond to Satan's speeches more strongly than to any other poetry I know, so it causes some anguish in me to counsel that currently we need Milton's sense of tradition much more than Emerson's revisionary tradition. Indeed, the counsel of necessity must be taken further: most simply, we need Milton, and not the Romantic return of the repressed Milton but the Milton who made his great poem identical with the process of repression that is vital to literary tradition. But a resistance even in myself is set up by my counsel of necessity, because even I want to know: what do I mean by "we"? Teachers? Students? Writers? Readers?

I do not believe that these are separate categories, nor do I believe that sex, race, social class can narrow this "we" down. If we are human, then we depend upon a Scene of Instruction, which is necessarily also a scene of authority and of priority. If you will not have one instructor or another, then precisely by rejecting all instructors, you will condemn yourself to the earliest Scene of Instruction that imposed itself upon you. The clearest analogue is necessarily Oedipal; reject your parents vehemently enough, and you will become a belated version of them, but compound with their reality, and you may partly free yourself. Milton's Satan failed, particularly as poet, after making a most distinguished beginning, because he became only a parody of the bleakest aspects of Milton's God. I greatly prefer Pynchon to Mailer as a writer because a voluntary parody is more impressive than an involuntary one, but I wonder if our aesthetic possibilities need to be reduced now to just such a choice. Do the dialectics of literary tradition condemn us, at this time, either to an affirmation of belatedness, via Kabbalistic inversion, or to a mock-vitalistic lie-against-time, via an emphasis upon the self-as-performer?

I cannot answer this hard question, because I am uneasy with the current alternatives to the ways of Pynchon and of Mailer, at least in fictional or quasi-fictional prose. Saul Bellow, with all his literary virtues, clearly shows the primal exhaustions of being a latecomer rather more strenuously in his way than Pynchon or Mailer do in theirs. I honestly don't enjoy Bellow more, and I would hesitate to find anything universal in such enjoyment even if I had it. Contemporary American poetry seems healthier to me, and provides alternatives to the voluntary parodies that Lowell has given us, or the involuntary parodies at which Ginsberg is so prominent. Yet even the poets I most admire, John Ashbery and A. R. Ammons, are rendered somewhat problematic by a cultural situation of such belatedness that literary survival itself seems fairly questionable. As Pynchon says in the closing pages of his uncanny book: "You've got much older. . . . Fathers are carriers of the virus of Death, and sons are the infected. . . ." And he adds a little further on in his Gospel of Sado-anarchism that this time we "*will* arrive, my God, too late."

I am aware that this must seem a Gospel of Gloom, and no one ought to be asked to welcome a kakangelist, a bearer of ill-tidings. But I cannot see that evasions of Necessity benefit anyone, least of all educationally. The teacher of literature now in America, far more than the teacher of history or philosophy or religion, is condemned to teach the presentness of the past, because history, philosophy and religion have withdrawn as agents from the Scene of Instruction, leaving the bewildered teacher of literature alone at the altar, terrifiedly wondering whether he is to be sacrifice or priest. If he evades his burden by attempting to teach only the supposed presence of the present, he will find himself teaching only some simplistic, partial reduction that wholly obliterates the present in the name of one or another historicizing formula, or past injustice, or dead faith, whether secular or not. Yet how is he to teach a tradition now grown so wealthy and so heavy that to accommodate it demands more strength than any single consciousness can provide, short of the parodistic Kabbalism of a Pynchon?

All literary tradition has been necessarily élitist, in every period, if only because the Scene of Instruction always depends upon a primal choosing and a being chosen, which is what "élite" means. Teaching, as Plato knew, is necessarily a branch of erotics, in the wide sense of desiring what we have not got, of redressing our poverty, of compounding with our fantasies. No teacher, however impartial he or she attempts to be, can avoid choosing among students, or being chosen by them, for this is the very nature of teaching. Literary teaching is precisely like literature itself; no strong writer can choose his precursors until first he is chosen by them, and no strong student can fail to be chosen by his teachers. Strong students, like strong writers, will find the sustenance they must have. And strong students, like strong writers, will rise in the most unexpected places and times, to wrestle with the internalized violence pressed upon them by their teachers and precursors.

Yet our immediate concern, as I am aware, is hardly with the strong, but with the myriads of the many, as Emersonian democracy seeks to make its promises a little less deceptive than they have been. Do the dialectics of literary tradition yield us no wisdom that can help with the final burden of the latecomer, which is the extension of the literary franchise? What is the particular inescapability of literary tradition for the teacher who must go out to find himself as a voice in the wilderness? Is he to teach *Paradise Lost* in preference to the Imamu Amiri Baraka?

I think these questions are self-answering, or rather will be, with the passage of only a few more years. For the literary teacher, more than ever, will find he is teaching *Paradise Lost* and the other central classics of Western literary tradition, whether he is teaching them overtly or not. The psychology of belatedness is unsparing, and the Scene of Instruction becomes ever more primal as our society sags around us. Instruction, in our late phase, becomes an antithetical process almost in spite of itself, and for antithetical teaching you require antithetical texts, that is to say, texts antithetical to your students as well as to yourself and to other texts. Milton's Satan may stand as representative of the entire canon when he challenges us to challenge Heaven with him, and he will provide the truest handbook for all those, of whatever origin, who as he says "with ambitious mind/Will covet more." Any teacher of the dispossessed, of those who assert *they* are the insulted and injured, will serve the deepest purposes of literary tradition and meet also the deepest needs of his students when he gives them possession of Satan's grand opening of the Debate in Hell, which I cite now to close this chapter on the dialectics of tradition:

> With this advantage then
> To union, and firm Faith, and firm accord,
> More than can be in Heav'n, we now return
> To claim our just inheritance of old,
> Surer to prosper than prosperity
> Could have assur'd us; and by what best way,
> Whether of open War or covert guile,
> We now debate; who can advise, may speak.

8   Poetry, Revisionism, Repression

Jacques Derrida asks a central question in his essay on Freud and the Scene of Writing: "What is a text, and what must the psyche be if it can be represented by a text?" My narrower concern with poetry prompts the contrary question: "What is a psyche, and what must a text be if it can be represented by a psyche?" Both Derrida's question and my own require exploration of three terms: "psyche," "text," "represented."

"Psyche" is ultimately from the Indo-European root *bhes*, meaning "to breath," and possibly was imitative in its origins. "Text" goes back to the root *teks*, meaning "to weave," and also "to fabricate." "Represent" has as its root *es* "to be." My question thus can be rephrased: "What is a breath, and what must a weaving or a fabrication be so as to come into being again as a breath?"

In the context of post-Enlightenment poetry, a breath is at once a *word*, and a *stance* for uttering that word, a word, and a stance *of one's own*. In this context, a weaving or a fabrication is what we call a poem, and its function is to represent, to bring back into being again, an individual stance and word. The poem, as text, is represented or seconded by what psychoanalysis calls the psyche. But the text *is* rhetoric, and as a persuasive system of tropes can be carried into being again only by another system of tropes. Rhetoric can be seconded only by rhetoric, for all that rhetoric can *intend* is more rhetoric. If a text and a psyche can be represented by one another, this can be done only because each is a departure from proper meaning. figuration turns out to be our only link between breathing and making.

The strong word and stance issue only from a strict will, a will that dares the error of reading all of reality as a text, and all prior texts as openings for its own totalizing and unique interpretations. Strong poets present themselves as looking for truth *in the world,* searching in reality and in tradition, but such a stance, as Nietzsche said, remains under the mastery of desire, of instinctual drives. So, in effect, the strong poet wants pleasure and not truth; he wants what Nietzsche named as "the belief in truth and the pleasurable effects of this belief." No strong poet can admit that Nietzsche was accurate in this insight, and no critic need fear that any strong poet will accept and so be hurt by demystification. The concern of this book, as of my earlier studies in poetic misprision, is only with strong poets, which in this series of chapters is exemplified by the major sequence of High Romantic British and American poets: Blake, Wordsworth, Shelley, Keats, Tennyson, Browning, Yeats, Emerson, Whitman, and Stevens, but also throughout by two of the strongest poets in the European Romantic tradition: Nietzsche and Freud. By "poet" I therefore do not mean only verse-writer, as the instance of Emerson also should make clear.

A poetic "text," as I interpret it, is not a gathering of signs on a page, but is a psychic battlefield upon which authentic forces struggle for the only victory worth winning, the divinating triumph over oblivion, or as Milton sang it:

> Attir'd with Stars, we shall for ever sit
> Triumphing over Death, and Chance, and Thee O Time.

Few notions are more difficult to dispel than the "commonsensical" one that a poetic text is self-contained, that it has an ascertainable meaning or meanings without reference to other poetic texts. Something in nearly every reader wants to say: "*Here* is a poem and *there* is a meaning, and I am reasonably certain that the two can be brought together." Unfortunately, poems are not things but only words that refer to other words, and *those* words refer to still other words, and so on, into the densely overpopulated world of literary language. Any poem is an inter-poem, and any reading of a poem is an inter-reading. A poem is not writing, but *rewriting,* and though a strong poem is a fresh start, such a start is a starting-again.

In some sense, literary criticism has known always this reliance of texts upon texts, but the knowing changed (or should have changed) after Vico, who uncovered the genuine scandal of poetic origins, in the complex defensive trope or troping defense he called "divination." Poetry began, according to Vico, out of the ignorance and mortal fear of the gentile giants, who sought to ward off danger and death through interpreting the auguries, through divination:"Their poetic wisdom began with this poetic metaphysics . . . and they were called theological poets . . . and were properly called divine in the sense of diviners, from *divinari,* to divine or predict." These were the giants or poets before the flood, for Vico a crucial image of two modes of encroachment always threatening the human mind, a divine deluge and a natural engulfment. Edward Said eloquently interprets Vico's own influence-anxieties:

> These threatening encroachments are described by Vico as the result of a divinely willed flood, which I take to be an image for the inner crisis of self-knowledge that each man must face at the very beginning of any conscious undertaking. The analogy, in Vico's *Autobiography,* of the universal flood is the prolonged personal crisis of self-alienation from full philosophic knowledge and self-knowledge that Vico faces until the publication of his major work, the *New Science.* His minor successes with his orations, his poems, his treatises, reveal bits of the truth to him, but he is always striving with great effort to come literally into his own.

Said's commentary illuminates the remarkable passage in Vico's early *On the Study Methods of Our Time,* where Vico suddenly appears to be the precursor of Artaud, arguing that the great masterpieces of anterior art must be destroyed, if any great works are still to be performed. Or, if great art is to be retained, let it be for "the benefit of lesser minds," while men of "surpassing genius, should put the masterpieces of their art out of their sight, and strive with the greatest minds to appropriate the secret of nature's grandest creation." Vico's primary precursor was Descartes, whom he repudiated in favor of Bacon as a more distant and antithetical

precursor, but it could be argued that Vico's *New Science* as a
"severe poem" is a strong misprision of Descartes.

Language for Vico, particularly poetic language, is always
and necessarily a revision of previous language. Vico, so far as I
know, inaugurated a crucial insight that most critics still refuse to
assimilate, which is that every poet is belated, that every poem is
an instance of what Freud called *Nachträglichkeit* or "retroactive
meaningfulness." Any poet (meaning even Homer, if we could
know enough about his precursors) is in the position of being
"after the Event," in terms of literary language. His art is necessarily an *aftering*, and so at best he strives for a selection, through
repression, out of the traces of the language of poetry; that is, he
represses some of the traces, and remembers others. This remembering is a misprision, or creative misreading, but no matter how
strong a misprision, it cannot achieve an autonomy of meaning,
or a meaning *fully* present, that is, free from all literary context.
Even the strongest poet must take up his stance *within* literary language. If he stands *outside* it, then he cannot begin to write poetry.
For poetry lives always under the shadow of poetry. The caveman
who traced the outline of an animal upon the rock always
retraced a precursor's outline.

The curse of an increased belatedness, a dangerously self-
conscious belatedness, is that creative envy becomes the ecstasy,
the Sublime, of the sign-system of poetic language. But this is,
from an altered perspective, a loss that can become a shadowed
gain, the blessing achieved by the latecomer poet as a wrestling
Jacob, who cannot let the great depart finally, without receiving a
new name all his own. Nothing is won for the reader we all need
to become if this wrestling with the dead is idealized by criticism.
The enormous distinction of Vico, among all critical theorists, is
that he idealized least. Vico understood, as almost no one has
since, that the link between poetry and pagan theology was as
close as the war between poetry and Hebrew-Christian theology
was perpetual. In Vico's absolute distinction between gentile and
Jew, the gentile is linked both to poetry and history, through the
revisionary medium of language, while the Jew (and subsequently

the Christian) is linked to a sacred origin transcending language, and so has no relation to human history or to the arts. We only know what we ourselves have made, according to Vico, and so his science excludes all knowledge of the true God, who can be left to the Church and its theologians. The happy consequence, for Vico, is that the world of the indefinite, the world of ambivalent and uncertain images, which is the universe of poetry, becomes identical with our fallen state of being in the body. To be in the body, according to Vico, is to suffer a condition in which we are ignorant of causation and of origins, yet still we are very much in quest of origins. Vico's insight is that poetry is born of our ignorance of causes, and we can extend Vico by observing that if any poet knows too well what causes his poem, then he cannot write it, or at least will write it badly. He must repress the causes, including the precursor-poems, but such forgetting, as this book will show, itself is a condition of a particular exaggeration of style or hyperbolical figuration that tradition has called the Sublime.

II

How does one read a strong poem? How does one write a strong poem? What makes a poem strong? There is a precarious identity between the Over-reader and the Over-poet, both of them perhaps forms of the Over-man, as prophesied by Nietzsche's Zarathustra. Strong poetry is a paradox, resembling nothing so much as Durkheim on Marxism, or Karl Kraus on Freudianism. Durkheim said that socialism was not a sociology or miniature science, but rather a cry of grief; not so much a scientific formulation of social facts, as itself a social fact. Following the aphorism of Kraus, that psychoanalysis itself was the disease for which it purported to be the cure, we can say that psychoanalysis is more a psychic fact than a formulation of psychic facts. Similarly, the reading of strong poetry is just as much a poetic fact as is the writing of such poetry. Strong poetry is strong only by virtue of a kind of textual usurpation that is analogous to what Marxism encompasses as its social usurpation or Freudianism as its psychic usurpation. A strong poem does not *formulate* poetic facts any more than strong reading or criticism formulates them, for a strong reading *is* the only poetic fact, the only revenge against time that endures, that is successful in canonizing one text as opposed to a rival text.

There is no textual authority without an act of imposition, a declaration of property that is made figuratively rather than properly or literally. For the ultimate question a strong reading asks of a poem is: Why? Why should it have been written? Why must we read it, out of all the too many other poems available? Who does the poet think he is, anyway? Why is his poem?

By defining poetic strength as usurpation or imposition, I am offending against civility, against the social conventions of literary scholarship and criticism. But poetry, when it aspires to strength, is necessarily a competitive mode, indeed an obsessive mode, because poetic strength involves a self-representation that is reached only through trespass, through crossing a daemonic threshold. Again, resorting to Vico gives the best insight available for the nature and necessity of the strong poet's self-proclamation.

Vico says that "the true God" founded the Jewish religion "on the prohibition of the divination on which all the gentile nations arose." A strong poet, for Vico or for us, is precisely like a gentile nation; he must divine or invent himself, and so attempt the impossibility of *originating himself.* Poetry has an origin in the body's ideas of itself, a Vichian notion that is authentically difficult, at least for me. Since poetry, unlike the Jewish religion, does not go back to a truly divine origin, poetry is always at work *imagining its own origin,* or telling a persuasive lie about itself, to itself. Poetic strength ensues when such lying persuades the reader that his own origin has been reimagined by the poem. Persuasion, in a poem, is the work of rhetoric, and again Vico is the best of guides, for he convincingly relates the origins of rhetoric to the origins of what he calls poetic logic, or what I would call poetic misprision.

Angus Fletcher, writing on *The Magic Flute,* observes that: "To begin is always uncertain, nextdoor to chaos. To begin requires that, uncertainly, we bid farewell to some thing, some one, some where, some time. Beginning is still ending." Fletcher, by emphasizing the uncertainty of a beginning, follows Vico's idea of the indefiniteness of all secular origins. But this indefiniteness, because it is made by man, can be interpreted by man. Vico says that "ignorance, the mother of wonder, made everything wonderful to men who were ignorant of everything." From this followed a poetic logic or language "not . . . in accord with the nature of things it dealt with . . . but . . . a fantastic speech making use of physical substances endowed with life and most of them imagined to be divine."

For Vico, then, the trope comes from ignorance. Vico's profundity as a philosopher of rhetoric, beyond all other ancient and modern except for his true son, Kenneth Burke, is that he views tropes as defenses. Against what? Initially, against their own origins in ignorance, and so against the powerlessness of man in relation to the world:

> . . . man in his ignorance makes himself the rule of the universe, for in the examples cited he has made of himself an entire world. So that, as rational metaphysics teaches that man becomes all things by understanding them, this imaginative metaphysics shows that man becomes all things by *not* understanding them; and perhaps the latter proposition is truer than the former, for when man understands he extends his mind and takes in the things, but when he does not understand he makes the things out of himself and becomes them by transforming himself into them.

Vico is asking a crucial question, which could be interpreted reductively as, What is a poetic image, or what is a rhetorical trope, or what is a psychic defense? Vico's answer can be read as a formula: poetic image, trope, defense are all forms of a ratio between human ignorance making things out of itself, and human self-identification moving to transform us into the things we have made. When the human ignorance is the trespass of a poetic repression of anteriority, and the transforming movement is a new poem, then the ratio measures a rewriting or an act of revision. As poetic image, the ratio is a phenomenal masking of the mind taking in the world of things, which is Vico's misprision of the Cartesian relationship between mind and the *res extensa*. An image is necessarily an imitation, and its coverings or maskings in poetic language necessarily center in certain fixed areas: presence and absence, partness and wholeness, fullness and emptiness, height and depth, insideness and outsideness, earliness and lateness. Why these? Because they are the inevitable categories of our makings and our becomings, or as inevitable as such categories can be, within the fixities and limits of space and time.

As trope, the ratio between ignorance and identification takes us back to the realization, by Vico, that the first language of the gentiles was not a "giving of names to things according to the nature of each," unlike the sacred Hebrew of Adam, but rather was fantastic and figurative. In the beginning was the trope, is in effect Vico's formula for pagan poetry. Kenneth Burke, the Vico of our century, gives us a formula for why rhetoric rises:

> In pure identification there would be no strife. Likewise, there would be no strife in absolute separateness, since opponents can join battle only through a mediatory ground that makes their communication possible, thus providing the first condition necessary for their interchange of blows. But put identification and division ambiguously together, so that you cannot know for certain just where one ends and the other begins, and you have the characteristic invitation to rhetoric. Here is a major reason why rhetoric, according to Aristotle, "proves opposites."

Vico saw rhetoric as being defensive; Burke tends to emphasize what he calls the realistic function of rhetoric: "the use of language as a symbolic means of inducing cooperation in beings that by nature respond to symbols." But Vico, compared to Burke, is more of a magical formalist, like his own primitives, his "theological poets." Vico's giants divinate so as to defend against death, and they divinate through the turns of figurative language. As a ratio between ignorance and identification, a psychic defense in Vichian terms is not significantly different from the Freudian notion of defense. Freud's "mechanisms" of defense are directed toward Vico's "ignorance," which in Freud is "instinct" or "drive."

For Freud and Vico alike the "source" of all our drives is the body, and defense is finally against drive itself. For though defense takes instinct as its object, defense becomes contaminated by instinct, and so becomes compulsive and at least partly repressed, which rhetorically means hyperbolical or Sublime.

A specific defense is for Freud an operation, but for Vico a trope. It is worth noting that the root-meaning of our word "defense" is "to strike or hurt," and that "gun" and "defense" are from the same root, just as it is interesting to remember that *tropos* meaning originally "turn, way, manner" appears also in the name *Atropos* and in the word "entropy." The trope-as-defense or ratio between ignorance and identification might be called at once a warding-off by turning and yet also a way of striking or manner of hurting. Combining Vico and Freud teaches us that the origin of any defense is its stance towards death, just as the origin of any trope is its stance towards proper meaning. Where the psychic defense and the rhetorical trope take the same particular phenomenal maskings in poetic images, there we might speak of the ultimate ratio between ignorance and identification as expressing itself in a somber formula: death is the most proper or literal of meanings, and literal meaning partakes of death.

Talbot Donaldson, commenting upon Chaucer's *Nun's Priest's Tale,* speaks of rhetoric as "a powerful weapon of survival in a vast and alien universe," a mode of satisfying our need for security. For a strong poet in particular, rhetoric is also what Nietzsche saw it as being, a mode of interpretation that is the will's revulsion against time, the will's revenge, its vindication against the necessity of passing away. Pragmatically, a trope's revenge is against an earlier trope, just as defenses tend to become operations against one another. We can define a strong poet as one who will not tolerate words that intervene between him and the Word, or precursors standing between him and the Muse. But that means the strong poet in effect takes up the stance of the Gnostic, ancestor of all major Western revisionists.

III

What does the Gnostic *know?* These are the injunctions of the Gnostic adept Monoimus, who sounds rather like Emerson:

> Abandon the search for God and the creation. . . . Look for him
> by taking *yourself* as the starting point. Learn who it is who *within you*
> makes everything his own and says, "*My* God, *my* mind, *my* thought,
> *my* soul, *my* body." Learn the sources of sorrow, joy, love, hate. Learn
> how it happens that one watches without willing, rests without will-
> ing, becomes angry without willing, loves without willing. If you
> search these matters you will find him *in yourself.*

What the Gnostic knows is his own subjectivity, and in that self-consciousness he seeks his own freedom, which he calls "salvation" but which pragmatically seems to be freedom from the anxiety of being influenced by the Jewish God, or Biblical Law, or nature. The Gnostics, by temperament, were akin both to Vico's magic primitives and to post-Enlightenment poets; their quarrel with the words dividing them from their own Word was essentially the quarrel of any belated creator with his precursor. Their rebellion against religious tradition as a process of supposedly benign transmission became the prophecy of all subsequent quarrels with poetic tradition. R. M. Grant, in his *Gnosticism and Early Christianity,* remarks of the proto-Gnostic yet still Jewish *Prayer of Joseph* that it "represents an attempt to supplant an archangel of the older apocalyptic by a new archangel who makes himself known by a new revelation." But Gnostics, as Grant indicates, go beyond apocalyptic thought, and abandon Judaism (and Christianity) by denying the goodness and true divinity of the Creator god, as well as the law of Moses and the vision of the Resurrection.

Part of the deep relevance of Gnosticism to any theory of poetic misprision is due to the attempt of Simon Magus to revise Homer as well as the Bible, as in this Simonian misreading of the *Iliad,* where Virgil's stationing of Helen is ascribed to Homer, an error wholly typical of all strong misinterpretation:

> She who at that time was with the Greeks and Trojans was the
> same who dwelt above before creation . . . . She is the one who now is

> with me; for her sake I descended. She waited for my coming; for she is the Thought called Helen in Homer. So Homer has to describe her as having stood on the tower and signaling with a torch to the Greeks the plot against the Phrygians. Through its shining he signified the light's display from above . . . . As the Phrygians by dragging in the wooden horse ignorantly brought on their own destruction, so the gentiles, the men apart from my gnosis, produce perdition for themselves.

Simon is writing his own poem, and calling it Homer, and his peculiar mixture in this passage of Homer, Virgil, the Bible, and his own Gnosis amounts to a revisionary freedom of interpretation, one so free that it transgresses all limits and becomes its own creation. Christianity has given Simon a bad name, but in a later time he might have achieved distinction as a truly audacious strong poet, akin to Yeats.

Valentinus, who came after Simon, has been compared to Heidegger by Hans Jonas, and I myself have found the Valentinian speculation to be rather more useful for poetic theory than the Heideggerian. Something of that usefulness I attempt to demonstrate in the chapter on Yeats in this book; here I want to cite only a single Valentinian passage, for its view of the Demiurge is precisely the view taken of a strong precursor poet by a strong ephebe or latecomer poet:

> When the Demiurge further wanted to imitate also the boundless, eternal, infinite and timeless nature of [the original eight Aeons in the Pleroma], but could not express their immutable eternity, being as he was a fruit of defect, he embodied their eternity in times, epochs, and great numbers of years, under the delusion that by the quantity of times he could represent their infinity. Thus truth escaped him and he followed the lie. Therefore he shall pass away when the times are fulfilled.

This is a misprision-by-parody of Plato, as Plotinus eloquently charged in his *Second Ennead IX,* "Against the Gnostics; or Against Those that Affirm the Creator of the Cosmos and the Cosmos Itself to be Evil." Hans Jonas observes the specific parody of the *Timaeus* 37C ff:

> When the father and creator saw the creature which he had made
> moving and living, the created image of the eternal gods, he
> rejoiced, and in his joy determined to make the copy still more like
> the original, and as this was an eternal living being, he sought to
> make the universe eternal, so far as might be. Now the nature of the
> ideal being was everlasting, but to bestow this attribute in its fullness
> upon a creature was impossible. Wherefore he resolved to have a
> moving image of eternity, and when he set in order the heaven, he
> made this image eternal but moving according to number, while
> eternity itself rests in unity, and this image we call time.

The Demiurge of Valentinus lies against eternity, and so, against the Demiurge, Valentinus lies against time. Where the Platonic model suggests a benign transmission (though with loss) through imitation, the Gnostic model insists upon a doubly malign misinterpretation, and a transmission through catastrophe. Either way, the belated creator achieves the uniqueness of his own consciousness through a kind of fall, but these kinds are very different, the Platonic model positing time as a necessity, the Valentinian misprision condemning time as a lie. While the major traditions of poetic interpretation have followed Platonic and/or Aristotelian models, I think that the major traditions of post-Enlightenment poetry have tended more to the Gnostic stance of misprision. The Valentinian doctrine of creation could serve my own revisionist purpose, which is to adopt an interpretative model closer to the stance and language of "modern" or post-Enlightenment poetry than the philosophically oriented models have proved to be. But, again like the poets, so many of whom have been implicitly Gnostic while explicitly even more occult, I turn to the medieval system of Old Testament interpretation known as Kabbalah, particularly the doctrines of Isaac Luria. Kabbalah, demystified, is a unique blend of Gnostic and Neoplatonic elements, of a self-conscious subjectivity founded upon a revisionist view of creation, combined with a rational but rhetorically extreme dialectic of creativity. My turn to a Kabbalistic model, particularly to a Lurianic and "regressive" scheme of creation, may seem rather eccentric, but the readings offered in this book should demonstrate the usefulness of the Lurianic dialectics for poetic interpretation.

The quest for interpretative models is a necessary obsession for the reader who would be strong, since to refuse models explicitly is only to accept other models, however unknowingly. All reading is translation, and all attempts to communicate a reading seem to court reduction, perhaps inevitably. The proper use of any critical paradigm ought to lessen the dangers of reduction, yet clearly most paradigms are, in themselves, dangerously reductive. Negative theology, even where it verges upon Theosophy, rather than the reasoning through negation of Continental philosophy, or structuralist linguistics, seems to me the likeliest "discipline" for revisionary literary critics to raid in their incessant quest after further metaphors for the act of reading. But so extreme is the situation of strong poetry in the post-Enlightenment, so nearly identical is it with the anxiety of influence, that it requires as interpretative model the most dialectical and negative of theologies that can be found. Kabbalah provides not only a dialectic of creation astonishingly close to revisionist poetics, but also a conceptual rhetoric ingeniously oriented towards defense.

Kabbalah, though the very word means "tradition" (in the particular sense of "reception"), goes well beyond orthodox tradition in its attempt to *restore* primal meanings to the Bible. Kabbalah is necessarily a massive misprision of both Bible and Talmud, and the initial sense in which it accurately was "tradition" is the unintentionally ironic one that means Neoplatonic and Gnostic traditions, rather than Jewish ones. The cosmology of Kabbalah, as Gershom Scholem definitively observes, is Neoplatonic. Scholem locates the originality in a "new religious impulse," yet understandably has difficulty in defining such an impulse. He distinguishes Kabbalistic theories of the emanation of the *sefirot*, from Neoplatonic systems, by noting that, in the latter, the stages of emanation "are not conceived as processes within the Godhead." Yet he grants that certain Gnosticisms also concentrated on the life within the Godhead, and we can notice the same emphasis in the analysis of the Valentinian Speculation by Hans Jonas: "The distinguishing principle . . . is the attempt to place the origin of darkness, and thereby of the dualistic rift of being, *within* the godhead itself." Jonas adds that the Valentinian vision relies on "terms of divine error" and this *is* the distinction between Gnosticism and Kabbalah, for Kabbalah declines to impute error to the Godhead.

Earlier Kabbalah from its origins until Luria's older contemporary Cordovero, saw creation as an outgoing or egressive process. Luria's startling originality was to revise the *Zohar's* dialectics of creation into an ingoing or regressive process, a creation by contraction, destruction, and subsequent restitution. This Lurianic story of creation-by-catastrophe is a genuine dialectic or dialectical process by the ordeal of the toughest-minded account of dialectic I know, the one set forth by the philosopher Karl Popper in his powerful collection, *Conjectures and Refutations: The Growth of Scientific Knowledge,* which has a decisive essay, "What Is Dialectic?" in which neither Hegel nor Marx passes the Popperian test.

The Lurianic story of creation begins with an act of self-limitation on God's part that finds its aesthetic equivalent in any new poet's initial rhetoric of limitation, that is, in his acts of re-seeing what his precursors had seen before him. These re-seeings are translations of desires into verbal acts, instances of substantive thinking, and tend to be expressed by a nominal style, and by an imagery that stresses states of absence, of emptiness, and of estrangement or "outsideness." In the language of psychoanalysis, these modes of aesthetic limitation can be called different degrees of sublimation, as I will explain in this chapter's last section. Lurianic *zimzum* or divine contraction, the first step in the dialectic of creation, can be called God's sublimation of Himself, or at least of His own Presence. God begins creation by taking a step inside Himself, by voiding His own Presence. This *zimzum,* considered rhetorically, is a composite trope, commencing as an irony for the creative act, since it says "withdrawal" yet means the opposite, which is absolute "concentration." Making begins with a regression, a holding-in of the Divine breath, which is also, curiously, a kind of digression.

Even so, the strong poems of the post-Enlightenment, from Blake through Stevens, begin with the parabasis of rhetorical irony. But the psychic defense concealed in the irony is the initial defense that Freud called reaction-formation, the overt attitude that opposes itself directly to a repressed wish, by a rigidity that expresses the opposite of the instinct it battles. The Kabbalistic contraction/withdrawal is both trope and defense, and in seeking an initial term for it I have settled upon the Epicurean-Lucretian *clinamen,* naturalized as a critical term long before me, by Coleridge in his *Aids to Reflection.* The *clinamen* or "swerve" is the trope-as-misreading, irony as a dialectical alternation of images of presence and absence, or the beginnings of the defensive process. Writing on *The Magic Flute,* Angus Fletcher ventures some very useful observations upon irony as an aesthetic limitation:

> Irony is merely a darkened awareness of that possibility of change, of transformation, which in its fixed philosophic definition is the "crossing over" of dialectic process. But we can never say too often that irony implies the potential defeat of action, defeat at the hands of introspection, self-consciousness, etc., modes of thought which sap the body and even the mind itself of its apparent motivation.

Kenneth Burke notes that dialectic irony provides us with a kind of technical equivalent for the doctrine of original sin, which for a strong new poem is simply a sin of transgression *against origins.* The Lurianic dialectic follows its initial irony of Divine contraction, or image of limitation, with a process it calls the breaking-of-the-vessels, which in poetic terms is the principle of rhetorical substitution, or in psychic terms is the metamorphic element in all defenses, their tendency to turn into one another, even as tropes tend to mix into one another. What follows in the later or regressive Kabbalah is called *tikkun* or "restitution" and is symbolic representation. Here again, Coleridge can be our guide, as he identified Symbol with the trope of synecdoche, just as Freud located the defense of turning-against-the-self, or masochistic reversal, within a thinking-by-synechdoche. Here, seeking for a broader term to hold together synechdoche and reversal within the part/whole image, I have followed Mallarmé and Lacan by using the word *tessera,* not in its modern meaning as a mosaic-building unit, but in its ancient, mystery-cult meaning of an antithetical completion, the device of recognition that fits together the broken parts of a vessel, to make a whole again.

There is an opening movement of *clinamen* to *tessera,* in most significant poems of our era, that is, of the last three centuries. I am aware that such a statement, between its homemade terminology and its apparent arbitrariness, is rather outrageous, but I offer it as merely descriptive and as a useful mapping of how the reading of poems begins. By "reading" I intend to mean the work both of poet and of critic, who themselves move from dialectic irony to synecdochal representation as they confront the text before them. The movement is from a troubled awareness of dearth, of signification having wandered away and gotten lost, to an even more troubled awareness that the self represents only part of a mutilated or broken whole, whether in relation to what it believes itself once to have been, or still somehow hopes to become.

Clinamen is a swerve or step inside, and so is a movement of internalization, just as *tessera* is necessarily an antithetical completion that necessarily fails to complete, and so is less full than a full externalization. That is reason enough for strong modern poems passing into a middle movement, where as terms-for-mapping I have employed *kenosis,* St. Paul's word for Christ's "humbling" or emptying-out of his own divinity, and *daemonization,* founded upon the ancient notion of the daemonic as the intervening stage between the human and the divine. *Kenosis* subsumes the trope of metonymy, the imagistic reduction from a prior fullness to a later emptiness, and the three parallel Freudian defenses of regression, undoing, and isolating, all of them repetitive and compulsive movements of the psyche.

Daemonization, which usually marks the climax or Sublime crisis point of the strong poem, subsumes the principal Freudian defense, repression, the very active defense that produces or accumulates much of what Freud calls the Unconscious. As trope, poetic repression tends to appear as an exaggerated representation, the overthrow called hyperbole, with characteristic imagery of great heights and abysmal depths. Metonymy, as a reification by contiguity, can be called an extension of irony, just as hyperbole extends synecdoche. But both extremes lack finality, as their psychic equivalents hint, since the reductiveness of metonymy is only the linguistic version of the hopelessly entropic backward movements of the regressing, undoing, and isolating psyche. The metonymizer is a compulsive cataloger, and the contents of the poetic self never can be wholly emptied out. Similarly, there is no end to repression in strong poetry, as again I will indicate in the last section of this chapter. The dialectics of revisionism compel the strong poem into a final movement of ratios, one that sets space against time, space as a metaphor of limitation and time as a restituting metalepsis or transumption, a trope that murders all previous tropes.

I take the name, *askesis,* for the revisionary ratio that subsumes metaphor, the defense of sublimation, and the dualistic imagery of inside consciousness against outside nature, from Walter Pater, who himself took it from pre-Socratic usage. Pater said of *askesis* (which he spelled *ascesis)* that in a stylistic context it equalled "self-restraint, a skillful economy of means," and in his usually subtle play on etymological meaning, he hinted at the athlete's self-discipline. Even more subtly, Pater was attempting to refine the Romantic legacy of Coleridge, with its preference for mind/nature metaphors over all other figurations. To Pater belongs the distinction of noting that the secularized epiphany, the "privileged" or good moment of Romantic tradition, was the ultimate and precarious form of this inside/outside metaphor. The third and final dialectical movement of modern strong poems tends to begin with such a sublimating metaphor, but again this is another limitation of meaning, another achieved dearth or realization of wandering signification. In the final breaking-of-the-vessels of Romantic figuration, an extraordinary substitution takes place, for which I have proposed the name *apophrades,* the unlucky days, dismal, when the Athenian dead return to reinhabit their former houses, and ritualistically and momentarily drive the living out of doors.

Defensively, this poetic final movement is frequently a balance between introjection (or identification) and projection (or casting-out the forbidden). Imagistically, the balance is between earliness and belatedness, and there are very few strong poems that do not attempt, somehow, to conclude by introjecting an earliness and projecting the affliction of belatedness. The trope involved is the unsettling one anciently called metalepsis or transumption, the only trope-reversing trope, since it substitutes one word for another in earlier figurations. Angus Fletcher follows Quintilian in describing transumption as a process "in which commonly the poet goes from one word to another that sounds like it, to yet another, thus developing a chain of auditory associations getting the poem from one image to another more remote image." Kenneth Burke, commenting upon my *A Map of Misreading*, sees daemonic hyperbole and transumption as heightened versions of synecdoche, representations related to Plato's transcendentalized eros:

> The *Phaedrus* takes us from seed in the sense of sheer sperm to the heights of the Socratic erotic, as transcendentally embodied in the idea of doctrinal insemination. And similarly, via hyperbole and metalepsis, we'd advance from an ephebe's sheer *physical* release to a potentially ejaculatory analogue.

Metalepsis or transumption thus becomes a total, final act of taking up a poetic stance in relation to anteriority, particularly to the anteriority of poetic language, which means primarily the loved-and-feared poems of the precursors. Properly accomplished, this stance figuratively produces the illusion of having fathered one's own fathers, which is the greatest illusion, the one that Vico called "divination," or that we could call poetic immorality.

What is the critic's defense for so systematic a mapping of the poet's defenses? Burke, in the preface to his first book, *Counter-Statement,* said that his set-piece, his "Lexicon Rhetoricae," was "frankly intended as a machine – machine for criticism, however, not for poetry," since poetry "is always beyond the last formula." I too offer a "machine for criticism," though I sometimes fear that poetry itself increasingly has become the last formula. Modern poetry, as Richard Rorty sums it up, lives under a triple curse: (1) Hegel's prophecy that any future will be transcended automatically by a future future, (2) Marx's prophecy of the end of all individual enterprise, (3) Freud's prophetic analysis of the entropic drive beyond the Pleasure Principle, an analysis uneasily akin to Nietzsche's vision of the death of Man, a vision elaborated by Foucault, Deleuze, and other recent speculators. As Rorty says, "Who can see himself as caught in a dialectical moment, enmeshed in a family romance, parasitic upon the last stages of capitalism, yet still in competition with the mighty dead?" The only answer I know is that the strongest artists, but only the strongest, can prevail even in this entrapment of dialectics. They prevail by reattaining the Sublime, though a greatly altered Sublime, and so I will conclude this chapter by a brief speculation upon that fresh Sublime, and its dependence upon poetic equivalents of repression.

IV

The grandfathers of the Sublime are Homer and the Bible, but in English, Milton is the severe father of the Sublime mode. Erich Auerbach said that "the *Divine Comedy* is the first and in certain respects the only European poem comparable in rank and quality to the sublime poetry of antiquity," a judgment that seems to exclude *Paradise Lost* from Europe. I suppose that Dante's superiority over Milton, insofar as it exists, best might be justified by Auerbach's beautiful observations upon Dante's personal involvement in his own Sublime:

> Dante . . . is not only the narrator; he is at the same time the suffering hero. As the protagonist of his poem which, far greater in scope than the Homeric epics, encompasses all the sufferings and passions, all the joys and blessings of human existence, he himself is involved in all the movements of his immense action. . . . it is he himself who, held fast in the depths of hell, awaits the savior in a moment of extreme peril. What he relates, accordingly, is not a mere

happening, but something that happens to him. He is not outside,
contemplating, admiring, and describing the sublime. He is in it, at a
definite point in the scene of action, threatened and hard pressed;
he can only feel and describe what is present to him at this particular
place, and what presents itself is the divine aid he has been awaiting.

Elsewhere in the same book *(Literary Language and Its Public
in Late Latin Antiquity and in the Middle Ages),* Auerbach sets
Petrarch above even Dante in one respect, which I believe is also
the one in which the English line that goes from Spenser through
Milton on to Wordsworth surpassed even Petrarch:

> The Italians learned to control the devices of rhetoric and gradually
> to rid them of their coldness and obtrusive pedantry. In this respect
> Petrarch's Italian is markedly superior even to Dante's, for a feeling
> for the limits of expressibility had become second nature to Petrarch
> and accounts in good part for his formal clarity, while Dante had to
> struggle for these acquisitions and had far greater difficulty in main-
> taining them in the face of his far greater and more profound under-
> taking. With Petrarch lyrical subjectivism achieved perfection for the
> first time since antiquity, not impaired but, quite on the contrary,
> enriched by the motif of Christian anguish that always accompanies
> it. For it was this motif that gave lyrical subjectivism its dialectical
> character and the poignancy of its emotional appeal.

The dialectical character of lyrical subjectivism is indeed my
subject, and is what I attempt to map through my interplay of revisionary ratios. Auerbach, in the same book, says of Vico that "In
the rhetorical figures of the schools he saw vestiges of the original,
concrete, and sensuous thinking of men who believed that in
employing words and concepts they were seizing hold of things
themselves." Auerbach is thus in Vico's tradition when he praises
Dante for being *in* his own Sublime, as though the Sublime were
not so much a word or concept but somehow was the thing itself,
or Dante was one with his own severe poem. The lyrical subjectivism of Petrarch knows more clearly its distance from the thing itself, its reliance upon words apart from things. Perhaps this is why
John Freccero so persuasively can nominate Petrarch as the first
strong instance in Western poetry of the anxiety of influence, an
anxiety induced by the greatness of Dante. Petrarch, like Spenser

and Milton after him, suffers several dialectical anguishes, besides the anguish of attempting to reconcile poetry and religion.

Milton does stand outside his own Sublime; his astonishing invention was to place Satan inside the Sublime, as even a momentary comparison of the Satans of Dante and Milton will show. I am an unreconstructed Romantic when I read *Paradise Lost;* I continue to be less surprised by sin than I am surprised by Satan. If I can recognize the Sublime in poetry, then I find it in Satan, in what he is, says, does; and more powerfully even in what he is not, does not say, and cannot do. Milton's Satan is his own worst enemy, but that is his strength, not his weakness, in a dualizing era when the self can become strong only by battling itself in others, and others in itself. Satan is a great rhetorician, and nearly as strong a poet as Milton himself, but more important he is Milton's central way through to the Sublime. As such, Satan prophesies the post-Enlightenment crisis-poem, which has become our modern sublime.

I find that my map of misprision with its dialectic of limitation/substitution/representation, and its three pairs of ratios, alternating with one another, works well enough for the pattern of Satan's major soliloquies, possibly because these are among the ancestors of the crisis-of-poetic-vision poem, by way of the eighteenth-century Sublime ode. Satan's hyperbolical rhetoric is wonderfully described by a theoretician of the Sublime, Martin Price, in a passage which tries only to explicate Longinus, but which nevertheless conveys the force of Satan's characteristic imagery:

> One finds, then, a conception of passion that transcends material objects, that moves through the sensible universe in search of its grandest forms and yet can never find outward grandeur adequate to its inherent vision and its capacities of devotion. The intensity of the soul's passions is measured by the immensity of its objects. The immensity is, at its extreme, quite literally a boundlessness, a surpassing of measurable extension.

The hyperbole or intensified exaggeration that such boundlessness demands exacts a psychic price. To "exaggerate" etymologically means "to pile up, to heap," and the function of the

Sublime is to heap us, as Moby Dick makes Ahab cry out "He heaps me!" Precisely here I locate the difference between the strong poets and Freud, since what Freud calls "repression" is, in the greater poets, the imagination of a Counter-Sublime. By attempting to show the poetic ascendancy of "repression" over "sublimation" I intend no revision of the Freudian trope of "the Unconscious," but rather I deny the usefulness of the Unconscious, as opposed to repression, as a literary term. Freud, in the context of poetic interpretation, is only another strong poet, though the strongest of modern poets, stronger even than Schopenhauer, Emerson, Nietzsche, Marx, and Browning; far stronger than Valéry, Rilke, Yeats, Stevens. A critic, "using" Freud, does nothing different in kind from "using" Milton or Valéry. If the critic chooses to employ Freud reductively, as a supposed sci-entist, whatever that is, then the critic forgets that tropes or defenses are primarily figures of willed falsification rather than figures of unwilled knowledge. There is willed knowing, but that process does not produce poems.

Whatever the criticism of poetry that I urge is, and whether it proves to be, as I hope, a necessary error, or just another useless mistake, it has nothing in common with anything now miscalled "Freudian literary criticism." To say that a poem's true subject is its repression of the precursor poem is not to say that the later poem reduces to the process of that repression. On a strict Freudian view, a good poem is a sublimation, and not a repres-sion. Like any work of substitution that replaces the gratification of prohibited instincts, the poem, as viewed by the Freudians, may contain antithetical effects but not unintended or counterintend-ed effects. In the Freudian valorization of sublimation, the sur-vival of those effects would be flaws in the poem. But poems are actually stonger when their counterintended effects battle most incessantly against their overt intentions.

Imagination, as Vico understood and Freud did not, is the faculty of self-preservation, and so the proper use of Freud, for the literary critic, is not so to apply Freud (or even revise Freud) as to arrive at an Oedipal interpretation of poetic history. I find

such to be the usual misunderstanding that my own work pro-
vokes. In studying poetry we are not studying the mind, nor the
Unconscious, even if there is an unconscious. We are studying a
kind of labor that has its own latent principles, principles that can
be uncovered and then taught systematically. Freud's lifework is a
severe poem, and its own latent principles are more useful to us,
as critics, than its manifest principles, which frequently call for
interpretation as the misprisions of Schopenhauer and Nietzsche
that they are, despite their own intentions.

Poems are not psyches, not things, nor are they renewable
archetypes in a verbal universe, nor are they architectonic units of
balanced stresses. They are defensive processes in constant
change, which is to say that poems themselves are *acts of reading*. A
poem is, as Thomas Frosch says, a fierce, proleptic debate *with
itself*, as well as with precursor poems. Or, a poem is a dance of
substitutions, a constant breaking-of-the-vessels, as one limitation
undoes a representation, only to be restituted in its turn by a fresh
representation. Every strong poem, at least since Petrarch, has
known implicitly what Nietzsche taught us to know explicitly: that
there is only interpretation, and that every interpretation answers
an earlier interpretation, and then must yield to a later one.

I conclude by returning to the poetic equivalent of repression, to the Sublime or the Counter-Sublime of a belated *daemonization*, because the enigma of poetic authority can be resolved
only in the context of repression. Geoffrey Hartman, in *The Fate
of Reading*, calls the poetic will "sublimated compulsion." I myself
would call it "repressed freedom." Freud, expounding repression,
was compelled to posit a "primal repression," a purely hypothetical first phase of repression, in which the very idea representing a
repressed instinct itself was denied any entrance into consciousness. Though the French Freudians courageously have tried to
expound this splendidly outrageous notion, their efforts have left
it in utter darkness. To explain repression at all, Freud overtly had
to create a myth of an archaic fixation, as though he were saying:
"In the beginning was repression, even before there was any drive
to be repressed or any consciousness to be defended by repres-

sion." If this is science, then so is the Valentinian Speculation, and so is Lurianic Kabbalah, and so is Ferenczi's *Thalassa,* and perhaps all of them are. But clearly they are also something else, poems that commence by defensive processes, and that keep going though an elaboration of those processes.

A primal fixation or repression, as I have tried to show in *A Map of Misreading,* takes us back not to the Freudian Primal Scene of the Oedipus Complex, not to the Freudian Primal History Scene of *Totem and Taboo,* nor to Derrida's Scene of Writing, but to the most poetically primal of scenes, the Scene of Instruction, a six-phased scene that strong poems must will to overcome, by repressing their own freedom into the patterns of a revisionary misinterpretation. Thomas Frosch's lucid summary is more admirably concise than I have been able to be, and so I borrow it here:

> . . . a Primal Scene of Instruction [is] a model for the unavoidable imposition of influence. The Scene – really a complete play, or process – has six stages, through which the ephebe emerges: election (seizure by the precursor's power); covenant (a basic agreement of poetic vision between precursor and ephebe); the choice of a rival inspiration (e.g., Wordsworth's Nature vs. Milton's Muse); the self-presentation of the ephebe as a new incarnation of the "Poetical Character"; the ephebe's interpretation of the precursor; and the ephebe's revision of the precursor. Each of these stages then becomes a level of interpretation in the reading of the ephebe's poem.

To this, I would add now only the formula that a poem both takes its origin in a Scene of Instruction and finds its necessary aim or purpose there as well. It is only by repressing creative "freedom," through the initial fixation of influence, that a person can be reborn as a poet. And only by revising that repression can a poet become and remain strong. Poetry, revisionism, and repression verge upon a melancholy identity, an identity that is broken afresh by every new strong poem, and mended afresh by the same poem.

9 Poetic Crossing: Rhetoric and Psychology

It is easy to find hidden things if their places are pointed out and marked, and, in like fashion, if we wish to track down an argument we should know places.

— *Richard McKeon*

Not through subtle subterranean channels need friend and fact be drawn to their counterpart, but, rightly considered, these things proceed from the eternal generation of the soul. Cause and effect are two sides of one fact.

— *Emerson*

A poem begins because there is an absence. An image must be given, for a beginning, and so that absence ironically is called a presence. Or, a poem begins because there is too strong a presence, which needs to be imaged as an absence, if there is to be any imaging at all. So Stevens began *Domination of Black,* suspended between these dialectics and troping for the first time against Shelley's fiction of the leaves:

At night, by the fire,
The colors of the bushes
And of the fallen leaves,
Repeating themselves,
Turned in the room,
Like the leaves themselves
Turning in the wind.

With just a few other poems written in 1915-16 (including *Blanche McCarthy, Sunday Morning,* the unfinished *For an Old Woman in a Wig,* and *Six Significant Landscapes),* this text was

Stevens's true starting-point as a poet. He was thirty-seven years
old as he wrote, yet the short lines carry the resonances of a master, who knows fully what it means to say that the colors of the fall-
en leaves are "*repeating* themselves." Thirty times and more in the
next forty years Stevens's poetry would repeat, crucially, some
form of the word "repeat," until Stevens could write of his
Penelope meditating the repetitious but never culminating advent
of her Ulysses:

> She would talk a little to herself as she combed her hair,
> Repeating his name with its patient syllables,
> Never forgetting him that kept coming constantly so near.

But that meditation, forty years later, though it turns upon a
dialectic of presence and absence, relies less upon images than
the image-named *Domination of Black*. In this early lyric we sit at
night by the fire and we associate the colors turning in the room,
by firelight, with the autumnal and the literary colors of bushes
and fallen leaves, in a repetition that is qualified by the closing
lines of the first stanza:

> Yes: but the color of the heavy hemlocks
> Came striding.
> And I remembered the cry of the peacocks.

As in Yeats, the cry of Juno's birds presages the end of an era, and
the domination of black plays against the multicolored and
Shelleyan trope of the leaves. "Colors" are a traditional synonym
for "tropes," and to trope is to execute a "turning." Stevens had
begun his poem with what the Freudians, in their tropological system, call a "reaction formation," a defensive movement of the
spirit that is opposed to a repressed desire and so manifests itself
as a reaction against that desire.

In 1940, Lionel Trilling, in his ambivalent and moving essay
Freud and Literature, remarked that "it was left to Freud to discover
how, in a scientific age, we still feel and think in figurative forma-
tions, and to create, what psychoanalysis is, a science of tropes, of
metaphors and its variants, synecdoche and metonymy." Trilling
prophesied many later recognitions, Gallic as well as American,
and we can add to his insight now by tracing the derivation of

Freud's formulations, from ancient rhetoric through the transitional discipline of associationist psychology. But I wish that Freud had used the ancient names, as well as the old notions, so that we could call a reaction formation what rhetorically it is, an *illusio* or simple irony, irony as a figure of speech. Stevens says that the autumnal colors troped in the room, yet he means mostly that they repeated themselves, with the repetition being a play of substitutions and not of the colors themselves. "Repeated themselves" requires to be read as its opposite, "failed to repeat themselves," which is why Stevens is vulnerable to the black dominant of the hemlocks and the other cry of mortality, that of the peacocks. To get started, his lyric had to say the exact opposite of what it meant.

To explain how and why that observation is accurate is to arrive at a theory of poetic interpretation. This theory depends upon the verifiable pronouncement that the language of British and American poetry, from at least Wordsworth to the present, is overdetermined in its patternings and so necessarily is underdetermined in its meanings. When Stevens turns against his lyric's opening figurations, he must give us a synecdoche for death in the domination of the black color of the heavy hemlocks, and it is equally predictable that the next movement of his little dejection should substitute a metonymic reduction as an obsessive undoing of that synecdoche:

> The colors of their tails
> Were like the leaves themselves
> Turning in the wind,
> In the twilight wind,
> They swept over the room,
> Just as they flew from the boughs of the hemlocks
> Down to the ground.

The peacocks, like the leaves, are in the room only as colors or turnings, and these momentarily repeal the sombre figuration of the hemlocks. But these colors too yield next to a hyperbolic figuration, the high dominant of the peacocks, wonderfully caught up in the synesthesia of "the loud fire":

> I heard them cry – the peacocks.
> Was it a cry against the twilight
> Or against the leaves themselves
> Turning in the wind,
> Turning as the flames
> Turned in the fire,
> Turning as the tails of the peacocks
> Turned in the loud fire,
> Loud as the hemlocks
> Full of the cry of the peacocks?
> Or was it a cry against the hemlocks?

These eleven lines about the cry can be termed one of Stevens's earliest achievements of the Sublime. If the cry is against the turning of the leaves, then it is a lament against mutablilty. But, as in *Sunday Morning,* the final form of change is death, and so the second question contains the first; the cry is against the trope of the hemlocks, against the color of mortality.

Had Stevens ended the poem there, it would have been little more than the Imagistic exercise some critics have praised it as being, a kind of Shelleyan lament assimilated to the mode of Laforgue or the early Eliot. But the final stanza has two sharply contrasting tropes, moving the entire poem into a very different mode. first, there is a fine transformation of one of Coleridge's best moments, when Stevens sets himself as inside observer against a cosmic outside, in a juxtaposition that prophesies the great confrontation of *The Auroras of Autumn:*

> Out of the window,
> I saw how the planets gathered
> Like the leaves themselves
> Turning in the wind.

In *Dejection: An Ode,* Coleridge looks out of the window at the western sky, just before a storm, "and with how blank an eye!" anticipating both Emerson's *Nature:* "The ruin or the blank that we see when we look at nature, is in our own eye," and Stevens's *Auroras:* "The man who is walking turns blankly on the sand." What Coleridge sees, stars and moon, he sees precisely, but without the capacity to rejoice in his own seeing:

> I see them all so exellently fair,
> I see, not feel, how beautiful they are!

Stevens, out of his window, sees his own (and Shelley's) trope; the gathering planets are *like* the leaves turning in the wind. This giant perspectivizing shrinks the cosmos to one autumnal metaphor, but Stevens ends his poem with a very different figuration:

> I saw how the night came,
> Came striding like the color of the heavy hemlocks.
> I felt afraid.
> And I remembered the cry of the peacocks.

This is a prolepsis again of the Stevens of the *Auroras,* who as "the scholar of one candle" gazes upon the flames of the northern lights, "and he feels afraid." Yet, in this early poem, Stevens is content to taste the defeat of belatedness. The length of the oncoming night's steps renders the blackness more vividly, because the tropic "striding" itself undoes an earlier trope in the first stanza, where "the color of the heavy hemlocks / Came striding." So the striding night tropes upon a trope, in a metaleptic reversal, raising the poem's final lines to an almost apocalyptic pitch of rhetoricity, of excessive word-consciousness (a text's equivalent of human self-consciousness).

I have been mapping *Domination of Black* as a tropological pattern, yet to do so is to invoke also a pattern of psychic defenses. Stevens concludes his poem by introjecting the imminence of death and so by projecting the fiction of the leaves, which in Shelley as in Wordsworth intimates an immortality. I want now to develop a technique for the antithetical mapping of poems, one that should bring us closer to the cognitive workings of poetry, from Wordsworth to Stevens and beyond, and that will return to *Domination of Black* as a later example. In order to make this suggestion, I must begin by entering again the problematic of Romantic imagery, by way of the largest inventor of the Romantic image, Wordsworth.

Owen Barfield's theory of Romantic imagery, in his brilliant theosophical study *Saving the Appearances,* depends on the notion he calls "participation," which is our awareness "of an extra-senso-

ry link between the percipient and the representations." As participation waned, down the centuries, memory-images were substituted for it, and we fell into an idolatry of these memory-images.
Barfield's high evaluation of Romanticism results from his conviction (in which he follows Rudolph Steiner) that the Romantic
image was an idol-smashing weapon meant to return men to their
original participation in the phenomena. For Barfield, the
Romantic image is thus certainly a figure of will:

> There *is* a close relation between language as it is used by a partici-
> pating consciousness and language as it is used, at a later stage,
> metaphorically or symbolically. When we use language metaphorical-
> ly, we bring it about of our own free will that an appearance means
> something other than itself. . . . We start with an idol, and we our-
> selves turn the idol into a representation. . . .
>
> As long as nature herself continued to be apprehended as image,
> it sufficed for the artist to imitate Nature. . . .
>
> Henceforth, if nature is to be experienced as representation, she
> will be experienced as representation of – Man. . . . It is part of the
> creed of idolatry that, when we speak of Man, we mean only the body
> of this or that man, or at most his finite personality.

Barfield says that the will gives us imagistic representations
of human personality, and he terms these representations images
of nature, or in effect pathetic fallacies, as Ruskin called them.
Romantic iconoclasm, for Barfield as for Ruskin, did not go far
enough. It is curious to find an exact parallel to this judgment in
the subtlest and most advanced essay yet ventured on these matters, Paul de Man's *Intentional Structure of the Romantic Image*. De
Man emphasizes the absolute separation between consciousness
and nature in early Romanticism:

> Poetic language can do nothing but originate anew over and over
> again: it is always constitutive, able to posit regardless of presence
> but, by the same token, unable to give a foundation to what it posits
> except as an intent of consciousness. The word is always a free pres-
> ence to the mind, the means by which the permanence of natural
> entities can be put into question and thus negated, time and again,
> in the endlessly widening spiral of the dialectic.

De Man's Romantic dialectic widens its spiral so endlessly that we
will see him concluding his essay by saying that the works of the

early Romantics, Rousseau and Wordsworth, give us *no* "actual examples" of Romantic imagery! Indeed, though de Man credits Rousseau and Wordsworth with being "the first modern writers to have put into question, in the language of poetry, the ontological priority of the sensory object," he is still compelled to say that they were "at most, *underway* towards renewed insights." Yet no one knows or asserts better than de Man the continued priority of Rousseau and Wordsworth over all later writers, who compared to those great precursors are scarcely even underway. And no one, in my judgment, has gone beyond de Man's statement about Wordsworth's concept of "imagination":

> This "imagination" has little in common with the faculty that pro-
> duces natural images born "as flowers originate." It marks instead a
> possibility for consciousness to exist entirely by and for itself, inde-
> pendently of all relationship with the outside world, without being
> moved by an intent aimed at a part of this world.

What de Man has done is to trace the intentional structure of the Romantic image in Rousseau and Wordsworth and also to assure us, convincingly, that this structure has yet to be interpreted accurately by scholarship, but then finally to assure us also that even Rousseau and Wordsworth actually could not carry out their own structural intentions. The Romantic image, on this account, turns out to be neither hyperbolical nor transumptive but purely visionary, an aspiration beyond the limits of art.

We might credit de Man with considerable irony in this essay, irony being his favorite trope. His formula, "to put into question," equals "to undergo the process of rhetorical substitution" by, as he says, "the word," *logos* in the sense of "meaning." Wordsworth's "word" puts into question "the permanence of natural entities," the *ethos* of nature, by substituting tropes of *pathos*, of passion and suffering, for tropes of *ethos*, of character and incident. I think that we can analyze Wordsworth's originality more fully than has been done if we continue and expand the study of the interplay of *ethos* and *pathos* in his poems, a study begun already by a group of scholars including Klaus Dockhorn, Herbert Lindenberger, Robert Langbaum, and Geoffrey Hartman.

Ethos, the Greek word for "custom," "image," "trait," goes back to a root meaning "self." We use it now to mean the character or attitude of a group, but Aristotle meant by it the character of an individual, as opposed to his emotions, or perhaps he meant what was permanent or ideal in anyone's character. *Pathos,* the Greek for "passion," goes back to a root meaning to "suffer." We use it now to mean a quality in someone that arouses feelings of pity or sympathy in anyone else, but Aristotle meant by it something like any person's transient and emotional frame of mind. Quintilian usefully remarks that *ethos* and *pathos* are different degrees of the same entity, the emotions, with *ethos* meaning the less violent and continuous emotions, such as affection, and *pathos* the more violent and momentary emotions, such as those we now call Romantic love. Quintilian's most useful insight is to associate *ethos* with irony and comedy, and *pathos* with tragedy; and so, by implication, with irony's rival as a master trope, synecdoche.

In more Freudian terms, *ethos* results from the successful translation of the will into an act, verbal or physical, whereas *pathos* ensues when there is a failure to translate will into act. In the terms I employed in *Poetry and Repression, ethos* is a reseeing and *pathos* a reaiming, with the middle position between them in the dialectic of revision being taken by *logos* as a re-esteeming or re-estimating. Rhetoric, conceived as a text or system of tropes, is an *ethos,* while rhetoric as persuasion falls under *pathos,* with an *aporia* between them as a *logos.* This formulation is de Man's, and I will use it more fully later in this chapter. But now I want to inquire, what is the value of analyzing Wordsworth's poetry in terms of *ethos, logos,* and *pathos,* rather than in terms of the revisionary dialectic I employed in *A Map of Misreading* and *Poetry and Repression,* the Kabbalistic triad of limitation, substitution, and representation?

The Kabbalistic terms themselves were derived, ultimately, from the Greek terms anyway, and this is certainly part of the answer. But Wordsworth himself uses his own variants of these traditional terms of rhetoric, as Dockhorn and Lindenberger have shown. *Ethos* in Wordsworth is "character" or "incident," or more structurally the spirit of place revealing its character, with or without incident, through images of voice. *Logos* in Wordsworth is what Hartman calls a "re-cognition leading to recognition," with "recognition" being another name for *pathos* as suffering and passion. We can surmise that Wordsworth surmounted his own epistemological confusions about the status of poetic images by making his great images *afterimages of voice,* usually the voice of the dead or of his own dead self. "Images of voice" is a tricky notion, worked out in different ways by Hartman, Angus fletcher, and John Hollander, and I will consider their formulations in a later book when I explain more fully the concept of *topos* that is involved in my theory of Poetic Crossing.

It is a truism of criticism from Aristotle through Sidney to Northrop Frye that poetry takes place between the concept and the example. In Wordsworth, this old realization becomes dialectical, in that poetic meaning or poetic thinking takes place in the substitution not only of *pathos* (example) for *ethos* (precept) but of *ethos* for *pathos* also. This dialectical movement supports Hartman's contention that Wordsworth was neither a "transcendentalist" nor an "associationist" or "sensationalist." Wordsworth's thinking, Hartman says, "starts with objects not as they *are* but as they *appear* to a mind fruitfully perplexed by their differing modes of appearance, and which does not try to reduce these to a single standard."

We can contrast Hartman's account with an accepted British scholarly analysis of the same problematic in Wordsworth, C. G. Clarke's *Romantic Paradox.* Clarke says that "if, like Wordsworth, we retain a layman's faith in the independent existence of everything – or virtually everything – given to sense, and yet remain covertly convinced that what the senses know is an attribute of *consciousness . . .* then we may well find perceptual experience contradictory." The result, in Clarke's judgment, is the equivocal status of Wordsworth's Romantic image, so that it is an appearance plus a thing. But here is Hartman, subtly tracing Wordsworth's dialectic of *ethos, logos, pathos,* or spirit of place haunted by images of voice, substituted for through a re-cognition

of the place and ensuing in a recognition that clarifies the image.
I run together in the following some widely separated passages
from Hartman's book on Wordsworth, so as to give a cento on the
dialectic of Wordsworthian imagery:

> The power of nature to retard, or to transmute from action to pas-
> sion the brief moment of truly individual being, is what raises the
> largest emotions: pity, perplexity, wonder. . . .

> The soul needs the "inscrutable workmanship " of its early associa-
> tion with nature in order to resist the crude interventions and imme-
> diate demands of reason. . . .

> Cognition is recognition as generation should be regeneration. . . .

> [The after-image] expresses the possibility of the renewal (or at
> least recurrence) of a certain experience by including that possibility
> in the very structure of the experience. . . .

> The after-image could be defined as a re-cognition that leads to
> recognition.

Hartman is arguing that Wordsworth refused to yield up a
residue of associationism because that would have meant starting
the poetic process at a point beyond object-consciousness, as
Blake did. Wordsworth raises himself to a transcendence of
object-consciousness through his faith that, as he remarked
against Ossian, "in nature everything is distinct, yet nothing
defined into absolute independent singleness." Or, as Wordsworth
phrased this elsewhere, in a letter to Landor, a truly imaginative
passage will follow such natural vision until, in a heightening,
"things are lost in each other, and limits vanish, and aspirations
are raised." We can sum this in a formula: The authentic temporal
moment is thwarted *by nature,* which reveals to the poet that
immediacy or presence is indeed an *illusio* or ironical dialectic, a
here and now always self-negating. But this natural thwarting edu-
cates the poet's mind, by reading the *ethos* of nature, its "action,"
without an immediately full significance. *Ethos* has become limitation, a contraction or withdrawal of meaning, that opens the way
for a rethinking that is necessarily a remeaning. This is very much

akin, as we will see, to the delayed signification that Freud calls *Nachträglichkeit,* or "aftering." *Ethos* or character or natural action is converted into a poet's fate, and the re-cognition becomes the path of imaginative freedom, until the power of self-recognition intervenes, completing the dialectic with a passage into the ultimate *pathos* of wonder.

Hartman, in his own later work, the essays on psychoesthetics in *The Fate of Reading,* uses this Wordsworthian dialectic of afterimaging as an excess-and-defect model that might replace I. A. Richards' stimulus-and-response psychic model for poetry. The topical image-of-voice becomes an excess of demand, the poem's redundancy of pressure upon both language and the self. *Ethos* thus is what language cannot sustain, or rather *ethos* works to limit unsustainable demands upon language. *Pathos* or recognition becomes a defect of response, or the survival of a will-to-representation after representation has been attained. I want now to translate these Hartmanian ideas into a stricter language of psychologized trope, but here I verge upon the barrier of what I take to be the most clarifying mode of criticism currently available to us, the "deconstruction" of Paul de Man and Jacques Derrida.

I have encountered no clear definitions of deconstruction as a criticism of poetry and so offer the following. Marie-Rose Logan sees Derridian philosophical deconstruction as a process aiming "at unveiling the implicit or uncritically accepted memory of any given concept," and she cites *Positions,* where Derrida says: "To deconstruct philosophy would thus mean to think the structured geneology of the philosophical concepts in the closest and most intimate way and yet to determine, at the same time, from a certain outside unwarrantable, unnamable by philosophy itself, what this history might have dissimulated or forbidden."

Let us transpose this from philosophy to poetry. To deconstruct a poem would mean to uncover whatever its rhetoricity conveyed, even if the poem, the poet, and the tradition of its interpretation showed no overt awareness of what implicitly was revealed by such word-consciousness. Rhetoricity, in this sense, is a questioning on the poem's part of its place in literary language, that is, the poem's *own* subversion of its own closure, its illusory status as independent poem. Again, this sense of rhetoricity (which is de Man's) would include both major aspects of word-consciousness, rhetoric as persuasion and rhetoric as a system of tropes. Between these aspects, in de Man's interpretation of Nietzsche's theories of rhetoric and of identity, there falls always an *aporia,* a figuration of doubt, which may be the principle of rhetorical substitution itself. To deconstruct a poem is to indicate the precise location of its figuration of doubt, its uncertain notice of that limit where persuasion yields to a dance or interplay of tropes.

Hartman keeps hinting that this process of deconstruction is not "reading," but necessarily Hartman's "reading" is itself a figuration for his own kind of interpretation, his own Will-to-Power over texts. *Contra* Hartman, it would not be unfair to say that the Derrida-de Man "deconstruction" is simply the most advanced form of a purely rhetorical criticism now available to us. "Deconstruction" *is* reading, but this is Over-Reading, or the reading of an Over-Man, who knows simultaneously how to fulfill and to transcend the text, or rather how to make the text expose the *aporia* between its self-fulfillment and its self-transcendence. For Over-Reader we could substitute "analytical or conceptual rhetorician" or simply "philosopher of rhetoric."

The limits of a purely rhetorical criticism, however advanced, are established by its inevitable reductiveness, its necessary attempt to see poetry as being a conceptual rhetoric, *and nothing more.* Rhetoric, considered as a system of tropes, yields much more readily to analysis than does rhetoric considered as persuasion, for persuasion, in poetry, takes us into a realm that also includes the lie. Poems lie primarily against three adversaries:

1) themselves
2) other poems
3) time

Why do we believe one liar rather than another? Why do we read one poet rather than another? We believe the lies we want to believe because they help us to survive. Similarly, we read (reread) the poems that keep our discourse with ourselves going.

Strong poems strengthen us by teaching us *how to talk to ourselves*, rather than how to talk to others. Satan is strongest when he talks to himself, like his Shakespearean precursors, though an immense loss in self-delight is felt when we move from Iago to Satan. Against whom does Satan lie most persuasively: himself, his precursor, time?

Deconstruction touches its limit because it cannot admit such a question. For the deconstructive critic, a trope is a figure of knowing and not a figure of willing, and so such a critic seeks to achieve, in relation to any poem – or to find in that poem – a cognitive moment, a moment in which the Negative is realized, but only insofar as a postponing substitution becomes an approximation of the Hegelian Negative. But what can a cognitive or epistemological moment in a poem be? Where the will predominates, even in its own despite, how much is there left to know? How can we speak of degrees of knowing in the blind world of the wish, where the truth is always elsewhere, always different, always to be encountered only by the acceptances and rejections of an energy that in itself is the antithesis of renunciation, a force that refuses all form?

A deconstructive reading of a poem must treat the poem's urging of us, to whatever, as the poem's own questioning of the language of urging. Here I cite John Hollander: "But the urging of a work of literature, perhaps accomplished by its formal frame, is no less an act of urging than any other kind of exhortation. The analysis of urging and exhorting can no longer be properly linguistic. And, finally, it is *as such* that it lies outside the realm of poetics." The issue of the limits of deconstruction will be resolved only if we attain a vision of rhetoric more comprehensive than the deconstructors allow, that is, if we can learn to see rhetoric as transcending the epistemology of tropes and as re-entering the space of the will-to-persuasion. Such a vision is a necessary prelude into what we never have had, and what the theorists of deconstruction are not attempting to give us: *a diachronic rhetoric.*

A diachronic rhetoric will emerge when we can begin to see that every synchronic concept of trope is itself necessarily only another trope. "All is trope save in games," Hollander rightly remarks. When de Man and Derrida (not to mention a whole crowd of Gallic linguistifiers far beneath them) speak of tropes as epistemological instruments, they have turned a considerable catachresis upon the traditional concept of trope. The strength of this catachresis comes from the long tradition of the polemic of philosophy against poetry, in which rhetoric has been at once the fought-over field and the weapons depot for both sides. If Empedocles indeed founded rhetoric, we might say that rhetoric rose out of shamanism or religious poetry, and so was more oracular than oratorical in its origins. But there is the fine speculation of Eric Havelock, in his *Preface to Plato,* that Empedocles was Plato's precursor in trying to wrest language from the image-thinking of the poets to the concept-thinking of the philosophers, or from *doxa* (opinion) to truth. Can we surmise that Empedocles invented rhetoric to help him in this transformation? Yet, though Plato tries to move the trope from Homer's figures of will to a figure of knowing, rhetoric remains incurably poetic, a drive toward will-to-identity rather than toward a knower/known dualism. Tropes are perverse; they are *para-phusis,* unnatural, deviant.

Whatever Empedocles might have meant rhetoric to do, his professed disciple, Gorgias, meant it to enchant his auditors into an awareness of the antithetical nature of all truth. Perhaps the alliance between rhetoric and psychology was inaugurated (however tentatively) by Plato, in opposition to this relativism. Aristotle's development of the alliance is more disinterested, and his example, not Plato's, dominated the subsequent history of rhetoric, until the apparent demise of rhetoric near the end of the seventeenth century.

There is a hidden relation between the "end" of classical rhetoric and the rise of the eighteenth-century psychology founded upon the association of ideas, and indeed an even more complex hidden relation between four modes that assert more diversity than they possess: Classical and Renaissance rhetoric; seventeenth-century and eighteenth-century association-of-ideas psychology; Romantic poetry, from Wordsworth to this moment; Freudian psychoanalysis. When the associationists – Locke, Hume,

Gay, Hartley, Tucker being the progression of founders – developed their psychology, they founded it (perhaps unconsciously) upon the topics or commonplaces of rhetoric, precisely because they wished to usurp the place and function of rhetoric. But Wordsworth, Coleridge, and their followers, by translating the commonplaces to their own purposes, brought back a powerful, implicit psychologized rhetoric in which topics regenerated tropes, and these tropes in turn elaborated themselves as defensive structures of consciousness. Happily unaware of this return of repressed rhetoric, the main associationist tradition passed on to Bentham and the Mills. Freud, translating the younger Mill, took over from him the Lockean notion of object-representation, which thus became the common ancestor both of Freud's system of defenses and of the tropological patterns of Romantic imagery.

Here I want to open again the large question of what rhetoric is: What is a trope? What is a topic or commonplace? What is the large relation of meaning to rhetoric, in poetry? Aristotle distinguished sophistic, as a mode of logic, from both analytical demonstration and dialectic. Sophistic relies upon premises that are not commonly held or even relevant, though they *appear* to be both. Aristotle says of the wielders of sophistic that they are those who argue as competitors and as rivals unto the death, which I believe to be one of the stigmata that necessarily afflict belated poets. This leads Aristotle to his crucial definition of rhetoric: it stems from dialectic or *logos* and from morals or *ethos* and *pathos,* yet it is only a faculty, or way of choosing, the best means of persuading an audience. Aristotle locates in the audience the *logos* or reason that needs to be satisfied, and also in that audience the *pathos* that needs to be moved, whereas the speaker is the locus of the *ethos* involved, since he must persuade his auditors of his own reliability or virtue.

That is the traditional vision of rhetoric, and we can say of it that it followed Plato's lead in "correcting" Gorgias, with his despised "relativism." Untersteiner, in his book *The Sophists,* illuminatingly defends Gorgias from the misrepresentations of Plato and of Aristotle. Gorgias exalted the orator as a *psychagosos,* a poet leading souls through incantation to the relativity of all truth, and doing this through an antithetical style, one which offered contrasts and alternatives for every definition ventured, in contrast to the Socratic mode of arriving at supposedly absolute truth. This ensues, in Gorgias, in the splendidly poetic notion he called *to kairon,* "the opportune," prophesying the opportunism that is the quick of every poetic invention. Since two antithetical statements can be made on anything, any subject involves a choice between or mixture of two antitheses, so that consideration of *kairos* (time, place, circumstance, or as Stevens or a modern Greek would say, the weather) must solve the *aporia* and lead first to a choice of a relative truth, and subsequently to action. *Kairos* then for orator or poet determines choice of organization, mode of proof, and stance and style. This, as Untersteiner says, is "the adaptation of the speech to the manifold variety of life, to the psychology of speaker and hearer: variegated, not absolute unity of tone." We can apply here, as a powerful ally for Untersteiner's defense of Gorgias, the insistence of Nietzsche that the Sophists were truly Hellenic, and the Socratic polemic against the Sophists a symptom of decadence. I now give a cento of Nietzsche's critique of Greek philosophy in aphorisms 427-30 of *The Will to Power:*

> Good and evil of differing origin are mingled: the boundary between good and evil is blurred – This is the "Sophist" – . . .
>
> It is a very remarkable moment: the Sophists verge upon the first *critique of morality,* the first *insight* into morality: – they juxtapose the multiplicity (the geographic relativity) of the moral value judgments. . . .
>
> What, then, is the significance of the reaction of Socrates, who recommended dialectics as the road to virtue . . . ?
>
> . . . *In praxi,* this means that moral judgments are torn from their conditionality, in which they have grown and alone possess any meaning, from their Greek and Greek-political ground and soil, to be denaturalized under the pretense of sublimation. The great concepts "good" and "just" are severed from the presuppositions to which they belong and, as liberated "ideas," become objects of dialectic. One looks for truth in them, takes them for entities or signs of entities: one *invents* a world where they are at home, where they originate –

I follow de Man when I observe that the "tearing" and "severing," of which Nietzsche speaks here, are linguistic events. These late Nietzschean aphorisms juxtapose illuminatingly with an early Nietzschean reflection on the process of rhetorical substitution that de Man has cited as basic to Nietzsche's theory of rhetoric:

> The abstract nouns are properties within and outside ourselves that are being torn away from their supports and considered to be autonomous entities. . . . Such concepts, which owe their existence only to our feelings, are posited as if they were the inner essence of things: we attribute to events a cause which in truth is only an effect. The abstractions create the illusion as if *they* were the entity that causes the properties, whereas they receive their objective, iconic existence only from us as a consequence of these very properties.

One of de Man's great contributions lies in his having shown us how Nietzsche links a theory of rhetoric with a theory of action and identity. The best commentary on both the Nietzschean passages I've quoted is de Man's vision of Nietzsche dismissing the reductive meaning of rhetoric as eloquence and concentrating instead upon the epistemology of the tropes:

> Nietzsche's final insight may well concern rhetoric itself, the discovery that what is called "rhetoric" is precisely the gap that becomes apparent in the pedagogical and philosophical history of the term. Considered as persuasion, rhetoric is performative but when considered as a system of tropes, it deconstructs its own performance. Rhetoric is a *text* in that it allows for two incompatible, mutually self-destructive points of view and therefore puts an insurmountable obstacle in the way of any reading or understanding. The *aporia* between performative and constative language is merely a version of the *aporia* between trope and persuasion that both generates and paralyzes rhetoric and thus gives it the appearance of history.

De Man's achievement is to have defined, following Nietzsche, the *aporia* or figuration of doubt that the principle of rhetorical substitution always constitutes in any poetic text. He locates this *between* rhetoric as the *art* of persuasion and rhetoric as *persuasion*. De Man does not attempt to name this mental dilemma or *topos* of liminality, yet he implies that such an *aporia* participates in the problematics of Derrida's "différance," the postponement or swerving repetition that is manifested in the dance and interplay of tropes within a poetic text. The de Manian *aporia,* despite its Nietzschean origins, is indistinguishable from a Gnostic formulation such as the Valentinian or Lurianic Breaking of the Vessels. Like a vision of the Gnosis, this *aporia* is a transgression that leads from taboo to transcendence, or in the imagery of Romance it serves as the threshold between temple and labyrinth. Because he is a conceptual rhetorician, defending poetry against the grammarian on one side and against the semiologist on the other, de Man valorizes the *aporia* between system of tropes and persuasion as the *logos,* a valorization that audaciously redefines poetic thinking *as* the process of rhetorical *substitution* rather than as a thinking by particular trope. In de Man's view, poetry cannot be reduced to the interplay between metonymic and metaphorical thinking, which is the Jakobsonian reduction, nor to ironic thinking (though this is a temptation for de Man), nor to the various forms of representational thinking – synecdochal, hyperbolic, even metaleptic – that have characterized Romantic and psychoanalytical conceptualizings. If the *aporia* is the only *logos* that modern poetry possesses, then the negative moment in any poem, the moment that locates the *aporia,* is necessarily an epistemological moment, with the authority to deconstruct its own text, that is, to indicate the text's cognitive awareness of its own limit as text, its own status as rhetoricity, its own demystification of the fiction of closure.

For de Man, then, criticism *begins* with the Nietzschean act of locating the *aporia* and continues by relocating it anew with each reading of each text. But here, up to now, de Man appears to me to limit himself by the asceticism of his own concept of trope, which isolates too purifyingly the trope from the *topos* or commonplace that generates it. With reverence for this advanced critical consciousness, the most rigorous and scrupulous in the field today, I now part from him to what I consider a larger and deeper concept of trope, a misprision of trope undoubtedly. Yet I believe that every critic necessarily tropes the concept of trope, for *there are no tropes,* but only concepts of tropes or figures of figures.

What is a trope? It is one of two possibilities only – either the will translating itself into a verbal act or figure of *ethos,* or else the will failing to translate itself and so abiding as a verbal desire or figure of *pathos.* But, either way, the trope *is* a figure of will rather than a figure of knowledge. The trope is a cut or gap made in or into the anteriority of language, itself an anteriority in which "language" acts as a figurative substitution for time. Just here, though it is rather late to be attempting fundamental definitions, I am compelled to explain the vision of rhetoric that my enterprise has taken as starting point. This vision is Gnostic and Kabbalistic in its ultimate origins.

Kabbalistic rhetorical theory, as formulated particularly by Cordovero in the figurations he called *behinot,* leads one to consider texts not as linguistic structures but as instances of *the will to utter within a tradition of uttering.* The *behinot,* as composite tropes, are magical devices for gaining the power that lies *beyond* the literal or proper truth. Such devices, as orthodox Talmudists said against Kabbalah, are dangerously close to wishes, equivocations, or lies told to the self by the self. John Hollander is knowingly within Talmudic tradition when he sums up the Lurianic dialectic of creation as "concepts of withdrawing from linguistic signification (or indeed from truth), filling it with meaning (as an effusion of will, of intending to utter) to overflowing, and a final restitution of meaning in a transformed significance." Hollander's summary is brilliantly apt, and yet its perspective is anything but Kabbalistic. Such a summary, in the tradition of the Gaon of Vilna, while it does not assume that proper or literal meaning necessarily exists *in* language, still implies that truth can be expressed *through* the interplay of proper and figurative meaning. Kabbalah, as a Gnosis, starts with the rival assumption, which is that all distinction between proper and figurative meaning in language has been totally lost since the catastrophe of creation. Another way of saying this is that a Kabbalistic or Gnostic theory of rhetoric must deny that there can be any *particular* semantic tension in language, because in the Kabbalistic vision all language is nothing but semantic tension raised to apocalyptic pitch.

The contemporary French rhetorician Gérard Genette says that a trope is nothing but a reader's awareness of a trope, an awareness that comes into existence only when the reader either recognizes or half recognizes that a text is problematic or ambiguous in its evasions of, or schematic deviations from, proper meaning. I would say rather that a trope is a reader's awareness of a poet's willed error and results only from a reader's *will to be lied to,* or to be repersuaded of persuasions already implicitly formulated that are crucial for the survival of the reader's own internal discourse, the hum of thoughts evaded in the reader's own mind. But I verge here upon the true outrageousness of Kabbalistic theory of rhetoric. Kabbalah misreads all language that is not Kabbalah, and I assert now that belated strong poetry misreads all language that is not poetry. Another way of saying this, in terms currently fashionable, is that all rhetoric as a system of tropes is a synchronic rhetoric, but all rhetoric as persuasion is diachronic, so that the *aporia* between the two indeed is beyond resolution. Poems misread earlier poems, yet they also misread every use of language that is not poetic, which means that the history of any language is an endless process of misprision. If a condition of poetic strength is a cunning in evading and distorting tradition, as I think it is, then what can persist and become tradition in any language must be a strength of misprision also.

Here I am compelled to clarify or perhaps even revise my own notion of misprision, to make a misprision of misprision, as it were. Misprision is the process by which the meanings of intentionality trope down to the mere significances of language, or conversely the process by which the significations of language can be transformed or troped upward into the meaningful world of our Will-to-Power over time and its henchman, language. Here I will cite Hollander again, and at length:

> Tropes, or turns that occur between the meanings of intention and the significances of linguistic utterances, are twisted through the plane of truth while yet all the more strongly connecting the will and the text which it flies like a flag "as it fitfully gleams, half-conceals, half-discloses" the impulses which raise it. Whereas formalist criti-

cisms have concerned themselves with the trope in the text alone, Bloom's sees this kind of study as two-dimensional and paradigmatic at best. For him, a trope is a twisted strand of transformational process, anchored deep in a rock of expressive need, and stretched upward, taut, to a connection at the surface with a flat sheet of text. Formalist and structuralist readings would be like more or less detailed plans of the textual surface, affording a view of the end-section only of the tropical rope. Bloom is concerned with the length of the rope, the layers of whatever it is through which it passes, the ways in which, at any particular level, the strands may seem in their twisting to be pointing away from the determined direction upward, the relative degrees of tension and slackness and so forth. His is the most recent manifestation in a strange history of troping the concept of trope itself.

If I may trope Hollander's troping of me, tropes have nothing to do with not being literal, since ordinarily nothing is literal anyway, or to quote again a line of Hollander's: "All is trope save in games." A trope is a stance or a ratio of revision; it defends against other tropes. But what, in language, is a stance? Ancient rhetoricians derived their notion of stance from boxers and wrestlers; modern rhetoric ought to derive its notion from batters and pitchers in baseball. Stevens's apparent ironies remind us of a batter swinging several bats together in the batter's circle before stepping up to the plate with a single bat, which will feel surprisingly light in his hands. The several bats do the work of "the final no" after which "there comes a yes / And on that yes the future world depends." The major Hellenistic *rhetor* Hermagoras, who taught misprision circa 150 B.C., said that *heuresis* or invention included *staseis* or stances, which were modes by which problems could be assaulted. Hermagoras perfected four stances: 1) the question, "Did my client do it?" 2) the end, "Was it a crime, anyway?" 3) the quality, "Was it an act of honor, or of expediency?" 4) the metalepsis, "It was all the victim's fault, anyway." I am delighted to find a precursor in Hermagoras and quote Hollander again to establish that I am a properly unscrupulous ephebe of Hermagoras:

> Bloom . . . , in his concern for the schematic and deep connections between stances toward a predecessor, stances taken by utterance itself against what one means to say, stances taken by what one

means to say against what the unconscious means for one to mean, and so forth, has undertaken to deal with a concept of trope far more general than that of the rhetorician. Operating in the realm in which the relation between realities and superstructures (Freudian, Marxian), between source and manifestation, usually seeks to reduce the latter to the former, he has propounded a kind of opening unscientific preface to a quest in these dialectical regions. [He sees] the war for authenticity and finality between surface (text) and depths (intentions variously clear and dark) as a true struggle of contraries.

To trope Hollander again, the conceptual rhetorician's notion of trope, whether de Man's or Genette's, does not interpret this war between text and intentions but fights instead on the side of text. Even de Man is thus part of the problem and not of the solution, for the pure rhetorician who regards the psyche as merely another text himself therefore argues on only one side of an authentic and ancient battle: with Socrates, Plato, and Aristotle against the sophists; with Plotinus against the Gnostics; with the Talmudists against the Kabbalists. Every notion of the will that we have is itself a trope, even when it tropes against the will, by asserting that the will is a linguistic fiction. Consciousness and writing alike take us back to the will and what it intends, and however such intentions are viewed they are being troped, for this history too has been adopted by both parties. But poets, at least belated strong poets or the ones we have who matter during the last two centuries, are less conceptual rhetoricians than they are masters of misprision, and to study them more truly and more strange we need a wider definition of trope than de Man or Genette affords us. We need, I think, to revivify the ancient identity between rhetoric and psychology that is still being partly obscured by that endless clearing or curing of the ground now being called "deconstruction." Such an identity, though itself figurative, momentarily takes us away from the tropological to the topological, to the commonplaces or places of invention, but only for a brief time, after which we can return not with one *aporia* or negative moment or crossing, but with three, thus going de Man two better in our quest after images for the act of reading poems.

Walter J. Ong regards the *topoi* as modes of information storage and of conceptualization characteristic of oral culture, which were preserved in the age of writing, and then in the age of print, as the *loci communes,* associated also with the history of Latin as a subject of academic rhetoric. Richard McKeon sees them as "arts of places." The oldest authorities describe them as a means of amplification, since they are "topics of invention." Cicero lists sixteen as being intrinsic to any subject: definition, division, genus, species, contraries, contradictories, comparison, similarity, dissimilarity, adjuncts, cause, effect, antecedent, consequences, notation, and conjugates. I will discuss these not in that traditional order but rather in the order that I believe they assumed in the tropological patterns of the Romantic and post-Romantic crisis-poem. Yet, to account for their reappearance in that patterning, I turn at last to the curious link between the "disappearance" of classical rhetoric in the seventeenth century and the rise of associationist psychology. W. J. Bate's formula for the complex movement I am trying to sketch envisions a five-stage process: from rhetoric to the Johnsonian universality of general nature to the growth of individualism first on the premise of associationism, and then of feeling or sensibility, until the Romanticism of Coleridge and Wordsworth arrived as a culmination. Associationism can be defined most simply as the psychological implications of the empirical tradition of Locke and Hume. It implies that ideas similar to one another, or ideas that have tended to recur in series or simultaneously, automatically call one another up. Locke, who invented the phrase "association of ideas," founded the notion on habit and memory as modes of repetition that fixed ideas through the accompaniment of pleasure and pain. Later associationists, culminating in Hartley, went from this process to the formation of habits of thought and feeling that resulted in principles, incentives, and actions. Hartley confected a visionary physiology of vibrations and tremblings that the more rational Scottish associationists graded down to a subtler intuitionism.

I will venture the speculation, not altogether playfully, that associationism was the "structuralism" of the eighteenth and nineteenth centuries and is not all that different from the "structuralism" of the twentieth century. Indeed, we can try a formula: associationism plus differential linguistics equals structuralism. Locke fathered Condillac, and can be called Lévi-Strauss's great-grandfather, so that structuralism can be regarded as belated Lockeanism flowering strangely upon alien soil. Hartley even invented the synchronic/diachronic distinction, which he called the synchronous and the successive. This is Part I, Proposition 10, of his *Observations of Man:* "Sensations may be said to be associated together, when their impressions are either made precisely at the same instant of time, or in the contiguous successive instants. We may therefore distinguish association into two sorts, the synchronous, and the successive."

The leading ideas of associationism, both synchronous and successive, were resemblance, contiguity, cause and effect, and contrariety, with occasional excursions into comparison and into division and definition. Essentially, associationism put the emphasis upon what we might call the topics of *ethos,* leading to reductive tropes of *ethos,* and rather less upon topics and figures of *pathos.* It could even be said that the advance beyond associationism taken by Wordsworth and Coleridge was to attempt to reconcile or balance a Romantic rhetoric of *pathos* with the associationist rhetoric of *ethos.* It is a mystery to me why neither the associationists nor their modern scholars have traced the clear displacement, by the associationists, of the places of invention into the psychological notions governing the formation of ideas. I suspect that the cause is inherent in an ambiguity in the topics of invention, which I will explore now en route to a theory as to how the imagistic and tropological patterns of the High Romantic crisis-poem were generated by associationist ideas and by the earlier forms of those ideas in the topics of classical rhetoric.

I take it that the shuttle or dialectic between topic and trope is a form of a larger struggle between speech and writing, or between wandering utterance and wandering signification. A *topos* truly is not so much a commonplace or a memory place as more nearly *the place of a voice,* the place from which the voice of the dead breaks through. Hence, a *topos* is an image of voice or of

speech, or the place where such an image is stored. The movement from *topos* to *topos,* the crossing, is always a crisis because it is
a kind of judgment or criticism between images of voice and
between the different kinds of figurative thinking that opposed
topics generate. Working from personally modified associationist
premises, Coleridge and Wordsworth wrote crisis-poems like *Frost
at Midnight* and *Tintern Abbey* by drawing their subjects through
the topics of invention, in an alteration of the Classical or
Ciceronian pattern. They opened with the topics of contraries
and contradictories, producing tropes of simple irony that by
naming one contrary intended another, so as to appear in images
of presence and absence. From this trope of *ethos* they then
moved to definition and division, the most fundamental of
artificial or poetic arguments, allied to the lesser topics of genus
and species, all of which tended to result in synecdochal figures.
The rhythm of invention then took them back to problems of spatial cause and effect, with the allied topics of associationist contiguity – characteristics, adjuncts, notations – all of which tended to
produce metonymic figurations, with attendant imagery of a prior
fullness emptying itself out as spatial effects were seen reducing to
spatial causes. The next step of this process of invention tended to
be that of comparison – greater, equal, less – with its conveying
trope of hyperbole, imagistically presented in the Sublime visions
of height and depth. I recall here two observations of Martin
Price, the first being that associationism had a way of dissolving
itself into a Platonism: "The recognition of a transcendental self
that lies behind its empirical experience is one of the most
intense expressions of the self-consciousness of the age. It absorbs
and transforms much of the interest in association of ideas." We
can combine this with another remark by Price concerning the
reliance of the Sublime poem upon hyperbole: "We are moving
from image to figure, from the picture to the dislocation of words
that indicates the inadequacy of any picture." This movement, I
would say, attains its climax in the Wordsworthian transformation
of the associationist topic of comparison into the hyperbole of the
Romantic Sublime.

But the curious rhythm of Romantic figuration then led Wordsworth and Coleridge back to the topics of similarity and dis-similarity, with their inevitable production of dualizing or High Romantic metaphors or "nature imagery," and subsequently into a final group of topics that commenced with reversible-cause-and-effect, or rather temporal effect-and-cause, which together with antecedents, consequences, and conjugates resulted in metaleptic or transumptive figurations, final reversals of temporal belated-ness. I am aware that this is heavy going, but I press on now to those "crossings" or crisis-points, the three negative moments or *aporias,* whose function seems to me crucial in post-Romantic poetry and particularly in Wallace Stevens, as the great inheritor of that poetry.

A crisis is a crucial point or turning point, going back to the Greek *krisis,* which derived from *krinein,* "to separate" or "to decide," from which came also the Greek *kritos,* "separated" or "chosen," and so *kritikos,* "able to discern," and so to be a critic. The Indo-European root is *skeri,* "to cut, separate, sift," from which stem such allied words as scribble, script, and hypocrisy, as well as crisis and critic. "Crossing" comes from a different root, a hypothetical one, *ger,* for "curving" or "crooked," but the acci-dents of linguistic history make it natural for us to associate "crossing" with the group that includes crisis, criticism, and script. I use "crossing" arbitrarily but precisely for the negative moments that collect meaning in the post-Romantic crisis-poem, insofar as meaning ever is present within a single text rather than wander-ing about between texts. But meaning also wanders about within a text, and its location by crossings ought to provide a perspective for interpretation that we haven't had before, a more certain link between rhetoric and psychology than my own ventures into iden-tifying tropes and defenses have thus far been able to establish.

Let us say (following de Man) that rhetoric *is* a text, and that its opposed aspects (system of tropes versus persuasion) make it an impossible text to read and understand, thus amassing all of rhetoric into One Enormous Poem (like Kabbalah, or like the Gnosis, or like Neoplatonism, or like Christianity, for that mat-ter!). Between theology (system of tropes) and belief (persuasion) there comes always the *aporia* (figuration of doubt, uncertain notice, mental dilemma, the necessity of misreading). Theology and a system of tropes are an *ethos;* belief and persuasion are a *pathos.* The *logos* of meaning is generated either by the repressive passage (representation) from *ethos* to *pathos* or by the sublimating passage (limitation) from *pathos* to *ethos.* The dynamism of the substituting process is the *logos,* which tells us that meaning in a poem is itself liminal, transgressive, a breaking as much as a making. But these violations of threshold are necessarily tropological *and* topological. A tropological deconstruction locates images of writing and then is forced to reduce to such images. Yet, the *places* of poetry are images of voice, even as the *figures* of poetry are images of writing. Poetry is a debate between voicing and writing, an endless crossing between topics *or* tropes, but also an endless shuttling between topics *and* tropes.

Of what use is my curious mixed discourse or Gnosis? How can we find the crossings in a poem, and what use can we make of them once they are found? I return to my map of misprision, with its three pairs of dialectical ratios, for I am going to complete it now by saying that a crossing is what intervenes at the crisis-point in each of the three pairs, that is, at the point where a figuration of *ethos* or Limitation yields to a figuration of *pathos* or Representation. I think that there are only two fundamental tropes, tropes of action and tropes of desire. Tropes of *ethos* are the language of what Emerson and Stevens call "poverty," of imaginative need, of powerlessness and necessity, *but also* of action, incident, and character. Tropes of *pathos* are the language of desire, possession, and power. In poetry, a trope of action is always an irony, until it is further reduced to metonymy and metophor; whereas a trope of imaginative desire always begins as a synecdoche, until it is further expanded to hyperbole and metalepsis, the trope that reverses temporality.

I follow the rhetoric of Kabbalah by calling the three degrees of *ethos* or verbal action three phases of limitation, since all of them, as Hartman says, point to a lack in language or a lack in the self, to a dearth of meaning, a withdrawal or contraction of the image (presence to absence, fullness to emptiness, insideness to outsideness). Yet all are instances of figures of will successfully translated into verbal act, a translation that leaves the will baffled at the inadequacy of language to its desires. The three degrees of *pathos*, as images of restitution or representation, strengthen or intend to strengthen both language and the self, but do so only through repression, or the failure to translate the will into act, which leaves will or desire rampant with *pathos*. These three degrees of *pathos* or representation point to a greater capacity to respond in language and in the self, and so to a willed excess in meaning, a restitution or expansion of the image (part to whole, low to high, late to early).

I go back now to the relation of associationism to the topics of rhetoric, so as to advance into the Wordsworthian crisis-poem and its crossings, and then to complete my circle by returning to Stevens's *Domination of Black*. Because of their distaste for the Neoclassical or Popean-Johnsonian universal or general truth, the associationists did not much use definition and division or synecdochal thinking, and also avoided comparison or hyperbolic thinking and the transumptive thinking that could reverse the temporal aspect of cause and effect. The major associationist faculties are contrariety, contiguity, cause and effect, and resemblance. There is thus very little *pathos* or representation in their system. They emphasize Lockean views of the object, and when Wordsworth reacts against them he emphasizes the category he calls "passion" or "excitement." Wordsworth got beyond his confusions on the image by making his greatest tropes *afterimages of voice*.

In the Wordsworthian crisis-poem, three crossings come together, even as they did in that place where Oedipus killed a stranger over the right to cross first. Let me name these crossings, though I will illustrate them here not from Wordsworth but from Stevens's *Domination of Black*, with which I began this discourse. Also, I will describe them primarily not in terms of trope but in those of psychoanalytic defense, following the schemes I set forth in *A Map of Misreading*.

Crossings, translated out of the abstract into the world of a poem's imaginings, address the mental dilemmas of confronting death, or the death of love, or the death of the creative gift, but in just the reverse order. The first crossing, which I have called the Crossing of Election, faces the death of the creative gift and seeks an answer to the question Am I still a poet, or, perhaps, am I truly a poet? This is the crossing between irony and synecdoche, or psychologically between reaction formation, where one defends against one's own instincts by manifesting the opposite of what one both wants and fears, and turning against the self, which is usually an exercise in sado-masochism.

The second crossing, which I have called the Crossing of Solipsism, struggles with the death of love, and tries to answer the fearful query Am I capable of loving another besides myself? This is the crossing between metonymy and hyperbole, or defensively between regressive and isolating movements of one's own psyche, and the massive repression of instinct that sublimely augments one's unconscious or inwardness at the expense of all the gregarious affects.

The third and final crossing, which I have called the Crossing of Identification, takes place between metaphor and metalepsis, or psychoanalytically between sublimation and introjection, that is between substituting some labor for one's own prohibited instincts and the psychic act of so identifying oneself with something or someone outside the self that time seems to stand still or to roll back or forward. The dilemma here is the confrontation with mortality, with total death, and the prohibited instinct is the drive toward death, the self-destructiveness that Freud hypothesized "beyond the pleasure principle."

I will add that each of these crossings seems to me to have three characteristic marks in nearly every poem in which they occur. These are:

1) A dialectical movement of the senses, usually between sight and hearing, though sometimes between different degrees of clarity in sight.

2) A movement of oscillation between mimetic and expressive theories of poetic representation, between mirror and lamp, to employ the terms that M. H. Abrams derived from Yeats.

3) A movement toward an even greater degree of internalization of the self, no matter how inward the starting point was.

I conclude by taking Stevens's *Domination of Black* as my text again, so as to trace its three crossings, the three negative moments or places where its rhetoric is most disjunctive and where paradoxically its meaning is therefore strongest, that is to say, where poetic or disjunctive thinking is going on most intensely. The Crossing of Election in *Domination of Black* takes place in the first stanza, between "Like the leaves themselves / Turning in the wind" and "Yes: but the color of the heavy hemlocks / Came striding," for this is the poem's first crisis or turning point, where Stevens meets the fear that he may not be able to become a poet or to maintain his own poethood. In the dialectic of the senses, he is moving from sight to sound, preluding the menace of hearing the cry of the peacocks. In the struggles of the growing inner self, he is threatened with loss of self through the loss of voice. As poet he is moving from the mimesis of the fallen leaves to the expressive cry of the peacocks, a cry to which the cry of his own poem is joined. Having seen that this is a Crossing of Election, successfully made, we can explain the puzzling and disjunctive "Yes," which thus becomes an affirmation of strength, an evidence of poetic election. In the midst of the longer second stanza, Stevens negotiates the Crossing of Solipsism, finding his way past his constant temptation to know both the externality of nature and the existence of other selves only as an irreality. The disjunction occurs between "They swept over the room, / Just as they flew from the boughs of the hemlocks / Down to the ground" and "I heard them cry – the peacocks." The movement is again from sight to sound (each more urgent than before) and again also from mimesis to expressiveness, but the internalizing movement is reversed, as the shadow of an external world comes near again. The surprise of meaning is clearest in the remarkable trope "loud fire," where the synesthesia hints at a lost eros, as it frequently does in Stevens, but here an eros directed toward the world that *Harmonium* calls "Florida."

The Crossing of Identification comes in the third stanza, between "I saw how the planets gathered / Like the leaves them-

selves / Turning in the wind" and "I saw how the night came,"
with its introjection of mortality. I cited earlier the prolepsis of
The Auroras of Autumn in "I felt afraid." The special quality of the
fear, in *Domination of Black*, is that it comes from a particular kind
of seeing, again akin to the seeing of *The Auroras of Autumn*. It is a
seeing that hears, because it hears a remembered cry, and so is
disjunctive with the seeing of "I saw how the planets gathered."
Adding to the fear are a sense of lost mimesis and the further
sense that the final internalization is the internalization of death.
A Crossing of Identification defensively tropes against death, and
also tropes toward it, confirming the ambivalence of Freud's
hypothetical yet Romantically based "death instinct."

I find that as poetry becomes more afflicted by a sense of its
belatedness the rhetoric of poetry becomes more and more disjunctive. The formal history of rhetoric tells us very little about
disjunctiveness, since whether it has been analyzed as system of
tropes or as persuasion it has been treated as though it were
always primarily conjunctive, as though one figuration joined
itself to another without rugged transitions taking place between,
say, ironic and synecdochal (or allegorical and symbolic) thinking.

I have described, in earlier works, the paradigm of the post-
Enlightenment crisis-poem as being a definite progression of six
tropes, which themselves might be troped as each strong poet's
version of the Six Days of Creation. Obviously, I am *not* saying that
every strong poem in English during the last two hundred years
follows a prescribed dance of tropes. Variations are profuse, per-
mutations abound, and yet there is a pattern to the dance. But
that pattern is conjunctive, and it is oddly enlightening to remember that the words "join" and "junction" have the same Indo-
European root as *yoga*, a root meaning "union." Against the unifying interplay of the steps that tropes constitute in the dance of
meaning, there is always a disjunctive or intertropical movement,
which is a missing element in our understanding of the reading
process. Stevens's grammar is as disjunctive as his syntax tends to
be conjunctive. His syntax affirms; his grammar is heavily condi-
tional and reductive; his rhetoric is complexly balanced but

becomes more and more disjunctive as his poetry advances. I hope to have demonstrated, in this book, that a theory of crossings can aid us in finding his poetry more truly and more strange than it has yet been found.

10 Reading Browning

A tower that crowns a country. But alas,
The soul now climbs it just to perish there!
For thence we have discovered ('Tis no dream –
We know this, which we had not else perceived)
That there's a world of capability
For joy, spread round about us, meant for us,
Inviting; and still the soul craves all. . . .

This is Browning's Cleon, describing what Shelley had called
"thought's crowned powers," the aesthetic dilemma of an elite
beyond religion. That dilemma was not Browning's own, as a
man, but in some ways it was his, as a poet. Yet it is cited here as
the inevitable dilemma of Browning's reader, and so as an epigraph to an introductory discussion of the difficulties of reading
one of the strongest and most perplexing poets in the English language.

Of all the problematic details in Browning's poetry, what
increasingly seems the central challenge to a reader is the peculiar nature of Browning's rhetorical stance. No poet has evidenced
more than Browning so intense a will-to-power over the interpretation of his own poems. The reader rides through the Browning
country with the poet always bouncing along at his side compulsively overinterpreting everything, very much in the manner of
his own Childe Roland, who thus usurps the reader's share.
Browning as self-interpreter has to be both welcomed and resist-
ed, and he makes the resistance very difficult. Such resistance,

though, may be Browning's greatest gift to his attentive reader. The Sublime, as Longinus formulated it, exists to compel readers to forsake easy pleasures in favor of more strenuous satisfactions, and Browning, like his master Shelley, crucially extends the possibilities of a modern Sublime.

One of the greatest achievements of English or Wordworthian Romanticism was an uneasily transitional Sublime, which retained just enough of a Miltonic aura of theophany without committing itself to biblical doctrine. This uneasy or skeptical sublimity, which Browning had learned to love by reading Shelley, was not available to Browning nor to the central poets after him, whether we take these to have been Pound and Eliot, or else Yeats and Stevens. Browning's quite nihilistic Sublime, founded upon the abyss of a figurative language always declaring its own status as figuration, became a major influence upon all four of these poets, and goes on working in contemporary poetry, though frequently in hidden ways.

To read Browning well we need to cope with his poetry's heightened rhetorical self-awareness, its constant consciousness that it *is* rhetoric, a personal system of tropes, as well as a persuasive rhetoric, an art that must play at transcendence. Browning is read very badly when that apparent and deeply moving transcendence is too easily accepted, as Browning in his social or public self tended to accept it. But Browning teaches his more strenuous readers not only the Sublime necessities of defense against his poems' self-interpretations, but also a healthy suspicion that the poet and reader alike are rhetorical systems of many selves, rather than any single or separate self. Here I think is the true center in reading Browning. The problems of rhetoric – of our being incapable of knowing what is literal and what figurative where all, in a sense, is figurative – and of psychology – is there as self that is not trope or an effect of verbal persuasion? – begin to be seen as one dilemma.

If Browning did not share this dilemma with all poets and their readers, then he would not be representative or even intelligible. However, his particular strength, which insures his permanent place in the canon, is that he appropriated the dilemma for his time with a singular possessiveness. An informed reader, brooding upon the rhetorical limits of interpretability, and upon the labyrinthine evasions of self-identity, will think very quickly of Browning when these problematic matters rise in the context of English poetic tradition. Browning's strength, like Milton's or Wordsworth's, is finally a strength of usurpation, in which a vast literary space is made to vacate its prior occupancy so as to permit a new formulation of the unresolvable dilemmas that themselves constitute poetry.

A number of the traditional issues that vex Browning criticism can be reoriented if we see them as burdens of rhetorical stance, when that stance itself determines Browning's psychopoetics. The dramatic monologue is revealed to be neither dramatic nor a monologue but rather a barely disguised High Romantic crisis lyric, in which antithetical voices contend for an illusory because only momentary mastery. The frequently grotesque diction appears a reaction formation away from Shelleyan verbal harmony, which means that the grotesquerie becomes a pure irony, a bitter digression away from meaning itself. The violent thematicism of Browning, including his exuberance in declaring a highly personalized evangelical belief in Christ, becomes something dangerously close to a thematics of violence, in which fervor of declaration far surpasses in importance the supposed spiritual content of the declaration. The notorious optimism begins to look rather acosmic and atemporal, so that the hope celebrated is much less Pauline than it is Gnostic. The faith demystifies as a Gnostic elitist knowledge of Browning's own divine spark, which turns out to be prior to and higher than the natural creation. Most bewilderingly, the love that Browning exalts becomes suspect, not because of its manifest Oedipal intensity, but because something in it is very close to a solipsistic transport, to a wholly self-delighting joy. He is a great lover – but primarily of himself, or rather of his multitude of antithetical selves.

The Browning I describe is hardly recognizable from much if not most of the criticism devoted to him, but few other poets have inspired so much inadequate criticism. Only Whitman and Dickinson among the major nineteenth-century poets seem to me as badly misrepresented as Browning has been. The prime fault of course is Browning's own, and so I return to his will-to-power over the interpretation of his own texts.

Hans Jonas remarks of the Gnostics that they delighted in "the intoxication of unprecedentedness," a poetic intoxication in which Browning, Whitman, and Dickinson share. Borges, with Gnostic irony, has pointed to Browning as one of the precursors of Kafka, an insight worthy of exploration. Against the Bible and Plato, the Gnostics refused the dialectics of sublimation and substitution, the Christian and Classical wisdom of the Second Chance. Like the Gnostics, Browning is interested in evasion rather than substitution, and does not wish to learn even the Wordsworthian version of the wisdom of the Second Chance. The "sober coloring" of a belated vision had no deep appeal to Browning, though he exemplifies it beautifully in the character and section of *The Ring and the Book* called "The Pope." The fire celebrated in the "Prologue" to his final volume, *Asolando: Fancies and Facts,* is the Gnostic fire of the First Chance, now "lost from the naked world." Browning appeals to "the purged ear," and a Voice rather clearly his own, at its most stentorian, proclaims: "God is it who transcends." "God" here is an hyperbole for poetic strength, which is Browning's violent and obsessive subject, whether in the overtly Shelleyan long poems that began his career or in the ostensibly dramatic romances, monologues, and lyrics of his more profoundly Shelleyan maturity.

Browning praised Shelley above all for

> his simultaneous perception of Power and Love in the absolute, and of Beauty and Good in the concrete, while he throws, from his poet's station between both, swifter, subtler, and more numerous films for the connection of each with each, than have been thrown by any modern artificer. . . .

Perhaps Browning's truest swerve away from this strong interpretation of Shelley, was an uncanny refusal to distinguish between Power and Love in the absolute, since for Browning both were forms of his own poetic self-recognition. What is Bishop Blougram but the strong poet taunting the weak critic?

If I'm a Shakespeare, let the well alone;
Why should I try to be what now I am?
If I'm no Shakespeare, as too probable, –
His power and consciousness and self-delight
And all we want in common . . .

. . .

We want the same things, Shakespeare and myself,
And what I want, I have: he, gifted more,
Could fancy he too had them when he liked. . . .

The reader who believes that the bishop means chair and wine by "what I want" is indeed another silent Mr. Gigadibs, who believes he sees "two points in Hamlet's soul / Unseized by the Germans yet." Sometimes Browning simply drops the mask and declares his precise agon:

For – see your cellarage!
    There are four big butts of Milton's brew.
How comes it you make old drips and drops
Do duty, and there devotion stops?
Leave such an abyss of malt and hops
    Embellied in butts which bungs still glue?
You hate your bard! A fig for your rage!
Free him from cellarage!

'Tis said I brew a stiff drink,
    But the deuce a flavour of grape is there.
Hardly a May-go-down, 'tis just
A sort of gruff Go-down-it-must –
No Merry-go-down, no gracious gust
    Commingles the racy with Springtide's rare!
'What wonder,' say you 'that we cough, and blink
At Autumn's heady drink?'

The strength of Browning's poetry is thus professedly an intoxication of belatedness, "Autumn's heady drink," and the weak reader's rage against both Milton and Browning is due to a weak head that doubts its own capacity. Browning's splendidly outrageous aggressivity is not so much latent as it is concealed in his more characteristic poems. Even in the charming and good-natured self-idealization of *Fra Lippo Lippi*, where Browning loves his monologist as himself, the appetite for a literal immortality is unabated. Poetic divination, in Browning, returns to its primal function, to keep the poet always alive: "Oh, oh, It makes me mad to see what men shall do / And we in our graves!" One of the Browning-selves evidently means *Cleon* to show how hopeless the Arnoldian or post-Christian aesthetic dilemma is, but a stronger Browning-self gets to work, and expresses a yet more poignant dilemma:

> Say rather that my fate is deadlier still,
> In this, that every day my sense of joy
> Grows more acute, my soul (intensified
> By power and insight) more enlarged, more keen;
> While every day my hairs fall more and more,
> My hand shakes, and the heavy years increase –
> The horror quickening still from year to year,
> The consummation coming past escape
> When I shall know most, and yet least enjoy –
> When all my works wherein I prove my worth,
> Being present still to mock me in men's mouths,
> Alive still, in the praise of such as thou,
> I, I the feeling, thinking, acting man,
> The man who loved his life so over-much,
> Sleep in my urn. It is so horrible. . . .

The rhetorical consciousness here characteristically makes us doubt the self-persuasiveness of this superb passage, since Cleon-Browning's death-in-life is livelier still than his life-in-death. His fate may be deadly, but the tropes are madly vigorous, even the "horror" *quickening*, and the "consummation" carrying its full range of significations, as it must, for what poet can fail to love his own life "so over-much"? The separate selves dance in the exuberant Browning when the reader juxtaposes to *Cleon* the now underpraised *Rabbi Ben Ezra*, where another poet, not imaginary, proclaims the life-affirming force of his supposedly normative Judaism:

> Thoughts hardly to be packed
>   Into a narrow act,
> Fancies that broke through language and escaped
>   All I could never be,
>   All, men ignored in me,
> This, I was worth to God, whose wheel the pitcher shaped.

> Ay, note that Potter's wheel,
>   That metaphor! and feel
> Why time spins fast, why passive lies our clay, –
>   Thou, to whom fools propound,
>   When the wine makes its round,
> 'Since life fleets, all is change; the Past gone, seize to-day!'
>
> Fool! All that is, at all,
>   Lasts ever, past recall;
> Earth changes, but thy soul and God stand sure:
>   What entered into thee,
>   *That* was, is, and shall be:
> Time's wheel runs back or stops: Potter and clay endure.

"That metaphor" is normative and prophetic, but the
poem's burden is Gnostic rather than Pharasaic. The "figured
flame which blends, transcends" all the stars is one with the
Gnostic *pneuma* or "spark" that preceded nature. Browning's
vision, and hardly the historical Ibn Ezra's, sees man as "a god
though in the germ." What Browning "shall know, being old" is
what he always knew, his own "*That* was, is, and shall be." Not the
Old Adam nor Christ as the New Adam is the paradigm, but what
we might call the Old Browning, the Gnostic primal Anthropos or
preexistent Adam.

Yeats remarked that he had feared always Browning's
influence upon him. In a deep sense, Yeats was right, not only
because of the shared Shelleyan ancestry, but because of the
shared Gnosticism, though the esoteric religion was quite overt in
Yeats. Browning does all he can to evade what Yeats (following
Nietzsche) named as the *antithetical* quest in Shelley, the drive
beyond nature to a nihilistic annihilation that is the poetic will's
ultimate revenge against time's "it was." But the evasion was only
half-hearted:

> For I intend to get to God,
>   For 'tis to God I speed so fast,
> For in God's breast, my own abode,
>   Those shoals of dazzling glory, passed,
> I lay my spirit down at last.
>   I lie where I have always lain,
> God smiles as he has always smiled. . . .

True that this is Johannes Agricola the Antinomian, chanting in his madhouse cell, but no reader would dispute such exuberance if he substituted the Gnostic alien god, the Abyss, for the "God" of these lines. Make the substitution and Johannes Agricola may be permitted to speak for another Browning-self or soul-side, and for the entire *antithetical* tradition.

Much of Tennyson's astonishing power was due to the Laureate's not knowing what it was that his daemon or antithetical self was writing about, but Browning was so daemonic that something in him always did know. Naming that something becomes the quest of Browning's capable reader, a quest unfulfillable in the Browning country where every self is a picnic of selves, every text a tropological entrapment. Browning's St John, in *A Death in the Desert,* gives us two passages whose juxtaposition helps us define his reader's quest for meaning:

> Therefore, I say, to test man, the proofs shift,
> Nor may he grasp that fact like other fact,
> And straightway in his life acknowledge it,
> As, say, the inevitable bliss of fire.
> Sigh ye, 'It had been easier once than now'?
> To give you answer I am left alive;
> Look at me who was present from the first!
> . . .
> Is this indeed a burthen for late days,
> and may I help to bear it with you all,
> Using my weakness which becomes your strength?

Browning's visionary is arguing against Cerinthus and other early Gnostics, but the argument is more Gnostic than Christian (which may have been Browning's shrewd reading of the Fourth Gospel). To be present from the first, at the origins, is to have priority over nature and history, and involves denying one's own belatedness, which is thus equated with weakness, while a return to earliness is strength. To do the deed and judge it at the same time is to impose interpretation, one's will-to-power over both text and the text of life. Browning is most uncanny as a poet when two or more of his selves contend within a poem to interpret that poem, a struggle that brings forth his greatest yet most problematic achievements, including *A Toccata of Galuppi's, By the Fireside, Master Hugues of Saxe-Gotha, Love Among the Ruins, The Heretic's Tragedy, Andrea del Sarto, Abt Vogler, Caliban Upon Setebos, Numpholeptos, Pan and Luna, Flute-Music, with an Accompaniment,* and *"Childe Roland to the Dark Tower Came."* These dozen poems alone would establish Browning's permanent importance, but I have space here only to glance briefly again at *Childe Roland,* which is a text that never lets go of a reader once it has found you. The poem may well be the definitive proof-text for the modern Sublime, more uncanny than Kafka, stronger than Yeats at his most uncompromising.

Browning's Roland descends ultimately from the Marlovian-Shakespearean hero-villain, by way of Milton's Satan and the High Romantic metamorphoses of Satan. Tennyson's Ulysses has something of the same complex ancestry, but he is less Jacobean than Roland, who like Webster's Lodovico in *The White Devil* could say he had limned his own night-piece, and it was his best. Roland is a savagely reductive interpreter whom the wary reader must resist, until at its close the poem so opens out that the reader suddenly wants Roland to interpret more, only to discover that the Childe is done with interpretation. The reader is left with the uncanny, which means with the self in Browning that finds both his aim and his origin in the Sublime, unlike the remorselessly reductive self that has spoken most of the poem.

The ogreless Dark Tower, where the quester must confront himself and his dead precursors, to "fail" at least as heroically as they have failed before him, is a composite trope for poetry if not for the Sublime poem itself. Indeed, the figuration is so suggestive that the Dark Tower can be read as the mental dilemma or *aporia* that Browning's reader faces in the poem. The Dark Tower is the black hole in the Browning cosmos, where Power and Love become one only through a supremely negative moment, in which loss of the self and loss of the fulness of the present pay the high price of achieved vision:

What in the midst lay but the Tower itself?
   The round squat turret, blind as the fool's heart,
   Built of brown stone, without a counterpart
In the whole world. The tempest's mocking elf
Points to the shipman thus the unseen shelf
   He strikes on, only when the timbers start.

Not see? because of night perhaps? – why day
   Came back for that! before it left
   The dying sunset kindled through a cleft:
The hills, like giants at a hunting, lay,
Chin upon hand, to see the game at bay, –
   'Now stab and end the creature – to the heft!'

Not hear? when noise was everywhere! it tolled
   Increasing like a bell. Names in my ears
   Of all the lost adventurers my peers, –
How such a one was strong, and such was bold,
And such was fortunate, yet each of old
   Lost, lost! one moment knelled the woe of years.

After a life spent training for the vision of the Dark Tower, you do not see it until burningly it comes on you all at once. How do we interpret the shock of "This was the place!" when we have learned to resist every one of Roland's earlier interpretations? Is it that we, like Roland, have overprepared the event, in Pound's fine phrasing? Roland is overtrained, which means that he suffers an acute consciousness of belatedness. We are overanxious not to be gulled by his reductiveness, which means that we suffer an acute consciousness that we have selves of our own to defend. In the Sublime agon between Roland and the reader, Browning stands aside, even at the very end, not because he is an "objective" as opposed to antithetical poet, but because he respects the *aporia* of the Dark Tower. Poetry is part of what the Gnostics called the Kenoma or cosmic and temporal emptiness, and not part of the Pleroma, the fullness of presence that is acosmic and atemporal. The Pleroma is always absent, for it inheres in the Abyss, the true, alien God who is cut off from nature and history.

    The name of that alien God in Roland's country is Shelley's trumpet of a prophecy, which enters by way of another precursor,

the boy-poet Chatterton, whose poetry provides the slug-horn that
is sounded:

> There they stood, ranged along the hillside, met
> > To view the last of me, a living frame
> > For one more picture! in a sheet of flame
> I saw them and I knew them all. And yet
> Dauntless the slug-horn to my lips I set,
> > And blew. 'Childe Roland to the Dark Tower came.'

The picture is Browning's, the frame or context is given by
the living but contradictory presence, where there can be no presence, of the precursors: Shelley, Chatterton, Keats, Tasso, who
lived and died in Yeats's Condition of Fire, Roland's "sheet of
flame." Browning as man and poet died old, but his anxiety seems
to have been that his poethood *could* have died young, when he
forswore the atheist Shelley in order to win back the approving
love of his evangelical mother. Roland's equivocal triumph
achieves the Sublime, and helps guarantee Browning's poetic
survival.

Roland sees and knows, like Keats's intelligences which are
at once atoms of perception and God. What he sees and knows
are the heroic precursors who are met to see *him*, but who cannot
know him, as presumably his readers can. Roland's knowledge
ought to daunt him, and yet against it he sets the trumpet of his
prophecy. His will is thus set in revenge against time's: "It was,"
but we do not know the content of his prophecy. After a full stop,
and not a colon, comes the poem's final statement, which is at
once its Shakespearean title and epigraph. Either the entire poem
begins again, in a closed cycle like Blake's *The Mental Traveller,* or
else Roland proclaims his story's inevitable lack of closure. What
seems clear is that Roland is not performing his own poem, in
direct contrast to Shelley at the close of the *Ode to the West Wind,*
where the words to be scattered among mankind are the text of
the *Ode.*

It is after all the many-selved Browning who is undaunted by
belatedness, by the dilemmas of poetic language, and by his own
struggle for authority as against both precursors and readers.

Poetic self-confidence delights us when we are persuaded that it can sustain itself, that it has usurped imaginative space and has forced its way into the canon. Again we are in the Sublime of Longinus, as the reader becomes one with the power he apprehends. The danger of sublimity is that the pit of the bathetic suddenly can open anywhere, and Browning (who wrote much too much) sometimes pulls us down with him. This hardly matters, where we are given so large a company of splendid self-deceivers and even more splendid deceivers of others, of all but the wariest readers. Browning, more than Yeats or Stevens, more than his disciple Pound or his secret student Eliot, is the last of the old High line, as in the audacious rhetorical gesture that concludes his magnificent, unread *Pan and Luna:*

> . . . The myth
> Explain who may! Let all else go, I keep
> – As of a ruin just a monolith –
> Thus much, one verse of five words, each a boon:
> Arcadia, night, a cloud, Pan, and the moon.

11   Freud and the Poetic Sublime

Jacques Lacan argues that Freud "derived his inspiration, his ways of thinking and his technical weapons" from imaginative literature rather than from the sciences. On such a view, the precursors of Freud are not so much Charcot and Janet, Brücke and Helmholtz, Breuer and Fliess, but the rather more exalted company of Empedocles and Heraclitus, Plato and Goethe, Shakespeare and Schopenhauer. Lacan is the foremost advocate of a dialectical reading of Freud's text, a reading that takes into account those problematics of textual interpretation that stem from the philosophies of Hegel, Nietzsche and Heidegger, and from developments in differential linguistics. Such a reading, though it has attracted many intellectuals in English-speaking countries, is likely to remain rather alien to us, because of the strong empirical tradition in Anglo-American thought. Rather like Freud himself, whose distate for and ignorance of the United States were quite invincible, Lacan and his followers distrust American pragmatism, which to them is merely irritability with theory. Attacks by French Freudians upon American psychoanalysis tend to stress issues of societal adjustment or else of a supposed American optimism concerning human nature. But I think Lacan is wiser in his cultural vision of Freud than he is in his polemic against ego psychology, interpersonal psychoanalysis or any other American school. Freud's power *as a writer* made him the contemporary not so much of his rivals and disciples as of the strongest literary minds of our century. We read Freud not as we read Jung or Rank, Abraham or Ferenczi, but as we read Proust or Joyce, Valéry or

Rilke or Stevens. A writer who achieves what once was called the Sublime will be susceptible to explication either upon an empirical *or* upon a dialectical basis.

The best brief account of Freud that I have read is by Richard Wollheim (1971), and Wollheim is an analytical philosopher, working in the tradition of Hume and Wittgenstein. The Freud who emerges in Wollheim's pages bears very little resemblance to Lacan's Freud, yet I would hesitate to prefer either Wollheim's or Lacan's Freud, one to the other. There is no "true" or "correct" reading of Freud because Freud is so strong a writer that he *contains* every available mode of interpretation. In tribute to Lacan, I add that Lacan in particular has uncovered Freud as the greatest theorist we have of what I would call the necessity of misreading. Freud's text both exemplifies and explores certain limits of language, and therefore of literature, insofar as literature is a linguistic as well as a discursive mode. Freud is therefore as much the concern of literary criticism as he is of psychoanalysis. His intention was to found a science; instead he left as legacy a literary canon and a discipline of healing.

It remains one of the sorrows, both of psychoanalysis and of literary criticsm, that as modes of interpretation they continue to be antithetical to one another. The classical essay on this antithesis is still Lionel Trilling's *Freud and Literature,* first published back in 1940, and subsequently revised in *The Liberal Imagination* (1950). Trilling demonstrated that neither Freud's notion of art's status nor Freud's use of analysis on works of art was acceptable to a literary critic, but nevertheless praised the Freudian psychology as being truly parallel to the workings of poetry. The sentence of Trilling's eloquent essay that always has lingered in my own memory is the one that presents Freud as a second Vico, as another great rhetorician of the psyche's twistings and turnings:

> In the eighteenth century Vico spoke of the metaphorical, imagistic language of the early stages of culture; it was left to Freud to discover how, in a scientific age, we still feel and think in figurative formations, and to create, what psychoanalysis is, a science of tropes, of metaphor and its variants, synecdoche and metonymy.

That psychoanalysis is a science of tropes is now an accepted commonplace in France, and even in America, but we do well to remember how prophetic Trilling was, since the *Discours de Rome* of Jacques Lacan dates from 1953. Current American thinkers in psychoanalysis like Marshall Edelson and Roy Schafer describe psychic defenses as fantasies, not mechanisms, and fantasies are always tropes, in which so-called "deep structures," like desires, become transformed into "surface structures," like symptoms. A fantasy of defense is thus, in language, the recursive process that traditional rhetoric named a trope or "turning," or even a "color," to use another old name for it. A psychoanalyst interpreting a symptom, dream or verbal slip and a literary critic interpreting a poem thus share the burden of having to become conceptual rhetoricians. But a common burden is proving to be no more of an authentic unifying link between psychoanalysts and critics than common burdens prove to be among common people, and the languages of psychoanalysis and of criticism continue to diverge and clash.

Partly this is due to a certain over-confidence on the part of writing psychoanalysts when they confront a literary text, as well as to a certain over-deference to psychoanalysis on the part of various critics. Psychoanalytic over-confidence, or courageous lack of wariness, is hardly untypical of the profession, as any critic can learn by conducting a seminar for any group of psychoanalysts. Since we can all agree that the interpretation of schizophrenia is a rather more desperately urgent matter than the interpretation of poetry, I am in no way inclined to sneer at psychoanalysts for their instinctive privileging of their own kinds of interpretation. A critical self-confidence, or what Nietzsche might have called a will-to-power over the text-of-life, is a working necessity for a psychoanalyst, who otherwise would cease to function. Like the shaman, the psychoanalyst cannot heal unless he himself is persuaded by his own rhetoric. But the writing psychoanalyst adopts, whether he knows it or not, a very different stance. As a writer he is neither more nor less privileged than any other writer. He cannot invoke the trope of the Unconscious as though he were doing more (or

TROPES OF:

PSYCHOANALYSTS / UNCONSCIOUS
POET-CRITIC / IMAGINATION
THEOLOGIAN / DEVINE

less) than the poet or critic does by invoking the trope of the Imagination, or than the theologian does by invoking the trope of the Divine. Most writing psychoanalysts privilege the realm of what Freud named as "the primary process." Since this privileging, or valorization, is at the center of any psychoanalytic account of creativity, I turn now to examine "primary process," which is Freud's most vital trope or fiction in his theory of the mind.

Freud formulated his distinction between the primary and secondary processes of the psyche in 1985, in his *Project for a Scientific Psychology*, best available in English since 1954 in *The Origins of Psychoanalysis* (ed. Bonaparte, A. Freud and Kris). In Freud's mapping of the mind, the primary process goes on in the system of the unconscious, while the secondary process characterizes the preconscious-conscious system. In the unconscious, energy is conceived as moving easily and without check from one idea to another, sometimes by displacement (dislocating) and sometimes by condensation (compression). This hypothesized energy of the psyche is supposed continually to reinvest all ideas associated with the fulfillment of unconscious desire, which is defined as a kind of primitive hallucination that totally satisfies, that gives a complete pleasure. Freud speaks of the primary process as being marked by a wandering-of-meaning, with meaning sometimes dislocated onto what ought to be an insignificant idea or image, and sometimes compressed upon a single idea or image at a crossing point between a number of ideas or images. In this constant condition of wandering, meaning becomes multiformly determined, or even over-determined, interestingly explained by Lacan as being like a palimpsest, with one meaning always written over another one. Dreaming is of course the principal Freudian evidence for the primary process, but wishing construed as a primitive phase of desiring may be closer to the link between the primary process and what could be called poetic thinking.

Wollheim calls the primary process "a primitive but perfectly coherent form of mental functioning." Freud expounded a version of the primary process in Chapter VII of his masterwork, *The Interpretation of Dreams* (1900), but his classic account of it is in the essay of 1911, *Formulations on the Two Principles of Mental Functioning*. There the primary process is spoken of as yielding to the secondary process when the person abandons the pleasure principle and yields to the reality principle, a surrender that postpones pleasure only in order to render its eventuality more certain.

The secondary process thus begins with a binding of psychic energy, which subsequently moves in a more systematic fashion. Investments in ideas and images are stabilized, with pleasure deferred, in order to make possible trial runs of thought as so many path-breakings towards a more constant pleasure. So described, the secondary process also has its links to the cognitive workings of poetry, as to all other cognitions whatsoever. The French Freudians, followers of Lacan, speak of the primary and secondary process as each having different laws of syntax, which is another way of describing these processes as two kinds of poetry or figuration, or two ways of "creativity," if one would have it so.

Anthony Wilden observes in his *System and Structure* (1972): "The concept of a primary process or system applies in both a synchronic and a diachronic sense to all systemic or structural theories." In Freudian theory, the necessity of postulating a primary process precludes any possibility of regarding the forms of that process as being other than abnormal or unconscious phenomena. The Lacanian psychoanalyst O. Mannoni concludes his study *Freud* (English translation 1971) by emphasizing the ultimate gap between primary process and secondary process as being the tragic, unalterable truth of the Freudian vision, since "what it reveals profoundly is a kind of original fracture in the way man is constituted, a split that opposes him to himself (and not to reality or society) and exposes him to the attacks of his unconscious."

In his book *On Art and the Mind* (1973), Wollheim usefully reminds us that the higher reaches of art "did not for Freud connect up with that other and far broader route by which wish and impulse assert themselves in our lives: Neurosis." Wollheim goes on to say that, in Freudian terms, we thus have no reason to think of art as showing any single or unitary motivation. Freud first had developed the trope or conceptual image of the unconscious in order to explain repression, but then had equated the unconscious with the primary process. In his final phase, Freud came to believe that the primary process played a positive role in the strengthening of the ego, by way of the fantasies or defenses of introjection and projection. Wollheim hints that Freud, if he had lived, might have investigated the role of art through such figures of identification, so as to equate art "with recovery or reparation on the path back to reality." Whether or not this surmise is correct, it is certainly very suggestive. We can join Wollheim's surmise to Jack Spector's careful conclusion in his *The Aesthetics of Freud* (1972) that Freud's contribution to the study of art is principally "his dramatic view of the mind in which a war, not of good and evil, but of ego, super-ego, and id forces occurs as a secular *psychomachia.*" Identification, through art, is clearly a crucial weapon in such a civil war of the psyche.

Yet it remains true, as Philip Rieff once noted, that Freud suggests very little that is positive about creativity as an intellectual process, and therefore explicit Freudian thought is necessarily antithetical to nearly any theory of the imagination. To quarry Freud for theories of creativity, we need to study Freud where he himself is most imaginative, as in his great phase that begins with *Beyond the Pleasure Principle* (1920), continues with the essay *Negation* (1925) and then with *Inhibitions, Symptoms, and Anxiety* (1926, but called *The Problem of Anxiety* in its American edition), and that can be said to attain a climax in the essay *Analysis Terminable and Interminable* (1937). This is the Freud who establishes the priority of anxiety over its stimuli, and who both imagines the origins of consciousness as a catastrophe and then relates that catastrophe to repetition-compulsion, to the drive-towards-death, and to the defense of life as a drive towards agonistic achievement, an agon directed not only against death but against the achievements of anteriority, of others, and even of one's own earlier self.

Freud, as Rieff also has observed, held a catastrophe theory of the genealogy of drives, but *not* of the drive-towards-creativity. Nevertheless, the Freudian conceptual image of a catastrophe-creation of our instincts is perfectly applicable to our will-to-creativity, and both Otto Rank and more indirectly Sandor Ferenczi made many suggestions (largely unacceptable to Freud himself) that can help us to see what might serve as a Freudian theory of the imagination-as-catastrophe, and of art as an achieved anxiety in the agonistic struggle both to repeat and to defer the repetition of the catastrophe of creative origins.

Prior to any pleasure, including that of creativity, Freud posits the "narcissistic scar," accurately described by a British Freudian critic, Ann Wordsworth, as "the infant's tragic and inevitable first failure in sexual love." Parallel to this notion of the narcissistic scar is Freud's speculative discovery that there are early dreams whose purpose is not hallucinatory wish-fulfillment. Rather they are attempts to master a stimulus retroactively by first developing the anxiety. This is certainly a creation, though it is the *creation of an anxiety,* and so cannot be considered a sublimation of any kind. Freud's own circuitous path-breaking of thought connects this creation-of-an-anxiety to the function of repetition-compulsion, which turns out, in the boldest of all Freud's tropes, to be a regressive return to a death-instinct.

Freud would have rejected, I think, an attempt to relate this strain in his most speculative thinking to any theory of creativity, because for Freud a successful repression is a contradiction in terms. What I am suggesting is that any theory of artistic creation that wishes to use Freud must depart from the Freudian letter in order to develop the Freudian spirit, which in some sense is already the achievement of Lacan and his school, though they have had no conspicuous success in speculating upon art. What the Lacanians *have* seen is that Freud's system, like Heidegger's, is a science of anxiety, which is what I suspect the art of belatedness, of the last several centuries, mostly is also. Freud, unlike Nietzsche, shared in the Romantics' legacy of over-idealizing art, of accepting an ill-defined trope of "the Imagination" as a kind of mythology of creation. But Freud, as much as Nietzsche (or Vico, before them both), provides the rational materials for demythologizing our pieties about artistic creation. Reading the later Freud teaches us that our instinctual life is agonistic and ultimately self-destructive and that our most authentic moments tend to be those of negation, contraction and repression. Is it so unlikely that our creative drives are deeply contaminated by our instinctual origins?

Psychoanalytic explanations of "creativity" tend to discount or repress two particular aspects of the genealogy of aesthetics: first, that the creative or Sublime "moment" is a negative moment; second, that this moment tends to rise out of an encounter with someone else's prior moment of negation, which in turn goes back to an anterior moment, and so on. "Creativity" is thus always a mode of repetition *and* of memory and also of what Nietzsche called the will's revenge against time and against time's statement of: "It was." What links repetition and revenge is the psychic operation that Freud named "defense," and that he identified first with repression but later with a whole range of figurations, including identification. Freud's rhetoric of the psyche, as codified by Anna Freud in *The Ego and the Mechanisms of Defense* (1946), is as comprehensive a system of tropes as Western theory has devised. We can see now, because of Freud, that rhetoric always was more the art of defense than it was the art of persuasion, or rather that defense is always *prior* to persuasion. Trilling's pioneering observation that Freud's science shared with literature a reliance upon trope has proved to be wholly accurate. To clarify my argument, I need to return to Freud's trope of the unconscious and then to proceed from it to his concern with catastrophe as the origin of drive in his later works.

"Consciousness," as a word, goes back to a root meaning "to cut or split," and so to know something by separating out one thing from another. The unconscious (Freud's *das Unbewusste*), is a purely inferred division of the psyche, an inference necessarily based only upon the supposed effects that the unconscious has upon ways we think and act that can be *known,* that are available to consciousness. Because there are gaps or disjunctions to be accounted for in our thoughts and acts, various explanatory concepts of an unconscious have been available since ancient times, but the actual term first appears as the German *Unbewusste* in the later eighteenth century, to be popularized by Goethe and by Schelling. The English "unconscious" was popularized by Coleridge, whose theory of a poem as reconciling a natural outside with a human inside relied upon a formula that "the consciousness is so impressed on the unconscious as to appear in it." Freud acknowledged often that the poets had been there before him, as discoverers of the unconscious, but asserted his own discovery as being the scientific *use* of a concept of the unconscious. What he did not assert was his intense narrowing down of the traditional concept, for he separated out and away from it the attributes of creativity that poets and other speculators always had ascribed to it. Originality or invention are not mentioned by Freud as rising out of the unconscious.

There is no single concept of the unconscious in Freud, as any responsible reading of his work shows. This is because there are two Freudian topographies or maps of the mind, earlier and later (after 1920), and also because the unconscious is a dynamic concept. Freud distinguished his concept of the unconscious from that of his closest psychological precursor, Pierre Janet, by emphasizing his own vision of a civil war in the psyche, a dynamic conflict of opposing mental forces, conscious against unconscious. Not only the conflict was seen thus as being dynamic, but the unconscious peculiarly was characterized as dynamic in itself, requiring always a contending force to keep it from breaking through into consciousness.

In the first Freudian topography, the psyche is divided into Unconscious, Preconscious, and Conscious, while in the second the divisions are the rather differnt triad of id, ego, and superego. The Preconscious, descriptively considered, is unconscious, but can be made conscious, and so is severely divided from the Unconscious proper, in the perspective given either by a topographical or a dynamic view. But this earlier system proved simplistic to Freud himself, mostly because he came to believe that our lives began with all of the mind's contents in the unconscious. This finally eliminated Janet's conception that the unconscious was a wholly separate mode of consciousness, which was a survival of the ancient belief in a creative or inaugurating unconscious. Freud's new topology insisted upon the dynamics of relationship between an unknowable unconscious and consciousness by predicating three agencies or instances of personality: id, ego, superego. The effect of this new system was to devaluate the unconscious, or at least to demystify it still further.

In the second Freudian topography, "unconscious" tends to become merely a modifier, since all of the id and very significant parts of the ego and super-ego are viewed as being unconscious. Indeed, the second Freudian concept of the ego gives us an ego which is *mostly* unconscious, and so "behaves exactly like the repressed – that is, which produces powerful effects without itself being conscious and which requires special work before it can be made conscious," as Freud remarks in *The Ego and the Id.* Lacan has emphasized the unconscious element in the ego to such a degree that the Lacanian ego must be considered, despite its creator's protests, much more a revision of Freud than what ordinarily would be accounted an interpretation. With mordant eloquence, Lacan keeps assuring us that the ego, every ego, is essentially paranoid, which as Lacan knows *sounds* rather more like Pascal than it does like Freud. I think that this insistence is at once Lacan's strength and his weakness, for my knowledge of imaginative literature tells me that Lacan's conviction is certainly true if by the ego we mean the literary "I" as it appears in much of the most vital lyric poetry of the last three hundred years, and indeed in all literature that achieves the Sublime. But with the literary idea of "the Sublime" I come at last to the sequence of Freud's texts that I wish to examine, since the first of them is Freud's theory of the Sublime, his essay *The "Uncanny"* of 1919.

The text of *The "Uncanny"* is the threshold to the major phase of Freud's canon, which begins the next year with *Beyond the Pleasure Principle.* But quite aside from its crucial place in Freud's writings, the essay is of enormous importance to literary criticism because it is the only major contribution that the twentieth century has made to the aesthetics of the Sublime. It may seem curious to regard Freud as the culmination of a literary and philosophical tradition that held no particular interest for him, but I would correct my own statement by the modification, no *conscious* interest for him. The Sublime, as I read Freud, is one of his major *repressed* concerns, and this literary repression on his part is a clue to what I take to be a gap in his theory of repression.

I come now, belatedly, to the definition of "the Sublime," before considering Freud as the last great theorist of that mode. As a literary idea, the Sublime originally meant a style of "lofti-ness," that is of verbal power, of greatness or strength conceived agonistically, which is to say against all possible competition. But in the European Enlightenment, this literary idea was strangely transformed into a vision of the terror that could be perceived both in nature and in art, a terror uneasily allied with pleasurable sensations of augmented power, and even of narcissistic freedom, freedom in the shape of that wildness that Freud dubbed "the omnipotence of thought," the greatest of all narcissistic illusions.

Freud's essay begins with a curiously weak defensive attempt to separate his subject from the aesthetics of the Sublime, which he insists deals only "with feelings of a positive nature." This is so flatly untrue, and so blandly ignores the long philosophical tradi-tion of the negative Sublime, that an alert reader ought to become very wary. A year later, in the opening paragraphs of *Beyond the Pleasure Principle,* Freud slyly assures his readers that "priority and originality are not among the aims that psycho-ana-lytic work sets itself." One sentence later, he charmingly adds that he would be glad to accept any philosophical help he can get, but that none is available for a consideration of the meaning of plea-sure and unpleasure. With evident generosity, he then acknowl-edges G. T. Fechner, and later makes a bow to the safely distant Plato as author of *The Symposium.* Very close to the end of *Beyond the Pleasure Principle,* there is a rather displaced reference to Schopenhauer, when Freud remarks that "we have unwittingly steered our course into the harbor of Schopenhauer's philoso-phy." The apogee of this evasiveness in regard to precursors comes where it should, in the marvelous essay of 1937, *Analysis*

Terminable and Interminable, which we may learn to read as being Freud's elegiac *apologia* for his life's work. There the true precursor is unveiled as Empedocles, very safely remote at two and a half millennia. Perhaps psychoanalysis does not set priority and originality as aims in its *praxis,* but the first and most original of psychoanalysts certainly shared the influence-anxieties and defensive misprisions of all strong writers throughout history, and particularly in the last three centuries.

Anxieties when confronted with anterior powers are overtly the concerns of the essay on the "uncanny." E. T. A. Hoffmann's *The Sand-Man* provides Freud with his text, and for once Freud allows himself to be a very useful practical critic of an imaginative story. The repetition-compulsion, possibly imported backwards from *Beyond the Pleasure Principle* as work-in-progress, brilliantly is invoked to open up what is hidden in the story. Uncanniness is traced back to the narcissistic belief in "omnipotence of thought," which in aesthetic terms is necessarily the High Romantic faith in the power of the mind over the universe of the senses and of death. *Das Heimliche,* the homely or canny, is thus extended to its only apparent opposite, *das Unheimliche,* "for this uncanny is in reality nothing new or foreign, but something familiar and old-established in the mind that has been estranged only by the process of repression."

Freud weakens his extraordinary literary insight by the latter part of his essay, where he seeks to reduce the "uncanny" to either an infantile or a primitive survival in our psyche. His essay knows better, in its wonderful dialectical play on the *Unheimlich* as being subsumed by the larger or parental category of the *Heimlich.* Philip Rieff finely catches this interplay in his comment that the effect of Freud's writing is itself rather uncanny, and surely never more so than in this essay. Rieff sounds like Emerson or even like Longinus on the Sublime when he considers the condition of Freud's reader:

> The reader comes to a work with ambivalent motives, learning what he does not wish to know, or, what amounts to the same thing, believing he already knows and can accept as his own intellectual property what the author merely "articulates" or "expresses" for him. Of course, in this sense, everybody knows everything – or nobody could learn anything. . . .

Longinus had said that reading a sublime poet ". . . we come to believe we have created what we have only heard." Milton, strongest poet of the modern Sublime, stated this version of the reader's Sublime with an ultimate power, thus setting forth the principle upon which he himself read, in Book IV of his *Paradise Regained,* where his Christ tells Satan:

> . . . who reads
> Incessantly, and to his reading brings not
> A spirit and judgment equal or superior
> (And what he brings, what needs he elsewhere seek?),
> Uncertain and unsettled still remains. . . .

Pope followed Boileau in saying that Longinus "is himself the great Sublime he draws." Emerson, in his seminal essay *Self-Reliance,* culminated this theme of the reader's Sublime when he asserted that "in every work of genius we recognize our own rejected thoughts; they come back to us with a certain alienated majesty." The "majesty" is the true, high, breaking light, aura or lustre of the Sublime, and this realization is at the repressed center of Freud's essay on the "uncanny." What Freud declined to see, at that moment, was the mode of conversion that alienated the "canny" into the "uncanny." His next major text, *Beyond the Pleasure Principle,* clearly exposes that mode as being catastrophe.

Lacan and his followers have centered upon *Beyond the Pleasure Principle* because the book has not lost the force of its shock value, even to Freudian analysts. My contention would be that this shock is itself the stigma of the Sublime, stemming from Freud's literary achievement here. The text's origin is itself shock or aura, the trauma that a neurotic's dreams attempt to master, *after the event.* "Drive" or "instinct" is suddenly seen by Freud as being catastrophic in its origins, and as being aimed, not at satisfaction, but at death. For the first time in his writing, Freud overtly assigns priority to the psyche's fantasizings over mere biology, though this valorization makes Freud uneasy. The pleasure principle produces the biological principle of constancy, and then is converted, through this principle, into a drive back to the constancy of death. Drive or instinct thus becomes a kind of defense, all but identified with repression. This troping of biology is so extreme, really so literary, that I find it more instructive to seek the aid of commentary here from a Humean empiricist like Wollheim than from Continental dialecticians like Lacan and Laplanche. Wollheim imperturbably finds no violation of empiricism or biology in the death-drive. He even reads "beyond," *jenseits*, as meaning only "inconsistent with" the pleasure principle, which is to remove from the word the transcendental or Sublime emphasis that Freud's usage gave to it. For Wollheim, the book is nothing more than the working through of the full implication of the major essay of 1914, *On Narcissism: An Introduction*. If we follow Wollheim's lead quite thoroughly here, we will emerge with conclusions that differ from his rather guarded remarks about the book in which Freud seems to have shocked himself rather more than he shocks Wollheim.

The greatest shock of *Beyond the Pleasure Principle* is that it ascribes the origin of all human drives to a catastrophic theory of creation (to which I would add: "of creativity"). This catastrophe theory is developed in *The Ego and the Id*, where the two major catastrophes, the drying up of ocean that cast life onto land and the Ice Age are said to be repeated psychosomatically in the way the latency period (roughly from the age of five until twelve) cuts a gap into sexual development. Rieff again is very useful when he says that the basis of catastrophe theory, whether in Freud or in Ferenczi's more drastic and even apocalyptic *Thalassa* (1921), "remains Freud's *Todestrieb*, the tendency of all organisms to strive toward a state of absence of irritability and finally 'the death-like repose of the inorganic world.'" I find it fascinating from a literary critical standpoint to note what I think has not been noted, that the essay on narcissism turns upon catastrophe theory also. Freud turns to poetry, here to Heine, in order to illustrate the psychogenesis of Eros, but the lines he quotes actually state a psychogenesis of creativity rather than of love:

> . . . whence does that necessity arise that urges our mental life to pass
> on beyond the limits of narcissism and to attach the libido to
> objects? The answer which would follow from our line of thought
> would once more be that we are so impelled when the cathexis of

the ego with libido exceeds a certain degree. A strong egoism is a protection against disease, but in the last resort we must begin to love in order that we may not fall ill, and must fall ill if, in consequence of frustration, we cannot love. Somewhat after this fashion does Heine conceive of the psychogenesis of the creation:

Krankheit ist wohl der letzte Grund
Des ganzen Schöpferdrangs gewesen;
Erschaffend konnte ich genesen,
Erschaffend wurde ich gesund.

To paraphrase Heine loosely, illness is the ultimate ground of the drive to create, and so while creating the poet sustains relief, and by creating the poet becomes healthy. Freud transposes from the catastrophe of creativity to the catastrophe of falling in love, a transposition to which I will return in the final pages of this chapter.

Beyond the Pleasure Principle, like the essay on narcissism, is a discourse haunted by images (some of them repressed) of catastrophe. Indeed, what Freud verges upon showing is that to be human is a catastrophic condition. The coloring of this catastrophe, in Freud, is precisely Schopenhauerian rather than, say, Augustinian or Pascalian. It is as though, for Freud, the Creation and the Fall had become one and the same event. Freud holds back from this abyss of Gnosticism by reducing mythology to psychology, but since psychology and cosmology have been intimately related throughout human history, this reduction is not altogether persuasive. Though he wants to show us that the daemonic is "really" the compulsion to repeat, Freud tends rather to the "uncanny" demonstration that repetition-compulsion reveals many of us to be daemonic or else makes us daemonic. Again, Freud resorts to the poets for illustration, and again the example goes beyond the Freudian interpretation. Towards the close of section III of *Beyond the Pleasure Principle,* Freud looks for a supreme instance of "people all of whose human relationships have the same outcome" and he finds it in Tasso:

... The most moving poetic picture of a fate such as this is given by Tasso in his romantic epic *Gerusalemme Liberata.* Its hero, Tancred, unwittingly kills his beloved Clorinda in a duel while she is disguised in the armor of an enemy knight. After her burial he makes his way into a strange magic forest which strikes the Crusaders' army with terror. He slashes with his sword at a tall tree; but blood streams from the cut and the voice of Clorinda, whose soul is imprisoned in the tree, is heard complaining that he has wounded his beloved once again.

Freud cites this episode as evidence to support his assumption "that there really does exist in the mind a compulsion to repeat which overrides the pleasure principle." The repetition in Tasso is not just incremental, but rather is qualitative, in that the second wounding is "uncanny" or Sublime, and the first is merely accidental. Freud's citation is an allegory of Freud's own passage into the Sublime. When Freud writes (and the italics are his): "*It seems, then, that a drive is an urge inherent in organic life to restore an earlier state of things,*" then he slays his beloved trope of "drive" by disguising it in the armor of his enemy, mythology. But when he writes (and again the italics are his): "*the aim of all life is death,*" then he wounds his figuration of "drive" in a truly Sublime or "uncanny" fashion. In the qualitative leap from the drive to restore pure anteriority to the apothegm that life's purpose is death, Freud himself has abandoned the empirical for the daemonic. It is the literary authority of the daemonic rather than the analytical which makes plausible the further suggestion that

... sadism is in fact a death instinct which, under the influence of the narcissistic libido, has been forced away from the ego. ...

This language is impressive, and it seems to me equally against literary tact to accept it or reject it on any supposed biological basis. Its true basis is that of an implicit catastrophe theory of meaning or interpretation, which is in no way weakened by being circular and therefore mythological. The repressed rhetorical formula of Freud's discourse in *Beyond the Pleasure Principle* can be stated thus: *literal meaning equals anteriority equals an earlier state of meaning equals an earlier state of things equals death equals literal meaning.* Only one escape is possible from such a formula, and it is a simpler formula: *Eros equals figurative meaning.* This is the dialectic that informs the proudest and most moving passage in

Beyond the Pleasure Principle, which comprises two triumphant sentences *contra* Jung that were added to the text in 1921, in a Sublime afterthought:

> Our views have from the very first been *dualistic,* and today they are even more definitely dualistic than before – now that we describe the opposition as being, not between ego-instincts and sexual instincts, but between life instincts and death instincts. Jung's libido theory is on the contrary *monistic;* the fact that he has called his one instinctual force "libido" is bound to cause confusion, but need not affect us otherwise.

I would suggest that we read *dualistic* here as a trope for "figurative" and *monistic* as a trope for "literal." The opposition between life drives and death drives is not just a dialectic (though it *is* that) but is a great writer's Sublime interplay between figurative and literal meanings, whereas Jung is exposed as being what he truly was, a mere literalizer of anterior mythologies. What Freud proclaims here, in the accents of sublimity, is the power of his own mind over language, which in this context *is* the power that Hegelians or Lacanians legitimately could term "negative thinking."

I am pursuing Freud as prose-poet of the Sublime, but I would not concede that I am losing sight of Freud as analytical theorist. Certainly the next strong Freudian text is the incomparable *Inhibitions, Symptoms, and Anxiety* of 1926. But before considering that elegant and somber meditation, certainly the most illuminating analysis of anxiety our civilization has been offered, I turn briefly to Freud's essay on his dialectic, *Negation* (1925).

Freud's audacity here has been little noted, perhaps because he packs into fewer than five pages an idea that cuts a considerable gap into his theory of repression. The gap is wide enough so that such oxymorons as "a successful repression" and "an achieved anxiety," which are not possible in psychoanalysis, are made available to us as literary terms. Repressed images or thoughts, by Freudian definition, *cannot* make their way into consciousness, yet their content can, on condition that it is *denied.* Freud cheerfully splits head from heart in the apprehension of images:

> Negation is a way of taking account of what is repressed; indeed, it is actually a removal of the repression, though not, of course, an acceptance of what is repressed. It is to be seen how the intellectual function is here distinct from the affective process. Negation only assists in undoing *one* of the consequences of repression – namely, the fact that the subject-matter of the image in question is unable to enter consciousness. The result is a kind of intellectual acceptance of what is repressed, though in all essentials the repression persists. . . .

I would venture one definition of the literary Sublime (which to me seems always a negative Sublime) as being that mode in which the poet, while expressing previously repressed thought, desire, or emotion, is able to continue to defend himself against his own created image by disowning it, a defense of *un-naming* it rather than *naming* it. Freud's word *Verneinung* means both a grammatical negation and a psychic disavowal or denial, and so the linguistic and the psychoanalytical have a common origin here, as Lacan and his school have insisted. The ego and the poet-in-his-poem both proceed by a kind of "misconstruction," a defensive process that Lacan calls *méconnaissance* in psychoanalysis, and that I have called "misprision" in the study of poetic influence (a notion formulated before I had read Lacan, but which I was delighted to find supported in him). In his essay *Aggressivity in Psychoanalysis* Lacan usefully connects Freud's notion of a "negative" libido to the idea of Discord in Heraclitus. Freud himself brings his essay on *Verneinung* to a fascinating double conclusion. First, the issue of truth or falsehood in language is directly related to the defenses of introjection and projection; a true image thus would be introjected and a false one projected. Second, the defense of introjection is aligned to the Eros-drive of affirmation, "while negation, the derivative of expulsion, belongs to the instinct of destruction," the drive to death beyond the pleasure principle. I submit that what Freud has done here should have freed literary discussion from its persistent over-literalization of his idea of repression. Freud joins himself to the tradition of the Sublime, that is, of the strongest Western poetry, by showing us that negation allows poetry to free itself from the aphasias and hysterias of repression, *without* however freeing the poets them-

selves from the unhappier human consequences of repression.
Negation is of *no* therapeutic value for the individual, but it *can*
liberate him into the linguistic freedoms of poetry and thought.

I think that of all Freud's books, none matches the work on
inhibitions, symptoms and anxiety in its potential importance for
students of literature, for this is where the concept of defense is
ultimately clarified. Wollheim says that Freud confused the issue
of defense by the "overschematic" restriction of repression to a
single species of defense, but this is one of the very rare instances
where Wollheim seems to me misled or mistaken. Freud's revised
account of anxiety *had* to distinguish between *relatively* non-repressive and the more severely repressive defenses, and I only wish
that both Freud and his daughter after him had been even more
schematic in mapping out the defenses. We need a rhetoric of the
psyche, and here the Lacanians have been a kind of disaster, with
their simplistic over-reliance upon the metaphor/metonymy distinction. Freud's revised account of anxiety is precisely at one with
the poetic Sublime, for anxiety is finally seen as a technique for
mastering anteriority by *remembering* rather than *repeating* the past.
By showing us that anxiety is a mode of expectation, closely
resembling desire, Freud allows us to understand why poetry,
which loves love, also seems to love anxiety. Literary and human
romance both are exposed as being anxious quests that could not
bear to be cured of their anxieties, even if such cures were possible. "An increase of excitation underlies anxiety," Freud tells us,
and then he goes on to relate this increase to a repetition of the
catastrophe of human birth, with its attendant trauma. Arguing
against Otto Rank, who like Ferenczi had gone too far into the
abysses of catastrophe-theory, Freud enunciated a principle that
can help explain why the terror of the literary Sublime must and
can give pleasure:

> Anxiety is an affective state which can of course be experienced
> only by the ego. The id cannot be afraid, as the ego can; it is not an
> organization, and cannot estimate situations of danger. On the con-
> trary, it is of extremely frequent occurrence that processes are initiat-
> ed or executed in the id which give the ego occasion to develop anxi-
> ety; as a matter of fact, the repressions which are probably the earli-

> est are motivated, like the majority of all later ones, by such fear on
> the part of the ego of this or that process in the id. . . .

Freud's writing career was to conclude with the polemical
assertion that "mysticism is the obscure self-perception of the
realm outside the ego, of the id," which is a splendid farewell
thrust at Jung, as we can see by substituting "Jung" for "the id" at
the close of the sentence. The id perceiving the id is a parody of
the Sublime, whereas the ego's earliest defense, its primal repression, is the true origin of the Sublime. Freud knew that "primal
repression" was a necessary fiction, because without some initial
fixation his story of the psyche could not begin. Laplanche and
Pontalis, writing under Lacan's influence in their *The Language of
Psychoanalysis,* find the basis of fixation

> in primal moments at which certain privileged ideas are indelibly
> inscribed in the unconscious, and at which the instinct itself
> becomes fixated to its psychical representative – perhaps by this very
> process constituting itself *qua* instinct.

If we withdrew that "perhaps," then we would return to the
Freudian catastrophe-theory of the genesis of all drives, with
fixation now being regarded as another originating catastrophe.
How much clearer these hypotheses become if we transpose them
into the realm of poetry! If fixation becomes the inscription in
the unconscious of the privileged idea of a Sublime poet, or
strong precursor, then the drive towards poetic expression origi-
nates in an agonistic repression, where the agon or contest is set
against the pattern of the precursor's initial fixation upon an
anterior figure. Freud's mature account of anxiety thus concludes
itself upon an allegory of origins, in which the creation of an
unconscious implicitly models itself upon poetic origins. There
was repression, Freud insists, before there was anything to be
repressed. This insistence is neither rational nor irrational; it is
a figuration that knows its own status as figuration, without
embarrassment.

My final text in Freud is *Analysis Terminable and Interminable.*
The German title, *Die Endliche und die Unendliche Analyse,* might
better be translated as "finite or indefinite analysis," which is

Lacan's suggestion. Lacan amusingly violates the taboo of discussing how long the analytic session is to be when he asks:

> . . . how is this time to be measured? Is its measure to be that of what Alexander Koyré calls "the universe of precision"? Obviously we live in this universe, but its advent for man is relatively recent, since it goes back precisely to Huyghens' clock – in other words, to 1659 – and the *malaise* of modern man does not exactly indicate that this precision is in itself a liberating factor for him. Are we to say that this time, the time of the fall of heavy bodies, is in some way sacred in the sense that it corresponds to the time of the stars as they were fixed in eternity by God who, as Lichtenberg put it, winds up our sundials?

I reflect, as I read Lacan's remarks, that it was just after Huyghens's clock that Milton began to compose *Paradise Lost,* in the early 1660's, and that Milton's poem is *the* instance of the modern Sublime. It is in *Paradise Lost* that temporality fully becomes identified with anxiety, which makes Milton's epic the most Freudian text ever written, far closer to the universe of psychoanalysis than much more frequently cited works, in Freudian contexts, as *Oedipus Tyrannus* and *Hamlet.* We should remember that before Freud used a Virgilian tag as epigraph for *The Interpretation of Dreams* (1908), he had selected a great Satanic utterance for his motto:

> Seest thou yon dreary plain, forlorn and wild,
> The seat of desolation, void of light,
> Save what the glimmering of these livid flames
> Casts pale and dreadful? Thither let us tend
> From off the tossing of these fiery waves,
> There rest, if any rest can harbour there,
> And reassembling our afflicted powers,
> Consult how we may henceforth most offend
> Our enemy, our own loss how repair,
> How overcome this dire calamity,
> What reinforcement we may gain from hope;
> If not, what resolution from despair.

This Sublime passage provides a true motto for all psychoanalysis, since "afflicted powers" meant "cast-down powers," or as Freud would have said, "repressed drives." But it would be an even apter epigraph for the essay on finite and indefinite analysis than it could have been for the much more hopeful *Interpretation of Dreams*, thirty years before. Freud begins his somber and beautiful late essay by brooding sardonically on the heretic Otto Rank's scheme for speeding up analysis in America. But this high humor gives way to the melancholy of considering every patient's deepest resistance to the analyst's influence, that "negative transference" in which the subject's anxiety-of-influence seeks a bulwark. As he reviews the main outlines of his theory, Freud emphasizes its *economic* aspects rather than the dynamic and topographical points of view. The *economic* modifies any notion that drives have an energy that can be measured. To estimate the magnitude of such excitation is to ask the classical, agonistic question that *is* the Sublime, because the Sublime is always a comparison of two forces or beings, in which the agon turns on the answer to three queries: more? equal to? or less than? Satan confronting hell, the abyss, the new world, is still seeking to answer the questions that he sets for himself in heaven, all of which turn upon comparing God's force and his own. Oedipus confronting the Sphinx, Hamlet facing the mystery of the dead father, and Freud meditating upon repression are all in the same economic stance. I would use this shared stance to re-define a question that psychoanalysis by its nature cannot answer. Since there is *no* biological warrant for the Freudian concept of libido, what is the energy that Freud invokes when he speaks from the economic point of view? Wollheim, always faithful to empiricism, has only one comment upon the economic theory of the mind, and it is a very damaging observation:

> ... though an economic theory allows one to relate the damming up of energy or frustration at one place in the psychic apparatus with discharge at another, it does not commit one to the view that, given frustration, energy will seek discharge along all possible channels indifferently. Indeed, if the system is of any complexity, an economic theory would be virtually uninformative unless some measure of selectivity in discharge was postulated. ...

But since Freud applied the economic stance to sexual drives almost entirely, no measure of selectivity *could* be postulated. This still leaves us with Freud's economic obsessions, and I suggest now that their true model was literary, and not sexual. This would mean that the "mechanisms of defense" are dependent for their formulaic coherence upon the traditions of rhetoric, and not upon biology, which is almost too easily demonstrable. It is hardly accidental that Freud, in this late essay which is so much his *summa,* resorts to the textual analogue when he seeks to distinguish repression from other defenses:

> Without pressing the analogy too closely we may say that repression is to the other methods of defense what the omission of words or passages is to the corruption of a text. . . . For quite a long time flight and an avoidance of a dangerous situation serve as expedients. . . . But one cannot flee from oneself and no flight avails against danger from within; hence the ego's defensive mechanisms are condemned to falsify the inner perception, so that it transmits to us only an imperfect and travestied picture of our id. In its relations with the id the ego is paralysed by its restrictions or blinded by its errors. . . .

What is Freud's motive for this remarkably clear and eloquent recapitulation of his theory of repression and defense (which I take to be the center of his greatness)? The hidden figuration in his discourse here is his economics of the psyche, a trope which is allowed an overt exposure when he sadly observes that the energy necessary to keep such defenses going "proves a heavy burden on the psychical economy." If I were reading this essay on finite and indefinite analysis as I have learned to read Romantic poems, I would be on the watch for a blocking-agent in the poetic ego, a shadow that Blake called the Spectre and Shelley a daemon or *Alastor.* This shadow would be an anxiety narcissistically intoxicated with itself, an anxiety determined to go on being anxious, a drive towards destruction in love with the image of self-destruction. Freud, like the great poets of quest, has given all the premonitory signs of this Sublime terror determined to maintain itself, and again like the poets he suddenly makes the pattern quite explicit:

> The crux of the matter is that the mechanisms of defense against former dangers recur in analysis in the shape of *resistances* to cure. It follows that the ego treats recovery itself as a new danger.

Faced by the patient's breaking of the psychoanalytic com-
pact, Freud broods darkly on the war between his true Sublime
and the patient's false Sublime:

> Once more we realize the importance of the quantitative factor
> and once more we are reminded that analysis has only certain limit-
> ed quantities of energy which it can employ to match against the hos-
> tile forces. And it does seem as if victory were really for the most part
> with the big battalions.

It is a true challenge to the interpreter of Freud's text to
identify the economic stance here, for what is the source of *the
energy of analysis,* however limited in quantity it may be?
Empiricism, whether in Hume or in Wittgenstein, does not discourse on the measurement of its own libido. But if we take Freud
as Sublime poet rather than empirical reasoner, if we see him as
the peer of Milton rather than of Hume, of Proust rather than of
the biologists, then we can speculate rather precisely about the
origins of the psychoanalytical drive, about the nature of the powers made available by the discipline that one man was able to
establish in so sublimely solitary a fashion. Vico teaches us that
the Sublime or severe poet discovers the origin of his rhetorical
drive, the catastrophe of his creative vocation, in *divination,* by
which Vico meant both the process of foretelling dangers to the
self's survival and the apotheosis of becoming a daemon or sort of
god. What Vico calls "divination" is what Freud calls the primal
instinct of Eros, or that "which strives to combine existing phenomena into ever greater unities." With moving simplicity, Freud
then reduces this to the covenant between patient and analyst,
which he calls "a love of truth." But, like all critical idealisms
about poetry, this idealization of psychoanalysis is an error. No
psychic economy (or indeed *any* economy) can be based upon "a
love of truth." Drives depend upon fictions, because drives *are*
fictions, and we want to know more about Freud's enabling
fictions, which grant to him his Sublime "energy of analysis."

We can acquire this knowledge by a very close analysis of the
final section of Freud's essay, a section not the less instructive for
being so unacceptable to our particular moment in social and cultural history. The resistance to analytical cure, in both men and

women, is identified by Freud with what he calls the "repudiation of femininity" *by both sexes,* the castration complex that informs the fantasy-life of everyone whatsoever: ". . . in both cases it is the attitude belonging to the sex opposite to the subject's own which succumbs to repression." This is followed by Freud's prophetic lament, with its allusion to the burden of Hebraic prophecy. Freud too sees himself as the *nabi* who speaks to the winds, to the winds only, for only the winds will listen:

> . . . At no point in one's analytic work does one suffer more from the oppressive feeling that all one's efforts have been in vain and from the suspicion that one is "talking to the winds" than when one is trying to persuade a female patient to abandon her wish for a penis on the ground of its being unrealizable, or to convince a male patient that a passive attitude towards another man does not always signify castration and that in many relations in life it is indispensable. The rebellious over-compensation of the male produces one of the strongest transference-resistances. A man will not be subject to a father-substitute or owe him anything and he therefore refuses to accept his cure from the physician. . . .

It is again one of Lacan's services to have shown us that this is figurative discourse, even if Lacan's own figurative discourse becomes too baroque a commentary upon Freud's wisdom here. Freud prophesies to the winds because men and women cannot surrender their primal fantasies, which are their poor but desperately prideful myths of their own origins. We cannot let go of our three fundamental fantasies: the primal scene, which accounts for our existence; the seduction fantasy, which justifies our narcissism; and the castration complex, which explains to us the mystery of sexual differentiation. What the three fantasy-scenes share is the fiction of an originating catastrophe, and so a very close relation to the necessity for defense. The final barrier to Freud's heroic labor of healing, in Freud's own judgment, is the human imagination. The original wound in man cannot be healed, as it is in Hegel, by the same force that makes the wound.

Freud became a strong poet of the Sublime because he made the solitary crossing from a realm where effect is always traced to a cause, to a mode of discourse which asked instead the economic and agonistic questions of comparison. The question of how an emptiness came about was replaced by the question that asks: more, less, or equal to? which is the agonistic self-questioning of the Sublime. The attempt to give truer names to the rhetoric of human defense was replaced by the increasing refusal to name the vicissitudes of drive except by un-namings as old as those of Empedocles and Heraclitus. The ambition to make of psychoanalysis a wholly positive *praxis* yielded to a skeptical and ancient awareness of a rugged negativity that informed every individual fantasy.

Lacan and his school justly insist that psychoanalysis has contributed nothing to biology, despite Freud's wistful hopes that it could, and also that the life sciences inform psychoanalysis hardly at all, again in despite of Freud's eager scientism. Psychoanalysis is a varied therapeutic *praxis,* but it is a "science" only in the peculiar sense that literature, philosophy and religion are also *sciences of anxiety.* But this means that no single rhetoric or poetic will suffice for the study of psychoanalysis, any more than a particular critical method will unveil all that needs to be seen in literature. The "French way" of reading Freud, in Lacan, Derrida, Laplanche, and others, is no more a "right" reading than the way of the ego-psychologists Hartmann, Kris, Erikson, and others, which Lacan and his followers wrongly keep insisting is the only "American reading." In this conflict of strong misreadings, partisans of both ways evidently need to keep forgetting what the French at least ought to remember: strong texts become strong by mis-taking all texts anterior to them. Freud has more in common with Proust and Montaigne than with biological scientists, because his interpretations of life and death are mediated always by texts, first by the literary texts of others, and then by his own earlier texts, until at last the Sublime mediation of otherness begins to be performed by his text-in-process. In the *Essays* of Montaigne or Proust's vast novel, this ongoing mediation is clearer than it is in Freud's almost perpetual self-revision, because Freud wrote no definitive, single text; but the canon of Freud's writings shows an increasingly uneasy sense that he had become his own precursor, and that he had begun to defend himself against himself by deliberately audacious arrivals at final positions.

12 Wrestling Sigmund

I begin with a parable, rather than a paradigm, but then I scarcely can distinguish between the two. The parable is Bacon's, and I have brooded on it before, as part of a meditation upon the perpetual (shall we say obsessive?) belatedness of strong poetry:

> The children of time do take after the nature and malice of the father. For as he devoureth his children, so one of them seeketh to devour and suppress the other, while antiquity envieth there should be new additions, and novelty cannot be content to add but it must deface . . .

I doubt that I have been able to add much to that dark observation of Bacon's, but I want again to swerve from it towards my own purposes. I don't read the ghastly image of malicious time devouring us as irony or allegory, but rather as sublime hyperbole, because of the terrible strength of the verb, "devouring." Time is an unreluctant Ugolino, and poems, as I read them, primarily are deliberate lies against that devouring. Strong poems reluctantly know, not Freud's parodistic Primal History Scene *(Totem and Taboo)* but what I have called the Scene of Instruction. Such a scene, itself both parable and paradigm, I have shied away from developing, until now, probably because of my own sense of trespass, my own guilt at having become a Jewish Gnostic after and in spite of an Orthodox upbringing. But without developing such a notion, I cannot go further, and so I must begin with it here.

We all choose our own theorists for the Scene of Instruction, or rather, as Coleridge would have said, we do not find their texts, but are found by them. More often than not, these days, the theorists that advanced sensibilities are found by are the German language fourfold of Marx, Nietzsche, Freud, and Heidegger, but the inevitable precursor for formulating a Scene of Instruction has to be Kierkegaard, allied to Marx and Heidegger, involuntarily, by his antithetical relationship to Hegel. It may be that any Scene of Instruction has to be, rather like Derrida's Scene of Writing, more an unwilling parody of Hegel's quest than of Freud's. But I am content with a misprision of Kierkegaard, while being uneasily aware that his "repetition" is a trope that owes more than he could bear to the Hegelian trope of "mediation."

To talk about paradigms, however parabolically, in the context of poetry and criticism, is to engage the discourse of "repetition," in Kierkegaard's rather than Freud's sense of that term. I haven't ever encountered a useful discursive summary of Kierkegaard's notion, and I myself won't try to provide one, because Kierkegaard's idea of repetition is more trope than concept, and tends to defeat discursiveness. His little book, *Repetition*, is subtitled "An essay in Experimental Psychology," but "experimental" there is the crucial and tricky term, and modifies "psychology" into an odd blend of psychopoetics and theology. Repetition, we are told first, "is recollected forwards" and is "the daily bread which satisfies with benediction." Later, the book's narrator assures us that "repetition is always a transcendence," and indeed is "too transcendent" for the narrator to grasp. The same narrator, Constantine Constantius, wrote a long open letter against a Hegelian misunderstanding of his work, which insisted that true or anxious freedom willed repetition: "it is the task of freedom to see constantly a new side of repetition." Each new side is a "breaking forth," a "transition" or "becoming," and therefore a concept of happening, and not of being. If repetition, in this sense, is always a transition or a crossing, then the power of repetition lies in what its great American theorist, Emerson, called the shooting of a gap or the darting to an aim. Kierkegaard, unlike Emerson, was a Christian, and so his repetition cannot be only a series of transitions; eternity becomes true repetition.

But if we are more interested in poetry than in eternity, we can accept a limited or transitional repetition. We can say, still following the aesthetic stage in Kierkegaard, that Wallace Stevens *is* the repetition of Walt Whitman, or that John Ashbery *is* the repetition of Stevens. In this sense, repetition means the re-creation or revision of a paradigm, but of what paradigm? When a strong poet revises a precursor, he re-enacts a scene that is at once a catastrophe, a romance, and a transference. All three paradigms technically are tainted, though favorably from the perspective of poetry. The catastrophe is also a creation; the romance is incestuous; the transference violates taboo and its ambivalences. Are these three categories or one? What kind of a relational or dialectical event is at once creatively catastrophic, incestuously romantic, and ambivalently a metaphor for a trespass that *works?*

For an instance, I go back to the example of Wallace Stevens, still the poet of our moment. When I was a youngster, the academy view of Stevens was that of a kind of hothouse exquisite, vaguely perfumed, Ronald Firbank grown fat, and transmogrified into a Pennsylvania Dutchman practising insurance in Hartford, Connecticut. Now, in 1981, this vision has its own archaic charm, but thirty years ago it filled me with a young enthusiast's fury. I remember still the incredulous indulgence displayed by one of the masters of Yale New Criticism, now heartbreakingly mourned by me, when I read an essay in his graduate seminar suggesting that the seer of Hartford was the true ephebe of Walt Whitman, one of the roughs, an American. Stevens himself, a few miles up the road then, would have denied his own poetic father, but that after all is the most ancient of stories. I cite here again a small poem by the sane and sacred Walt that even Stevens confesses he had pondered deeply. The poem is called *A Clear Midnight:*

This is thy hour O Soul, thy free flight into the wordless,
Away from books, away from art, the day erased, the lesson done,
Thee fully forth emerging, silent, gazing, pondering the themes
    thou lovest best,
Night, sleep, death and the stars.

The Whitmanian soul, I take it, is the Coleridgean moon, the Arab of *Notes toward a Supreme Fiction*. Perhaps the ocean would have been redundant had it been lined up with night, sleep and death, instead of "the stars," since moon and the tides are so intimately allied in the most pervasive of feminine tropes. We don't need the ocean anyway, since the moon as mother of the months is always the mother proper, Whitman's and our "fierce old mother," moaning for us to return whence we came. The mother's face is the purpose of the poem, as Keats told us implicitly, and Stevens in so many words. But the purpose of the poem, for the poet *qua* person, is Kenneth Burke's purpose, and not my own. The poet *qua* poet is my obsessive concern, and the Scene of Instruction creates the poet as or in a poet.

The Scene of Instruction in Stevens is a very belated phenomenon, and even Whitman's origins, despite all his mystifications, are shadowed by too large an American foreground. A better test for my paradigms is provided by the indubitable beginning of a canonical tradition. The major ancient possibilities are the Yahwist, the strongest writer in the Bible, and Homer. Beside them we can place Freud, whose agon with the whole of anteriority is the largest and most intense of our century. Because Freud has far more in common with the Yahwist than with Homer, I will confine myself here to the two Jewish writers, ancient and modern.

I want to interpret two difficult and haunting texts, each remarkable in several ways, but particularly as a startling manifestation of originality. One goes back to perhaps the tenth century before the Common Era; the other is nearly three thousand years later, and comes in our own time. The first is the story of Wrestling Jacob, and tells how Jacob achieved the name Israel, in Genesis 32:23-32, the author being that anonymous great writer, fully the equal of Homer, whom scholars have agreed to call by the rather Kafkan name of the letter J, or the Yahwist. The second I would call, with loving respect, the story of Wrestling Sigmund, and tells how Freud achieved a theory of the origins of the human sexual drive. As author we necessarily have the only possible modern rival of the Yahwist, Freud himself, the text being mostly the second of the *Three Essays on the Theory of Sexualtiy.*

Here is the text of Jacob's encounter with a daemonic being, as rendered literally by E. A. Speiser in the Anchor Bible (pp. 253–54):

> In the course of that night he got up and, taking his two wives, the two maidservants, and his eleven children, he crossed the ford of the Jabbok. After he had taken them across the stream, he sent over all his possessions. Jacob was left alone. Then some man wrestled with him until the break of dawn. When he saw that he could not prevail over Jacob, he struck his hip at its socket, so that the hip socket was wrenched as they wrestled. Then he said, "Let me go, for it is daybreak." Jacob replied, "I will not let you go unless you bless me." Said the other, "What is your name?" He answered, "Jacob." Said he, "You shall no longer be spoken of as Jacob, but as Israel, for you have striven with beings divine and human, and have prevailed." Then Jacob asked, "Please tell me your name." He replied, "You must not ask my name." With that, he bade him good-by there and then.
>
> Jacob named the site Peniel, meaning, "I have seen God face to face, yet my life has been preserved." The sun rose upon him just as he passed Penuel, limping on his hip.

I shall enhance my reputation for lunatic juxtapositions by citing next to this Sublime passage a cento of grotesque passages from Freud, the first two being from the second *Essay*, "Infantile Sexuality," and the third from *Essay* III, but summarizing the argument of the second *Essay:*

> It was the child's first and most vital activity, his sucking at his mother's breast, or at substitutes for it, that must have familiarized him with this pleasure. The child's lips, in our view, behave like an *erotogenic zone,* and no doubt stimulation by the warm flow of milk is the cause of the pleasurable sensation. The satisfaction of the erotogenic zone is associated, in the first instance, with the satisfaction of the need for nourishment. To begin with, sexual activity props itself upon functions serving the purpose of self-preservation and does not become independent of them until later. No one who has seen a baby sinking back satiated from the breast and falling asleep with flushed cheeks and a blissful smile can escape the reflection that this picture persists as a prototype of the expression of sexual satisfaction in later life. The need for repeating the sexual satisfaction now becomes detached from the need for taking nourishment.

> . . . Our study of thumb-sucking or sensual sucking has already
> given us the three essential characteristics of an infantile sexual man-
> ifestation. At its origin it props itself upon one of the vital somatic
> functions; it has as yet no sexual object, and is thus *auto-erotic;* and its
> sexual aim is dominated by an *erotogenic zone.*
>   . . . At a time at which the first beginnings of sexual satisfaction are
> still linked with the taking of nourishment, the sexual instinct has a
> sexual object outside the infant's own body in the shape of his moth-
> er's breast. It is only later that he loses it, just at the time, perhaps,
> when he is able to form a total idea of the person to whom the organ
> that is giving him satisfaction belongs. As a rule the sexual drive then
> becomes auto-erotic, and not until the period of latency has been
> passed through is the original relation restored. There are thus good
> reasons why a child sucking at his mother's breast has become the
> prototype of every relation of love. The finding of an object is in fact
> a re-finding of it.

Wrestling with a divine being or angel is rather a contrast to sucking at one's mother's breast, and achieving the name Israel is pretty well unrelated to the inauguration of the sexual drive. All that the Yahwist's and Freud's breakthroughs have in common is that they *are* breakthroughs, difficult to assimilate because these curious stories are each so *original.* But before I explore that common difficulty, I need to give a commentary upon each of these passages. What is the nature of Jacob's agon, and what does it mean to see Freud's own agon as being central to his theory of sexual origins?

To consider the Yahwist as being something other than a religious writer would be as eccentric as to consider Freud a religious writer despite himself. But who sets the circumferences? All the academies, from the Academy of Ezra through the Academies of Alexandria on down to our own institutions, have in common their necessity for consensus. The Yahwist may have written to persuade, but he remains hugely idiosyncratic when compared either to the Elohist, who probably came a century after him, or to the much later Priestly Author, who may have belonged to the age of Ezra and the Return from Babylon, some six centuries after the Yahwist. E and P are far more normative than J, and far less original, in every meaning of "original." But I want to specify a particular aspect of J's originality, and it is one that I have never seen discussed as such. We are familiar, since the work of Nietzsche and of Burckhardt, with the ancient Greek concept of the agonistic, but we scarcely recognize an ancient Hebrew notion of agon, which is crucial throughout J's writing. J is an *unheimlich* writer, and perhaps the greatest master of the literary Sublime in what has become Western tradition. But J is also the most remarkable instance of what Blake meant, when in *The Marriage of Heaven and Hell* he characterized the history of all religions as choosing forms of worship from poetic tales. J's poetic tales of Yahweh and the Patriarchs are now so much the staple of Judaism and Christianity, and have been such for so long, that we simply cannot read them. Yet they were and are so original that there is quite another sense in which they never have been read, and perhaps cannot be read. If we allowed them their strangeness, then their uncanniness would reveal that tradition never has been able to assimilate their originality.

Yahweh appears to Abraham by the terebinths of Mamre; Abraham sits at the entrance of his tent as the day grows hot. He looks up, sees three men, one of them Yahweh, whom he recognizes, and invites them for an immediate meal. Yahweh and his angels devour rolls, curd, milk, and roast calf, while Abraham stands nearby. Yahweh then prophesies that Sarah, well past a woman's periods, will have a son. Sarah, listening behind Yahweh's back, at the tent entrance, laughs to herself. Yahweh, offended, asks rhetorically if anything is too much for him. Poor, frightened Sarah says she didn't laugh, but Yahweh answers: "Yes, you did."

What can we do with a Yahweh who sits on the ground, devours calf, is offended by an old woman's sensible derision, and then walks on to Sodom after being argued down by Abraham to a promise that he will spare that wicked city if he finds just ten righteous among the inhabitants? The silliest thing we can do is to say that J has an anthropomorphic concept of god. J doesn't have a concept of Yahweh; indeed we scarcely can say that J even has a conceptual image of Yahweh. J is nothing of a theologian, and everything of a storyteller, and his strong interest is personality, particularly the personality of Jacob. J's interest in Yahweh is intense, but rather less than J's concern for Jacob, because Jacob is cannier and more agonistic even than Yahweh. Yahweh just about *is* the uncanny for J; what counts about Yahweh is that he is the source of the Blessing, and the Blessing is the aim of the agon, in total distinction from the Greek notion of agon.

The contest among the Greeks was for the foremost place, whether in chariot racing, poetry, or civic eminence. The subtle and superb Jacob knows only one foremost place, the inheritance of Abraham and of Isaac, so that tradition will be compelled to speak of the God of Abraham, the God of Isaac, the God of Jacob, the God of Judah. The Blessing means that the nation shall be known as Israel, the name that Jacob wins as agonist, and that the people shall be known as Jews after Judah, rather than say as Reubens, if that first-born had been chosen. Such a blessing achieves a pure temporality, and so the agon for it is wholly temporal in nature, whereas the Greek agon is essentially spatial, a struggle for the foremost place, and so for place, and not a mastery over time. That, I take it, is why temporality is at the center of the nightlong wrestling between Jacob and some nameless one among the Elohim, and I am now ready to describe that most significant of J's visions of agon.

I quote again Speiser's literal version of J's text:

> In the course of that night he got up and, taking his two wives, the two maidservants, and his eleven children, he crossed the ford of the Jabbok. After he had taken them across the stream, he sent over all his possessions. Jacob was left alone. Then some man wrestled with him until the break of dawn. When he saw that he could not prevail over Jacob, he struck his hip at its socket, so that the hip socket was wrenched as they wrestled. Then he said, "Let me go, for it is daybreak." Jacob replied, "I will not let you go unless you bless me." Said the other, "What is your name?" He answered, "Jacob." Said he, "You shall no longer be spoken of as Jacob, but as Israel, for you have striven with beings divine and human, and have prevailed." Then Jacob asked, "Please tell me your name." He replied, "You must not ask my name." With that, he bade him good-by there and then.
>
> Jacob named the site Peniel, meaning, "I have seen God face to

face, yet my life has been preserved." The sun rose upon him just as
he passed Penuel, limping on his hip.

So great is the uncanniness of this that we ought to
approach J with a series of questions, rather than rely upon any
traditional or even modern scholarly commentary whatsoever.
Jacob has left Laban, and is journeying home, uneasily expecting
a confrontation with his defrauded brother Esau. On the night
before this dreaded reunion, Jacob supervises the crossing, into
the land of the Blessing, of his household and goods. But then
evidently he crosses back over the Jabbok so as to remain alone at
Penuel in Transjordan. Why? J does not tell us, and instead suddenly confronts Jacob and the reader with "some man" who wres-
tles with Jacob until the break of dawn. About this encounter,
there is nothing that is other than totally surprising. J's Jacob has
been an agonist literally from his days in Rebecca's womb, but his
last physical contest took place in that womb, when he struggled
vainly with his twin Esau as to which should emerge first, Esau
winning, but dragging out his tenacious brother, whose hand held
on to his heel. Popular etymology interpreted the name Jacob as
meaning "heel." Craft and wiliness have been Jacob's salient characteristics, rather than the physical strength evidently displayed in
this nocturnal encounter. Yet that strength is tropological, and
substitutes for the spiritual quality of persistence or endurance
that marks Jacob or Israel.

Who is that "man," later called one of the Elohim, who wres-
tles with Jacob until dawn? And why should they wrestle anyway?
Nothing in any tradition supports my surmise that this daemonic
being is the Angel of Death, yet such I take him to be. What Jacob
rightly fears is that he will be slain by the vengeful Esau on the
very next day. Something after all is curiously negative and even
fearful about Jacob's opponent. Rabbinical tradition explains this
strange being's fear of the dawn as being an angel's pious fear lest
he be late on Yahweh's business, but here as so often the Rabbis
were weak misreaders of J. Everything about the text shows that
the divine being's dread of daybreak is comparable to Count
Dracula's, and only the Angel of Death is a likely candidate

among the Elohim for needing to move on before sunrise. This wrestling match is not a ballet, but is deadly serious for both contestants. The angel lames Jacob permanently, yet even this cannot subdue the patriarch. Only the blessing, the new naming Israel, which literally means "May God persevere," causes Jacob to let go even as daylight comes. Having prevailed against Esau, Laban and even perhaps against the messenger of death, Jacob deserves the agonistic blessing. In his own renaming of the site as Peniel, or the divine face, Jacob gives a particular meaning to his triumphal declaration that: "I have seen one of the Elohim face to face, and yet my life has been preserved." Seeing Yahweh face to face was no threat to Abraham's life, in J's view, but it is not Yahweh whom Jacob has wrestled to at least a standstill. I think there is no better signature of J's sublimity than the great sentence that ends the episode, with its powerful implicit contrast between Israel and the fled angel. Here is Jacob's true epiphany: "The sun rose upon him just as he passed Penuel, limping on his hip."

If there is an aesthetic originality in our Western tradition beyond interpretive assimilation, then it inheres in J's texts. We do not know Homer's precursors any more than we know J's, yet somehow we can see Homer as a revisionist, whereas J seems more unique. Is this only because Homer has been misread even more strongly than J has? The prophet Hosea is our first certain interpreter of wrestling Jacob, and Hosea was a strong poet, by any standards, yet his text is not adequate to the encounter he describes. But Hosea's Yahweh was a rather more remote entity than J's, and Hosea did not invest himself as personally in Jacob as J seems to have done. What interpretive paradigm can help us read Jacob's contest strongly enough to be worthy of the uncanniness of J, an author who might be said impossibly to combine the antithetical strengths of a Tolstoy and a Kafka?

I recur to the distinction between the Hebrew temporal Sublime agon and the Greek spatial striving for the foremost place. Nietzsche, in his notes for the unwritten "untimely meditation" he would have called *We Philologists,* caught better even than Burckhardt the darker aspects of the Greek agonistic spirit:

> The agonistic element is also the danger in every development; it
> overstimulates that creative impulse . . .
>
> The greatest fact remains always the precociously pan-hellenic
> HOMER. All good things derive from him; yet at the same time he
> remained the mightiest obstacle of all. He made everyone else
> superficial, and that is why the really serious spirits struggled against
> him. But to no avail. Homer always won.
>
> The destructive element in great spiritual forces is also visible
> here. But what a difference between Homer and the Bible as such a
> force!
>
> The delight in drunkenness, delight in cunning, in revenge, in
> envy, in slander, in obscenity – in everything which was *recognized* by
> the Greeks as human and therefore built into the structure of society
> and custom. The wisdom of their institutions lies in the lack of any
> gulf between good and evil, black and white. Nature, as it reveals
> itself, is not denied, but only ordered, limited to specified days and
> religious cults. This is the root of all spiritual freedom in the ancient
> world; the ancients sought a moderate release of natural forces, not
> their destruction and denial . . .
>
> [translated by William Arrowsmith]

Whatever Nietzsche means by "the Bible" in that contrast to
Homer, he is not talking accurately about J, the Bible's strongest
writer. Not that J, with his obsessive, more-than-Miltonic sense of
temporality, essentially agrees with Homer upon what constitutes
spiritual freedom; no, perhaps J is further from Homer in that
regard than even Nietzsche states. J does not discourse in good
and evil, but in blessedness and unblessedness. J's subject, like
Homer's, is strife, including the strife of gods and men. And
drunkenness, delight in cunning, in revenge, in envy, in slander,
in obscenity are at least as much involved in the expression of J's
exuberance as they are of Homer's. But J's temporal nature is not
Homer's spatial realm, and so the agonistic spirit manifests itself
very differently in the linguistic universes of these two masters. In
Homer, the gods transcend nature spatially, but Yahweh's transcendence is temporal. The overcoming of nature by means of the
Blessing must be temporal also. Jacob's temporal victory over one
of the Elohim is a curious kind of creative act which is one and
the same as Jacob's cunning victories over Esau and Laban. In
Greek terms this makes no sense, but in ancient Hebrew thinking

this corresponds to that vision in which Yahweh's creation of the world, his rescue of the Israelites at the Red Sea, and the return of his people from Babylon are all one creative act on his part. Thorleif Boman defines the Hebrew word for eternity, *olam,* as meaning neither otherworldliness nor chronological infinity, but rather time without boundaries. Something like that is the prize for which agonists strive in J. When Jacob becomes Israel, the implication is that his descendants also will prevail in a time without boundaries.

That Jacob is, throughout his life, an agonist, seems beyond dispute, and certainly was the basis for Thomas Mann's strong reading of J's text in the beautiful *Tales of Jacob* volume which is the glory of Mann's Joseph tetralogy. Yet distinguishing Hebrew from Greek agon is not much beyond a starting point in the interpretation of the recalcitrant originality of J's text. Whoever it is among the Elohim, the angel fears a catastrophe, and vainly inflicts a crippling wound upon Jacob, averting one catastrophe at the price of another. And yet, as agonists, the angel and Jacob create a blessing, the name of Israel, a name that celebrates the agonistic virtue of persistence, a persistence into unbounded temporality. That creation by catastrophe is one clear mark of this encounter. Another is the carrying across from Jacob's struggles in earlier life, veritably in the womb, his drive to have priority, where the carrying across is as significant as the drive. If the drive for priority is a version of what Freud has taught us to call family romance, then the conveyance of early zeal and affect into a later context is what Freud has taught us to call transference.

Catastrophe creation, family romance, and transference are a triad equally central to J and to Freud, and in some sense Freud's quest was to replace J and the other biblical writers as the legitimate exemplar of these paradigms. Ambivalence is the common element in the three paradigms, if we define ambivalence strictly as a contradictory stance mixing love and hate towards a particular object. Before returning to Wrestling Jacob, I want to cite the most shocking instance of Yahweh's ambivalence in the Hebrew Bible, an ambivalence manifested towards his particular favorite, Moses. The text is Exodus 4:24-26, translated literally:

> Yahweh encountered Moses when Moses camped at night on his
> way [to Egypt] and Yahweh sought to kill Moses. So Zipporah
> [Moses' wife] cut off her son's foreskin with a flint and touched
> Moses on his legs with it, saying: "Truly you are a bridegroom of
> blood to me." And when Yahweh let Moses alone, she added, "A
> bridegroom of blood due to the circumcision."

Confronted by this passage, normative interpretation has
been very unhappy indeed, since in it the uncanny of originality
has gone beyond all limits. Indeed only Gnostics, ancient and
modern, could be happy with this text, in which the agonistic
seems truly to have crossed over into a really shocking divine mur-
derousness. Whoever it was among the Elohim, even if the Angel
of Death, Jacob undauntedly confronted an agonist. Yet Zipporah
is even more courageous in her rescue of Moses. Perhaps the
Hebraic concept of agon is more extensive even than I have indi-
cated. Consider, though only briefly, the opening of Psalm 19,
which I cite in the extraordinary King James version:

> The heavens declare the glory of God; and the firmament
> showeth his handiwork.
> Day unto day uttereth speech, and night unto night showeth
> knowledge.
> There is no speech nor language, where their voice is not heard.
> Their line is gone out through all the earth, and their words to
> the end of the world. In them hath he set a tabernacle for the sun,
> Which is as a bridegroom coming out of his chamber, and
> rejoiceth as a strong man to run a race.
> His going forth is from the end of the heaven, and his circuit unto
> the ends of it: and there is nothing hid from the heat thereof.

That marvelous fifth verse reverberates in Spenser,
Shakespeare, Milton, and Wordsworth, and is the most curiously
Pindaric moment in the Bible, with the Hebrew agonistic vision
coinciding just this once with the Greek. But against whom is this
rejoicing bridegroom of a sun contending? Not with God but with
man, must be the answer. The Psalmist is far more normative than
the Yahwist. Who could conceive of a Psalm in the uncanny mode
of the Yahwist? One way of arriving at a reading of Wrestling
Jacob's night encounter is to contrast it with the characteristic
stances and attitudes of the poets of Psalms confronting their

Maker. Voices in the Psalms do not demand blessings; they implore. The sun emerges from his chamber like a bridegroom, and rejoicing at his own skill as an agonist, but the sun reflects the glory of God. It is not God's glory but Israel's, meaning Jacob just transformed into Israel, which is celebrated so sublimely by the Yahwist:

> The sun rose upon him just as he passed Penuel, limping on his hip.

What allies Freud to the Yahwist is this agonistic Sublime, as manifested in the power of the uncanny, in what cannot be rendered normative. We might think of the school of Ego Psychology, of Heinz Hartmann, Lowenstein, Kris, and Erikson, as being Psalmists in relation to Freud-as-Yahwist, an analogy that could be continued by describing Lacan and his school as Gnostics. Scenes of Instruction like the agon of Jacob or Yahweh's night attack upon Moses are akin to Freud's fantasies of catastrophe, because the outrage to normative sensibilities is beyond assimilation. Even our difficulties in recovering the uncanny originality of J are matched by our difficulties in acknowledging how peculiar and extreme a writer Freud sometimes compels himself to be, for reasons nearly as unknowable as the Yahwist's motives.

Wittgenstein, who resented Freud, and who dismissed Freud as a mythologist, however powerful, probably was too annoyed with Freud to read him closely. This may explain Wittgenstein's curious mistake in believing that Freud had not distinguished between the Primal Scene and the somewhat later Primal Scene fantasy. Freud's Primal Scene takes place in the beginning, when an infant sees his parents in the act of love, without in any way understanding that sight. Memory, according to Freud, holds on to the image of copulation until the child, between the ages of three and five, creates the Primal Scene fantasy, which is an Oedipal reverie. One of my former students, Cathy Caruth, caught me in making this same error, so that in my literary transformation of Freud into the Primal Scene of Instruction, I referred to such a Primal Scene as being at once oral and written. I would clarify this now by saying that the "oral" scene is the topos or Primal Scene proper, the negative moment of being influenced, a perpetually lost origin, while the "written" scene is the trope or Primal Scene fantasy. This means, in my terms, that in a poem a topos or rhetorical commonplace is *where* something can be *known*, but a trope or inventive turning is *when* something is desired or *willed*. Poems, as I have written often, are verbal utterances that cannot be regarded as being simply linguistic entities, because they manifest their will to utter *within* traditions of uttering, and as soon as you will that "within," your mode is discursive and topological as well as linguistic and tropological. As a Primal Scene, the Scene of Instruction is a Scene of Voicing; only when fantasized or troped does it become a Scene of Writing.

That Scene of Voicing founds itself upon the three models of family romance, transference, and catastrophe creation, and here I assert no novelty in my own formulation, since Dryden for one deals with the family romance of poets in his *Preface to Fables, Ancient and Modern,* with poetic transference in stating his preference for Juvenal over Horace in his *Discourse Concerning . . . Satire,* and even with a kind of catastrophe creation in his *Parallel Betwixt Poetry and Painting.* Dryden's mastery of dialectical contrasts between related poets seems to me now as good a guide for an antithetical practical criticism as I can find. Dryden is dialectical both in the open sense that Martin Price expounds, an empirical testing by trial and error, and also in the antithetical sense in which his description of one poet always points back to the contrasting poet from whom the critic is turning away.

What Dryden and the English tradition cannot provide is a third sense of critical dialectic, which in Freudian or Hegelian terms is the problematic notion of the overdetermination of language, and the consequent underdetermination of meaning. Hegelian terms do not much interest me, even in their Heideggerian and deconstructive revisions, since they seem to me just too far away from the pragmatic workings of poetry. Catastrophe creation, whether in its explicit Gnostic and Kabbalistic versions, or its implicit saga in the later Freud, contributes a model for distinguishing between the meanings of things in non-verbal acts, and the meaning of words in the linguistic and discursive acts of poetry. By uttering truths of desire within traditions of uttering, the poetic will also gives itself a series of overdetermined names. Gnosis and Kabbalah are attempts to explain how the overdetermination of Divine names has brought about an underdetermination of Divine meanings, a bringing about that is at once catastrophe and creation, a movement from fullness to emptiness.

Freud is not only the powerful mythologist Wittgenstein deplored, but also *the* inescapable mythologist of our age. His claims to science should be shrugged aside forever; that is merely his mask. Freudian literary criticism I remember comparing to the Holy Roman Empire: not holy, or Roman, or an empire; not Freudian, or literary, or criticism. Any critic, theoritical or practical, who tries to *use* Freud ends up being used *by* Freud. But Freud has usurped the role of the mind of our age, so that more than forty years after his death we have no common vocabulary for discussing the works of the spirit except what he gave us. Philosophers, hard or soft, speak only to other philosophers; theologians mutter only to theologians; our literary culture speaks to us in the language of Freud, even when the writer, like Nabokov or Borges, is violently anti-Freudian. Karl Kraus, being Freud's contemporary, said that psychoanalysis itself was the disease of which it purported to be the cure. We come after, and we must say that psychoanalysis itself is the culture of which it purports to be the description. If psychoanalysis and our literary culture no longer can be distinguished, then criticism is Freudian whether it wants to be or not. It relies upon Freudian models even while it pretends to be in thrall to Plato, Aristotle, Coleridge, or Hegel, and all that I urge is that it achieve a clearer sense of its bondage.

Freudian usurpation as a literary pattern is uniquely valuable to critics because it is *the* modern instance of poetic strength, of the agonistic clearing-away of cultural rivals, until the Freudian tropes have assumed the status of priority, while nearly all precedent tropes seem quite belated in comparison. When we think of earliness we now think in terms of primal repression, of the unconscious, of primary process, and of the drives or instincts, and all these are Freud's figurative language in his literary project of representing the civil wars of the psyche. The unconscious turns out alas not to be structured like *a* language, but to be structured like *Freud's* language, and the ego and superego, in their conscious aspects, are structured like Freud's own texts, for the very good reason that they *are* Freud's texts. We have become Freud's texts, and the *Imitatio Freudi* is the necessary pattern for the spiritual life in our time.

Ferenczi, a great martyr of that *Imitatio,* urged us in his apocalyptic *Thalassa*

> to drop once and for all the question of the beginning and end of life, and conceive the whole inorganic and organic world as a perpetual oscillating between the will to live and the will to die in which an absolute hegemony on the part of either life or death is never attained . . . it seems as though life had always to end catastrophically, even as it began, in birth, with a catastrophe . . .

Ferenczi is following yet also going beyond Freud's apocalyptic *Beyond the Pleasure Principle,* where the Nirvana Principle or Death Drive is described as an *"urge inherent in organic life to restore an earlier state of things* which the living entity has been obliged to abandon under the pressure of external disturbing forces."* Such an urge, Freud insists, takes priority over the Pleasure Principle, and so *"the aim of all life is death."* Three years later, in *The Ego and the Id,* Freud speculated upon the two aboriginal catastrophes dimly repeated in every human development under the ill-starred dominance of the death-drive. Our curious pattern of sexual development, particularly the supposed latency period between the ages of five and twelve, is related to those great cataclysms when all the cosmos became ice and again when the oceans went dry and life scrambled up upon the shore. These are Freud's scientistic versions of the Gnostic escapades of the Demiurge, or the great trope of the Breaking of the Vessels in the Lurianic Kabbalah.

But why should Freud have been haunted by images of catastrophe, however creative? It is not, I think, hyperbolic to observe that, for the later Freud, human existence is quite as catastrophic a condition as it was for Pascal and for Kierkegaard, for Dostoevsky and for Schopenhauer. There is a crack in everything that God has made, is one of Emerson's cheerful apothegms. In Freud, the fissure in us between primary process and secondary process insures that each of us is her or his own worst enemy, exposed endlessly to the remorseless attacks of the superego, whose relation to the hapless ego is shockingly like the Gnostic vision of the relation of Yahweh to human beings.

The horror of the family romance, as Freud expounds it, is one version of this human fissure, since the child attempts to trope one of the stances of freedom, yet makes the parents into the numinous shadows that Nietzsche called ancestor gods. As a revision of the Primal Scene, the family romance's falsification shows us that Oedipal fantasies are only ironies, or beginning moments merely, for truly strong poets and poems. This limitation makes the family romance a model neither catastrophic nor creative enough, and gives us the necessity for advancing to another model, the psychoanalytic transference, whose workings are closer to the dialectical crises of poetic texts.

The Freudian transference, as I have attempted to demonstrate elsewhere, depends for its pattern upon the sublimely crazy myth that Freud sets forth in *Totem and Taboo*. Briefly and crudely, the totem is the psychoanalyst and the taboo is the transference. All the ambivalences of the Oedipal situation are transferred from the individual's past to the analytic encounter, and the agon thus threatens to act out again the erotic defeat and tragedy of every psyche whatsoever. Against this threat, Freud sought to muster the strength of what he called "working through" but his beautiful late essay, "Analysis Terminable and Interminable," confesses that the benign powers of the totemic analyst tend to be confounded by the malign intensity of each patient's fantasy-making power. Working-through is replaced by repetition, and so by the death-drive, which deeply contaminates all repressive defenses. This mutual contamination of drive and defense is the clearest link between Freud's visionary cosmos and the arena of Post-Enlightenment poetry. Contamination is not a trope but the necessary condition of all troping (or all defending); another word for contamination here might be "blurring" or even "slipping." There may be boundaries between the ego and the id, but they blur always in the transference situation, just as poet and precursor slip together in the Scene of Instruction or influence relationship.

I am suggesting that neither my use of Freud's images of Oedipal ambivalence, nor those images themselves, are generally read strongly enough. Identification in the Oedipal agon is not the introjection of the paternal superego but rather is a violent narcissistic metamorphosis. I rely here upon a formulation by the psychoanalyst Joseph H. Smith:

> The poet as poet is taken over by a power with which he has chosen to wrestle. It is not essentially a matter of passivity. The experience of a negative moment that coincides with the negative moment of a precursor is to be understood as an achieved catastrophe. It reaches beyond the ordinary understanding of oedipal identification to those primal internalizations which are and yet cannot be because no boundary is yet set across which anything could be said to be internalized. They are, rather, boundary-establishing phenomena which presuppose the possibility of internalization proper. But who is to say that there is not such a reestablishment of boundaries even in oedipal identifications?

I would go further than Smith in suggesting that every ambivalent identification with another self, writer or reader, parent or child, is an agon that makes ghostlier the demarcations between self and other. That blurring or slipping creates, in that it restores the abyss in the Gnostic sense, where the abyss is the true, alien godhead that fell away into time when the Demiurge sickened to a catastrophic false creation. The transference shakes the foundations of the ego more authentically than the family romance does, even though the transference is an artificial Eros and the family romance a natural one. After all, the transference, like a poem, is a lie against time, a resistance that must be overcome if we are to accept unhappy truth. Let us call a transference a kind of parody of a Sublime poem, since the taboo protects the totem analyst from the patient, yet no taboo can protect a precursor poet from the fresh strength or daemonic counter-sublime of an authentic new poet. To call a transference a parody of a poem is to suggest that catastrophe creations and family romances are also parodies of poetic texts. How can a parody be a model or paradigm for interpretation? We are accustomed to thinking of poems as parodies of prior poems, or even as parodies of paradigms. Yet reversing the order gets us closer, I am convinced, to the actualities of poetic interpretation.

Yeats wrote that "Plato thought nature but a spume that plays / Against a ghostly paradigm of things." Freud thought of nature very differently, yet he had his own version of a transcendentalism, in what he called "reality testing." Yet his paradigms for object attachments play uncanny tricks upon nature, or perhaps rely upon the uncanny tricks that nature seems to play with human sexuality. I go back here to the passages I quoted from the *Three Essays on the Theory of Sexuality* earlier in this chapter. The child sucking at his mother's breast becomes the paradigm for all sexual pleasure in later life, and Freud asserts that to begin with, sexual activity props itself upon the vital function of nourishment by the mother's milk. Thumb-sucking and the sensual smacking of the lips then give Freud the three characteristics of infantile sexual manifestation. These are: (1) Propping, at the origin, upon a vital somatic function; (2) auto-eroticism, or the lack of a sexual object; (3) domination of sexual aim by an erotogenic zone; here, the lips. It is at this point in his discussion that Freud makes one of his uncanniest leaps, relying upon his extraordinary trope of *Anlehnung* or propping (or anaclisis, as Strachey oddly chose to translate it). While the propping of the sexual drive upon the vital order still continues, the sexual drive finds its first object outside the infant's body in the mother's breast, and in the milk ensuing from it. Suddenly Freud surmises that just at the time the infant is capable of forming a total idea of the mother, quite abruptly the infant loses the initial object of the mother's breast, and tragically is thrown back upon auto-eroticism. Consequently, the sexual drive has no proper object again until after the latency period has transpired, and adolescence begins. Hence that dark and infinitely suggestive Freudian sentence: "The finding of an object is in fact a re-finding of it."

Thus human sexuality, alas, on this account has not had, from its very origins, any real object. The only real object was milk, which belongs to the vital order. Hence the sorrows and the authentic anguish of all human erotic quest, hopelessly seeking to rediscover an object, which never was the true object anyway. All human sexuality is thus tropological, whereas we all of us desperately need and long for it to be literal. As for sexual excitation, it is merely what Wrestling Sigmund terms a marginal effect *(Nebenwirkung)*, because it reflects always the propping process, which after all has a double movement, of initial leaning, and then deviation or swerving. As Laplanche says, expounding Freud: "Sexuality in its entirety is in the slight deviation, the *clinamen* from the function." Or as I would phrase it, our sexuality is in its very origins a misprision, a strong misreading, on the infant's part, of the vital order. At the crossing (Laplanche calls it a "breaking or turning point") of the erotogenic zones, our sexuality is a continual crisis, which I would now say is not so much mimicked or parodied by the High Romantic crisis poem, but rather our sexuality itself is a mimicry or parody of the statelier action of the will which is figured forth in the characteristic Post-Enlightenment strong poem.

I call Freud, in the context of these uncanny notions, "Wrestling Sigmund," because again he is a poet of Sublime agon, here an agon between sexuality and the vital order. Our sexuality is like Jacob, and the vital order is like that one among the Elohim with whom our wily and heroic ancestor wrestled, until he had won the great name of Israel. Sexuality and Jacob triumph, but at the terrible expense of a crippling. All our lives long we search in vain, unknowingly, for the lost object, when even that object was a *clinamen* away from the true aim. And yet we search incessantly, do experience satisfactions, however marginal, and win our real if limited triumph over the vital order. Like Jacob, we keep passing Penuel, limping on our hips.

How can I conclude? Paradigms are not less necessary, but more so, when the power and the originality of strong poets surpass all measure, as Freud and the Yahwist go beyond all comparison. Sexuality, in Freud's great tropological vision, is at once a catastrophe creation, a transference, and a family romance. The blessing, in the Yahwist's even stronger vision, is yet more a catastrophe creation, a transference, a family romance. Those strategems of the spirit, those stances and attitudes, those positions of freedom, or ratios of revision and crossings, that I have invoked as aids to reading strong poems of the Post-Enlightenment, are revealed as being not wholly inadequate to the interpretation of the Yahwist and of Freud. So I conclude with the assertion that strength demands strength. If we are to break through normative or weak misreadings of the Yahwist and of Freud, of Wordsworth and Whitman and Stevens, then we require strong paradigms, and these I have called upon agonistic tradition to provide.

13 From Sensibility to Romanticism: Collins's "Ode to Fear"

Doubtless there are many perspectives that could reveal to us the essential continuities between four apparently disjunctive entities: the topics of classical rhetoric, the ideas of Associationist psychology, the tropes of High Romantic poetry, the mechanisms of defense named by Sigmund Freud and eventually codified by his daughter Anna. But I have only my own perspective to offer, and I seek here to develop certain critical notions that have obsessed me in a series of works, culminating in an essay called "Poetic Crossing," to be found as a coda to my book on Stevens. Much that I have to say will be rather technical, but at least it will not be dry. I propose to take William Collins's "Ode to Fear" and to read it rhetorically and psychologically, so as to contrast within it the representations of two related but distinct poetic modes, Sensibility (as Northrop Frye suggested we call it) and Romanticism.

The "Ode to Fear," a remarkable poem by any standards, is perhaps too Spenserian in its diction, and too Miltonic in its procedures, to sustain its own implicit prayer for originality, its own yearnings for strength. Collins was a very learned young poet of real genius, and he seems to have intuited how few years of sanity and control would be available to him. His "Ode to Fear" is a daemonic exercise, a desperate gamble with his poetic limits that rightly reminds us how attractive he was to Coleridge and to Hart Crane, poets who shared his temperament and his ambitions. The

modern critical theorist who best illuminates daemonic or
Sublime poetry is Angus Fletcher, both in his remarkable early
book, *Allegory* (1964), and in his more recent essays on threshold
rhetoric and personification. But before I expound Fletcher's liminal visions, I need to say something about the puzzling gap
between the poets, in their advanced conceptions of rhetoric and
psychology, and the critics of later eighteenth- and early nineteenth-century Britain.

We are currently in a literary situation where much critical
theory and *praxis* is more on the frontier than most of our best
poetry tends to be, a situation infrequent though hardly unique
in the history of culture. The criticism and formal psychology of
the Age of Sensibility and of Romantic times lagged considerably
behind the experiments of Collins and of Shelley. When I began
to write criticism, in the middle fifties, it seemed to me that
Wallace Stevens was well out in front of available criticism, though
not of the speculations of Freud. We are catching up to Stevens,
and perhaps we begin to see precisely what Freud was *not* doing,
anyway. Collins implicitly had a Miltonic theory of imagination, as
presumably the commentaries on Aristotle that he wished to write
would have shown. But what marks both British psychology and
literary theory from the mid-1740's down to (and beyond) the
time of Coleridge is its conservatism. Hazlitt is a formidable
exception, and his theories helped to free Keats from some of the
inadequacies of British intellectual tradition, but the main story is
elsewhere, with Wordsworth and Coleridge, where the puzzles of
the relation between thought and art are still just beyond the analytical range of our critical scholarship.

Dr. Johnson, who wrote of Collins with personal warmth but
lack of critical discernment (rather like Allen Tate on Hart
Crane) was of course the strong critic contemporary with Collins's
experiments in the ode. With his Neoclassic bias, Johnson was
critically just not what Collins needed, though humanly the compassionate and sensible Johnson did Collins much good.
Poetically, I would say, Collins needed a vital critic to tell him that
the trope for time, particularly *literary* time, could be only irony or
else metalepsis (also called transumption) and Collins was delib-

erately one of the least ironic of all gifted poets. He needed a critic rather like Angus Fletcher, who is discussing Coleridge in the
passages I am about to quote, but who might as well be describing
Collins:

> Coleridge, whose heart is so full, if sometimes only of its own empti-
> ness, its desire to be filled, seems fully aware that the betweenness of
> time-as-moment, pure thresholdness, barren liminality, at least in
> what Einstein would call a "space-like" way, must be a nothingness.
> Between the temple and labyrinth there must be a crossing which,
> viewed from the perspective of time, does not stand, stay, hold or
> persist. Yet the poet craves persistence and duration . . .
> A new or renewed Renaissance mode of personification would seem
> to be the main yield of the poetry of threshold . . .
>
> . . . Formally, we can say that personification is the figurative emer-
> gent of the liminal scene . . . Personifications come alive the
> moment there is psychological breakthrough, with an accompanying
> liberation of utterance, which in its radical form is a first deep breath
> . . .

A Sublime or Longinian critic this acute would have
strengthened Collins where he needed it most, in his own sense of
poetic election. The "Ode to Fear" could have been called "Ode
to Poetic Election," and its opening invocation makes us wonder
just what the personification Fear can mean:

> Thou, to whom the world unknown
> With all its shadowy shapes is shown;
> Who see'st appalled the unreal scene,
> While Fancy lifts the veil between:
> > Ah Fear! Ah frantic Fear!
> > I see, I see thee near.

Why name one's own daemon or genius as Fear? Indeed as
"frantic Fear"? Is this a free choice among available personifica-
tions, a kind of Aristotelian "fear" to be dispelled by an aesthetic
catharsis, or is it an overdetermined fear, belonging more to
Freud's cosmos than Aristotle's? Perhaps these questions reduce
to: is there not a sexual, perhaps a sado-masochistic element, in
what Collins calls Fear? The "mad Nymph," Fear, is nothing less
than Collins's Muse, rather in the sense that Lacan called Freud's

earliest patients, those gifted and charming hysterical young women of Jewish Vienna, Freud's Muses.

The most illuminating reading of the "Ode to Fear" that I know is by Paul Sherwin in his superb book, *Precious Bane: Collins and the Miltonic Legacy* (Austin, 1977). Sherwin rightly emphasizes Collins's teasing technique; we never do see anything of the presumably attractive mad Nymph beyond her "hurried step" and "haggard eye." I agree with Sherwin that there is an affinity here between Collins and Burke. Collins too favors sympathy over imitation, the effect of things on the mind over a clear idea of the things themselves. Milton's "judicious obscurity," as Burke admiringly called it, is followed by Collins, who also rejects mere mimesis. Sherwin approvingly quotes Mrs. Barbauld, that Mrs. Alfred Uruguay of her age, as remarking that Collins's Fear is at once the inspirer of passion and its victim. And so, in Sherwin's reading, is Collins:

> If, on the one hand, his sympathy is drawn out by Fear's all-too-human vulnerability, it is perplexed by her apparent divinity; and whereas the former aspect of the personification establishes the possibility of intimacy, it is the latter aspect, enticing the speaker with the dangerous allure of numinous experience and heightening his sense of self, that provokes him to seek out this precarious communion.

I don't wish to be accused of assimilating William Collins to Ernest Dowson, but I am going to urge a reading rather less ontological and more sexual even than Sherwin's. How after all, experientially speaking, how does one go about renewing the link between rhetorical personification and daemonic possession? There is religion of course, presumably more in its esoteric than in its normative aspects. There is intoxication, by drink and by drug, and there is, yet more poetically, the always beckoning abyss of sexuality as taken to its outer limits, where pleasure and pain cease to be antithetical entities. I am not going to give us a William Collins as heroic precursor of the Grand Marquis, or a critical vision of the "Ode to Fear" as a grace note preceding *The Hundred and Twenty Days of Sodom and Gomorrah*. But the pleasures of the "Ode to Fear" are uneasily allied to its torments, and there is an element of sexual bondage in those torments. That even this element should be, ultimately, a trope for influence-anxieties is hardly a revelation, since I know no ampler field for the study of belatedness than is constituted by the sadomasochistic elements in our psyches.

Is it too much to say that Collins, throughout his Ode, attempts to work himself up into a frenzy of fearful apprehension, in the hope that such frenzy will grant him the powers of the tragic poet, of Aeschylus, Sophocles, but above all of Shakespeare? Yes, that is to say too much, because we then underestimate what Freud would have called Collins's overvaluation of the object, when his Fear is that object. Fear indeed is Collins's wounded Narcissism, and so becomes the entire basis for the aggressivity of his poetic drive. But that requires us to name more clearly the Nymph or daemon, since Aristotle's tragic fear hardly seems an apt name for the Sublime hysteria that Collins confronts and desires.

Shall we not call her the Muse of repression, and so of the Counter-Sublime? Perhaps, in Freudian terms, we could call her the Counter-Transference, the analyst's totemic and repressed apprehension that he is in psychic danger of being, as it were, murdered and devoured by his devoted patient. Fear, as Fletcher and Sherwin tell us, is Collins's *own* daemon, his indwelling Urania. Our twentieth-century Collins was Hart Crane, and I turn to Crane for his versions of Collins's Nymph. In a late, unfinished lyric, "The Phantom Bark," Crane rather strangely alludes to Collins, and evidently not to any actual poem Collins wrote:

> So dream thy sails, O phantom bark
> That I thy drownèd man may speak again
> Perhaps as once Will Collins spoke the lark,
> And leave me half adream upon the main.

The reference is purely visionary, as though Collins came back from the dead say in Shelley's "Skylark." In some truer sense Collins speaks to his Nymph Fear again when Crane addresses his nymph Helen in *For the Marriage of Faustus and Helen*. Crane too cries out: "Let us unbind our throats of fear and pity," while he goes on to give us his version of *"Vengeance, in the lurid Air, / Lifts her red Arm, expos'd and bare"* as "the ominous lifted arm / That lowers down the arc of Helen's brow / To saturate with blessing and dismay." Crane's later versions of this antithetical Muse include the Paterian Venus of *Voyages* VI, who "rose / Conceding dialogue with eyes / That smile unsearchable repose – ," and the woman of "The Broken Tower," a Collinsian poem where the Muse's "sweet mortality stirs latent power" in her poet. A late fragment by Collins actually prophesies Crane's death lyric: "Whatever dark aerial power, / Commission'd, haunts the gloomy tower." Like Collins, Crane invokes the Evening Star as the gentlest form of his Daemon, though Crane's invocation necessarily is more desperate: "O cruelly to inoculate the brinking dawn / With antennae toward worlds that glow and sink; – "

What Crane helps us see is that Collins's Fear is a Muse not so much called on to help the poet remember, as one invoked to help the poet forget. A Muse who forgets, or who needs to forget, is *en route* to Moneta in *The Fall of Hyperion,* but Collins is rather more Coleridge's precursor than he is Keats's. Except for Scripture and Milton, and perhaps Shakespeare, what passage in poetry haunted Coleridge more productively than this:

> Through glades and glooms the mingled measure stole,
> Or o'er some haunted stream with fond delay,
>   Round an holy calm diffusing,
>   Love of peace and lonely musing,
> In hollow murmers died away.

From "The Passions" to "Kubla Khan" is a movement from one threshold to another, and liminal poets have a particularly intense way of recognizing their family romance and its nuances. Fletcher, the theoretician of thresholds, reminds us that etymologically the *daemon* is the spirit of division, a reminder that I remember using as a starting-point in working out the revisionary ratio of *daemonization* or the Counter-Sublime. The Sublime trope for such dividing tends to be breaking, a making by breaking, or catastrophe creation. I return to the "Ode to Fear" to trace just such a breaking.

How specific ought we to be in finding an identity for
Collins's "world unknown" and "unreal scene"? The late Thomas
Weiskel brilliantly argued for something like Freud's Primal Scene
Fantasy, but here as elsewhere I would prefer some version of
what I have theorized as the Scene of Instruction. Not that the
two fantasies are wholly exclusive, since what passes between the
Poetic Father and the Muse has its sexual overtones in the
evening ear of the belated ephebe. Yet Collins's scene can be
called more Yeatsian than Freudian, more at home in the world of
Per Amica Silentia Lunae than in that of *Totem and Taboo*. This may
be simply because Collins's "sources" are mostly Spenserian
(Masque of Cupid, Temple of Venus), but I suspect a more crucial
reason also; Fear is indeed Collins's own Daemon, but he has not
yet possessed her or been possessed by her. The scene she partly
inhabits by seeing is populated by the fathers, by Spenser,
Shakespeare and Milton, but not by Collins himself. As the Ode
begins, Fear sees the visionary world, but all that Collins sees is
Fear. We are in the ancient topos of Contraries and
Contradictories but not yet in the trope of Romantic Irony. And
there I touch at last upon my first theoretical speculation in this
essay; Sublime Personification seems to me an uneasy transitional
phase or crossing between Associationist topos and Romantic
trope. Collins's Fear is a commonplace burgeoning but not yet
burgeoned into an irony, or as Freud called it, a reaction-formation. Fear *sees* and is frantic; Collins sees *her,* and becomes rather
less persuasively frantic:

> Ah Fear! Ah frantic Fear!
> I see, I see thee near.
> I know thy hurried step, thy haggard eye!
> Like thee I start, like thee I disordered fly.

That repetition of "I see, I see" is already quite Coleridgean,
so that we almost expect Collins to burst forth with "And still I
gaze – and with how blank an eye!" What restrains Collins is an
awareness still just short of irony, certainly short of Spenserian
irony, regardless of all the Spenserian diction. The contraries of
seeing and not-seeing the visionary scene yield to the topoi of

definition and division in the remainder of the strophe, as Collins enumerates the monsters appearing in Fear's train. Division is properly daemonic here, with one giant form, a Spenserian Danger, thousands of phantoms: "Who prompt to deeds accursed the mind," as well as an indefinite number of fiends who: "O'er nature's wounds and wrecks preside." All these lead up to a highly sadistic Vengeance, who requires considerable scrutiny. But even Danger has his peculiarities:

> Danger, whose limbs of giant mould
> What mortal eye can fixed behold?
> Who stalks his round, an hideous form,
> Howling amidst the midnight storm,
> Or throws him on the ridgy steep
> Of some loose hanging rock to sleep;

The sources here – in Spenser and Pope – are not developed with any particular zest or inventiveness on Collins's part. But we should note the obsessive emphasis again upon the eye of the beholder, the horrified fixation that is one of the stigmata of repression. Spenser's Danger, that hideous Giant, was associated with hatred, murder and treason, which may have been daily intimations for Spenser to dread, whether in Ireland or at court, but cannot have had much reality for Collins in the years when he still was sane. His Danger "stalks his round" amid more commonplace sublimities, storm and impending rock fall. These represent surely the psyche's potential for violence, whether aggressivity is to be turned against others or against the self:

> And with him thousand phantoms joined,
> Who prompt to deeds accursed the mind;
> And those, the fiends who, near allied,
> O'er nature's wounds and wrecks preside;

Those wounds and wrecks of nature include internalized disorders, which is what prompts the vision of a ferociously personified feminine superego, as it were, an image of sadomasochistic Vengeance:

> Whilst Vengeance in the lurid air
> Lifts her red arm, exposed and bare,
> On whom that ravening brood of fate,
> Who lap the blood of sorrow, wait;

Again the sources (Milton, Dryden, Pope) are of little consequence except for Collins's own noted reference to the hounds of vengeance in Sophocles's *Electra*. The curious doubling almost redundant, of Vengeance's lifted arm as both "exposed and bare" enforces how lurid Collins's scopic drive dares to become. There is a troubling ambiguity in the image, as Weiskel noted. Vengeance is a kind of phallic woman, appropriate to a masochistic fantasy, and in some curious way Collins blends her into an Artemis figure, waited upon by destined hounds. There is thus a hint of an Actaeon identity for poor Collins himself, a hint taken up in the couplet closing the strophe:

> Who, Fear, this ghastly train can see,
> And look not madly wild like thee?

Like his daemonic Muse, Collins really does expect to be hunted down and torn apart by the Furies, for his tone lacks any playful element. That he more than half desires his fate is clear enough also. What is beautifully not clear is just who is seeing what in this rather confused scene of sadomasochistic instruction. Fear sees it all, yet Collins is by no means as yet fully one with his own Fear. She sees and yet does not wish to see; Collins sees only in and by visionary fits, yet he does want to see, whatever the cost. Lacan's grim jest about the scopic drive comes to mind: that which we are fixated upon, obsessively stare upon, is precisely what cannot be seen. Only the creativity of Fear can impel Collins beyond this daemonic threshold.

Of course, like Weiskel or to some extent also Sherwin, or Paul Fry in his fine reading of this Ode, I am giving a kind of Freudian reading (broadly speaking) and Collins's own overt psychology was Associationist. But the line between Associationism and Freud is a blurred one, for a number of reasons. One is merely genetic, despite all Freudian denials. Freud's theory of language essentially came from John Stuart Mill (whom Freud had translated) and so was essentially a late version of Associationism. But far more crucially, both the Associationist categories and the Freudian mechanisms or fantasies of defense rely implicitly upon rhetorical models, these being the topoi or commonplaces for Associationism and the prime tropes or figures for Freud. Romanticism is of course the connecting link here between topos and trope, association and defense, or to phrase this more salient-ly, Collins's "Ode to Fear," though a monument of and to Sensibility, is itself a version of that connecting link, a poem verg-ing on High Romanticism and kept back from it mostly by two barriers. Call one of these decorum or diction, and the other Collins's own anxieties, human and creative, and you may be call-ing a single entity by two misleadingly different names.

I am aware that I am telling what is hardly a new story, schol-arly or critical, but this twice-told tale always does need to be told again. The story's troublesome phantom is what we go on calling personification, an old term I have no desire to protest provided we keep remembering that primarily it means not humanization but masking, or as Fletcher has taught us, masking at the thresh-old, at the crossing between labyrinth and temple, or as I want to say, between limitation and a representation that is a restitution. Such masking, in Associationist terms, is a movement through cat-egorical places. In Romantic or Freudian terms, it is a movement between tropological or defensive configurations, marked always by ambivalence and duplicity.

The masterpiece of emotive ambivalence, in Freud or in the poets, is called variously the Oedipal conflict, taboo, and transfer-ence, and this is where Collins chooses to center his Epode:

> In earliest Greece to thee with partial choice
>   The grief-full Muse addressed her infant tongue;
> The maids and matrons on her awful voice,
>   Silent and pale, in wild amazement hung.
>
> Yet he, the bard who first invoked thy name,
>   Disdained in Marathon its power to feel:
> For not alone he nursed the poet's flame,
>   But reached from Virtue's hand the patriot's steel.
>
> But who is he whom later garlands grace,
>   Who left awhile o'er Hybla's dews to rove,
> With trembling eyes thy dreary steps to trace,
>   Where thou and Furies shared the baleful grove?

> Wrapped in thy cloudy veil the incestuous queen
>> Sighed the sad call her son and husband heard,
> When once alone it broke the silent scene,
>> And he, the wretch of Thebes, no more appeared.

Sophocles of course is hardly Collins's poetic father, but the Oedipal scene is very much Collins's own, and the echo of *Comus* in the condition of the maids and matrons has considerable force. Freud has taught us to look for meaningful mistakes, and the learned Collins errs remarkably here. The "sad call" in *Oedipus Coloneus* is not sighed once by Jocasta, but frequently by the god, who is summoning Oedipus to join him. I take it that Collins himself is being summoned, not by Apollo, but by the Oedipal Muse, for whom another name, we now can see, is Fear:

> O Fear, I know thee by my throbbing heart,
>> Thy withering power inspired each mournful line,
> Though gently Pity claim her mingled part,
>> Yet all the thunders of the scene are thine!

Pity here is as little Aristotelian as Fear has been. Collins now recognizes Fear as being not only daemon and Muse but as mother, a recognition scene that is the Sublime crisis-point of the Ode. In Associationist terms, the Epode has moved from the categories of Contiguity to those of Comparison, from matters of cause and effect to those lying, beyond causation, in the heights and depths of the daemonic Sublime. Collins's heart recognizes what his occluded sight could not, and so he learns, as Stevens phrased it, that the mother's face is the purpose of the poem. But a mother who is more fear than pity, whose power is withering, and who inspires a thunderous Scene of Instruction, is a most extraordinary version of the mother, and suggests an Orphic as well as an Oedipal fate for poor Collins.

But this is of course Collins's own direct suggestion, and the puzzle of the "Ode to Fear" grows ever greater. The Pindaric, from its origins through Collins on to Shelley courts disaster, as suits the most overtly agonistic of all lyric forms. Paul Fry charmingly suggests that all the "monsters" Collins invokes "appear to be nothing other than Pindaric odes." I would modify Fry by observing that Collins is a strong enough poet as to know that anything he wishes to get into his Pindaric ode must be treated as if it already was a Pindaric ode. A motherly Muse so fearful, indeed so hysterical as to require the analogue of Jocasta, belongs to the same principle of strength and its costs. Collins is frightening himself to some purpose, and I swerve for a brief interval from Collins into Freud not to seek a reductive version of that purpose but rather to show that every strong anxiety is in some sense an *achieved* anxiety, so that Collins mimes a profound constant in the civil wars of the psyche.

Freud, in his later (post-1926) revision of his theory of anxiety, wrote a kind of commentary upon the Sublime ode, not least upon the "Ode to Fear." In Freud's earlier theory, neurotic anxiety and realistic anxiety were rigidly distinguished from one another, since neurotic anxiety was dammed-up libido, caused by unsuccessful repression, while realistic anxiety was caused by real danger. But after 1926, Freud gave up the notion that libido could be transformed into anxiety. Anxiety, Freud came to insist, is prior to repression, and indeed was the motive for repression. The causal distinction between neurotic anxiety and real fear was thus abandoned for good. The doctrine of the priority of anxiety depends upon a mapping of the psyche in which the ego itself is viewed as being in large part unconscious, so that we must say we are lived by the id. Oppressed from the other side by the superego, or the ego's own abandoned earlier affections, the poor ego is exposed to the death drive, the final form of sadomasochistic ambivalence aggressively turned in against the self. Real fear and neurotic anxiety alike become interchangeable with the fear of castration, which is to say, the fear of death. But the hapless ego's surrender of its aggressivity, whether against the self or others, does not appease the superego, which progressively grows more murderous towards the ego.

Associationist psychology had no such vision of man, but Collins's "Ode to Fear" does, probably against Collins's own desires and intentions. Weiskel shrewdly observed that Collins had discovered "a fantasy code appropriate to the special crisis of discourse in his day." Freud admitted that the poets had been there before him, and it is uncanny that Collins was more *there* than poets far stronger. We think of Blake in this dark area, but Blake was enough of an heroic vitalist to disengage from his own Spectre of Urthona. Collins, like Cowper, is all but one with that Spectre, with the temporal anxiety that cannot be distinguished from the poetic ambitions of the Sensibility poets.

If we glance back at the Strophe of the "Ode to Fear" we can see that its hidden subject is the tormented question: "Am I a poet?" Collins indeed is the Muse's true son, but can the Muse be Fear and nothing more? In the Epode the question is altered, since there the true poet, Aeschylus, is revealed as being fearless. The question therefore becomes: "Can I love, or get beyond poetic self-love?," and the answer seems to be highly equivocal, since Oedipal love is narcissistic beyond measure. In the Antistrophe, much the strongest of the poem's three divisions, Collins makes a fierce endeavor to introject poetic immortality, but the Miltonic shadow intervenes, with startling results. The question becomes not what it should be, more life or a wasting death, but the truth and decorum of the romance mode. Collins is, I think, creatively confused throughout the Antistrophe but the confusion, as in so much of Tennyson, becomes an aesthetic gain:

> Thou who such weary lengths hast passed,
> Where wilt thou rest, mad nymph, at last?
> Say, wilt thou shroud in haunted cell,
> Where gloomy Rape and Murder dwell?
> Or in some hollowed seat,
> 'Gainst which the big waves beat,
> Hear drowning seamen's cries in tempests brought!

The sentiment here, though not the mode, suggests Thomas Lovell Beddoes and George Darley, a good three generations later. The "mad nymph" desperately requires rest, but the Miltonic verb "shroud" for "shelter" suggests that no rest is possible for this personification of the poetic. A rested Fear would cease to fear, and so the poem would have to close prematurely. But the transmogrification of personification into phantasmagoria moves Fear from visual to auditory hallucination, which increases psychic disorder, both in the Muse and in her poet. What seem to me the poem's most effective lines mark Collins's crisis of identification, as he seeks to internalize Miltonic power while continuing his avoidance of naming that source of paternal strength:

> Dark power, with shuddering meek submitted thought
> Be mine to read the visions old,
> Which thy awakening bards have told:
> And, lest thou meet my blasted view,
> Hold each strange tale devoutly true;

The Archangel Michael, instructing Adam just before the expulsion from Eden, says it is time to wake up Eve, who has been calmed with gentle dreams: "and all her spirits compos'd / To meek submission." Collins here takes up that feminine and passive stance imposed upon Eve by angelic power, and so I think that his union with his Muse Fear now has become a very radical interpenetration. In this progressive internalization, the topos of Resemblance engenders characteristic metaphor, in which nature and consciousness bewilderingly perspectivize one another. Weiskel, acutely aware of this progress from Sensibility to Romanticism, caught it up in an eloquent formulation:

> The "reader's" mind is deeply divided between the powerful and dark appeal the fantasies are making and his conscious renunciation of the desires they excite. An attitude of meek submission holds off his recognition of these desires, but it also prevents his Longinian appropriation of the precursor's power as his own. The power remains dark, instinct with danger; the liberating power of a symbolic identification with the bards is just what is missing . . .

Sherwin emphasizes "the radical bivalence of the daemon" here, saying of Collins that:

> . . . He has so thoroughly absorbed the rage of his dark angel that the daemon, no longer threatening the poet with engulfment, is viewed as a guide leading beyond itself to the special prerogatives of the prophetic seer . . .

Both these critics of Collins's Sublime help us to see that Collins is on the verge of strength, yet hesitant to cross over into it, though Sherwin's tone is more positive than Weiskel's. I would add that Collins's baffled version of the Longinian or reader's Sublime is very difficult indeed to interpret. Unlike the idealized Eve's, Collins's meek submission is a "shuddering" one, and that modifier "shuddering" is his ironic response to Milton as an "awakening" bard, that is, a bard who imposes upon the reader a very intense affective burden. So empathic is this response, however ironic, that Collins's eyes are threatened with being blasted, darkened by shock, unless he assents to the Miltonic fable, however strange. If the precise tale here be the expulsion from Eden, then one sees why Collins's subsequent passage returns to the Milton of *L'Allegro* and *Il Penseroso,* and of *Comus,* and perhaps to the Shakespeare of *A Midsummer Night's Dream:*

> Ne'er be I found, by thee o'erawed,
> In that thrice-hallowed eve abroad,
> When ghosts, as cottage-maids believe,
> Their pebbled beds permitted leave,
> And goblins haunt, from fire or fen
> Or mine or flood, the walks of men!

That an urbane tone has entered cannot be questioned, but what has departed is the voice of William Collins. We hear the octosyllabic Milton, and not his venturesome and daring ephebe. Had Collins dared further, he would have found the Miltonic rhetoric of transumption or metalepsis for a triumphant closure, but instead he ends quite elegantly but weakly, in an interplay of the topoi of Antecedents and Consequences:

> O thou whose spirit most possessed
> The sacred seat of Shakespeare's breast!
> By all that from thy prophet broke,
> In thy divine emotions spoke,
> Hither again thy fury deal,
> Teach me but once like him to feel:
> His cypress wreath my meed decree,
> And I, O Fear, will dwell with thee!

Collins was capable of strong closure, as the "Ode on the Poetical Character" demonstrates. What defeated him here? Paradoxically, I would assert that the relative failure is in the generation of sufficient anxiety. What fails in Collins is his own capacity for an infinite Fear. Not that courage becomes the issue, but trauma. Apathy dreadly beckons, and Collins prays for the power *to feel.* Yet I do not think he means affect. His knowing failure is in cognition, and I want to look closely at Dr. Johnson's moving dispraise of his learned and gifted young friend in order to see if we can recover a clue to Collins's self-sabotage:

> . . . He had employed his mind chiefly upon works of fiction, and subjects of fancy; and, by indulging some peculiar habits of thought, was eminently delighted with those flights of imagination which pass the bounds of nature . . .
>
> This was however the character rather of his inclination than his genius; the grandeur of wildness, and the novelty of extravagance, were always desired by him, but were not always attained . . . His poems are the productions of a mind not deficient in fire . . . but somewhat obstructed in quest of mistaken beauties.

To pass natural bounds, to wander beyond limits, *extra vagans,* that surely was Collins's poetic will, his intended revenge against time's: "It was." Johnson is shrewd, as always, in saying that Collins not only desired too much, but beyond the range of his genius. The fault was not ambition, but rather that Collins had to ask his inventive powers to give him what neither contemporary criticism nor contemporary psychology afforded. Milton stands on the verge of the European Enlightenment, but when it begins to reach him it breaks over him, confirming only his recalcitrant furies. Collins puzzles us because he is spiritually close enough to Milton to acquire more of the Miltonic power than actually came to him. Geoffrey Hartman's sad summary is just, noble and restrained, and joins Johnson as the classical verdict upon Collins:

> Collins rarely breaks through to the new poetry . . .
>
> Collins does teach us, however, that the generic subject of the sublime ode (as distinct from that of individual poems) is the poetical character: its fate in an Age of Reason. The odes are generally addressed to invited powers and, like the gothic novel, raise the

ghosts they shudder at. Their histrionic, sometimes hysterical, character stems from the fact that they are indeed theatrical machines,
evoking a power of vision that they fear to use. Collins, like a sorcerer's apprentice, is close to being overpowered by the spirit he sum-
mons . . .

My friend's simile of the sorcerer's apprentice is particularly
effective if associated with the version of Dukas in Disney's
Fantasia. The vision of William Collins as Mickey Mouse overcome
by a host of mops is more than any poet's reputation could sustain. Poor Collins indeed! I would prefer another vision of
Collins's limitations, one that emphasizes the odd splendor, or
splendid oddness, of his liminal achievements. Daemonic poetry
is a strange mode, whether in Collins, Coleridge, Shelley, Beddoes
or Hart Crane. When Collins gets it exactly right, then he has the
uncanniness of an original, as this cento intends to illustrate:

> And she, from out the veiling Cloud,
> Breath'd her magic Notes aloud:
> And Thou, Thou rich-hair'd Youth of Morn,
> And all thy subject Life was born!

* * *

> To the blown *Baltic* then, they say
> The wild Waves found another way,
> Where *Orcas* howls his wolfish Mountains rounding;
> Till all the banded West at once gan rise,
> A wide wild Storm ev'n Nature's self confounding,
> With'ring her Giant Sons with strange uncouth Surprise.

* * *

> Now Air is hush'd, save where the weak-ey'd Bat,
> With short shrill Shriek flits by on leathern Wing,
> Or where the Beetle winds
> His small but sullen Horn,
> As oft he rises midst the twilight Path,
> Against the Pilgrim born in heedless Hum:

* * *

> What though far off, from some dark dell espied
> His glimm'ring mazes cheer th'excursive sight,
> Yet turn, ye wand'rers, turn your steps aside,

> Nor trust the guidance of that faithless light;
> For watchful, lurking mid th'unrustling reed,
>> At those mirk hours the wily monster lies,
> And listens oft to hear the passing steed,
>> And frequent round him rolls his sullen eyes,
> If chance his savage wrath may some weak wretch surprise.

These are among the breakthroughs from Sensibility into Romanticism, though never into the Wordsworthian mode. What Collins could not learn was what Wordsworth had to invent, a transumptive or time-reversing kind of troping as original as Milton's own, yet plainly *not* Miltonic. Collins's stance was neither ironic nor transumptive, and so temporality remained for Collins a choking anxiety. If Collins was no mere sorcerer's apprentice, it must be admitted he was also no sorcerer, as the baffled closure of the "Ode to Fear" renders too obvious. I circle back to the question prevalent in all criticism of Collins: what made him poor? Why was his psychic poverty, his imaginative need, so scandalously great. To have crossed into the Romantic Sublime only a year or two after the death of Pope was hardly the act of a weak poet, yet Collins will never lose the aura that Johnson gave him and that Hartman has confirmed.

I go back to Collins's true spiritual companion among the critics, Fletcher, though Fletcher alas has published only a few remarks about Collins. In his early masterpiece, *Allegory*, Fletcher has a fine observation on the function of the Sublime:

> Graver poems like the sublime odes of Collins and Gray, and later of Shelley, have the direct and serious function of destroying the slavery of pleasure . . .

I interpret Fletcher as meaning that Collins, Gray, Shelley in their uncanny Pindarics are bent on persuading the reader to foresake easier in exchange for more difficult pleasures. Paul Fry, acutely but perhaps too severely, says of the School of Collins and Gray: "An ode that remembers the pastness of others and not the otherness of the past can have nothing to say of fallen experience as a distinct phase." I think that Collins met Fry's challenge by refusing to admit that fallen experience *was* a distinct phase. As

Coleridge's precursor, Collins pioneered in representing what Thomas McFarland calls the "modalities of fragmentation" or "forms of ruin" in Romantic poetry. As McFarland is showing us, these *are* modalities, these *are* achieved forms, with aesthetic arguments and structured intensities all their own.

Repetition, as Paul Fry has noted in this context, is very much the issue when we bring Collins to an aesthetic judgment:

> Repetition is what unlearns the genealogical knowledge of the
> ode, which creates a world and a god with every stroke of the pen,
> only in the same movement to absent these creations from the poet's
> field of vision.

Fry knowingly follows Paul de Man's theory of lyric here, but I would suggest Kierkegaard's "repetition" rather than de Man's as being closer to Collins's Sublime project. Kierkegaard's "repetition" literally means in Danish "a taking again," and is described by Mark Taylor as "the willed taking-again of a transcendental possibility." Collins wills to take again the transcendental possibility of poetry as he knows it in Spenser, Shakespeare and Milton. Or rather, he wills to will such a taking-again, so as to affirm again the possibility of poetic strength. But a will two degrees from the possibility is a troubled will, too troubled to attempt what McFarland, following Plato, calls "the Place Beyond the Heavens," the "true being, transcendence, and the symbolic indication of wholeness" that make up the synecdoches of visionary poetry. Collins's synecdoches are wounded aggressivities, turned in against themselves, sadomasochistic vicissitudes of the thwarted poetic drive against time's "It was." Collins cannot say: "I am," in his poems. Instead of the synecdoches of wholeness, Wordsworthian or Keatsian, he can offer only the Associationist categories of Definition and Division.

Yet the "Ode to Fear" remains a unique poem, as do three or four other major performances by Collins, and its deep mutual contamination of drive and defense is far closer to the psychic cartography of Freud than to Locke. Collins survives not so much as a voice, but as the image of a voice, perhaps even as the topos of image-of-voice itself. What Collins knows in that daemonic place is the "continuous present" that Northrop Frye said was representative of the mode of Sensibility and of its exercise of repetition.

Gray and Cowper and Smart perhaps were more at home in that "continuous present" than Collins was, and what we know of his life shows us how little Collins ever felt at home anywhere. Only the place of the daemon could have been home for Collins, and to that occult place I turn for my conclusion.

Collins, as all his critics rightly say, is a poet always engaged at invocation, in calling, until he seems quite giddy with the strain. Recall that our word "god" goes back to a root meaning "called" or "invoked," and that the word "giddy," possessed by god, has the same root. Yeats, in his beautiful daemonic reverie, *Per Amica Silentia Lunae,* gives us the formula for Collins's sense of place, for the exact topos of Sensibility:

> The Daimon, by using his mediatorial shades, brings man again and again to the place of choice, heightening temptation that the choice may be as final as possible, imposing his own lucidity upon events, leading his victim to whatever among works not impossible is the most difficult . . .

Collins's odes enact that drama over and again. That there should have been a religious element in his final mania is not surprising, for he is nothing but a religious poet, as Shelley and Hart Crane are Orphic religionists also. But to be an Orphic prophet in the mode of Sensibility was plainly not possible, and again it was not surprising that Collins, and his odes, alike were slain upon the stems of Generation, to adapt a Blakean conceptual image. Yeats, so much stronger a poet then Collins could ever be, must have the final words here. The tragedy of Sensibility is that it could suffer but not write this liminal passage of High Romantic self-revelation, which again I quote from *Per Amica Silentia Lunae:*

> . . .when I have closed a book too strirred to go on reading, and in those brief intense visions of sleep, I have something about me that, though it makes me love, is more like innocence. I am in the place where the Daimon is, but I do not think he is with me until I begin to make a new personality, selecting among those images, seeking always to satisfy a hunger grown out of conceit with daily diet; and yet, as I write the words 'I select,' I am full of uncertainty, not knowing when I am the finger, when the clay . . .

14 Sunset Hawk:
Warren's Poetry and Tradition

The beginning is like a god which as long as it dwells among men saves all things.
— Plato, *Laws* 775

Where can an authentic poet begin again, when clearly the past has ceased to throw its illumination upon the future? Robert Penn Warren's poetry spans nearly sixty years, from "Pondy Woods" to his long poem upon Chief Joseph, against whom the United States fought its last serious Indian war. No final perspective is possible upon a strong poet whose own wars are far from over. I have been reading Warren's poetry for thirty years, since I first came to Yale, but only in the second half of that period have I read him with the deep absorption that his poetry demands and rewards. Before the publication of *Incarnations: Poems 1966-1968*, I would have based my judgment of Warren's aesthetic eminence primarily upon his most ambitious novels, *All the King's Men* and *World Enough and Time*. The poetry seemed distinguished, yet overshadowed by Eliot, and perhaps of less intrinsic interest than the best poems of Ransom and Tate. But from *Incarnations* on, without a break, Warren consciously has taken on his full power over language and the world of the senses. In his varied achievement, his poetry now asserts the highest claims upon us.

Incarnations is an extraordinary book, and so it may be arbitrary to single out just one poem, but I still remember the shock with which I first read its strongest poem, "The Leaf." Few moments in the varied history of the American Sublime match Warren's sudden capture of that mode:

Near the nesting place of the hawk, among
Snag-rock, high on the cliff, I have seen
The clutter of annual bones, of hare, vole, bird, white
As chalk from sun and season, frail
As the dry grass stem. On that

High place of stone I have lain down, the sun
Beat, the small exacerbation
Of dry bones was what my back, shirtless and bare, knew.
   I saw

The hawk shudder in the high sky, he shudders
To hold position in the blazing wind, in relation to
The firmament, he shudders and the world is a metaphor, his eye
Sees, white, the flicker of hare-scut, the movement of vole.

It may be gratuitous, but I am tempted to find, just here, a
textual point of crossing, the place Warren's poetry turned about,
on his quest for an ultimate strength. Certainly his stance, style,
and thematics are different, in and after this passage through to
the Sublime. "This is the place," Warren had written earlier in the
poem, adding: "To this spot I bring my grief." His grief, as we
might expect from so experiential and dramatic a writer, doubtless presented itself to him as temporal guilt. But poetry is a mediated mode of expression, in which poems are mediated primarily
by other poems. I will read Warren's guilt in "The Leaf" as a literary anxiety, appropriate to a poem's inescapable dilemma, which
is that it must treat literal anguish as being figurative, in order to
find appropriate figuration which would justify yet another poem.
Warren actually may have lain down on that high place of stone,
but the actuality matters only as another order or degree of trope.
"The Leaf" is a crisis poem of a very traditional kind, and in that
kind the crisis concerns the fate of poetic voice, in a very precise
sense of voice. The sense is American, though the tradition of the
crisis poem is Biblical in its origins, and British in its major developments. Like his poetic father, Eliot, Warren rehearses the crisis
poem's origins, but more even than Eliot, Warren develops an
acutely American sense of poetic voice. "The Leaf" occupies a
place in Warren's canon analogous to the place of *Ash-Wednesday*

in Eliot's work, but with an American difference necessarily more emphasized in Warren.

Rather than qualify that "necessarily" I would emphasize its double aspect: historical and personal. Both the historical necessity and the personal modification are agonistic. The agon, whether with tradition or with Eliot as tradition's contemporary representative, is ambivalent in Warren, but a loving struggle is not less a struggle. When Warren writes "my tongue / Was like a dry leaf in my mouth," he is writing Eliot's language, and so the tongue still is not quite his own. *Incarnations* has two epigraphs, the first being the opening of Nehemiah 5:5, when the people say to Nehemiah: "Yet now our flesh is as the flesh of our brethren." Warren omits the remainder of the verse, which concludes: "for other men have our lands and our vineyards." The context is the rebuilding of Jerusalem, after the return from exile in Babylon. *Incarnations'* other epigraph is the heroic defiance of John Henry in his ballad: "A man ain't nuthin but a man" – which of course is less an expression of limitation than an assertion of individuality against overwhelming force. The epigraphs point to the secret plot of *Incarnations,* culminating in "The Leaf." Let us call the plot "deferred originality," and with that calling return to everything problematic in the poem. Here is its extraordinary first section:

> Here the fig lets down the leaf, the leaf
> Of the fig five fingers has, the fingers
> Are broad, spatulate, stupid,
> Ill-formed, and innocent – but of a hand, and the hand,
>
> To hide me from the blaze of the wide world, drops,
> Shamefast, down. I am
> What is to be concealed. I lurk
> In the shadow of the fig. Stop.
> Go no further. This is the place.
>
> To this spot I bring my grief.
> Human grief is the obscenity to be hidden by the leaf.

Warren portrays himself as Adam just after the Fall, with partial reference to earlier lyrics about the fig in the first sequence of *Incarnations,* a sequence concluding in "The Leaf." Whether by intuition or by acquired knowledge, Warren seems to have a sense of the ancient Jewish tradition that identified the forbidden fruit with the fig rather than the grape or apple of paradise *(Etrog)*. Only the fig-tree therefore granted Adam permission to take of its leaves when he sought to cover himself. Warren concentrates upon a single leaf, more an emblem or trope of voice than of sexuality. In the second lyric of the "Island of Summer" sequence that closes with the crucial poem called "The Leaf," Warren introduces the trope as a version of death:

> . . . a single
> Leaf the rest screens, but through it, light
> Burns, and for the fig's bliss
> The sun dies . . .

The image of the leaf resumes in the sardonic poem bearing the long and splendid title: "Paul Valéry Stood on the Cliff and Confronted the Furious Energies of Nature." Whether Warren triumphs over the formidable seer of the marine cemetery is perhaps questionable, but we are left with a vivid critique of a transcendental consciousness:

> He sways high against the blue sky,
> While in the bright intricacies
> Of wind, his mind, like a leaf,
> Turns. In the sun, it glitters.

Warren would say that this is a disincarnation, and to it he opposes a further lyric in his sequence:

> Where purples now the fig, flame in
> Its inmost flesh, a leaf hangs
> Down, and on it, gull-droppings, white
> As chalk, show, for the sun has
>
> Burned all white, for the sun, it would
> Burn our bones to chalk – yes, keep
> Them covered, oh flesh, oh sweet
> Integument, oh frail, depart not
>
> And leave me thus exposed, like Truth.

Fig, flame, flesh, leaf, and sun are drawn together here into
the dark intricacy that is an incarnation, the truth that is the body
of death. With this as prelude, we are ready to return to "The
Leaf" as Warren's great poem of the threshold, of a crossing over
into his own image of voice. To see how drastic a swerve into originality is made here from the start, we have to recall something of
the fiction of the leaves in Western poetry. I've written about this
extensively, in *A Map of Misreading* and the more recent *The
Breaking of the Vessels*, and don't wish to repeat here the long train
of transumptions that holds together the history of this conceptual image from Homer and the Bible through Virgil, Dante,
Spenser, and Milton on to Shelley, Whitman, and Wallace Stevens.
Warren's fiction of the leaf is a baroque figuration, in a very different tradition. Unlike the transumptive line, Warren does not
seek an ellipsis of further figuration. Most simply, Stevens does;
Stevens wants the reader of "The Rock" or "The Course of a
Particular" to believe that the fiction of the leaves attains a completion in those poems. This is the Romantic and Emersonian cre-
dence that Warren refuses, in favor of a more Eliotic vision of tradition and the individual talent. Hence Warren's moral vocabulary of shame and guilt, or should we call it rather his moral
refusal to acknowledge that poetry refuses the distinction between
shame culture and guilt culture? To refuse that distinction is to
attempt an individual closure to tradition; to accept it, as Warren
does, is to affirm that one's role is to extend tradition, to hold it
open for a community of others. Warren's fundamental postu-
lates, however tempered by skepticism, are Biblical and Classical,
but his rhetoric and his poetic dilemmas are High Romantic. He
thus repeats the fundamental conflicts of his precursor Eliot,
whose actual rhetorical art stemmed from Whitman and
Tennyson, and not from more baroque sensibilities. Warren's
dilemmas in some ways are both simpler and harsher than Eliot's.
A shamanistic intensity, a sense of the abruptness of poetic force
more suitable to Yeats or Hart Crane than to Eliot, somehow has
to be reconciled with a cultural sense that demands rational

restraints and the personal acceptance of historical guilt.

The hand-like leaf of the fig has fingers that are "broad, spatulate, stupid, / Ill-formed, and innocent," which is pretty well Warren's judgment upon the Adamic condition, a judgment not exactly Emersonian. On what basis are we to accept Warren's peculiarly harsh line: "Human grief is the obscenity to be hidden by the leaf," unless the grief indeed is merely the poet's, any poet's, anxious resentment *as poet* in regard to the almost organic sadness of poetic origins? I am not under the illusion that Warren would accept this reading, but I set aside here my personal reverence for the man and my critical worship of the poet in order to enter again that area of grief that no strong poet will acknowledge as a poet. As I keep discovering, this is not enchanted ground upon which I am driven, doubtless obsessively, to trespass. But I would cite here a touch of external evidence of the most persuasive because most developmental kind. In the decade 1943-1953, when he wrote his most accomplished novels, *All the King's Men* and *World Enough and Time,* Warren's poetry simply stopped. So fecund an imagination does not cease from poetry only because its energies are caught up by the novel. As with Stevens's silence between 1924 and 1934, we have a very problematic gap in a major poetic career, and later in this essay I intend to return to Warren's poetic silence.

In my circular way I have come back to the Sublime second section of "The Leaf," and to the shock of my personal conversion to Warren when I first read the poem in 1969. Ransom and Tate were poets of enormous talent, but not exactly visionaries who favored shamanistic symbolic acts in their work, despite Tate's troubled relation to the primal exuberance of Hart Crane's poetry. Any close reader of Warren's poetry in 1969 would have known that the flight of hawks meant a great deal to him, but even that was hardly adequate preparation for the hawk's shudder in "The Leaf." In Warren's earliest book, *Thirty-Six Poems* (1935), there is a remarkable sequence, "Kentucky Mountain Farm," which I continue to hope he will reprint entire in his next *Selected Poems.* Section VI, "Watershed," not now available in print, has a memorable and crucially prophetic image: "The sunset hawk now rides / The tall light up the climbing deep of air." While men sleep, the hawk flies on in the night, scanning a landscape of disappearances with "gold eyes" that make all shriveling reappear. This sunset hawk, first a vision in boyhood, keeps returning in Warren's poems. In the still relatively early "To a Friend Parting," the inadequacy of "the said, the unsaid" is juxtaposed to seeing "The hawk tower, his wings the light take," an emblem of certainty in pride and honor. Perhaps it was the absence of such emblems in his confrontation of reality that stopped Warren's poetry in the decade 1943-1953.

Whatever the cause of his silence in verse, it seems significant that *Promises: Poems 1954-1956* opens with an address to the poet's infant daughter that culminates in a return of the hawk image. Viewing the isolated spot to which he has brought his daughter, Warren celebrates "the hawk-hung delight / Of distance unspoiled and bright space spilled." In *Tale of Time: Poems 1960-1966,* he explicitly compares "hawk shadow" with "that fugitive thought which I can find no word for," or what we might call the poetry that would begin anew when he wrote *Incarnations.* I quote again the central vision from the second section of "The Leaf," but extending the quotation now to the entire section:

> We have undergone ourselves, therefore
> What more is to be done for Truth's sake? I
>
> Have watched the deployment of ants, I
> Have conferred with the flaming mullet in a deep place.
>
> Near the nesting place of the hawk, among
> Snag-rock, high on the cliff, I have seen
> The clutter of annual bones, of hare, vole, bird, white
> As chalk from sun and season, frail
> As the dry grass stem. On that
>
> High place of stone I have lain down, the sun
> Beat, the small exacerbation
> Of dry bones was what my back, shirtless and bare, knew.
>   I saw

The hawk shudder in the high sky, he shudders
To hold position in the blazing wind, in relation to
The firmament, he shudders and the world is a metaphor,
   his eye
Sees, white, the flicker of hare-scut, the movement of vole.

Distance is nothing, there is no solution, I
Have opened my mouth to the wind of the world like wine,
   I wanted
To taste what the world is, wind dried up

The live saliva of my tongue, my tongue
Was like a dry leaf in my mouth.

Destiny is what you experience, that
Is its name and definition, and is your name, for

The wide world lets down the hand in shame:
Here is the human shadow, there, of the wide world,
   the flame.

The poet offers himself here not to the hawk, but to the hawk's shudder and the hawk's vision, and so to what shudder and vision incarnate, a stance or holding of position. That stance casts out shame even as it accepts guilt. That Warren practices a private ritual is palpable, even though we could only guess at the ritual until he wrote and published the extraordinary long autobiographical "Red-Tail Hawk and Pyre of Youth" that is the glory of *Now and Then: Poems 1976-1978.* Though the later poem is finer even than "The Leaf," it is not as pivotal, because it focuses on the young Warren alone, and not on the agon with forebears. What "The Leaf" discovers, with a clarity not often matched in our poetry, is the necessity of mediation despite the poet's longing for an unmediated relation between his mouth and the wind of the world. Both these terms, as Warren well knows, are Shelley's, a poet not much to Warren's taste, and so his treatment of the terms submits them to the stylistic cosmos of Eliot: "wind dried up / The live saliva of my tongue, my tongue / Was like a dry leaf in my mouth." We recognize that this is the Waste Land, and not an

Italy waiting for the Revolution. But the revelation that comes is not much more Eliotic than it is Shelleyan:

> The world is fruitful. In this heat
> The plum, black yet bough-bound, bursts, and the gold ooze is,
> Of bees, joy, the gold ooze has striven
> Outward, it wants again to be of
> The goldness of air and – blessedly – innocent. The grape
> Weakens at the juncture of the stem. The world
>
> Is fruitful, and I, too,
> In that I am the father
> Of my father's father's father. I,
> Of my father, have set the teeth on edge. But
> By what grape? I have cried out in the night.
>
> From a further garden, from the shade of another tree,
> My father's voice, in the moment when the cicada ceases, has called
>   to me.

"The moment when the cicada / ceases" deliberately alludes to Eliot's "not the cicada" in "What the Thunder Said"; but the prophetic trope, in its reversal, overcomes the rhetoric of *The Waste Land*. There is a curious ambiguity as to whose is the father's voice that calls out this ambivalent blessing:

> The voice blesses me for the only
> Gift I have given: *teeth set on edge.*
>
> In the momentary silence of the cicada,
> I can hear the appalling speed,
> In space beyond the stars, of
> Light. It is
>
> A sound like wind.

It is Warren's gift, by the reversal of the influence process, that has set Eliot's teeth on edge. Which is to say, it is Warren's rhetorical strength to have converted the Eliotic trope of orthodoxy, the light, into the appalling speed that sounds the wind of time, for time is Warren's trope, the center of his poetics. The hawk shudders to hold position in the blazing wind of time, and so transforms the world into a temporal metaphor. Warren's merger of identity with the hawk's shudder affirms the pride of his own stance and theme, the unforgiving shudder of poetic time. I want to hold on to Warren's vision of the hawk in order to trace something of the development of his poetry from *Incarnations* on to this moment. If my procedure is arbitrary, I defend it by the persistence of this vision, or something near to it, throughout his work.

Warren's best volume, *Or Else – Poem/Poems 1968-1974* ends with an extraordinary poem bearing the curious title, "A Problem in Spatial Composition." The first section composes the space, a senset through a high window, an eternity that is always beyond, a Sublime from which we are detached, as is traditional. But this is Warren setting us up for his original power in the second section and the closure in a single line of his third:

> [2]
> While out of the green, up-shining ramshackle of leaf, set
> In the lower right foreground, the stub
> Of a great tree, gaunt-blasted and black, thrusts.
>
> A single
> Arm jags upward, higher goes, and in that perspective, higher
> Than even the dream-blue of distance that is
> The mountain.
>
> Then
> Stabs, black, at the infinite saffron of sky.
>
> All is ready.
>
> The hawk,
> Entering the composition at the upper left frame
> Of the window, glides,
> In the pellucid ease of thought and at
> His breathless angle,
> Down.
>
> Breaks speed.
>
> Hangs with a slight lift and hover.

Makes contact.

The hawk perches on the topmost, indicative tip of
The bough's sharp black and skinny jag skyward.

[3]
The hawk, in an eyeblink, is gone.

This is a different kind of hawk's vision, and shall we not call
it a deliberate and triumphant figuration for the poet's new style?
"The hawk, / ... glides, / In the pellucid ease of thought and at /
His breathless angle, / Down." As the hawk breaks speed and hovers, he "makes contact," giving us a trope that stands, part for
whole, for the tense power of Warren's mature art: "The hawk
perches on the topmost, indicative tip of / The bough's sharp
black and skinny jag skyward." The emphasis is upon the immanent thrust of the natural object, rather than its transcendent possibilities. Another emphasis, as characteristic of Warren, is the
temporal swiftness of this fiction of duration, or poem – gone in
an eyeblink.

In 1975, Warren wrote a group of poems to form the first
section of his *Selected Poems: 1923-1975*. The second of these
poems, "Evening Hawk," is surely one of his dozen or so lyric masterpieces, a culmination of forty years of his art:

From plane of light to plane, wings dipping through
Geometries and orchids that the sunset builds,
Out of the peak's black angularity of shadow, riding
The last tumultuous avalanche of
Light above pines and the gutteral gorge,
The hawk comes.

His wing
Scythes down another day, his motion
Is that of the honed steel-edge, we hear
The crashless fall of stalks of Time.

The head of each stalk is heavy with the gold of our error.

Look! look! he is climbing the last light

Who knows neither Time nor error, and under
Whose eye, unforgiving, the world, unforgiven, swings
Into shadow.

                   Long now,
The last thrush is still, the last bat
Now cruises in his sharp hieroglyphics. His wisdom
Is ancient, too, and immense. The star
Is steady, like Plato, over the mountain.

If there were no wind we might, we think, hear
The earth grind on its axis, or history
Drip in darkness like a leaking pipe in the cellar.

The hawk's motion is that of a scythe reaping time, but Warren has learned more than his distance from the hawk's state of being. I know no single line in him grander than the beautifully oxymoronic "The head of each stalk is heavy with the gold of our error." What is being harvested is our fault, and yet that mistake appears as golden grain. When the poet sublimely cries "Look! look!" to us, I do not hear a Yeatsian exultation, but rather an acceptance of a vision that will forgive us nothing, and yet does not rejoice in that stance. Emerson, Warren once snapped in a now notorious poem, "had forgiven God everything," which is true enough, since Emerson sensibly had forgiven himself everything, and God was identical with what was oldest in Emerson himself. Warren goes on forgiving God, and himself, nothing, and implies that this is the only way to love God or the self. One does not imagine Ralph Waldo Emerson invoking the flight of a hawk as an image of the truth, but the poets of his tradition – notably Whitman, Stevens, and Hart Crane – have their own way of coming to terms with such an image. But, to Emersonians, the hawk is firmly part of Nature, of the Not-Me. Warren's trespasses upon a near-identity with the hawk clearly are no part of *that* American tradition.

    Warren is not interested in similitudes when he achieves a Sublime vision, but rather in identifying with some aspect of the truth, however severely he indicates his own distance from the truth. I am not much interested in rehearsing Warren's polemic against Emerson because I voted for Emerson a long time ago, and my love for Warren's poetry is therefore against the grain. As I wrote once, I read Warren's poetry with a shudder that is simultaneously spiritual revulsion and total aesthetic satisfaction, a shudder that only Yeats also evokes for me in this century.

Much in what is problematic in Warren's hawk poems was clarified permanently by "Red-Tail Hawk and Pyre of Youth" in *Now and Then,* the poem in which Warren himself seems to have arrived at a full awareness of his creative obsession. Yet the poem, perhaps as the price of so full a knowing, is in many ways at variance with Warren's other hawk visions. Beginning with the boy hunter's confrontation of the hawk's gaze ("Gold eyes, unforgiving, for they, like God, see all"), Warren moves rapidly past the miraculous shot to center upon his clay-burlap stuffed hawk, mounted in his room on a bookshelf of the poets and of Augustine, set over them as an emblem of the boy's own ambitions. Vividly as this is portrayed, it is less memorable than Warren's later return to the emblem, and his placing of the hawk upon a pyre:

> Flame flared. Feathers first, and I flinched, then stood
> As the steel wire warped red to defend
> The shape designed godly for air. But
> It fell with the mass, and I
> Did not wait.
>
> What left
> To do but walk in the dark, and no stars?

What is not consumed is the ecstasy of confrontation, the memory of the encounter shared with the hawk:

> Some dreams come true, some no.
> But I've waked in the night to see
> High in the late and uncurdled silver of summer
> The pale vortex appear once again – and you come
> And always the rifle swings up, though with
> The weightlessness now of dream,
> The old .30-30 that knows
> How to bind us in air-blood and earth-blood together
> In our commensurate fate,
> Whose name is a name beyond joy.

The vortex is what matters, and part of the point is surely that the stuffed hawk was merely text, while the vortex was the truth, the fate beyond joy but also beyond language. Warren's insistence upon truth puts the value of any fiction, including the poem he is writing, perhaps too severely into question. It is hardly possible not to be moved by the final section of "Red-Tail Hawk and Pyre of Youth," and yet the reader needs an answer to the query as to just what flared up on that sacrificial pyre:

> And I pray that in some last dream or delusion,
> While hospital wheels creak beneath
> And the nurse's soles make their *squeak-squeak* like mice,
> I'll again see the first small silvery swirl
> Spin outward and downward from sky-height
> To bring me the truth in blood-marriage of earth and air –
> And all will be as it was
> In that paradox of unjoyful joyousness,
> Till the dazzling moment when I, a last time, must flinch
> From the regally feathered gasoline flare
> Of youth's poor, angry, slapdash, and ignorant pyre.

The hawk spins outward and downward not to bring the truth *as* blood-marriage between boy and bird, but *in* that sacrament of slaughter. The killing is not the truth, but only an angry and youthful way to the truth. What can the truth be except solipsistic transport, the high and breaking light of the Sublime? If Warren were Stevens, he might have written, "Am I that imagine this hawk less satisfied?," but being Warren, he would deny that he had *imagined* the hawk. Warren longs to be what Stevens once termed "a hawk of life." Stevens said he wanted his poems "To meet that hawk's eye and to flinch / Not at the eye but at the joy of it." Such an ambition stops at similitudes, and shies away from identification. But Warren is about halfway between the shrewd Stevens and the fanatical Yeats, whose hawk-like hero, Cuchulain, could confront death by crying out, "I make the truth." Like Whitman, Stevens chooses a fiction that knows itself to be a fiction. Warren, in his prose "Afterthought" to *Being Here: Poetry 1977-1980,* somberly ends by remarking "that our lives are our own supreme fiction." There is an implicit thrust here against

Stevens, who would not have agreed. Yet Warren is a dramatic lyricist, whose boys and hawks are not fictive. Stevens, infinitely nuanced, would not have deigned to write a dramatic lyric. In Stevens, "the truth" sagely reduces to "the the," but Warren wants and needs the truth, and will risk placing all his own poems and stories upon the pyre if that will spur the truth to appear.

The risk is extended all through recent Warren, with necessarily mixed results. We are given a poetic art that dares constantly the root meaning of *hamartia:* to shoot wide of the mark. From the Sublime lyric, this very late Warren has passed to the tragic mode, which fails sometimes very badly in *Being Here,* and then suddenly gives us perfection, as in "Eagle Descending":

Beyond the last flamed escarpment of mountain cloud
The eagle rides air currents, switch and swell,
With spiral upward now, steady as God's will.

Beyond black peak and flaming cloud, he yet
Stares at the sun – invisible to us,
Who downward sink. Beyond new ranges, shark-

Toothed, saw-toothed, he stares at the plains afar
By ghostly shadows eastward combed, and crossed
By stream, steel-bright, that seems to have lost its way.

No silly pride of Icarus his! All peril past,
He westward gazes, and down, where the sun will brush
The farthermost bulge of earth. How soon? How soon

Will the tangent of his sight now intersect
The latitudinal curvature where the sun
Soon crucial contact makes, to leave him in twilight,

Alone in glory? The twilight fades. One wing
Dips, slow. He leans. – And with that slightest shift,
Spiral on spiral, mile on mile, uncoils

The wind to sing with joy of truth fulfilled.

This is parenthetically subtitled "To a dead friend," identified by Warren as Allen Tate, and is an elegy worthy of its subject, with eagle replacing the personal emblem of the hawk. Hovering throughout, there is a sense of the precursor poem, the first section of Eliot's *Ash Wednesday,* a poem equally influential upon Tate and Warren. The despairing voice that opens *Ash Wednesday* has abandoned the agonistic intensities of poetic tradition: "Desiring this man's gift and that man's scope / I no longer strive to strive towards such things." Warren says of his eagle that it too has given up the poetic quest if that quest is only a Sublime battle against human limitations: "No silly pride of Icarus his!" This eagle's pride is rather in persistence of sight; he goes on staring at the sun, at the plains of Hades, at the westward sweep outwards and downwards of human speculation. And this gaze *is* instrumental, for unless it intersects the sunlight there will not be a final vision "in twilight, / Alone in glory." That Sublime will survive the fading of twilight, the survival being manifest in the slow dip of wing with which the descending eagle makes its last exercise of will. Echoing the *clinamen* of Lucretius, Warren celebrates "that slightest shift" which is poetic and human freedom. Tradition becomes the spiral on spiral, mile on mile, uncoiling of a singing wind whose message is the fulfilled truth of the eagle's dying will. This does seem to me a Lucretian rather than a Christian elegy, but so vexed is the issue of Warren's unforgiving emphasis upon an identity of truth and poetry that I express my own judgment here with considerable qualms.

Warren in his current phase, exemplified by *Rumor Verified: Poems 1979-1980* and by *Chief Joseph,* still under revision, is in the midst of undergoing yet another stylistic change, comparable in scope to the one that ensued in *Incarnations* and *Audubon: A Vision.* Clearly he is not one of the poets who unfold, like Stevens, but one of those who develop, like Yeats. But the alteration in idiom shows no signs of modifying his obsession with the identity of poetic truth and the fierce but entropic freedom emblematic in the image of the hawk. I quote from *Chief Joseph* with a gingerly feeling, so revisionary is Warren, but there is a striking and relevant passage spoken by the Chief as he leads his people's flight from their oppressors:

> Past lava, past schist, past desert and sand –
> A strange land we wandered to eastern horizons
> Where blueness of mountains swam in their blue –
> In blue beyond name. The hawk hung high.
> Gleamed white. A sign. It gleamed like a word in the sky.
> Cleanse hearts and pray. Pray to know what the Sky-Chief
> Would now lean to tell. To the pure heart, Truth speaks.

By now, then, a high-hanging hawk is for Warren not just a sign, but the inevitable sign of the truth. Nothing is more dangerous for a belated poetry (and as Americans we can have no other) than to establish a proper sign for the truth. I want to put Warren's poetry to the test by showing how much that danger both mutilates and enhances his achievement. As a final exemplary text, I give the final poem of *Now and Then*, "Heart of Autumn," primarily because I love it best of all Warren's poems:

> Wind finds the northwest gap, fall comes.
> Today, under gray cloud-scud and over gray
> Wind-flicker of forest, in perfect formation, wild geese
> Head for a land of warm water, the *boom*, the lead pellet.
>
> Some crumple in air, fall. Some stagger, recover control,
> Then take the last glide for a far glint of water. None
> Knows what has happened. Now, today, watching
> How tirelessly *V* upon *V* arrows the season's logic,
>
> Do I know my own story? At least, they know
> When the hour comes for the great wing-beat. Sky-strider,
> Star-rider – they rise, and the imperial utterance,
> Which cries out for distance, quivers in the wheeling sky.
>
> That much they know, and in their nature know
> The path of pathlessness, with all the joy
> Of destiny fulfilling its own name.
> I have known time and distance, but not why I am here.
>
> Path of logic, path of folly, all
> The same – and I stand, my face lifted now skyward,
> Hearing the high beat, my arms outstretched in the tingling
> Process of transformation, and soon tough legs,

With folded feet, trail in the sounding vacuum of passage,
And my heart is impacted with a fierce impulse
To unwordable utterance –
Toward sunset, at a great height.

This seems to me the essential Warren poem, as much his own invention as "The Course of a Particular" is Stevens's or "Repose of Rivers" is Hart Crane's. Eliot, prime precursor, is so repressed here that one might think more readily of Melville or Hardy – both Shelleyans – as closer to Warren's mode, though certainly not to his stance or vision. But how much has that stance and vision changed from the poetry of the young Warren? I quote pretty much at random from Warren's earliest verse, and what I hear is the purest Eliot:

What grief has the mind distilled?
The heart is unfulfilled
The hoarse pine stilled
I cannot pluck
Out of this land of pine and rock
Of red bud their season not yet gone
If I could pluck
(In drouth the lizard will blink on the hot limestone)

* * *

At the blind hour of unaimed grief,
Of addition and subtraction,
Of compromise,
Of the smoky lecher, the thief,
Of regretted action,
At the hour to close the eyes,
At the hour when lights go out in the houses –
Then wind rouses
The kildees from their sodden ground.
Their commentary is part of the wind's sound.
What is that other sound,
Surf or distant cannonade?

Both passages would fit well enough in "Gerontion" or *The Waste Land,* but that was Warren more that a half-century ago. In an older way of critical speaking, you might say that he had weathered Eliot's influence, while extending both Eliot's tradition and Eliot's sense of *the* tradition, the sense we associate with Cleanth Brooks, as with Warren. But I tend to a different kind of critical speaking, one which would emphasize Warren's passage into poetic strength as an agonistic process that the Eliot-Warren-Brooks tradition tends to deprecate, or even to deny. Does a poem like "Heart of Autumn" show Warren in a benign relation to tradition, and does Warren's desire to embody the truth find a place within Eliot's sense of the tradition?

Whitman began the final section of *Song of Myself* by juxtaposing himself to the spotted hawk, who swoops by and accuses the poet, complaining "of my gab and my loitering." For the Emersonian Whitman, identification took place not with the hawk, but between one's own empirical and ontological selves. In late Warren, the ontological self is identified with and as the flight of wild birds, and "the imperial utterance," crying out for distance, is beyond the human. The "high beat" transforms Warren himself, and he crosses the threshold of a wordless Sublime, as his heart identifies with the heart of autumn. Whatever such an identification is, its vitalism has broken the canons both of Whitman's American Romantic tradition and of Eliot's counter-tradition of neo-orthodoxy. Warren chooses an identification not available to poets like Whitman, Stevens, and Hart Crane, who know their estrangement from the universe of sense. But this choice of identification also brings to an end Eliot's firm separation between poetry and shamanism. For the tradition of Emerson, Warren feels a range of reaction that varies from genial contempt to puzzled respect. For Eliot's poetry, Warren has the agonistic and ambivalent love that always marks the family romance. A poem like "Heart of Autumn" possesses an extraordinary *ethos,* one that mixes memory and desire, where the memory is of a tradition that clearly could distinguish the path of logic from the path of folly, and the desire is to know the shamanistic path of pathlessness, since the traditional paths have proved to be all the same.

Warren, on this reading, is a sunset hawk at the end of a tradition. His usurpation of the Sublime has about it the aura of a solitary grandeur. "I thirst to know the power and nature of Time . . ." is the Augustinian epigraph of *Being Here,* to which Warren adds: "Time is the dimension in which God strives to define His own being." The epigraph is truer to Warren than the addition is, because the trope of a hawk's shuddering immanence is not wholly appropriate for the God of Abraham, the God of Isaac, the God of Jacob, the God of Jesus. Such a trope, whether in Hopkins or Warren, Yeats or Hart Crane, shows rather the poet's agonistic striving, not so much for the foremost place, but for the blessing of a time without boundaries. In *Audubon,* Warren found the inevitable trope for that time: "They fly / In air that glitters like fluent crystal / And is hard as perfectly transparent iron, they cleave it / With no effort." Such a trope is not an Eliotic baroque extension of tradition, but marks rather an ellipsis of further figuration. Warren stands, his face lifted now skyward, toward sunset, at a great height.

15 Elizabeth Bishop: The Lion Sun

The principal poets of Elizabeth Bishop's generation included
Roethke, Lowell, Berryman, Jarrell and, in a different mode,
Olson. Whether any of these articulated an individual rhetorical
stance with a skill as sure as hers may be questioned. Her way of
writing was closer to that of Stevens and Marianne Moore, in the
generation just beyond, than to any of her exact contemporaries.
Despite the differences in scale, her best poems rival the Stevens
of the shorter works, rather than the perhaps stronger Stevens of
the sequences.

Bishop stands then securely in a tradition of American poetry that began with Emerson, Very and Dickinson, and culminated
in aspects of Frost as well as of Stevens and Moore. This tradition
is marked by firm rhetorical control, overt moral authority, and
sometimes by a fairly strict economy of means. The closing lines
in *Geography III* epitomize the tradition's self-recognition:

> He and the bird know everything is answered,
> all taken care of,
> no need to ask again. .
> — Yesterday brought to today so lightly!
> (A yesterday I find almost impossible to lift.)

These poignant lines have more overt pathos than the poet
ever allowed herself elsewhere. But there is a paradox always in
the contrast between a poetry of deep subjectivity, like
Wordsworth's or Stevens's or Bishop's, and a confessional poetry,
like Coleridge's or that of Bishop's principal contemporaries.

When I read say "The Poems of Our Climate," by Stevens, or "The End of March," by Bishop, I encounter eventually the overwhelming self-revelation of a profoundly subjective consciousness. When I read say "Skunk Hour" by Lowell or one of Berryman's sonnets, I confront finally an opacity, for that is all the confessional mode can yield. It is the strength of Bishop's tradition that its clarity is more than a surface phenomenon. Such strength is cognitive, even analytical, and surpasses philosophy and psychoanalysis in its power to expose human truth.

There are grander poems by Bishop than the relatively early "The Unbeliever," but I center upon it here because I love it best of all her poems. It does not compare in scope and power to "The Monument," "Roosters," "The Fish," "The Bight, " "At the Fishhouses," "Brazil, January 1, 1502," "First Death in Nova Scotia," or the extraordinary late triad of "Crusoe in England," "The Moose" and "The End of March." Those ten poems have an authority and a possible wisdom that transcend "The Unbeliever." But I walk around, certain days, chanting "The Unbeliever" to myself, it being one of those rare poems you never evade again, once you know it (and it knows you). Its five stanzas essentially are variations upon its epigraph, from Bunyon: "He sleeps on the top of a mast." Bunyon's trope concerns the condition of unbelief; Bishop's does not. Think of the *personae* of Bishop's poem as exemplifying three rhetorical stances, and so as being three kinds of poet, or even three poets: cloud, gull, unbeliever. The cloud is Wordsworth or Stevens. The gull is Shelley or Hart Crane. The unbeliever is Dickinson or Bishop. None of them has the advantage; the spangles sea wants to destroy them all. The cloud, powerful in introspection, regards not the sea but his own subjectivity. The gull, more visionary still, beholds neither sea nor air but his own aspiration. The unbeliever observes nothing, but the sea is truly observed in his dream:

> which was, "I must not fall.
> The spangled sea below wants me to fall.
> It is hard as diamonds; it wants to destroy us all."

I think that is the reality of Bishop's famous eye. Like Dickinson's, its truest precursor, it confronts the truth, which is that what is most worth seeing is impossible to see, at least with open eyes. A poetry informed by that mode of observation will station itself at the edge where what is most worth saying is all but impossible to say. I will conclude here by contrasting Bishop's wonderful trope of the lion, in "The End of March," to Stevens's incessant use of the same figure. In Stevens, the lion tends to represent poetry as a destructive force, as the imposition of the poet's will-to-power over reality. This image culminates in "An Ordinary Evening in New Haven":

> Say of each lion of the spirit

> It is a cat of a sleek transparency
> That shines with a nocturnal shine alone.
> The great cat must stand potent in the sun.

Against that destructive night in which all cats are black, even the transparent ones, Stevens sets himself as a possible lion, potent in the light of the idea-of-ideas. Here, I take it, is Bishop's affectionate riposte:

> They could have been teasing the lion sun,
> except that now he was behind them
> — a sun who'd walked the beach the last low tide,
> making those big, majestic paw-prints,
> who perhaps had batted a kite out of the sky to play with.

A somewhat Stevensian lion sun, clearly, but with something better to do than standing potent in itself. The path away from poetry as a destructive force can only be through play, the play of trope. Within her tradition so securely, Bishop profoundly plays at trope. Dickinson, Moore and Bishop resemble Emerson, Frost and Stevens, in that tradition, with a difference due not to mere nature or mere ideology but to superb art.

16 Inescapable Poe

I

Valéry, in a letter to Gide, asserted that: "Poe is the only impeccable writer. He was never mistaken." If this judgment startles an
American reader, it is less remarkable than Baudelaire's habit of
making his morning prayers to God and to Edgar Poe. If we add
the devotion of Mallarmé to what he called his master Poe's
"severe ideas," then we have some sense of the scandal of what
might be called "French Poe," perhaps as much a Gallic
mystification as "French Freud." French Poe is less bizarre than
French Freud, but more puzzling, because its literary authority
ought to be overwhelming, and yet vanishes utterly when confronted by what Poe actually wrote. Here is the second stanza of
the impeccable writer's celebrated lyric, "For Annie":

> Sadly, I know
>   I am shorn of my strength,
> And no muscle I move
>   As I lie at full length –
> But no matter! – I feel
>   I am better at length.

Though of a badness not to be believed, this is by no means
unrepresentative of Poe's verse. Aldous Huxley charitably supposed that Baudelaire, Mallarmé and Valéry simply had no ear for
English, and so just could not hear Poe's palpable vulgarity.
Nothing even in Poe's verse is so wickedly funny as Huxley's paro-

dy in which a grand Miltonic touchstone is transmuted into the
mode of Poe's "Ulalume." First Milton, in *Paradise Lost,* IV,
268–73:

> Not that fair field
> of Enna, where Proserpine gathering flowers
> Her self a fairer flower by gloomy Dis
> Was gathered, which cost Ceres all that pain
> To seek her through the world;

Next, Huxley's Poe:

> It was noon in the fair field of Enna,
>   When Proserpina gathering flowers –
>   Herself the most fragrant of flowers,
> Was gathered away to Gehenna
>   By the Prince of Plutonian powers;
> Was borne down the windings of Brenner
>   To the gloom of his amorous bowers –
> Down the tortuous highway of Brenner
>   To the God's agapemonous bowers.

What then did Baudelaire hear, what music of thought,
when he read the actual Poe of "Ulalume"?

> Here once, through an alley Titanic,
>   Of cypress, I roamed with my Soul –
>   Of cypress, with Psyche, my Soul.
> These were days when my heart was volcanic
>   As the scoriac rivers that roll –
>   As the lavas that restlessly roll
> Their sulphurous currents down Yaanek,
>   In the ultimate climes of the Pole –
> That groan as they roll down Mount Yaanek,
>   In the realms of the Boreal Pole.

If this were Edward Lear, poet of "The Dong with the
Luminous Nose" or "The Jumblies," one might not question
Baudelaire and the other apostles of French Poe. But the hard-
driven Poe did not set out to write nonsense verse. His desire was
to be the American Coleridge or Byron or Shelley, and his poetry,
at its rare best, echoes those High Romantic forerunners with
some grace and a certain plangent urgency. Yet even "The City in
the Sea" is a touch too close to Byron's "Darkness," while "Israfel"

weakly revises Shelley's "To a Skylark." Nineteenth-century
American poetry is considerably better than it is generally
acknowledged to be. There are no other figures comparable to
Whitman and Dickinson, but at least the following are clearly
preferable to Poe, taking them chronologically: Bryant, Emerson,
Longfellow, Whittier, Jones Very, Thoreau, Melville, Timrod and
Tuckerman. Poe scrambles for twelfth place with Sidney Lanier; if
this judgment seems harsh, or too arithmetical, it is prompted by
the continued French overevaluation of Poe as lyricist. No reader
who cares deeply for the best poetry written in English can care
greatly for Poe's verse. Huxley's accusation of vulgarity and bad
taste is just: "To the most sensitive and high-souled man in the
world we should find it hard to forgive, shall we say, the wearing
of a diamond ring on every finger. Poe does the equivalent of this
in his poetry; we notice the solecism and shudder."

II

Whatever his early ambitions, Poe wrote relatively little verse;
there are scarcely a hundred pages of it in the remarkable new
edition of his complete writings, in two substantial volumes, published by The Library of America. The bulk of his work is in tale-
telling and criticism, with the exception of the problematic
Eureka: A Prose Poem, a hundred page cosmology that I take to be
Poe's answer to Emerson's Transcendental manifesto, *Nature*.
Certainly *Eureka* is more of a literary achievement than Poe's
verse, while the popularity and influence of the shorter tales has
been and remains immense. Whether either *Eureka* or the famous
stories can survive authentic criticism is not clear, but nothing
could remove the stories from the canon anyway. They are a permanent element in Western literary culture, even though they are
best read when we are very young. Poe's criticism has mixed
repute, but in fact has never been made fully available until The
Library of America edition.
  Poe's survival raises perpetually the issue as to whether literary merit and canonical status necessarily go together. I can think
of no other American writer, down to this moment, at once so

inevitable and so dubious. Mark Twain catalogued Fenimore
Cooper's literary offenses, but all that he exuberantly listed are
minor compared to Poe's. Allen Tate, proclaiming Poe "our
cousin" in 1949, at the centenary of Poe's death, remarked: "He
has several styles, and it is not possible to damn them all at once."
Uncritical admirers of Poe should be asked to read his stories
aloud (but only to themselves!). The association between the acting style of Vincent Price and the styles of Poe is alas not gratuitous, and indeed is an instance of deep crying out unto deep.
Lest I be considered unfair by those devoted to Poe, I hasten to
quote him at his strongest as a storyteller. Here is the opening
paragraph of "William Wilson," a tale admired by Dostoevski and
still central to the great Western topos of the double:

> Let me call myself, for the present, William Wilson. The fair page
> lying before me need not be sullied with my real appellation. This
> has already been too much an object for the scorn – for the horror –
> for the detestation of my race. To the utter-most regions of the globe
> have not indignant winds bruited its unparalleled infamy? Oh, out-
> cast of all outcasts most abandoned! – to the earth art thou not forev-
> er dead? to its honors, to its flowers, to its golden aspirations? – and a
> cloud, dense, dismal, and limitless, does it not hang eternally
> between thy hopes and heaven?

This rhetoric, including the rhetorical questions, is British
Gothic rather than German Gothic, Ossian or Monk Lewis rather
than Tieck or E.T.A. Hoffmann. Its palpable squalors require no
commentary. The critical question surely must be: how does
"William Wilson" survive its bad writing? Poe's awful diction,
whether here or in "The Fall of the House of Usher" or "The
Purloined Letter" seems to demand the decent masking of a com-
petent French translation. The tale somehow is stronger than its
telling, which is to say that Poe's actual text does not matter. What
survives, despite Poe's writing, are the psychological dynamics and
mythic reverberations of his stories about William Wilson and
Roderick Usher. Poe can only gain by a good translation, and
scarcely loses if each reader fully retells the stories to another. C.
S. Lewis, defending the fantasies of George Macdonald (*George
Macdonald: An Anthology* by C. S. Lewis, Doubleday Dolphin

Books, 1962), formulated a curious principle that seems to me more applicable to Poe than to Macdonald:

> The texture of his writing as a whole is undistinguished, at times fumbling. . . . But this does not quite dispose of him even for the literary critic. What he does best is fantasy – fantasy that hovers between the allegorical and the mythopoeic. And this, in my opinion, he does better than any man. The critical problem with which we are confronted is whether this art – the art of mythmaking – is a species of the literary art. The objection to so classifying it is that the Myth does not essentially exist in words at all. We all agree that the story of Balder is a great myth, a thing of inexhaustible value. But of whose version – whose words – are we thinking when we say this?

Lewis replies that he is not thinking of anyone's words, but of a particular pattern of events. Of course that means Lewis is thinking of his own words. He goes so far as to remember:

> . . . when I first heard the story of Kafka's *Castle* related in conversation and afterwards read the book for myself. The reading added nothing. I had already received the myth, which was all that mattered.

Clearly mistaken about Kafka, Lewis was certainly correct about Macdonald's *Lilith,* and I think the insight is valid for Poe's stories. Myths matter because we prefer them in our own words, and so Poe's diction scarcely distracts us from our retelling, to ourselves, his bizarre myths. There is a dreadful universalism pervading Poe's weird tales. The Freudian reductions of Marie Bonaparte pioneered at converting Poe's universalism into the psychoanalytical universalism, but Poe is himself so reductive that the Freudian translations are in his case merely redundant. Poe authentically frightens children, and the fright can be a kind of trauma. I remember reading Poe's tales and Bram Stoker's *Dracula,* each for the first time, when I was about ten. *Dracula* I shrugged off (at least until I confronted Bela Lugosi murmuring: "I never drink – wine!") but Poe induced nasty and repetitious nightmares that linger even now. Myth may be only what the Polish aphorist Stanislaw Lec once called it, "gossip grown old," but then Poe would have to be called a very vivid gossip, though not often a very eloquent one.

III

Critics, even good ones, admire Poe's stories for some of the oddest of reasons. Poe, a true Southerner, abominated Emerson, plainly perceiving that Emerson (like Whitman, like Lincoln) was not a Christian, not a royalist, not a classicist. Self-reliance, the Emersonian answer to Original Sin, does not exist in the Poe cosmos, where you necessarily start out damned, doomed and dismal. But I think Poe detested Emerson for some of the same reasons Hawthorne and Melville more subtly resented him, reasons that persist in the most distinguished living American writer, Robert Penn Warren, and in many current academic literary critics in our country. If you dislike Emerson, you probably will like Poe. Emerson fathered pragmatism; Poe fathered precisely nothing, which is the way he would have wanted it. Yvor Winters accused Poe of obscurantism, but that truthful indictment no more damages Poe than does tastelessness and tone-deafness. Emerson, for better and for worse, was and is the mind of America, but Poe was and is our hysteria, our uncanny unanimity in our repressions. I certainly do not intend to mean by this that Poe was deeper than Emerson in any way whatsoever. Emerson cheerfully and consciously threw out the past. Critics tend to share Poe's easy historicism; perhaps without knowing it, they are gratified that every Poe story is, in too clear a sense, over even as it begins. We don't have to wait for Madeline Usher and the house to fall in upon poor Roderick; they have fallen in upon him already, before the narrator comes upon the place. Emerson exalted freedom, which he and Thoreau usefully called "wildness." No one in Poe is or can be free or wild, and some academic admirers of Poe truly like everything and everyone to be in bondage to a universal past. To begin is to be free, god-like and Emersonian-Adamic, or Jeffersonian. But for a writer to be free is bewildering and even maddening. What American writers and their exegetes half-unknowingly love in Poe is his more-than-Freudian oppressive and curiously original sense and sensation of overdetermination. Walter Pater once remarked that museums depressed him because they made him doubt that anyone had ever once been young. No one in a Poe story was ever young. As D. H. Lawrence once angrily observed, everyone in Poe is a vampire – Poe himself in particular.

IV

Among Poe's tales, the near-exception to what I have been saying is the longest and most ambitious, *The Narrative of Arthur Gordon Pym*, just as the best of Poe's poems is the long prose-poem, *Eureka*. Alas, even these works are somewhat over-valued, if only because Poe's critics understandably become excessively eager to see him vindicated. *Pym* is readable, but *Eureka* is extravagantly repetitious. Auden was quite taken with *Eureka*, but he could remember very little of it in conversation, and one can doubt that he read it through, at least in English. Poe's most advanced critic is John T. Irwin, in his book *American Hieroglyphics* (New Haven, 1980; paperback edition, Baltimore, 1983). Irwin rightly centers upon *Pym*, while defending *Eureka* as an "aesthetic cosmology" addressed to what in each of us Freud called the "bodily ego." Irwin is too shrewd to assert that Poe's performance in *Eureka* fulfills Poe's extraordinary intentions:

> What the poem Eureka, at once pre-Socratic and post-Newtonian, asserts is the truth of the feeling, the bodily intuition, that the diverse objects which the mind discovers in contemplating external nature form a unity, that they are all parts of one body which, if not infinite, is so gigantic as to be beyond both the spatial and temporal limits of human perception. In Eureka, then, Poe presents us with the paradox of a "unified" macrocosmic body that is without a totalizing image – an alogical, intuitive belief whose "truth" rests upon Poe's sense that cosmologies and myths of origin are forms of internal geography that, under the guise of mapping the physical universe, map the universe of desire.

Irwin might be writing of Blake, or of other visionaries who have sought to map total forms of desire. What Irwin catches, by implication, is Poe's troubling anticipation of what is most difficult in Freud, the "frontier concepts" between mind and

body, such as the bodily ego, the non-repressive defense of introjection, and above all, the drives or instincts. Poe, not just in
Eureka and in *Pym,* but throughout his tales and even in some of
his verse, is peculiarly close to the Freudian speculation upon the
bodily ego. Freud, in *The Ego and the Id* (1923), resorted to the
uncanny language of E. T. A. Hoffmann (and of Poe) in describing this difficult notion:

> The ego is first and foremost a bodily ego; it is not merely a surface
> entity, but is itself the projection of a surface. If we wish to find an
> anatomical analogy for it we can best identify it with the 'cortical
> homunculus' of the anatomists, which stands on its head in the cor-
> tex, sticks up its heels, faces backwards and, as we know, has its
> speech-area on the left-hand side.

A footnote in the English translation of 1927, authorized by Freud
but never added to the German editions, elucidates the first sentence of this description in a way analogous to the cricial
metaphor in Poe that concludes *The Narrative of Arthur Gordon
Pym:*

> I. e. the ego is ultimately derived from bodily sensations, chiefly from
> those springing from the surface of the body, besides, as we have
> seen above, representing the superficies of the mental apparatus.

A considerable part of Poe's mythological power emanates
from his own difficult sense that the ego is always a bodily ego.
The characters of Poe's tales live out nearly every conceivable fantasy of introjection and identification, seeking to assuage their
melancholia by psychically devouring the lost objects of their
affections. D. H. Lawrence, in his *Studies in Classic American
Literature* (1923), moralized powerfully against Poe, condemning
him for "the will-to-love and the will-to-consciousness, asserted
against death itself. The pride of human conceit in KNOWL-
EDGE." It is illuminating that Lawrence attacked Poe in much the
same spirit as he attacked Freud, who is interpreted in
Psychoanalysis and the Unconscious as somehow urging us to violate
the taboo against incest. The interpretation is as extravagant as
Lawrence's thesis that Poe urges vampirism upon us, but there
remains something suggestive in Lawrence's violence against both

Freud and Poe. Each placed the elitist individual in jeopardy, Lawrence implied, by hinting at the primacy of fantasy not just in the sexual life proper, but in the bodily ego's constitution of itself through acts of incorporation and identification.

The cosmology of *Eureka* and the narrative of *Pym* alike circle around fantasies of incorporation. *Eureka*'s subtitle is "An Essay on the Material and Spiritual Universe" and what Poe calls its "general proposition" is heightened by italics: *"In the Original Unity of the First Thing lies the Secondary Cause of all Things, with the Germ of their Inevitable Annihilation. "* Freud, in *his* cosmology, *Beyond the Pleasure Principle,* posited that the inorganic had preceded the organic, and also that it was the tendency of all things to return to their original state. Consequently, the aim of all life was death. The death drive, which became crucial for Freud's later dualisms, is nevertheless pure mythology, since Freud's only evidence for it was the repetition compulsion, and it is an extravagant leap from repetition to death. This reliance upon one's own mythology may have prompted Freud's audacity when, in the *New Introductory Lectures,* he admitted that the theory of drives was, so to speak, his own mythology, drives being not only magnificent conceptions but particularly sublime in their indefiniteness. I wish I could assert that *Eureka* has some of the speculative force of *Beyond the Pleasure Principle* or even of Freud's disciple Ferenczi's startling *Thalassa: A Theory of Genitality,* but *Eureka* does badly enough when compared to Emerson's *Nature,* which itself has only a few passages worthy of what Emerson wrote afterwards. And yet Valéry in one sense was justified in his praise for *Eureka.* For certain intellectuals, *Eureka* performs a mythological function akin to what Poe's tales continue to do for hosts of readers. *Eureka* is unevenly written, badly repetitious, and sometimes opaque in its abstractness, but like the tales it seems not to have been composed by a particular individual. The universalism of a common nightmare informs it. If the tales lose little, or even gain, when we retell them to others in our own words, *Eureka* gains by Valéry's observations, or by the summaries of recent critics like John Irwin or Daniel Hoffman. Translation even into his own language always benefits Poe.

I haven't the space, or the desire, to summarize *Eureka,* and no summary is likely to do anything besides deadening both my readers and myself. Certainly Poe was never more passionately sincere than in composing *Eureka,* of which he affirmed: *"What I here propound is true."* But these are the closing sentences of *Eureka:*

> Think that the sense of individual identity will be gradually merged in the general consciousness – that Man, for example, ceasing imperceptibly to feel himself Man, will at length attain that awfully triumphant epoch when he shall recognize his existence as that of Jehovah. In the meantime bear in mind that all is Life-Life-Life within Life – the less within the greater, and all within the Spirit Divine.

To this, Poe appends a "Note":

> The pain of the consideration that we shall lose our individual identity, ceases at once when we further reflect that the process, as above described, is, neither more nor less than that of the absorption, by each individual intelligence of all other intelligences (that is, of the Universe) into its own. That God may be all in all, *each* must become God.

Allen Tate, not unsympathetic to his cousin, Mr. Poe, remarked of Poe's extinction in *Eureka* that "there is a lurid sublimity in the spectacle of his taking God along with him into a grave which is not smaller than the universe." If we read closely, Poe's trope is "absorption," and we are where we always are in Poe, amid ultimate fantasies of introjection in which the bodily ego and the cosmos become indistinguishable. That makes Poe the most cannibalistic of authors, and seems less a function of his "angelic" theological imagination than of his mechanisms of defense. Again, I suspect this judgment hardly weakens Poe, since his strength is no more cognitive than it is stylistic. Poe's mythology, like the mythology of psychoanalysis that we cannot yet bear to acknowledge as primarily a mythology, is peculiarly appropriate to any modernism, whether you want to call it early, high or postmodernism. The definitive judgment belongs here to T.W. Adorno, certainly the most authentic theoretician of all modernisms, in his last book, *Aesthetic Theory* (translated by C. Lenhardt, Routledge & Kegan Paul, London and Boston, 1948). Writing on "reconciliation and mimetic adaptation to death,"

Adorno blends the insights of Jewish negative theology and psychoanalysis:

> Whether negativity is the barrier or the truth of art is not for art to decide. Art works are negative *per se* because they are subject to the law of objectification; that is, they kill what they objectify, tearing it away from its context of immediacy and real life. They survive because they bring death. This is particularly true of modern art, where we notice a general mimetic abandonment to reification, which is the principle of death. Illusion in art is the attempt to escape from this principle. Baudelaire marks a watershed, in that art after him seeks to discard illusion without resigning itself to being a thing among things. The harbingers of modernism, Poe and Baudelaire, were the first technocrats of art.

Baudelaire was more than a technocrat of art, as Adorno knew, but Poe would be only that except for his myth-making gift. C.S. Lewis may have been right when he insisted that such a gift could exist even apart from other literary endowments. Blake and Freud are inescapable myth-makers who were also cognitively and stylistically powerful. Poe is a great fantasist whose thoughts were commonplace and whose metaphors were dead. Fantasy, mythologically considered, combines the stances of Narcissus and Prometheus, which are ideologically antithetical to one another, but figuratively quite compatible. Poe is at once the Narcissus and the Prometheus of his nation. If that is right, then he is inescapable, even though his tales contrast weakly with Hawthorne's, his poems scarcely bear reading, and his speculative discourses fade away in juxtaposition to Emerson's, his despised Northern rival.

V

To define Poe's mythopoeic inevitability more closely, I turn to his story, "Ligeia," and to the end of *Pym*. Ligeia, a tall, dark, slender transcendentalist, dies murmuring a protest against the feeble human will, which cannot keep us forever alive. Her distraught and nameless widower, the narrator, endeavors to comfort himself, first with opium, and then with a second bride, "the fair-

haired and blue-eyed Lady Rowena Trevanian, of Tremaine."
Unfortunately, he has little use for this replacement, and so she
sickens rapidly and dies. Recurrently, the corpse revivifies, only to
die yet again and again. At last, the cerements are stripped away,
and the narrator confronts the undead Ligeia, attired in the
death-draperies of her now evaporated successor.

As a parable of the vampiric will, this works well enough.
The learned Ligeia presumably has completed her training in the
will during her absence, or perhaps merely owes death a substitute, the insufficiently transcendental Rowena. What is mythopoe-
ically more impressive is the ambiguous question of the narrator's
will. Poe's own life, like Walt Whitman's, is an American mythology, and what all of us generally remember about it is that Poe married his first cousin, Virginia Clemm, before she turned fourteen.
She died a little more than ten years later, having been a semi-
invalid for most of that time. Poe himself died less than three
years after her, when he was just forty. "Ligeia," regarded by Poe as
his best tale, was written a bit more than a year into the marriage.
The later Freud implicitly speculates that there are no accidents;
we die because we will to die, our character being also our fate. In
Poe's myth also, ethos is the daemon, and the daemon is our destiny. The year after Virginia died, Poe proposed marriage to the
widowed poet Sarah Helen Whitman. Biographers tell us that the
lady's doubts were caused by rumors of Poe's bad character, but
perhaps Mrs. Whitman had read "Ligeia"! In any event, this marriage did not take place, nor did Poe survive to marry another
widow, his childhood sweetheart Elmira Royster Skelton. Perhaps
she too might have read "Ligeia" and forborne.

The narrator of "Ligeia" has a singularly bad memory, or
else a very curious relationship to his own will, since he begins by
telling us that he married Ligeia without ever having troubled to
learn her family name. Her name itself is legend, or romance,
and that was enough. As the story's second paragraph hints, the
lady was an opium dream with the footfall of a shadow. The implication may be that there never was such a lady, or even that if you
wish to incarnate your reveries, then you must immolate your con-

substantial Rowena. What is a touch alarming, to the narrator, is the intensity of Ligeia's passion for him, which was manifested however only by glances and voice so long as the ideal lady lived. Perhaps this baffled intensity is what kills Ligeia, through a kind of narcissistic dialectic, since she is dominated not by the will of her lust but by the lust of her will. She wills her infinite passion towards the necessarily inadequate narrator and when (by implication) he fails her, she turns the passion of her will against dying and at last against death. Her dreadful poem, "The Conqueror Worm," prophesies her cyclic return from death: "Through a circle that ever returneth in / To the self-same spot." But when she does return, the spot is hardly the same. Poor Rowena only becomes even slightly interesting to her narrator-husband when she sickens unto death, and her body is wholly usurped by the revived Ligeia. And yet the wretched narrator is a touch different, if only because his narcissism is finally out of balance with his first wife's grisly Prometheanism. There are no final declarations of Ligeia's passion as the story concludes. The triumph of her will is complete, but we know that the narrator's will has not blent itself into Ligeia's. His renewed obsession with her eyes testifies to a continued sense of her daemonic power over him, but his final words hint at what the story's opening confirms: she will not be back for long – and remains "my lost love."

The conclusion of *Pym* has been brilliantly analyzed by John Irwin, and so I want to glance only briefly at what is certainly Poe's most effective closure:

> And now we rushed into the embraces of the cataract, where a chasm threw itself open to receive us. But there arose in our pathway a shrouded human figure, very far larger in its proportions than any dweller among men. And the hue of the skin of the figure was of the perfect whiteness of the snow.

Irwin demonstrates Poe's reliance here upon the Romantic topos of the Alpine White Shadow, the magnified projection of the observer himself. The chasm Pym enters is the familiar Romantic Abyss, not a part of the natural world but belonging to eternity, before the creation. Reflected in that abyss, Pym beholds his own shrouded form, perfect in the whiteness of the natural context. Presumably, this is the original bodily ego, the Gnostic self before the fall into creation. As at the close of *Eureka*, Poe brings Alpha and Omega together in an apocalyptic circle. I suggest we read Pym's, which is to say Poe's, white shadow as the American triumph of the will, as illusory as Ligeia's usurpation of Rowena's corpse.

Poe teaches us, through Pym and Ligeia, that as Americans we are both subject and object of our own quests. Emerson, in Americanizing the European sense of the abyss, kept the self and the abyss separate as facts: "There may be two or three or four steps, according to the genius of each, but for every seeing soul there are two absorbing facts – I and the Abyss." Poe, seeking to avoid Emersonianism, ends with only one fact, and it is more a wish than a fact: "I will to be the Abyss." This metaphysical despair has appealed to the Southern American literary tradition and to its Northern followers. The appeal cannot be refuted, because it is myth, and Poe backed the myth with his life as well as his work. If the Northern or Emersonian myth of our literary culture culminates in the beautiful image of Walt Whitman as wound-dresser, moving as a mothering father through the Civil War Washington, D.C. hospitals, then the Southern or counter-myth achieves its perfect stasis at its start, with Poe's snow-white shadow shrouding the chasm down which the boat of the soul is about to plunge. Poe's genius was for negativity and opposition, and the affirmative force of Emersonian America gave him the impetus his daemonic will required.

VI

It would be a relief to say that Poe's achievement as a critic is not mythological, but the splendid, new and almost complete edition of his essays, reviews and marginalia testifies otherwise. It shows Poe indeed to have been Adorno's "technocrat of art." Auden defended Poe's criticism by contrasting the subjects Baudelaire was granted – Delacroix, Constantin Guys, Wagner – with the books Poe was given to review, such as *The Christian Florist, The History of Texas* and *Poetical Remains of the Late Lucretia Maria Davidson.* The answer to Auden is that Poe also wrote about Bryant, Byron, Coleridge, Dickens, Hawthorne, Washington Irving, Longfellow, Shelley and Tennyson; a ninefold providing scope enough for any authentic critical consciousness. Nothing that Poe had to say about these poets and storytellers is in any way memorable or at all an aid to reading them. There are no critical insights, no original perceptions, no accurate or illuminating juxtapositions or historical placements. Here is Poe on Tennyson, from his *Marginalia,* which generally surpass his other criticism:

> Why do some persons fatigue themselves in attempts to unravel such phantasy-pieces as the "Lady of Shalott"? . . . If the author did not deliberately propose to himself a suggestive indefiniteness of meaning, with the view of bringing about a definiteness of vague and therefore of spiritual effect – this, at least, arose from the silent analytical promptings of that poetic genius which, in its supreme development, embodies all orders of intellectual capacity.

I take this as being representative of Poe's criticism, because it is uninterestingly just plain *wrong* about "The Lady of Shalott." No other poem, even by the great word-painter Tennyson, is deliberately so definite in meaning and effect. Everything vague precisely is excluded in this perhaps most Pre-Raphaelite of all poems, where each detail contributes to an impression that might be called hard-edged phantasmagoria. If we take as the three possibilities of nineteenth-century practical criticism the sequence of Arnold, Pater and Wilde, we find Poe useless in all three modes: Arnold's seeing the object as in itself it really is, Pater's seeing accurately one's own impression of the object, and the divine Oscar's sublime seeing of the object as in itself it really is not. If "The Lady of Shalott" is the object, then Poe does not see anything: the poem as in itself it is, one's impression of the poem as that is, or best of all the Wildean sense of what is missing or excluded from the poem. Poe's descriptive terms are "indefinitiveness" and "vague," but Tennyson's poem is just the reverse:

> She left the web, she left the loom,
> She made three paces through the room,
> She saw the water-lily bloom,
> She saw the helmet and the plume,
>   She looked down to Camelot.
> Out flew the web and floated wide;
> The mirror cracked from side to side;
> "The curse is come upon me," cried
>   The Lady of Shalott.

No, Poe as practical critic is a true match for most of his contemporary subjects, such as S. Anna Lewis, author of *The Child of the Sea and other Poems* (1948). Of her lyric, "The Forsaken," Poe wrote: "We have read this little poem more than twenty times and always with increasing admiration. *It is inexpressibly beautiful*" (Poe's italics). I quote only the first of its six stanzas:

> It hath been said – for all who die
>   there is a tear;
> Some pining, bleeding heart to sigh
>   O'er every bier:
> But in that hour of pain and dread
>   Who will draw near
> Around my humble couch and shed
>   One farewell tear?

Well, but there is Poe as theoretician, Valéry has told us. Acute self-consciousness in Poe was strongly misread by Valéry as the inauguration and development of severe and skeptical ideas. Presumably, this is the Poe of three famous essays: "The Philosophy of Composition," "The Rationale of Verse," and "The Poetic Principle." Having just reread these pieces, I have no possibility of understanding a letter of Valéry to Mallarmé which prizes the theories of Poe as being "so profound and so insidiously learned." Certainly we prize the theories of Valéry for just those qualities, and so I have come full circle to where I began, with the mystery of French Poe. Valéry may be said to have read Poe in the critical modes of both Pater and of Wilde. He saw his impression of Poe clearly, and he saw Poe's essays as in themselves they really were not. Admirable, and so Valéry brought to culmination the critical myth that is French Poe.

VII

Whose head is swinging from the swollen strap?
Whose body smokes along the bitten rails,
Bursts from a smoldering bundle far behind
In back forks of the chasms of the brain –
Puffs from a riven stump far out behind
In interborough fissures of the mind . . .?

Hart Crane's vision of Poe, in "The Tunnel" section of *The Bridge*, tells us again why the mythopoeic Poe is inescapable for American literary mythology. Poe's nightmare projections and introjections suggest the New York city subway as the new underground, where Coleridge's "deep Romantic chasm" has been internalized into "the chasms of the brain." Whatever his actual failures as poet and critic, whatever the gap between style and idea in his tales, Poe is central to the American canon, both for us and for the rest of the world. Hawthorne implicitly and Melville explicitly made far more powerful critics of the Emersonian national hope, but they were by no means wholly negative in regard to Emerson and his pragmatic vision of American Self-Reliance. Poe was savage in denouncing minor transcendentalists like Bronson Alcott and William Ellery Channing, but his explicit rejection of Emerson confined itself to the untruthful observation that Emerson was indistinguishable from Thomas Carlyle. Poe should have survived to read Carlyle's insane and amazing pamphlet on "The Nigger Question," which he would have adored. Mythologically, Poe is necessary because all of his work is a hymn to negativity. Emerson was a great theoretician of literature as of life, a good practical critic (when he wanted to be, which was not often), a very good poet (sometimes) and always a major aphorist and essayist. Poe, on a line-by-line or sentence-by-sentence basis, is hardly a worthy opponent. But looking in the French way, as T. S. Eliot recommended: "we see a mass of unique shape and impressive size to which the eye constantly returns." Eliot was probably right, in mythopoeic terms.

17 Walt Whitman: The Real Me

I

As poet and as person, Walt Whitman remains large and evasive. We cannot know, even now, much that he desired us not to know, despite the best efforts of many devoted and scholarly biographers. The relation between his life and his poetry is far more uncertain than most of his readers believe it to be. Yet Whitman is so important to us, so crucial to an American mythology, so absolutely central to our literary culture, that we need to go on trying to bring his life and his work together. Our need might have delighted Whitman, and might have troubled him also. Like his master, Emerson, Whitman prophesied an American religion that is post-Christian, but while Emerson dared to suggest that the Crucifixion was a defeat and that Americans demand victory, Whitman dared further, and suggested that he himself had satisfied the demand. Here is Emerson:

> The history of Christ is the best document of the power of character which we have. A youth who owed nothing to fortune and who was "hanged at Tyburn" – by the pure quality of his nature has shed this epic splendor around the facts of his death which has transfigured every particular into a grand universal symbol for the eyes of all mankind ever since.
>
> He did well. This great Defeat is hitherto the highest fact we have. But he that shall come shall do better. The mind requires a far higher exhibition of character, one which shall make itself good to the senses as well as to the soul; a success to the senses as well as to the soul. This was a great Defeat; we demand Victory. . . .

This grand journal entry concludes, magnificently: "I am *Defeated* all the time; yet to Victory I am born." And here is Whitman, "he that shall come," doing better:

> That I could forget the mockers and insults!
> That I could forget the trickling tears and the blows of the bludgeons and hammers!
> That I could look with a separate look on my own crucifixion and bloody crowning.
> I remember now,
> I resume the overstaid fraction,
> The grave of rock multiplies what has been confided to it, or to any graves,
> Corpses rise, gashes heal, fastenings roll from me.
>
> I troop forth replenish'd with supreme power, . . .

This is Walt Whitman "singing and chanting the things that are part of him, / The worlds that were and will be, death and day," in the words of his involuntary heir, Wallace Stevens. But which Walt Whitman is it? His central poem is what he finally entitled "Song of Myself," rather than, say, "Song of My Soul." But which self? There are two in the poem, besides his soul, and the true difficulties of reading Whitman begin (or ought to begin) with his unnervingly original psychic cartography which resists assimilation to the Freudian maps of the mind. Freud's later system divides us into the "I" or ego, the "above-I" or superego, and the "it" or id. Whitman divided himself (or recognized himself as divided) into "my self," "my soul," and the "real Me" or "Me myself," where the self is a kind of ego, the soul not quite a superego, and the "real Me" not at all an id. Or to use a vocabulary known to Whitman, and still known to us, the self is personality, the soul is character, and again the "real Me" is a mystery. Lest these difficulties seem merely my own, and not truly Whitman's, I turn to the text of "Song of Myself." Here is Walt Whitman, "My self," the *persona* or mask, the personality of the poet:

> Walt Whitman, a kosmos, of Manhattan the son,
> Turbulent, fleshy, sensual, eating, drinking and breeding,
> No sentimentalist, no stander above men and women or apart from them,
> No more modest than immodest.

This is Walt Whitman, one of the roughs, an American, but hardly Walter Whitman Jr., whose true personality, "real Me" or "Me myself," is presented in the passage I love best in the poem:

> These come to me days and nights and go from me again,
> But they are not the Me myself.
>
> Apart from the pulling and hauling stands what I am,
> Stands amused, complacent, compassionating, idle, unitary,
> Looks down, is erect, or bends an arm on an impalpable certain rest,
> Looking with side-curved head curious what will come next,
> Both in and out of the game and watching and wondering at it.

This "Me myself" is not exactly "hankering, gross, mystical, nude," nor quite "turbulent, fleshy, sensual, eating, drinking and breeding." Graceful and apart, cunningly balanced, charming beyond measure, this curious "real Me" is boylike and girllike, very American yet not one of the roughs, provocative, at one with itself. Whatever the Whitmanian soul may be, this "Me myself" evidently can have no equal relationship with it. When the Whitmanian "I" addresses the soul, we hear a warning:

> I believe in you my soul, the other I am must not abase itself to you,
> And you must not be abased to the other.

The "I" here is the "Myself" of "Song of Myself," poetic personality, robust and rough. "The other I am" is the "Me myself," in and out of the game, and clearly not suited for embraces with the soul. Whitman's wariness, his fear of abasement, whether of his soul or of his true, inner personality, one to the other, remains the enigma of his poetry, as of his life, and accounts for his intricate evasions both as poet and as person.

II

Whitman's critics thus commence with a formidable disadvantage as they attempt to receive and comprehend his work. The largest puzzle about the continuing reception of Whitman's poetry is the still prevalent notion that we ought to take him at his word, whether about his self (or selves) or about his art. No other poet insists so vehemently and so continuously that he will tell us all, and tell us all without artifice, and yet tells us so little, and so cunningly. Except for Dickinson (the only American poet comparable to him in magnitude), there is no other nineteenth-century poet as difficult and hermetic as Whitman; not Blake, not Browning, not Mallarmé. Only an elite can read Whitman, despite the poet's insistence that he wrote for the people, for "powerful uneducated persons," as his "By Blue Ontario's Shore" proclaims. His more accurate "Poets to Come" is closer to his readers' experience of him:

> I am a man who, sauntering along without fully stopping, turns a
> casual look upon you and then averts his face. . . .

Whitman was surely too sly to deceive himself, or at least both of his selves, on this matter of his actual poetic evasiveness and esotericism. Humanly, he had much to evade, in order to keep going, in order to start writing and then to keep writing. His biographers cannot give us a clear image of his childhood which was certainly rather miserable. His numerous siblings had mostly melancholy life histories. Madness, retardation, marriage to a prostitute, depressiveness and hypochondria figure among their fates. The extraordinary obsession with health and cleanliness that oddly marks Whitman's poetry had a poignant origin in his early circumstances. Of his uneasy relationship with his father we know a little, though not much. But we know nothing really of his mother, and how he felt towards her. Perhaps the most crucial fact about Whitman's psyche we know well enough; he needed, quite early, to become the true father of all his siblings, and perhaps of his mother also. Certainly he fathered and mothered as many of his siblings as he could, even as he so beautifully became a surrogate father and mother for thousands of wounded and sick soldiers, Union and Confederate, white and black, in the hospitals of Washington, D.C. throughout the Civil War.

The extraordinary and truthful image of Whitman that haunts our country; the vision of the compassionate, unpaid, volunteer wound-dresser comforting young men in pain and soothing the dying, is the climax of Paul Zweig's book on how the man

Walter Whitman Jr. became the poet Walt Whitman. This vision informs the finest pages of Zweig's uneven but moving study; I cannot recall any previous Whitman biographer or critic so vividly and humanely portraying Whitman's hospital service. Searching for the authentic Whitman, as Zweig shows, is a hopeless quest; our greatest poet will always be our most evasive, and perhaps our most self-contradictory. Whitman, at his greatest, has overwhelming pathos as a poet; equal I think to anything in the language. The *Drum-Taps* poem called "The Wound-Dresser" is far from Whitman at his astonishing best, and yet its concluding lines carry the persuasive force of his poetic and human images for once unified:

> Returning, resuming, I thread my way through the hospitals,
> The hurt and wounded I pacify with soothing hand,
> I sit by the restless all the dark night, some are so young,
> Some suffer so much, I recall the experience sweet and sad,
> (Many a soldier's loving arms about this neck have cross'd and rested,
> Many a soldier's kiss dwells on these bearded lips.)

Zweig is admirably sensitive in exploring the ambiguities in Whitman's hospital intensities, and more admirable still in his restraint at not voicing how much all of us are touched by Whitman's pragmatic saintliness during those years of service. I cannot think of a Western writer of anything like Whitman's achievement who ever gave himself or herself up so directly to meeting the agonized needs of the most desperate. There are a handful of American poets comparable to Whitman in stature: Emily Dickinson certainly, Wallace Stevens and Robert Frost perhaps, and maybe one or two others. Our image of them, or of our greatest novelists, or even of Whitman's master, Emerson, can move us sometimes, but not as the image of the wound-dresser Whitman must move us. Like the Lincoln whom he celebrated and lamented, Whitman is American legend, a figure who has a kind of religious aura even for secular intellectuals. If Emerson founded the American literary religion, Whitman alone permanently holds the place most emblematic of the life of the spirit in America.

These religious terms are not Zweig's, yet his book's enterprise usefully traces the winding paths that led Whitman on to his apotheosis as healer and comforter. Whitman's psychosexuality, labyrinthine in its perplexities, may have been the central drive that bewildered the poet into those ways, but it was not the solitary, overwhelming determinant that many readers judge it to have been. Zweig refreshingly is not one of these overdetermined readers. He surmises that Whitman might have experienced little actual homosexual intercourse. I suspect none, though Whitman evidently was intensely in love with some unnamed man in 1859, and rather differently in love again with Peter Doyle about five years later. Zweig accurately observes that: "Few poets have written as erotically as Whitman, while having so little to say about sex. For the most part, his erotic poetry is intransitive, self-delighting." Indeed, it is precisely auto-erotic rather more than it is homo-erotic; Whitman overtly celebrates masturbation, and his most authentic sexual passion is always for himself. One would hardly know this from reading many of Whitman's critics, but one certainly knows it by closely reading Whitman's major poems. Here is part of a crucial crisis-passage from "Song of Myself," resolved through successful masturbation:

> I merely stir, press, feel with my fingers, and am happy,
> To touch my person to some one else's is about as much as I can
>   stand.
> Is this then a touch? quivering me to a new identity,
> Flames and ether making a rush for my veins,
> Treacherous tip of me reaching and crowding to help them,
> My flesh and blood playing out lightning to strike what is hardly dif-
>   ferent from myself, . . .
> I went myself first to the headland, my own hands carried me there.
> You villain touch! what are you doing? my breath is tight in its throat,
> Unclench your floodgates, you are too much for me.
> Blind loving wrestling touch, sheath'd hooded sharp-tooth'd touch!
> Did it make you ache so, leaving me?
> Parting track'd by arriving, perpetual payment of perpetual loan,
> Rich showering rain, and recompense richer afterward.
> Sprouts take and accumulate, stand by the curb prolific and vital,
> Landscapes projected masculine, full-sized and golden.

I take it that this celebratory mode of masturbation, whether read metaphorically or literally, remains the genuine scandal of Whitman's poetry. This may indeed be one of the kernel passages in Whitman, expanded and elaborated as it is from an early note-book passage that invented the remarkable trope of "I went myself first to the headland," the headland being the psychic place of *extravagance*, of wandering beyond limits, from which you cannot scramble back to the shore, place of the father, and from which you may topple over into the sea, identical with night, death and the fierce old mother. "My own hands carried me there," as they fail to carry Whitman in "When Lilacs Last in the Dooryard Bloom'd":

> Oh great star disappear'd – O the black murk that hides the star!
> O cruel hands that hold me powerless – O helpless soul of me!

These are Whitman's own hands, pragmatically cruel because they cannot hold him potently, disabled as he is by a return of repressed guilt. Lincoln's death has set going memories of filial guilt, the guilt that the mortal sickness of Walter Whitman Sr. should have liberated his son into the full blood of creativity that ensued in the 1855 first edition of *Leaves of Grass* (the father died a week after the book's publication). What Whitman's poetry does not express are any reservations about auto-eroticism, which more than sado-masochism remains the last Western taboo. It is a peculiar paradox that Whitman, who proclaims his love for all men, women and children, should have been profoundly solipsistic, narcissistic and self-delighting, but that paradox returns us to the Whitmanian self or rather selves, the cosmological *persona* as opposed to the daemonic "real Me."

III

The most vivid manifestation of the "real Me" in Whitman comes in the shattering "Sea-Drift-" poem, "As I Ebb'd with the Ocean of Life":

> O baffled, balk'd bent to the very earth,
> Oppress'd with myself that I have dared to open my mouth,

> Aware now that amid all that blab whose echoes recoil upon me I
>   have not once had the least idea who or what I am,
> But that before all my arrogant poems the real Me stands yet
>   untouch'd, untold, altogether unreach'd,
> Withdrawn far, mocking me with mock-congratulatory signs and
>   bows,
> With peals of distant ironical laughter at every word I have written,
> Pointing in silence to these songs, and then to the sand beneath.
> I perceive I have not really understood any thing, not a single object,
>   and that no man ever can,
> Nature here in sight of the sea taking advantage of me to dart upon
>   me and sting me,
> Because I have dared to open my mouth to sing at all.

It is Walt Whitman, Kosmos, American, rough, who is
mocked here by his real self, a self that knows itself to be a mystery, because it is neither mother, nor father, nor child; neither
quite female nor quite male; neither voice nor voicelessness.
Whitman's "real Me" is what is best and oldest in him, and like the
faculty Emerson called "Spontaneity," it is no part of the creation,
meaning both nature's creation and Whitman's verbal cosmos. It
is like a surviving fragment of the original Abyss preceding
nature, not Adamic but pre-Adamic. This "real Me" is thus also
presexual, and so plays no role either in the homo-erotic
"Calamus" poems or in the dubiously heterosexual "Children of
Adam" group. Yet it seems to me pervasive in the six long or
longer poems that indisputably are Whitman's masterpieces: "The
Sleepers," "Song of Myself," "Crossing Brooklyn Ferry," "As I
Ebb'd with the Ocean of Life," "Out of the Cradle Endlessly
Rocking," and "When Lilacs Last in the Dooryard Bloom'd."
Though only the last of these is overtly an elegy, all six are in
covert ways elegies for the "real Me," for that "Me myself" that
Whitman could not hope to celebrate as a poet and could not
hope to fulfill as a sexual being. This "real Me" is not a spirit that
denies, but rather one that always remains out of reach, an autistic spirit. In English Romantic poetry and in later nineteenth-century prose romance there is the parallel being that Shelley called
"the Spirit of Solitude," the daemon or shadow of the self-destructive young Poet who is the hero of Shelley's *Alastor*. But Whitman's

very American "real Me" is quite unlike a Shelleyan or Blakean Spectre. It does not quest or desire, and it does not want to be wanted.

Though Zweig hints that Whitman has been a bad influence on other writers, I suspect that a larger view of influence would reverse this implicit judgment. Whitman has been an inescapable influence not only for most significant American poets after him (Frost, indebted directly to Emerson, is the largest exception) but also for the most gifted writers of narrative fiction. This influence transcends matters of form, and has everything to do with the Whitmanian split between the *persona* of the rough Walt and the ontological truth of the "real Me." Poets as diverse as Wallace Stevens and T. S. Eliot have in common perhaps only their hidden, partly unconscious reliance upon Whitman as prime precursor. Hemingway's acknowledged debt to *Huckleberry Finn* is real enough, but the deeper legacy came from Whitman. The Hemingway protagonist, split between an empirical self of stoic courage and a "real Me" endlessly evasive of others while finding its freedom only in an inner perfection of loneliness, is directly descended from the dual Whitman of "Song of Myself." American elegiac writing since Whitman (and how surprisingly much of it *is* covertly elegiac) generally revises Whitman's elegies for the self. *The Waste Land* is "When Lilacs Last in the Dooryard Bloom'd" rewritten, and Stevens's "The Rock" is not less Whitmanian than Hart Crane's *The Bridge*.

Zweig's book joins itself to the biographical criticism of Whitman by such scholars as Bliss Perry, Gay Wilson Allen, Joseph Jay Rubin, Justin Kaplan and others whose works are all part of a useful tradition that illuminates the Americanism of Whitman and yet cannot do enough with Whitman's many paradoxes. Of these, I judge the most crucial to be expressed by this question: how did someone of Whitman's extraordinarily idiosyncratic nature become so absolutely central to nearly all subsequent American literary high culture? This centrality evidently cannot ebb among us, as can be seen in the most recent poems of John Ashbery in his book, *The Wave*, or in the stories of Harold Brodkey, excerpted from his vast and wholly Whitmanian work-in-progress. Whitman's powerful yet unstable identities were his own inheritance from the Orphic Emerson, who proclaimed the central man or poet-to-come as necessarily metamorphic, Bacchic and yet original, and above all American and not British or European in his cultural vistas. This prescription was and is dangerous, because it asks for pragmatism and yet affirms impossible hopes. The rough Whitman is democratic, "real Me" an elitist, but both selves are equally Emersonian.

Politically, Whitman was a Free Soil Democrat who rebelled against the betrayal by the New York Democratic Party of its Jacksonian tradition, but Zweig rightly emphasizes the survival of Emersonian "Prudence" in Whitman which caused him to oppose labor unions. I suspect that Whitman's politics paralleled his sexual morality; the rough Walt homo-erotic and radical, the "real Me" auto-erotic and individualistically elitist. The true importance of this split emerges neither in Whitman's sexuality nor in his politics, but in the delicacy and beauty of his strongest poems. Under the cover of an apparent rebellion against traditional literary form, they extend the poetic tradition without violating it. Whitman's elegies for the self have much in common with Tennyson's, but are even subtler, more difficult triumphs of High Romanticism. Here I dissent wholly from Zweig, who ends his book with a judgment I find both wrong and puzzling:

> . . . *Leaves of Grass* was launched on a collision course with its age. Whitman's work assaulted the institution of literature and language itself and, in so doing, laid the groundwork for the anti-cultural ambition of modernist writing. He is the ancestor not only of Henry Miller and Allen Ginsberg but of Kafka, Beckett, Andre Breton, Borges – of all who have made of their writing an attack on the act of writing and on culture itself.

To associate the subtle artistry, delicate and evasive, of Whitman's greatest poems with Miller and Ginsberg rather than with Hemingway and Stevens and Eliot, is already an error. To say that Kafka, Beckett, and Borges attack, by their writing, the act of writing and culture, is to mistake their assault upon certain interpretive conventions for a war against literary culture. But the gravest misdirection here is to inform readers that Whitman truly attacked the institutions of language and literature. Whitman's "real Me" has more to do with the composition of the great poems than the rough Walt ever did. "Lilacs," which Zweig does not discuss, is as profoundly traditional an elegy as *In Memoriam* or *Adonais*. Indeed, "Lilacs" echoes Tennyson, while "As I Ebb'd" echoes Shelley and "Crossing Brooklyn Ferry" invokes *King Lear*. Zweig is taken in by the prose Whitman who insists he will not employ allusiveness, but the poet Whitman knew better, and is brilliantly allusive, as every strong poet is compelled to be, echoing his precursors and rivals but so stationing the echoes as to triumph with and in some sense over them.

Zweig's study is an honorable and useful account of Whitman's poetic emergence, but it shares in some of the severe limitations of nearly all Whitman criticism so far published. More than most of the biographical critics, Zweig keeps alert to Whitman's duality, and I am grateful to him for his eloquent representations of the poet's war years. Yet Whitman's subtle greatness as a poet seems to me not fully confronted, here or elsewhere. The poetry of the "real Me," intricate and forlorn, is addressed to the "real Me" of the American reader. That it reached what was oldest and best in Eliot and Stevens is testified to by their finest poetry, in contradistinction to their prose remarks upon Whitman. Paradoxically, Whitman's best critic remains, not an American, but D. H. Lawrence, who lamented that, "The Americans are not worthy of their Whitman." Lawrence believed that Whitman had gone further, in actual living expression, than any other poet. The belief was extravagant, certainly, but again the Whitmanian poems of Lawrence's superb final phase show us what Lawrence meant. I give the last word here though, not to Lawrence, but to Emerson, who wrote the first words about Whitman in his celebrated 1855 letter to the poet, words that remain true nearly 130 years further on in our literary culture:

> I am not blind to the worth of the wonderful gift of *Leaves of Grass*. I find it the most extraordinary piece of wit and wisdom that America has yet contributed. . . .

18 Emerson: Power at the Crossing

I

Emerson is an experiential critic and essayist, and not a
Transcendental philosopher. This obvious truth always needs
restating, perhaps now more than ever, when literary criticism is
so overinfluenced by contemporary French heirs of the German
tradition of Idealist or Transcendental philosophy. Emerson is the
mind of our climate, the principal source of the American difference in poetry, criticism and pragmatic post-philosophy. That is a
less obvious truth, and it also needs restating, now and always.
Emerson, by no means the greatest American writer, perhaps
more an interior orator than a writer, is the inescapable theorist
of all subsequent American writing. From his moment to ours,
American authors either are in his tradition, or else in a counter-
tradition originating in opposition to him. This continues even in
a time when he is not much read, such as the period from 1945 to
1965 or so. During the last twenty years, Emerson has returned,
burying his undertakers. "The essays of Emerson," T. S. Eliot
remarked, "are already an encumbrance," one of those judicial
observations that governed the literary academy during the Age
of Eliot, but that now have faded into an antique charm.

Other judicial critics, including Yvor Winters and Allen Tate,
sensibly blamed Emerson for everything they disliked in
American literature and even to some extent in American life.
Our most distinguished living poet, Robert Penn Warren, culminated the counter-traditional polemic of Eliot and Tate in his live-

ly sequence, "Homage to Emerson, on Night-Flight to New York."
Reading Emerson's essays in the "pressurized gloom" of the airlin-
er, Warren sees the glowing page declare: "There is / No sin. Not
even error." Only at a transcendental altitude can Warren's heart
be abstract enough to accept the Sage of Concord, "for / At
38,000 feet Emerson / Is dead right." At ground level, Emerson
"had forgiven God everything" because "Emerson thought that
significance shines through everything."

Sin, error, time, history, a God external to the self, the visit-
ing of the crimes of the fathers upon the sons: these are the topoi
of the literary cosmos of Eliot and his Southern followers, and
these were precisely of no interest whatsoever to Ralph Waldo
Emerson. Of Emerson I am moved to say what Borges said of Oscar Wilde: he was always right. But he himself always says it better:

> That is always best which gives me to myself. The sublime is excited
> in me by the great stoical doctrine, obey thyself. That which shows
> God in me, fortifies me. That which shows God out of me, makes me
> a wart and wen. There is no longer a necessary reason for my being.

One might say that the Bible, Shakespeare and Freud show
us as caught in a psychic conflict, in which we need to be everything in ourselves while we go on fearing that we are nothing in
ourselves. Emerson dismisses the fear, and insists upon the necessity of the single self achieving a total autonomy, of becoming a
cosmos without first ingesting either nature or other selves. He
wishes to give us to ourselves, although these days supposedly he
preaches to the converted, since it is the fashion to assert that we
live in a culture of narcissism, of which our smiling President is
the indubitable epitome. Emerson, in this time of Reagan, should
be cited upon the limitations of all American politics whatsover:

> We might as wisely reprove the east wind, or the frost, as a political
> party, whose members, for the most part, could give no account of
> their position, but stand for the defense of those interests in which
> they find themselves. . . . A party is perpetually corrupted by person-
> ality. Whilst we absolve the association from dishonesty, we cannot
> extend the same charity to their leaders. They reap the rewards of
> the docility and zeal of the masses which they direct. . . . Of the two
> great parties, which, at this hour, almost share the nation between

them, I should say, that, one has the best cause, and the other contains the best men. The philosopher, the poet, or the religious man, will, of course, wish to cast his vote with the democrat, for free trade, for wide suffrage, for the abolition of legal cruelties in the penal code, and for facilitating in every manner the access of the young and the poor to the sources of wealth and power. But he can rarely accept the persons whom the so-called popular party propose to him as representatives of these liberalities.

Emerson writes of the Democrats and of the Whigs (precursors of our modern Republicans) in the early 1840's, when he still believes that Daniel Webster (foremost of "the best men") will never come to advocate the worst cause of the slaveholders. Though his politics have been categorized as "transcendental anarchism," Emerson was at once a believer in pure power and a prophet of the moral law, an apparent self-contradiction that provoked Yvor Winters in an earlier time, and President Giamatti of Yale more recently. Yet this wise inconsistency led Emerson to welcome Whitman in poetry for the same reasons he had hailed Daniel Webster in politics, until Webster's Seventh of March speech in 1850 moved Emerson to the most violent rhetoric of his life. John Jay Chapman, in a great essay on Emerson, remarked that, in his polemic against Webster, Emerson "is savage, destructive, personal, bent on death." Certainly no other American politician has been so memorably denounced in public as Webster was by Emerson:

> Mr. Webster, perhaps, is only following the laws of his blood and constitution. I suppose his pledges were not quite natural to him. He is a man who lives by his memory; a man of the past, not a man of faith and of hope. All the drops of his blood have eyes that look downward, and his finely developed understanding only works truly and with all its force when it stands for animal good; that is, for property.

All the drops of his blood have eyes that look downward; that bitter figuration has outlived every phrase Webster himself ventured. Many modern historians defend Webster for his part in the compromise of 1850, by which California was admitted as a free state while the North pledged to honor the Fugitive Slave Law. This defense maintains that Webster helped preserve the Union for another decade, while strengthening the ideology of Union that culminated in Lincoln. But Emerson, who had given Webster every chance, was driven out of his study and into moral prophecy by Webster's support of the Fugitive Slave Law:

> We are glad at last to get a clear case, one on which no shadow of doubt can hang. This is not meddling with other people's affairs: this is hindering other people from meddling with us. This is not going crusading into Virginia and Georgia after slaves, who it is alleged, are very comfortable where they are: – that amiable argument falls to the ground: but this is befriending in our own State, on our own farms, a man who has taken the risk of being shot or burned alive, or cast into the sea, or starved to death, or suffocated in a wooden box, to get away from his driver: and this man who has run the gauntlet of a thousand miles for his freedom, the statute says, you men of Massachussetts shall hunt, and catch, and send back again to the dog-hutch he fled from. And this filthy enactment was made in the nineteenth century, by people who could read and write. I will not obey it, by God.

As late as 1843, Emerson's love of Webster as incarnate Power had prevailed: "He is no saint, but the wild olive wood, ungrafted yet by grace." After Webster's defense of the Fugitive Slave Law, even Emerson's decorum was abandoned: "The word *liberty* in the mouth of Mr. Webster sounds like the word *love* in the mouth of a courtezan." I suspect that Emerson's deep fury, so uncharacteristic of him, resulted partly from the violation of his own cheerfully amoral dialectics of power. The extraordinary essay on "Power" in *The Conduct of Life* appears at first to worship mere force or drive as such, but the Emersonian cunning always locates power in the place of crossing over, in the moment of transition:

> In history, the great moment is, when the savage is just ceasing to be a savage, with all his hairy Pelasgic strength directed on his opening sense of beauty; – and you have Pericles and Phidias, – not yet passed over into the Corinthian civility. Everything good in nature and the world is in that moment of transition, when the swarthy juices still flow plentifully from nature, but their astringency or acridity is got out by ethics and humanity.

A decade or so before, in perhaps his central essay, "Self-Reliance," Emerson had formulated the same dialectic of power, but with even more exuberance:

> Life only avails, not the having lived. Power ceases in the instant of repose; it resides in the moment of transition from a past to a new state, in the shooting of a gulf, in the darting to an aim. This one fact the world hates, that the soul *becomes;* for that for ever degrades the past, turns all riches to poverty, all reputation to shame, confounds the saint with the rogue, shoves Jesus and Judas equally aside. Why, then, do we prate of self-reliance? Inasmuch as the soul is present, there will be power not confident but agent. To talk of reliance is a poor external way of speaking. Speak rather of that which relies, because it works and is.

Magnificent, but surely even the Webster of 1850 retained his Pelasgic strength, surely even *that* Webster works and is? Emerson's cool answer would have been that Webster had failed the crossing. I think Emerson remains *the* American theoretician of power – be it political, literary, spiritual, economic – because he took the risk of exalting transition for its own sake. Admittedly, I am happier when the consequence is Whitman's "Crossing Brooklyn Ferry" than when the Emersonian product is the first Henry Ford, but Emerson is canny enough to prophesy both disciples. There is a great chill at the center of his cosmos, which remains ours, both the chill and the cosmos:

> But Nature is no sentimentalist, – does not cosset or pamper us. We must see that the world is rough and surly, and will not mind drowning a man or a woman; but swallows your ship like a grain of dust. The cold, inconsiderate of persons, tingles your blood, benumbs your feet, freezes a man like an apple.

This is from the sublime essay "Fate," which leads off *The Conduct of Life,* and culminates in the outrageous question: "Why should we fear to be crushed by savage elements, we who are made up of the same elements?" Elsewhere in "Fate," Emerson observes: "The way of Providence is a little rude," while in "Power" he restates the law of Compensation as "nothing is got for nothing." Emerson is no sentimentalist, and it is something of a puzzle how he ever got to be regarded as anything other than a rather frightening theoretician of life or of letters. But then, his personality also remains a puzzle. He was the true American charismatic, and founded the actual American religion, which is Protestant without being Christian. Was the man one with the essayist, or was only the wisdom uncanny in our inescapable sage?

II

A biography of Emerson is necessarily somewhat redundant at best, because Emerson, like Montaigne, is almost always his own subject, though hardly in Montaigne's own mode. Emerson would not have said: "I am myself the matter of my book," yet Emerson on "History" is more Emerson than history. Though he is almost never overtly autobiographical, his best lesson nevertheless is that all true subjectivity is a difficult achievement, while supposed objectivity is merely the failure of having become an amalgam of other selves and their opinions. Though his is in the oral tradition, his true genre was no more the lecture than it had been the sermon, and certainly not the essay, though that is his only formal achievement, besides a double handful of strong poems. His journals are his authentic work, and seem to me poorly represented by all available selections. Perhaps the journals simply ought not to be condensed, because Emerson's reader needs to be immersed in their flow and ebb, their own experience of the influx of insight followed by the perpetual falling back into skepticism. They move endlessly between a possible ecstasy and a probable shrewdness, while knowing always that neither daemonic intensity nor worldly irony by itself can constitute wisdom.

The essential Emerson begins to emerge in the journals in the autumn of 1830, when he was twenty-seven, with his first entry on Self-Reliance, in which he refuses to be "a secondary man" imitating any other being. A year later (October 27, 1831) we hear the birth of Emerson's *reader's Sublime*, the notion that what moves us in the eloquence, written or oral, of another, must be what is oldest in oneself, which is not part of the Creation, and indeed is God in oneself:

> Were you ever instructed by a wise and eloquent man? Remember then, were not the words that made your blood run cold, that brought the blood to your cheeks, that made you tremble or delight- ed you, – did they not sound to you as old as yourself? Was it not truth that you knew before, or do you ever expect to be moved from the pulpit or from man by anything but plain truth? Never. It is God in you that responds to God without, or affirms his own words trem- bling on the lips of another.

On October 28, 1832, Emerson's resignation from the Unitarian ministry was accepted (very reluctantly) by the Second Church, Boston. The supposed issue was the proper way of cele- brating the Lord's Supper, but the underlying issue, at least for Emerson himself, was celebrating the self as God. Stephen Whicher in his superb *Emerson: An Organic Anthology* (still the best one-volume Emerson) gathered together the relevant notebook texts of October 1832. We find Emerson, sustained by daemonic influx, asserting: "It is light. You don't get a candle to see the sun rise," where clearly Jesus is the candle and Emerson is the sunrise (prophetic, like so much else in early Emerson, of Nietzsche's *Zarathustra*). The most outrageous instance of an inrush of God in Emerson is the notorious and still much derided Transparent Eyeball passage in *Nature* (1836), which is based upon a journal entry of March 19, 1835. But I give the final text from *Nature:*

> Crossing a bare common, in snow puddles, at twilight, under a clouded sky, without having in my thoughts any occurence of special good fortune, I have enjoyed a perfect exhileration. I am glad to the brink of fear. . . . There I feel that nothing can befall me in life, – no disgrace, no calamity, (leaving me my eyes,) which nature cannot repair. Standing on the bare ground, – my head bathed by the blithe air, and uplifted into infinite space, – all mean egotism vanishes. I become a transparent eyeball; I am nothing; I see all; the currents of the Universal Being circulate through me; I am part or particle of God.

Nature, in this passage as in the title of the little book, *Nature,* is rather perversely the wrong word, since Emerson does

not mean "nature" in any accepted sense whatsoever. He means
Man, and not a natural man or fallen Adam, but original man or
unfallen Adam, which is to say America, in the transcendental
sense, just as Blake's Albion is the unfallen form of Man.
Emerson's primal Man, to whom Emerson is joined in this
epiphany, is all eye, seeing earliest, precisely as though no
European, and no ancient Greek or Hebrew, had seen before
him. There is a personal pathos as well, which Emerson's contemporary readers could not have known. Emerson feared blindness
more than death, although his family was tubercular and frequently died young. But there had been an episode of hysterical
blindness during his college years, and its memory, however
repressed, hovers throughout his work. Freud's difficult "frontier
concept" of the bodily ego, which is formed partly by introjective
fantasies, suggests that thinking can be associated with any of the
senses or areas of the body. Emerson's fantastic introjection of the
transparent eyeball as bodily ego seems to make thinking and seeing the same activity, one that culminated in self-deification.

Emerson's power as a kind of interior orator stems from this
self-deification. Nothing is got for nothing, and perhaps the
largest pragmatic consequence of being "part or particle of God"
is that your need for other people necessarily is somewhat diminished. The transparent eyeball passage itself goes on to manifest
an estrangement from the immediacy of other selves:

> The name of the nearest friend sounds then foreign and accidental:
> to be brothers, to be acquaintances, master or servant, is then a trifle
> and a disturbance.

This passage must have hurt Emerson himself, hardly a person for whom "to be brothers" ever was "a trifle and a distur-
bance." The early death of his brother Charles, just four months
before *Nature* was published in 1836, was one of his three terrible
losses, the others being the death of Ellen Tucker, his first wife, in
1831, after little more than a year of marriage, and the death of
his first born child, Waldo, in January 1842, when the boy was
only five years old. Emerson psychically was preternaturally
strong, but it is difficult to interpret the famous passage in his
great essay, "Experience," where he writes of Waldo's death:

An innavigable sea washes with silent waves between us and the things we aim at and converse with. Grief too will make us idealists. In the death of my son, now more than two years ago, I seem to have lost a beautiful estate – no more. I cannot get it nearer to me. If tomorrow I should be informed of the bankruptcy of my principal debtors, the loss of my property would be a great inconvenience to me, perhaps, for many years; but it would leave me as it found me, – neither better nor worse. So is it with this calamity; it does not touch me; something which I fancied was a part of me, which could not be torn away without tearing me nor enlarged without enriching me, falls off from me and leaves no scar.

Perhaps Emerson should have written an essay entitled "The Economic Problem of Grief," but perhaps most of his essays carry that as a hidden subtitle. The enigma of grief in Emerson, after all, may be the secret cause of his strength, of his refusal to mourn for the past. Self-reliance, the American religion he founded, converts solitude into a firm stance against history, including personal history. That there is no history, only biography, is the Emersonian insistence, which may be why a valid biography of Emerson appears to be impossible. John McAleer's biography sets out shrewdly to evade the Emersonian entrapment, which is that Emerson knows only biography, a knowledge that makes personal history redundant. What then is the biographer of Emerson to do?

Such worthy practitioners of the mode as Ralph Rusk and Gay Wilson Allen worked mightily to shape the facts into a life, but are evaded by Emerson. Where someone lives so massively *from within,* he cannot be caught by chroniclers of events, public and private. McAleer instead molds his facts as a series of encounters between Emerson and all his friends and associates. Unfortunately, Emerson's encounters with others – whether his brothers, wives, children, or Transcendental and other literary colleagues, are little more revelatory of his inner life than are his encounters with events, whether it be the death of Waldo or the Civil War. All McAleer's patience, skill and learning cannot overcome the sage's genius for solitude. A biography of Emerson becomes as baffling as a biography of Nietzsche, though the two lives have nothing in common, except of course for ideas. Nietzsche acknowledged Emerson, with affection and enthusiasm,

but he probably did not realize how fully Emerson had anticipated him, particularly in unsettling the status of the self while proclaiming simultaneously a greater overself to come.

III

The critic of Emerson is little better off than the biographer, since
Emerson, again like Nietzsche and remarkably also akin to Freud,
anticipates his critics and does their work for them. Emerson
resembles his own hero, Montaigne, in that you cannot combat
him without being contaminated by him. T. S. Eliot, ruefully contemplating Pascal's hopeless agon with Montaigne, observed that
fighting Montaigne was like throwing a hand grenade into a fog.
Emerson, because he appropriated America, is more like a climate than an atmosphere, however misty. Attempting to write the
order of the variable winds in the Emersonian climate is a hopeless task, and the best critics of Emerson, from John Jay Chapman
and O.W. Firkins through Stephen Whicher to Barbara Packer
and Richard Poirier, wisely decline to list his ideas of order. You
track him best, as writer and as person, by learning the principle
proclaimed everywhere in him: that which you can get from
another is never instruction, but always provocation.

But what is provocation, in the life of the spirit? Emerson
insisted that he called you forth only to your self, and not to any
cause whatsoever. The will to power, in Emerson as afterwards in
Nietzsche, is reactive rather than active, receptive rather than
rapacious, which is to say that it is a will to interpretation.
Emerson teaches interpretation, but not in any of the European
modes fashionable either in his day or in our own, modes currently touching their nadir in a younger rabblement celebrating itself
as having repudiated the very idea of an individual reader or an
individual critic. Group criticism, like group sex, is not a new idea,
but seems to revive whenever a sense of resentment dominates the
aspiring clerisy. With resentment comes guilt, as though societal
oppressions are caused by how we read, and so we get those academic covens akin to what Emerson, in his 1838 journal, called

"philanthropic meetings and holy hurrahs," for which read now "Marxist literary groups" and "Lacanian theory circles":

> As far as I notice what passes in philanthropic meetings and holy hurrahs there is very little depth of interest. The speakers warm each other's skin and lubricate each other's tongue, and the words flow and the superlatives thicken and the lips quiver and the eyes moisten, and an observer new to such scenes would say, Here was true fire; the assembly were all ready to be martyred, and the effect of such a spirit on the community would be irresistible; but they separate and go to the shop, to a dance, to bed, and an hour afterwards they care so little for the matter that on slightest temptation each one would disclaim the meeting.

Emerson, according to President Giamatti of Yale, "was as sweet as barbed wire," a judgment recently achieved independently by John Updike. Yes, and doubtless Emerson gave our politics its particular view of power, as Giamatti laments, but a country deserves its sages, and we deserve Emerson. He has the peculiar dialectical gift of being precursor for both the perpetual New Left of student non-students and the perpetual New Right of preacher non-preachers. The American Religion of Self-Reliance is a superb *literary* religion, but its political, economic and social consequences, whether manifested Left or Right, have now helped place us in a country where literary satire of politics is impossible, since the real thing is far more outrageous than even a satirist of genius could invent. Nathanael West presumably was parodying Calvin Coolidge in *A Cool Million's* Shagpoke Whipple, but is this Shagpoke Whipple or President Reagan speaking?

> America is the land of opportunity. She takes care of the honest and industrious and never fails them as long as they are both. This is not a matter of opinion, it is one of faith. On the day that Americans stop believing it, on that day will America be lost.

Emerson unfortunately believed in Necessity, including "the offence of superiority in persons," and he was capable of writing passages that can help to justify Reagan's large share of the Yuppie vote, as here in "Self-Reliance":

> Then again, do not tell me, as a good man did today, of my obligation to put all poor men in good situations. Are they *my* poor? I tell

> thee, thou foolish philanthropist, that I grudge the dollar, the dime,
> the cent I give to such men as do not belong to me and to whom I do
> not belong. There is a class of persons to whom by all spiritual
> affinity I am bought and sold; for them I will go to prison if need be;
> but your miscellaneous popular charities; the education at college of
> fools; the building of meeting-houses to the vain end to which many
> now stand; alms to sots; and the thousand-fold Relief Societies; –
> though I confess with shame I sometimes succumb and give the dol-
> lar, it is a wicked dollar, which by and by I shall have the manhood to
> withhold.

True, Emerson meant by his "class of persons" men such as
Henry Thoreau and Jones Very and the Reverend William Ellery
Channing, which is not exactly Shagpoke Whipple, Ronald
Reagan and the Reverend Jerry Falwell, but Self-Reliance translated out of the inner life and into the marketplace is difficult to distinguish from our current religion of selfishness, as set forth so
sublimely in the recent grand epiphany at Dallas. Shrewd Yankee
that he was, Emerson would have shrugged off his various and
dubious paternities. His spiritual elitism could only be misunderstood, but he did not care much about being misread or misused.
Though he has been so oddly called "the philosopher of democracy" by so many who wished to claim him for the Left, the
political Emerson remains best expressed in one famous and
remarkable sentence by John Jay Chapman: "If a soul be taken
and crushed by democracy till it utter a cry, that cry will be
Emerson."

IV

I return with some relief to Emerson as literary prophet, where
Emerson's effect, *pace* Yvor Winters, seems to me again dialectical
but in the end both benign and inevitable. Emerson's influence,
from his day until ours, has helped to account for what I would
call the American difference in literature, not only in our poetry
and criticism, but even in our novels and stories – ironic since
Emerson was at best uneasy about novels. What is truly surprising

about this influence is its depth, extent and persistence, despite many concealments and even more evasions. Emerson does a lot more to explain most American writers than any of our writers; even Whitman or Thoreau or Dickinson or Hawthorne or Melville serve to explain *him*. The important question to ask is not "How?" but "Why?" Scholarship keeps showing the "how" (though there is a great deal more to be shown) but it ought to be a function of criticism to get at that scarcely explored "why."

Emerson was controversial in his own earlier years, and then became all but universally accepted (except, of course, in the South) during his later years. This ascendancy faded during the Age of Literary Modernism *(circa* 1915-1945) and virtually vanished, as I remarked earlier, in the heyday of academic New Criticism or Age of Eliot *(circa* 1945-1965). Despite the humanistic protests of President Giamatti, and the churchwardenly mewings of John Updike, the last two decades have witnessed an Emerson revival, and I prophesy that he, rather than Marx or Heidegger, will be the guiding spirit of our imaginative literature and our criticism for some time to come. In that prophecy, "Emerson" stands for not only the theoretical stance and wisdom of the historical Ralph Waldo, but for Nietzsche, Walter Pater and Oscar Wilde, and much of Freud as well, since Emerson's elitist vision of the higher individual is so consonant with theirs. Individualism, whatever damages its American ruggedness continues to inflict on our politics and social economy, is more than ever the only hope for our imaginative lives. Emerson, who knew that the only literary and critical method was oneself, is again a necessary resource in a time beginning to weary of Gallic scientism in what are still called the Humanities.

Lewis Mumford, in *The Golden Day* (1926), still is the best guide as to *why* Emerson was and is the central influence upon American letters: "With most of the resources of the past at his command, Emerson achieved nakedness." Wisely seeing that Emerson was a Darwinian before Darwin, a Freudian before Freud, because he possessed "a complete vision," Mumford was able to make the classic formulation as to Emerson's strength: "The past for Emerson was neither a prescription nor a burden: it was rather an esthetic experience." As a poem already written, the past was not a force for Emerson; it had lost power, because power for him resided only at the crossing, at the actual moment of transition.

The dangers of this repression of the past's force are evident enough, in American life as in its literature. In our political economy, we get the force of secondary repetition; Reagan as Coolidge out-Shagpoking Nathanael West's Whipple. We receive also the rhythm of ebb and flow that makes all our greater writers into crisis-poets. Each of them echoes, however involuntarily, Emerson's formula for dicontinuity in his weird, irrealistic essay, "Circles":

> Our moods do not believe in each other. Today I am full of thoughts and can write what I please. I see no reason why I should not have the same thought, the same power of expression, tomorrow. What I write, whilst I write it, seems the most natural thing in the world; but yesterday I saw a dreary vacuity in this direction in which now I see so much; and a month hence, I doubt not, I shall wonder who he was that wrote so many continuous pages. Alas for this infirm faith, this will not strenuous, this vast ebb of a vast flow! I am God in nature; I am a weed by the wall.

From God to weed and then back again; it is the cycle of Whitman from "Song of Myself" to "As I Ebb'd with the Ocean of Life," and of Emerson's and Whitman's descendants ever since. Place everything upon the nakedness of the American self, and you open every imaginative possibility from self-deification to absolute nihilism. But Emerson knew this, and saw no alternative for us if we were to avoid the predicament of arriving too late in the cultural history of the West. Nothing is got for nothing; Emerson is not less correct now than he was 150 years ago. On November 21, 1834, he wrote in his journal: "When we have lost our God of tradition and ceased from our God of rhetoric then may God fire the heart with his presence." Our God of tradition, then and now, is as dead as Emerson and Nietzsche declared him to be. He belongs, in life, to the political clerics and the clerical politicians and, in letters, to the secondary men and women. Our

God of rhetoric belongs to the academies, where he is called by the name of the Gallic Demiurge, Language. That leaves the American imagination free as always to open itself to the third God of Emerson's prayer.

19 Martin Buber on the Bible

The Hebrew Bible, in whatever version we read it, is an immensely difficult sequence or series of books. This difficulty cannot be too much emphasized. It has been masked by familiarity and by two thousand years of normative interpretation, ranging from the subtlest analyses of possible meaning to the astonishing literalism we confront nightly when viewing evangelists on television. Stories and poems that are so worn by repetition as to be beyond surprise, and yet remain so esoteric, are texts necessarily in Freud's category of "the uncanny." We read them and feel at once estranged and yet at home.

Modern Biblical scholarship, though now two hundred years old, is inadequate as literary criticism. Much of what this scholarship insists upon calling literary criticism would be dismissed as trivial or rudimentary by the advanced criticism of secular literature. Martin Buber's writings on the Bible were not intended as scholarship or as specifically literary criticism but as a religious testimony. In my judgment, at their best they are precisely instances of an authentic *literary* criticism and, as such, are likely to survive Buber's writings on Hasidism or his more direct presentations of his own spiritual stance.

Buber on Hasidism and on the concept of Judaism has suffered the formidable criticism of Gershom Scholem, the leading scholar of myth and mysticism in Jewish tradition. Acknowledging Buber as precursor in the exploration of esoteric Judaism, Scholem nevertheless puts into question the descriptive accuracy of his older contemporary:

> In the reports of the Torah, which he considers unhistorical, he seeks the "core" of an original event, namely that "encounter" in the highest sense, and he finds the latter by the application of a purely pneumatic exegesis, the subjectivity of which bewilders the reader.

"Pneumatic exegesis" is Scholem's sly irony at Buber's expense, since the phrase can mean "gnostic interpretation," and so much of Buber's work is a moral polemic directed against Gnosticism. But the essence of Hasidism, as Scholem has shown against Buber, is the Gnosticism of the Lurianic Kabbalah. Scholem's contention is that both he and Buber are religious anarchists, but Buber is a subjectivist masking as a Hasidic sage, while Scholem is an objective historian of Kabbalism. This is a little misleading, since Scholem's Kabbalah is in some sense as much his own creation as Buber's Hasidism is Buber's kind of strong misreading. But there is a vital difference, which establishes Scholem as the stronger of these two demonic interpreters. Scholem's "history" is essentially analytic and descriptive, however colored it may be by his his own prophetic force of spiritual anarchy. Buber is rarely analytic and almost never descriptive.

Yet Buber on the Bible survives Scholem's critiques, precisely because he is the more literary of the two expositors. Buber, as Scholem once remarked, was an eloquent rhetorician, and his spiritual commentaries on the Bible tend to be remarkable instances of rhetorical criticism. Here is one example, in the vivid discussion of "The Burning Bush" from Buber's *Moses:*

> As reply to his question about the name, Moses is told: *Ehyeh asher ehyeh.* This is usually understood to mean "I am that I am" in the sense that YHVH describes Himself as the Being One or even the Everlasting One. . . . Should we, however, really assume that in the view of the narrator the God who came to inform His people of their liberation wishes, at that hour of all hours, merely to secure His distance, and not to grant and warrant proximity as well?

From this powerful rhetorical question follows Buber's reading of the *ehyeh asher ehyeh* as, in effect, "I shall be present where and when I shall be present," the covenant promise of perpetual presence. Buber in some sense shrewdly answers his own rhetorical prophecy, as stated in the 1926 lecture that the editor, Nahum

Glatzer, selected as the inaugural essay of *On the Bible*. Confronting the Bible, the person of today must read it:

> . . . as though it were something entirely unfamiliar, as though it had not been set before him ready-made, as though he has not been confronted all his life with sham concepts and sham statements that cited the Bible as their authority. He must face the Book with a new attitude, as something new. He must yield to it, withhold nothing of his being, and let whatever will occur between himself and it.

Buber seems to be describing the process of falling in love, but his paradigm indeed is *'ahabah* or Yahweh's Election-Love for Israel. That paradigm accounts for Buber's love of the Bible and for his intense confrontational reading of *ehyeh asher ehyeh* as the uncanny or sublime presence of Divine Love. Scholem, with his customary exemplary harshness, criticized Buber's use of Rosenzweig's terminology of creation, revelation, and redemption as the basic categories of Judaism, observing that Buber's "revelation" is purely mystical, Kabbalistic even, as Buber denied any reliance upon mysticism. Certainly Buber's *rhetorical* defense of his enterprise betrays the aura of a Kabbalistic or gnostic critique of Darwin, Freud, and Marx:

> We have already answered the question of whether the man of today can believe by saying that, while he is denied the certainty of faith, he has the power to hold himself open to faith. But is not the strangeness of biblical concepts a stumblingblock to his readiness to do so? Has he not lost the reality of creation in his concept of evolution, that of revelation in the theory of the unconscious, and that of redemption in the setting up of social or national goals?

In his rejection of "scientific" views, Buber still insists that he does not resort to "the mystic interpretation, according to which the acts of creation are not acts, but emanations." Scholem's polemical point nevertheless holds, since Buber also asserts a freedom from all historical considerations that might circumscribe concepts of creation, revelation, and redemption. His rhetoric grants Buber only a pragmatic freedom from the entrapments of temporality, a freedom unearned dialectically. Skilled at detecting the ironies of apprehension and of expression in Biblical texts, Buber seems blind to the ironies implicit in his own discourse. His

"I – Thou" doctrine, as Scholem demonstrates so often, is essentially rhetorical rather than spiritual or philosophical. It is a grand turning operation dependent upon the traditional trope of apostrophe, the confrontation between life and life, subject and subject, that always conditions Western lyric poetry, and that attained its apotheosis in a radical lyricist like Shelley.

After this problematic introductory essay on "The Man of Today and the Jewish Bible," the next seven pieces in this volume address themselves to texts in Genesis and Exodus by the greatest of Biblical authors, known to scholarly convention as the Jahvist, or J for shorthand. Buber had little interest in what is called the "documentary hypothesis" of Biblical scholarship, yet it is about as well established as internal evidence can establish anything textual. In his book, *The Prophetic Faith,* Buber says that the J document is "very much more comprehensive than had been supposed," but scholars like E. A. Speiser hardly show J as being less than comprehensive. Buber's real point about J ought to have been that this author was badly misrepresented by normative commentary. Unfortunately, Buber sought to demonstrate that J was more prophet than priest and was even prophetic of Buber's dialogical vision. But J was more storyteller than prophet, and more interested in the relation of God's blessing to human struggle than in the blessing as an index to revelation and redemption. The Jahvist is the most problematic of writers, and though his work is the foundation of Western religion, he is hardly a religious writer as such. Something in Buber knew this and helped spark Buber's fury at Freud, whose *Moses and Monotheism,* problematic as it was, is so ferociously denounced in the opening footnote of Buber's book, *Moses.*

What allies Freud to the Jahvist in particular, and to Biblical writers in general, is the double problematic of authority and transference, a problematic more Hebraic than Greek. I mean by this a very specific and limited sense of both authority and transference, having to do with the representation of what Freud called "reality-testing," and of what the Biblical writers regarded as the transcendent reality of Yahweh. In Freud and the Bible, representation is antimimetic, in the uncanny mode that attains an apotheosis whenever Messianic speculations attempt to embody themselves in appropriate images. Scholem once associated a majestic saying from the *Zohar:* "The Messiah will not come until the tears of Esau will be exhausted," with the even more mysterious apothegm of the Hasidic Rabbi Israel of Rizhin: "The Messianic world will be a world without images in which the image and its object can no longer be related." In a postscript to his critique of Buber on Hasidism, Scholem recalled an exchange with Buber in which the expounder of Hasidism confessed his inability to understand that apothegm. Scholem's implication is, again, that Buber lacked imaginative sympathy for the apocalyptic impulse, an implication that suggests a correspondent weakness in Buber's Biblical criticism. But this weakness prevails in all Biblical criticism, which must confront the most difficult of all literary texts.

Our difficulties in reading J or the Jahvist stem primarily from his almost unique authority, an authority so long established that it cannot be undermined by mere disbelief, or by any supposed advances in modes of interpretation, or in historical knowledge. J's invention, so far as we can tell, was Yahweh, not the Yahweh of normative tradition, but the Yahweh who inspired the awe that made the tradition both necessary and inevitable. What texts concerning Yahweh were available to J we cannot know, though it seems likely that his sources were not confined to an oral tradition. We must read what we have, and the strongest and earliest chronicler of Yahweh available to us is J. What characterized Yahweh as J gives him to us?

To ask that question, from a literary perspective, is to ask also just *how* J presents Yahweh to us. What is J's tone or stance, and what modes of representation does he favor? Much scholarship, falling victim to J's irony, calls him a simple and naive writer, which is neither helpful nor true. Like Tolstoy or the early Wordsworth, both his close descendants, J is a massively self-confident writer, fierce and primal in his approach to human personality and totally daring in his apprehension of divine realities.

Unlike Tolstoy and Wordsworth, J is almost invariably ironic when human personality and divine reality collide. But the irony of one age or culture is rarely the irony of another, and J's irony is neither classical nor romantic, Greek nor European. If irony is saying one thing while meaning another or provoking an expectation that will not be fulfilled, then J is no ironist. However, there is a more sublime irony, the irony say of Kafka's fragmentary story, "The Hunter Gracchus," which ends with a fussy seaport mayor nervously asking Gracchus (an undead phantasm floating about on his death ship) whether he means to go on docking in the mayor's domain and being answered that the hunter thinks not, since his ship is rudderless and is driven by a wind from the region of death. In Kafka, and more massively in J, irony comes from clashes or encounters between totally incommensurate orders of reality. J's most peculiar gift is his preternatural ease in so writing about Yahweh, in so making Yahweh act and speak, that no uncertainty or reservation is experienced when the reader moves from Yahweh to Jacob or to Moses. Yet this authority is quite knowingly ironic, in that no one is clearer than J as to where Yahweh ends and man begins.

One way of estimating J's extraordinary success in representing God is to contrast it with the vicissitudes of later representations of Yahweh in the normative tradition, both Jewish and Christian. The prophet Isaiah makes us a little uneasy by giving us a Yahweh seated upon a throne surrounded by an assembly of seraphs. Isaiah is a sublime poet, but his images of a high throne, six-winged angels, smoke, and a train of glory mix earthly emblems of power with aspects of the grotesque. Prophecy takes its point of origin from J's account of Moses (Buber would say from Abraham), but J's preternatural greatness as a writer transcended the necessity for the later prophetic imagery of kingly pomp. J does not need to see himself as standing in the presence of God in the heavenly council, there to receive the God-word. Jeremiah says: "The God-word was (came) to me," but that would be a weak perspective, to J. J precedes and has spiritual authority over kings and prophets alike. The prophet Micaiah ben Imlah (1 Kings

22:17) actually reports a dialogue in the heavenly court just as the poet of Job does, thus setting the bad precedent that causes Milton such esthetic grief in Book III of *Paradise Lost.* J's God does not preside over a royal council in the heavens, and indeed such a role or image is not conceivable for the uncanny Yahweh J chronicles.

To confine oneself only to J's share in Genesis, these are some of the representations of God that he gives us. Yahweh molds a man out of clods in the soil and plants a garden so as to make a home for this creature. Even in his creation, God is not unironic, since he first makes animals *as an aid for man's loneliness* and fashions woman only as an afterthought. Yahweh likes to walk around his garden toward sundown, as even he prefers to keep cool, but this charming touch is qualified by his bad temper after Adam and Eve have devoured prohibited fruit. Still, this is a very intimate God, who never shrinks from face-to-face conversation with his creatures. Presumably the presence of this God is not just a voice, though J is too canny to describe him. But then J, and nearly all biblical writers after him, are not interested in how persons or objects look anyway. Thorleif Boman acutely notes that in biblical theophanies, "sight and hearing pass imperceptibly into one another," since the Hebraic images of God were never visual but rather were motor, dynamic, and auditive. So, in J's story of the tower of Babel, God descends to look at the tower, though presumably he had a good enough view of its presumption from above. But J's God is highly dynamic; he *likes* to go down, walk about amidst places, persons, and things, and see for himself from the ground level. Indeed, without such periodic descents, Yahweh evidently does not allow himself to make covenants, since these are very much on-the-ground affairs.

The intercessions at Mamre and on the road to Sodom illustrate Yahweh's penchant for abrupt visits, but only our consciousness feels the abruptness; J and Abraham do not feel it. Rather than continue a citation of instances, I move to what I would name as the esthetic principle involved, which governs our responses: originality. J's strength, and difficulty, is that he remains more original than any other writer in the entire tradition that he fostered. Such a statement makes little literary sense unless I can define my use of the critical term, "originality," within the context of biblical tradition. That context is a history of interpretation, but by "interpretation" I mean also the use and readings of J that take place as early as E, P, and D, the other narrative strands in the Pentateuch.

Perhaps it was absolutely arbitrary that nearly all of the biblical writers took J as their point of origin. But once they did, the teleology of Jewish tradition became absolutely inescapable. A kind of brute factuality or contingency inheres forever in every historical tradition, be it philosophy or religion, literature or psychoanalysis, though such factuality usually blinds later representatives of a tradition from seeing that it is indeed factuality that imprisons them. J may have been a kind of idiosyncratic accident, as Shakespeare perhaps was, but once writers as overwhelming as J or Shakespeare or Freud set a tradition, that tradition is doomed to shy away from them even as it exalts them. J and the Priestly Author or authors are as separated in time as say Chaucer and Yeats were, and we would have grave trouble in trying to interpret Chaucer through Yeats, though in some respects we are doomed to do so. J is more original than Chaucer or Shakespeare, in that his central creation, Yahweh, had to undergo a metamorphosis in the work even of the Priestly Author. The prophets present a God who has more in common with P's God than with J's, a process of progressive alteration that culminated in the God of normative and rabbinical Judaism.

J's originality thus can be defined as another name for his difficulty, for something in him that tradition never has been able to assimilate. His uncanny Yahweh defies conceptualization and derives much of his literary and spiritual authority from that defiance. If to begin is to be free, such freedom in an originator like J becomes the freedom to rule those who come later, and such freedom to rule is authority, in a textual sense. Plato rose among the Greeks to contest the authority of Homer, but among the Hebrews no one contested the authority of J, except through the subtle techniques of redaction, of joining oneself to J's text by interpolation and addition, by adumbrations peculiarly interpretative.

II

Though the difficulties (and rewards) of reading J are the largest in the Bible, there are few biblical texts, whatever their authorship, that are not particularly difficult this late in the history of Western culture. Christian, Jewish, or secular, the contemporary reader has been nurtured by literary suppositions that frequently are alien to the nature of the ancient Hebrew text. It is mistaken to call J an epic writer, or the maker of a saga, or a historian, or even an originator of prose fiction in something like the modern sense, though any of these is preferable to calling him a religious writer. Even calling J a storyteller is rather misleading. He chronicles the vicissitudes of an agonistic blessing and is therefore not only the first but still the most Jewish of writers, just as his Jacob, most agonistic of his characters, remains the most Jewish of all personages. But even the term "agonistic" is a Greek importation, and Greek, particularly Platonic, importations have been prevalent in Jewish interpretations from the days of Rabbi Akiba until now. The Judaism of Ezekiel, in the Exile, and of Ezra, in the Return, already had moved a considerable way from the doctrine implicit in J, but a partly Platonized Judaism, in Akiba and after, which we inherit, has little possibility of interpreting J accurately. Martin Buber was as little interested in his imprisonment by the brute contingency of tradition as more normative interpreters have been, but his impatience with the normative was a true advantage for him as a literary critic of the Bible.

J, the strongest of the Biblical writers, is also the most enigmatic from a normative stance. I hold to the odd formula I have expressed elsewhere, that J improbably is an amalgam of Tolstoy and of Kafka, as though Hadji Murad and the Hunter Gracchus could be accommodated by the same fictive universe. Despite his prevalent tendency, so vigorously protested by Scholem, to reduce every Biblical text to an *I-Thou* confrontation, Buber at least puts J's uncanniness in the foreground and teaches the reader to distrust normative misreadings of J. Thus, Buber's account of "The Tree of Knowledge" is superb at seeing J's irony in the story of the "Fall," though odd in ascribing the irony to a theme of oppositeness rather than to J's rhetorical stance. Buber emphasizes play and dream rather than good and evil, an emphasis that restores the primal strangeness with which J recounts origins. J's Yahweh is without doubt the most bewildering representation in the world's literature. Whether or not J invented the Hebraic mode of the anti-iconic or developed it from tradition is beyond investigation, particularly since J, for all pragmatic purposes, simply *became* the tradition, even as Homer did. J, much more than Homer, shows us that tradition depends upon the processes, strong and weak, of misreading an overwhelming precursor. J's starkness is beyond assimilation, which is to say that reading J without crippling presuppositions is not possible, since prior readings of J, starting with the Elohist, the Priestly Author, and the Deuteronomist, have established all the available presuppositions concerning Yahweh and mankind and their relationships.

A careful reading of Genesis 3 might begin with the realization that Adam's wife (not yet named, until after Yahweh's curses) is in no way surprised by the talking, standing, shrewd serpent, whether in itself or in its message. J does not say the serpent was evil or even ill-intentioned but merely rather sly, a craftiness which in the Hebrew is connected to nakedness by a pun. Nor does J have the serpent lie; a half-truth is enough to encourage human catastrophe. The woman eats so as to gain wisdom and gains instead death and the knowledge of death, but only after Yahweh takes action. What she gains eventually, therefore, is the darkest of wisdoms, yet the immediacy of the supposed gain is the previously nonexistent consciousness of sexuality, through its sign of nakedness. What the serpent teaches must be called consciousness or a sense of nakedness, and it is the largest irony of J that his God

Yahweh had created consciousness in the serpent but not in the woman or in Adam. J's saga begins not with the autumnal and cosmic harvest of the Priestly Author in Genesis 1, but with the harsh Judean spring of Genesis 2, a moment in the history of Yahweh's will when a lump of earth can be formed into an earthling. It is instructive that J's text, except for his part in the Book of Joshua, may end with Yahweh's return of his prophet, Moses, to an unmarked grave in the earth. Here, interpolated as Deuteronomy 34:6, are what may be J's concluding words about Moses:

> Yahweh buried Moses in the valley in the land of Moab, near Beth-peor; no one to this day knows his burial place.

From earth to earth is J's cycle while J's God Yahweh goes from a first speech forbidding the tree of knowledge of good and bad, lest man die, to a final speech forbidding Moses to cross over into the land sworn to Abraham, Isaac, and Jacob. The speeches have the same pattern, first giving, but then taking away. "I have let you see it with your own eyes," Yahweh says to Moses, and to Adam: "You are free to eat of every tree in the garden," but the limitation or final narrowing down of choice follows in each instance. Yahweh is unconditioned; Moses and Adam must accept conditions. Moses and Adam cannot will to be present wherever and whenever they choose to be present. That power belongs to presence itself.

Buber's essay, "Abraham the Seer," strongly reads Genesis 12 to 25 as a mediation of presence, covering the gap between Adam and Moses by way of a contrast between the covenants of Noah and of Abraham with Yahweh. Buber's Abraham is the first *nabi* or prophet of Yahweh, and so the precise precursor of Moses, Elijah, and Isaiah. Buber's Noah "has received no call that goes beyond his 'generations' and no *historical* task," but Abraham matters because of "what he does, and what he becomes." Tracing the seven revelations made to Abraham, Buber emphasizes the sixth and seventh, respectively at Mamre and at Beersheba. The Mamre episode is J almost at his uncanniest, giving us a Yahweh so

humanized as to make scholarly categories like "anthropomor-
phism" laughably inadequate. A Yahweh who sits upon the
ground, devouring roast calf, curds, milk, and rolls, and then is
offended by an old woman's sensible derision, is beyond all normative understanding. Buber praises Abraham in this episode for
"the boldest speech of man in all Scripture," surpassing Job
(though not, I would say, surpassing the one bold outcry of Job's
wife). What Buber, like normative commentary, ignores is the
peculiarity of J's Yahweh, who is argued down stage by stage and
with obvious recalcitrance. Buber's achievement here as an *esthetic* critic lies in his emphasis upon Abraham's *seeing*, particularly in
the vision on Mount Moriah, a seeing that allows Isaac to be
spared. The birth of prophecy, as Buber strikingly suggests, is a
birth of a particular kind of sight: "The man sees, and sees also
that he is being seen."

Buber's essay on "The Burning Bush," already glanced at in
this Introduction, primarily meditates upon Yahweh as a name,
yet in passing considers also one of J's greatest and most demonic
incidents, Jacob's wrestling at the Jabbok with a nameless one
from among the Elohim. In the powerful section on "Divine
Demonism," placed directly after "The Burning Bush" in his
Moses, Buber returned to wrestling Jacob in connection with J's
weirdest passage, Yahweh's attempt to murder Moses (Exodus
4:24-26). By associating the two incidents, Buber in my judgment
is far superior to any rivals at this point as a critic of J and of J's
God:

> It is part of the basic character of this God that he claims the
> entirety of the one he has chosen; he takes complete possession of
> the one to whom he addresses himself. It is told of him that once in
> the early days of the human race a human being (Enoch) was
> allowed to accompany him in his wanderings; this human being had
> then suddenly vanished, because the God had taken him away. Such
> taking away is part of his character in many respects. He promises
> Abraham a son, gives him and demands him back in order to make a
> gift of him afresh; and for this son he remains a sublime "Terror."
> His character finds even more direct expression when he first tells
> the son of that son to return from Aram to Canaan, and thereafter
> attacks him or causes him to be attacked and dislocates his hip while

wrestling. At this point the tradition is not yet fully interested in ascribing everything to YHVH himself, and so the one who performs the action is "a man," but that the God stands behind cannot be doubted. Unlike the narrative of the attack on Moses, the motif of the "dread night," which is merely hinted at there, is expanded in repeated keywords. By the nocturnal struggle with the divine being, by holding the "man" fast until a blessing is obtained, Jacob passes his test. His leading God had ordered him to wander, the same God who had once promised him: "See, I am with you, I shall protect you wherever you go, and shall bring you back to this land." And now that he had returned to this land, the wanderer had to face the perilous encounter before he enjoyed the final grace of God.

The strange episode in the Exodus story is associated and yet different. YHVH attacks the messenger whom he has just sent, clearly because the man's devotion to him after his resistance has been surmounted does not appear full enough. . . .

We know from the life of the founders of religions, and also from that of other souls who live in the deeps of faith, that there is such an "event of the night"; the sudden collapse of the newly-won certainty, the "deadly factual" moment when the demon working with apparently unbounded authority appears in the world where God alone had been in control but the moment before. The early stage of Israelite religion knows no Satan; if a power attacks a man and threatens him, it is proper to recognize YHVH in it or behind it, no matter how nocturnally dread and cruel it may be; and it was proper to withstand Him, since after all He does not require anything else of me than myself.

Only a few normative traces obscure Buber's insights here. For "the tradition," J should be substituted, and the text in itself does not justify Buber's conclusion that the devotion of God to Moses was not yet complete. J's abruptness is absolute. Yahweh has just spoken to Moses, instructing him on the message to Pharoah, and Moses has just taken the rod of God in his hand. Hastening to Egypt, Moses necessarily camps by night, and there and then Yahweh encountered him and sought to kill him. But these minor points aside, Buber has broken through thousands of years of pious misreadings, or at least he has begun the break. J's God, whether through a nameless "some man" among the Elohim (the Angel of Death?), who cripples Jacob, or in his own person, can behave in modes that almost might have been designed to render normative interpretation gratuitous. No moral meanings can be ascribed to this Yahweh, in our terms, that will not be weak misreadings. Buber's vision of a God who desires complete possession, the entirety of the elected one, restores to J much of his primal force as a writer.

This primal force again is placed in the foreground in the meditation, "Holy Event," excerpted in this volume from Buber's *The Prophetic Faith*. The Holy Event is the account in Exodus 19 to 27 of Yahweh's epiphany at Mount Sinai, but Buber resumes in it his own account of divine demonism. Scholem's critique of Buber's "pneumatic exegesis" asserts that the specific and historical occurrences of revelation are subverted here by a purely personal mysticism. The issue, I think, is more problematic than Scholem makes it out to be. What Buber clearly does subvert is the normative tradition of reading, but Buber's own reading is again closer to the uncanniness of the Biblical text. Buber's obsession with the kingship of God helps him in conveying the supermimetic force of the Sinai text.

"The Election of Israel: A Biblical Inquiry" continues this reading by juxtaposing Exodus 3 and 19 with aspects of Deuteronomy. "Election without obligation" is Buber's succinct formula, illuminating again the texts' own departures from normative conventions. Buber's personalism and religious anarchism are at the center of his account of "The Words on the Tablets," his reading of Exodus 20 in *Moses*, to which "What Are We To Do about The Ten Commandments" forms a coda. For Buber, the Decalogue is no catechism but an address to the "Thou." Here, perhaps, Scholem is vindicated again, since Buber's idealizings soften the text in ways that the normative tradition does not countenance and thus weaken Buber's truest justification for his own stance, which is the cleansing of the text from its more barren commentaries.

Much richer is the brief article on "The Prayer of the First Fruits," possibly because the text (from Deuteronomy 26) is so cunningly integrated by Buber with Jeremiah's great trope: "Israel was holy to the Lord, the first fruits of his harvest." Buber goes on to cite the Mishnah's report of the actual ceremony of the offering, with its vivid realization of the prayer's figurations. Halfway through this volume, we are thus given a graceful transition from the Pentateuch to the prophets and from the thematic concern with revelation to the adjacent problematics of redemption.

The brief examination of "Samuel and the Ark" enforces Buber's characteristic exaltation of prophet over priest by way of a questionable transmogrification of Samuel from judge to prophet. Yet Buber goes so far here as to add Deborah to the line of prophets. The operative definition of prophet, for Buber, is a proclaimer of the kingship of Yahweh against any other authority, priestly or royal. This persuasive definition allows Buber unquestioned insights, as when he points out that "Samuel is made to utter the first non-anonymous prophecy of doom in the Bible," or when he names Samuel as the *nabi* because he is "one who speaks also of his own accord, *unasked,* the message of revelation." These insights are more impressively set forth in the much earlier lecture, on "Biblical Leadership," which follows in this volume and represents Buber at his most eloquent.

Here Buber begins with the surprising assertion that the Bible is not concerned with character nor with individuality, but only with "persons in situations," and so not with the differences between persons, but only with the different degrees of success or failure in those situations. Palpably this is untrue, since we have an overwhelming sense of Jacob and of Moses, as J represents them, or of Jeremiah as he represents himself. Probably Buber means that *he* is concerned only with "persons in situations," and with their dialogical situation in particular. This personal stance on Buber's own part causes him to exclude as biblical leaders "all those who are not called, elected, appointed anew, as the Bible says, directly by God," such as Joshua and Solomon, for these do not transcend both nature and history. Buber looks instead to "the younger sons who are chosen – from Abel, through Jacob, Joseph and Moses, to David." He looks also to Gideon, who deliberately reduces his army from ten thousand to three hundred, a reduction here interpreted as another incident in the struggle against merely natural and historical strength.

There is something impressively hyperbolical about Buber's emphasis, which is a kind of sublime trope of the thematics of his entire life and work. The reader is likely to be carried along when

Buber asserts that Moses and David were somehow *failures,* an assertion that can only be judged a sublime misreading or creative misunderstanding on Buber's part. Yet, I would call Buber's vehement rhetoric and its effect here his greatest strength as a *literary* critic of the Bible. As criticism, Buber's figurative, hyperbolical language does the work of breaking down our preconceived response and restores the strangeness of the Bible. Here, it particularly stresses the problematic but authentic continuity between Moses and David as precursors, Isaiah and Jeremiah as latecomers *in the same spiritual grouping.* For Buber, the prophets find their essence in historical and natural failure:

> The prophet is the man who has been set up against his own natural instincts that bind him to the community, and who likewise sets himself up against the will of the people to live on as they have always lived, which, naturally, for the people is identical with the will to live.

Despite its eloquence, Buber's formulation is again vulnerable to Scholem's characteristic critique, which is that this is more Buber than it is Isaiah or Jeremiah. Buber himself was fated to become a prophet more accepted by the Gentiles than by the Jews. Certainly the anti-historical element in Buber's vision is never more vehement than in the peroration of this astonishing lecture:

> The real work, from the biblical point of view, is the late-recorded, the unrecorded, the anonymous work. The real work is done in the shadow, in the quiver. Official leadership fails more and more, leadership devolves more and more, upon the secret. The way leads through the work that history does not write down, and that history cannot write down.

This *sounds* much more like a gnostic or Kabbalistic point of view than like the biblical one. Even Buber's beautiful allusion to Second Isaiah (49:2) subverts the meaning of that lament, whose point is that the true prophet ought *not* to be concealed in the shadow and the quiver. Buber's personal darkening of the prophetic faith is in some ways intensified in his pages on "Plato

and Isaiah," excerpted from his introductory lecture at the
Hebrew University in 1938. In a contrast between Plato's failure to
found a perfect state in Syracuse, through his pupil Dion, and
Isaiah's failure to keep the kings of Judah from disaster, Buber
insists that the prophet's failure is more fruitful. Plato's truth was
timeless and so could never be realized in time, but paradoxically
Isaiah's truth was timely, failed in its own temporal moment, and
yet survives perpetually through and in that failure. A reader's
puzzlement at Buber's judgment can be tested by contrasting
these two Buberian lectures with "Jerusalem and Athens," two lectures given by Leo Strauss in New York City in 1967. Strauss also
compares Plato and the prophets, or rather Socrates and the
prophets, since Socrates has the call or mission, as Isaiah and
Jeremiah did. For Strauss, neither Socrates nor the prophets are
failures, paradoxical or otherwise, and more crucially their primary difference is not in the temporal nature of their work. In a fine
discrimination, Strauss reminds us that Socrates expects the truth
always to be knowable only to philosophers, whereas Isaiah chants
of when "the earth shall be full of knowledge of the Lord, as the
waters cover the earth." Like Kierkegaard, Socrates speaks to the
single one, to a man who can be made to understand, but the
nabi is a public orator. Isaiah and Jeremiah sometimes speak to
the king, but sometimes to all the people of Jerusalem.

Shall we say that Strauss is the better scholar here, while
Buber is the more literary interpreter? Buber's pages on
"Redemption" in Isaiah and Second Isaiah emphasize the way in
which Solomon's temple becomes a Messianic trope, a Zionist
prophecy to which Buber himself can assent. Again the reader is
left uncertain as to the the historical difference between the two
Isaiahs, a difference that Strauss would not have voided.
Something of the spirit of Strauss would have been a useful corrective for Buber, as we can see by a further contrast between
these two sages. Buber considers Jeremiah 28 in "False Prophets,"
where he grants that the false prophet Hananiah was an honest
patriot but condemns him nevertheless for supposed worship of

success, unlike Jeremiah, who embraced failure. Strauss, in his lecture on Socrates and the prophets, astutely traces Hananiah's downfall to something subtler than the worship of success:

> The false prophets trust in flesh, even if that flesh is the temple in Jerusalem, the promised land, nay, the chosen people itself, nay, God's promise to the chosen people if that promise is taken to be an unconditional promise and not as a part of a Covenant. The true prophets, regardless of whether they predict doom or salvation, predict the unexpected, the humanly unforeseeable – what would not occur to men, left to themselves, to fear or to hope.

False prophecy, on this view, is a failure of imagination, rather than a failure to accept the burden of temporal failure. If Strauss is persuasive here, more than Buber, it is because *he* is closer to literature this time or to the critical insight that literature fosters and demands. But Buber is a formidable theorist of prophecy, and even his obsession with prophetic failure has links to his lasting achievement as an interpreter of what he calls the prophetic faith.

Buber's central ideas on prophecy exist only in dialectical tension with his polemic against the apocalyptic. Presumably Buber would have endorsed the formula that failed prophecy becomes apocalyptic, while failed apocalyptic becomes Gnosticism. Scholem again identifies Buber's refusal of the apocalyptic vision with Buber's insistence upon projecting his own dialogical spirituality into the prophetic impulse. Even if true, this does not invalidate the intense essay on "Prophecy, Apocalyptic, and the Historical Hour," where the true subject is individual freedom, and the telling contrast is between Jeremiah the prophet and Karl Marx. Jeremiah's crucial image is the double wheel of the potter, a figure for God's making and unmaking of the house of Israel. The immanent dialectic of Marx, substituting for Yahweh's will, obliterates the will and the act of the individual, such an obliteration representing, for Buber, the authentic stigma of the apocalyptic. Buber, in my judgment, is never more powerful as a critic than in his characteristic juxtaposition of prophetic *voice* and apocalyptic *writing*, with its illuminating preference for voice:

> The time the prophetic voice calls us to take part in is the time of the actual decision; to this the prophet summons his hearers, not seldom at the risk of martyrdom to himself. In the world of the apocalyptic this present historical-biographical hour harldy ever exists. . . . The prophet addresses persons who hear him, who should hear him. He knows himself sent to them in order to place before them the stern alternatives of the hour. Even when he writes his message or has it written, whether it is already spoken or is still to be spoken, it is always intended for particular men, to induce them, as directly as if they were hearers, to recognize their situation's demand for decision and to act accordingly. The apocalyptic writer has no audience turned toward him; he speaks into his notebook.

Unquestionably powerful, this is also unquestionably unfair to the apocalyptic, scorned here as mere literature. Buber's animus against the apocalyptic is at one with his polemic against gnosis; both are modes of self-absorption, of the I obsessed with I, on this view. Persuasive as a rhetorician because of his own certainty as to what prophecy was or was not, Buber represses our authentic inability to know exactly where and how the prophetic voice edges into the apocalyptic. Yet he relies upon the literary experience that is increasingly our only authority for recognizing prophetic voice. The paradigm for this experience is unforgettably the abrupt entry of Elijah into the biblical text:

> Now Elijah the Tishbite, of Tishbe in Gilead, said to Ahab, "As the Lord the God of Israel lives, before whom I stand, there shall be neither dew nor rain these years, except by my word."

It is not that any material has been lost, as unimaginative scholars have insisted, but rather that nothing less in esthetic force could convey the ethos of this precursor of Amos and Hosea, Isaiah and Jeremiah. But it seems to me that scholarship has failed with the Hebrew prophets, even in the massive achievement of Gerhard von Rad or the sympathetic psychologizing of Abraham J. Heschel. Poets of action as well as of words, or overwhelmingly the exemplification of the range of meanings of *davar* (word, thing, deed), the prophets remain still to be read in all the difficulties of what a genuine reading would have to be. I know of no more difficult text than Jeremiah. He has in common with J a quality that defeats interpretation, and I suspect at last we must call the quality "originality." Buber's great virtue is that almost uniquely he does not underemphasize biblical originality, but as that is the burden of his last essay in this volume, I defer comment on this quality until my own conclusion.

The essay on prophecy and the apocalyptic does not mention Nietzsche, but the shadow of his Zarathustra is very dark as Buber moves towards closure:

> ... only the unbelief remains in the broken yet emphatic apocalyptic of our time. It steps forward with a heroic mien, to be sure; it holds itself to be the heroic acknowledgement of the inevitable, the embodiment of *amor fati*. But this convulsive gesture has nothing in common with real love.

I read this as Buber's unmastered anxiety of influence in regard to Nietzsche, who far more than Buber himself fulfilled Buber's program for prophecy as set forth in *The Prophetic Faith:*

> But the word of God ... breaks into the whole order of the word world and breaks through. The aforementioned is an addition to rite, and is even nothing but rite in the form of language; whereas the other, the divine word, which suddenly descends into the human situation, unexpected and unwilled by man, is free and fresh like lightning. And the man who has to make it heard is over and over again subdued by the word before He lets it be put in his mouth.

Buber's reference is to the exemplary sufferings of Jeremiah, but Nietzsche, as Jeremiah's truest descendant, could be described here. It is from *The Prophetic Faith* also, Buber's finest single book, that the remarkable analysis of Job is excerpted in the present volume. The Book of Job has had Calvin, Blake, Kierkegaard, and Newman among its commentators, and it cannot be said that Buber rivals them, but then no biblical scholar does either. What Buber does uncover, with great clarity, is a pattern of four very diverse views of God's relationship to Job's sufferings. There is the "popular" view of the prologue, with a God too easily "enticed" by Satan. There is the "dogmatic" view of Job's "comforters": if sufferings, then sin. There is Job's own view, which became Buber's theology: the "eclipse" of God. But most powerfully, there is God's own view, his answer. As Buber phrases it, this is "not *the* divine justice, which remains hidden, but *a* divine justice, namely that manifest in creation." Buber cites Rudolf Otto here on the playful riddle of God's creative power. Karl Barth in his *Church Dogmatics* makes a nice point illuminating this riddle, which is that God shrewdly allows creation to speak for him:

> He obviously counts upon it that they belong so totally to Him,
> that they are so subject to Him and at His disposal, that in speaking
> of themselves they will necessarily speak of Him.

Buber's Job is a "faithful rebel" and therefore a servant of God. Perhaps toward this text Buber was not audacious enough. A reader is likelier to remember the bitter irony of Calvin on Job: "God would have to create new worlds, if He wished to satisfy us"; or the more complex irony of Kierkegaard: "Fix your eyes upon Job; even though he terrifies you, it is not this he wishes, if you yourself did not wish it." But Buber is not Calvin nor Kierkegaard, Blake nor Kafka. If he *gentles* Job, it is because as exegete he seeks consolation as well as wisdom.

I judge Buber to be as valuable a commentator as the wisdom Psalms have had, and "The Heart Determines," his reading of Psalm 73, is without critical parallel. This intricate exegesis defies summary, and so I restrict myself to indicating its subtle technique of continuously undermining apparent meaning until only the trope of the Psalmist's "nearness" remains. Here Buber is at last wholly beyond Scholem's strictures, for the interpretation is normative, in no way "pneumatic," and yet wholly original.

Originality is the crucial concern of the address on "Biblical Humanism," dating back to the fateful year 1933, that fittingly ends this volume. When one seeks Buber's central apothegm on the Bible, one finds: "The purity of the Hebrew Bible's word resides not in form but in originality." Buber's word,

Ursprünglichkeit, relates in his view to "the immediacy of spoken-ness." At the least, as a critic Buber returns us to the uncanniness of J, of the court personage who wrote of David, of Jeremiah, of the author of Job. These writers are the spring of the longest normative tradition in the West, yet that tradition has never subdued the strangeness of its origins, never overcome the originality of its God. Buber's biblical criticism has the final virtue of being a kind of threshold rhetoric, beckoning the reader on to the wandering of further criticism. As a sustained body of work, Buber on the Bible is more vitalizing than any other critic has been. Kafka once complained of Buber that "no matter what he says, something is missing." One can hazard what Kafka missed in Buber by finding it in Kafka himself:

> The essence of Wandering in the Wilderness. A man who leads his people along this way with a shred (more is unthinkable) of consciousness of what is happening. He is on the track of Canaan all his life; it is incredible that he should see the land only when on the verge of death. This dying vision of it can only be intended to illustrate how incomplete a moment is human life, incomplete because a life like this could last forever and still be nothing but a moment. Moses fails to enter Canaan not because his life is too short but because it is a human life. This ending of the Pentateuch bears a resemblance to the final scene of [Flaubert's] *Education sentimentale*.

That final sentence is magnificently beyond audacity. Moses gazing at the land promised but not to be entered "resembles" two men thinking back to a Sunday of their adolescence, when first they entered but then too quickly fled a bordello, yet in recall seeing the incident as the happiest time they ever had. Even Kafka is more strangely studying the nostalgias than being ironic here. That splendor aside, the rest of the passage is simply the finest criticism I have read of J's saga of Moses, and of much else as well. Kafka, as I remarked earlier, is half of J; Tolstoy perhaps is the rest. So unlikely a writer may never find his adequate critic. Buber, though much indeed is missing in him, surely represents better than anyone else certain qualities that a true critic of the Bible will have to possess.

20 Jewish Culture and Jewish Identity

I

"American Jewish Culture," considered merely as a phrase, is as
problematic say as "Freudian Literary Criticism," which I recall
once comparing to the Holy Roman Empire: not holy, not
Roman, not an empire; not Freudian, not literary, not criticism.
Much that is herded together under the rubric of American
Jewish Culture is not American, not Jewish, not culture. Here I
will take these terms backwards, starting with "culture," which
began as a Roman concept, became European, has not quite yet
become American, and never could be Jewish, if by Jewish we
mean anything religious at all, since culture is a stubbornly secular concept. Whether we know what we mean by "Jewish" is so
problematic that I will begin on "culture" with one of our enemies, since our enemies have known well enough what they
meant. I will quote an eminent speculator upon culture, Carl
Gustav Jung. Of course, he has his followers and apologists, but I
will let him speak for himself, in an essay of 1934:

> The Jew as a relative nomad has never created, and presumably will
> never create, a cultural form of his own, for all his instincts and tal-
> ents are dependent on a more or less civilized host people. . .

By the "cultural," Jung would appear to have meant his
divinely creative Collective Unconscious, very fecund in Aryans,
but lacking in Freudians, who to Jung were identical with all Jews.
Culture, in some of its Germanic overtones, rightly makes us a

touch nervous, in consequence, when it is applied to Jewish matters. Yet we hardly can resign the term to the conceptual contexts of anthropologists and sociologists. We *were* a text-centered people, perhaps as much as any people ever has been. If we still *are* a people, it can only be because we have some texts in common. Culture in our context broadly must mean literary culture, if by "literary" one means Biblical and post-Biblical *written* tradition. Even our oral tradition was more text-oriented than not, since it too was commentary upon the ultimate book.

Culture, in the sense expounded by the Matthew Arnold – Lionel Trilling tradition, essentially is the culture of the highly literate, an elite class whose ideology is determined by a relationship between text and society, rather than between folkways and society. Whether that sense of culture still prevails is clearly dubious. Deep reading is a vanished phenomenon, practiced now only at selected academies, where already it shows a token of decline. In some large sense, such reading was one of the residues of Platonic tradition, since even the Hebraic emphasis upon study as salvation was a Platonic importation, though we are uneasy at acknowledging this. But I do not want to repeat here my melancholy prophecy in regard to the cultural prospects of American Jewry, uttered in Jerusalem at an American Jewish Congress dialogue a few years ago; since that essay is now available in my book, *Agon*. Rather than speculate upon the probable further decline of American Jewish culture, I prefer here to ask whether there ever *could* have been such a culture anyway, in the literary or Arnoldian sense of culture. What is truly problematic in the question has little to do with definitions of culture, and everything to do with the difficult definition of being American, and the impossible definition of being Jewish. "Culture" is a nagging term however, even in its essentially literary sense, whether we seek its meaning in Arnold and Trilling, or in T. S. Eliot, or in a Marxist critic like Raymond Williams. So, before abandoning it here, I want to start with its origins, particularly as set forth by Hannah Arendt.

Arendt wrote an essay on the social and political significance of "The Crisis in Culture," first published in 1960, and still available in what I believe to be her most useful book, *Between Past and Future*. She gives there a true starting-point for our inquiry:

> Culture, word and concept, is Roman in origin. The word "culture" derives from *colere* – to cultivate, to dwell, to take care, to tend and preserve – and it relates primarily to the intercourse of man with nature in the sense of cultivating and tending nature until it becomes fit for human habitation. . .
>
> The Greeks did not know what culture is because they did not cultivate nature but rather tore from the womb of the earth. . . closely connected with this was that the great Roman reverence for the testimony of the past as such, to which we owe not merely the preservation of the Greek heritage but the very continuity of our tradition, was quite alien to them. . .

Arendt stresses the agricultural metaphor of loving care for the earth, which by extension became loving care for the testimony of tradition. In Matthew Arnold, these Roman concepts were broadened and modernized into the most famous of all definitions of culture: "being a pursuit of our total perfection by means of getting to know on all matters which most concern us, the best which has been thought and said in the world." T. S. Eliot's revision of Arnold, in a less than generous work called *Notes Towards the Definition of Culture* emphasized the conflict between culture and equalitarianism. Lionel Trilling, rather than Eliot, became the true heir of Arnold by compounding Arnold with Freud:

> To make a coherent life, to confront the terrors of the outer and inner world, to establish the ritual and art, the pieties and duties which make possible the life of the group and the individual – these are culture. . .
>
> This intense conviction of the existence of the self apart from culture is, as culture well knows, its noblest and most generous achievement. . . We can speak no greater praise of Freud than to say that he placed this idea at the very center of his thought.

We are left then, by Trilling, with what has become the Freudian or normative notion of culture in American intellectual society. The self stands within yet beyond culture, culture being that ideology which helps produce such a self: coherent, capable of standing apart, yet dutiful and pious toward the force of the best which has been thought and said in the past. This noble idealization has become a *shibboleth* of what the academy regards as its humanism, but it is already sadly dated, and truly it does seem to me far more Arnoldian than Freudian. Not that our high culture is less literary than it used to be; quite the contrary, as a darker view of Freud and culture might show us. Freud thought that the prime intellectual enemy of psychoanalysis was religion, with philosophy a kind of poor third in the contest, and literature too harmless to compete. We see now that Freud fought shadows; religion and philosophy alike no longer inform our culture, and psychoanalysis, merged with our culture, has been revealed as another branch of literature. The ideology of the Western world, whether sounded forth within or beyond the universities, depends upon a literary culture, which explains why teachers of literature, more than those of history or philosophy or politics, have become the secular clergy or clerisy of the West. A culture becomes literary when its conceptual modes have failed it, and when its folkways have been homogenized into a compost heap of ocular junk, nightly visible upon our television screens.

I think that this is the somber context in which the supposed achievement of any American Jewish culture has to be examined. Such an examination requires touchstones, and there seem to me only two candidates for greatness in modern Jewish cultural achievement: Freud and Kafka. But what is Jewish about the work of Freud and Kafka, rather than Austrian German or Czech German, respectively? Vienna and Prague are neither of them Jerusalem, and Freud and Kafka were not traditional or religious Jews, in any way crucially indebted to our normative tradition. I grant the apparent absurdity of touchstones for Jewish culture whose own Jewish culture was essentially so peripheral, but American Jewish culture is at least as much an oxymoronic phrase as German Jewish culture was, and without the conscious use of paradox there is no way into the dilemmas of my subject. If American Jewish identity is a cultural puzzle, and it is, why then let us acknowledge also that all Jewish identity in the Diaspora is a permanent enigma. But I want now to go against all current

Israeli polemic, by multiplying the enigma. There are three areas of Jewish identity today: Israel, the Diaspora, and the United States. I doubt that Israel, in its Western cultural and so non-normative Jewish aspects, is in much more continuity with Diaspora traditions than we are. As for our identity, well where shall we begin, how could I ever end? However, we seem from the perspective of Jerusalem we know that we are not in Exile. I am aware that many German Jews had deluded themselves into a similar knowledge, but American Jewry is unlike any previous Jewry in supposed Exile, with the single possible exception being the Hellenized Jewry of Alexandria, from roughly the third century before the Common Era until the third century after. But everything that is problematic about our identity is capable of sustaining some illumination from my touchstones, so I return to Freud and to Kafka. Why do we think of their cultural achievement as having been Jewish, and what about those idiosyncratic spirits *was* incontrovertibly Jewish?

Peter Gay, in his book, *Freud, Jews, and Other Germans,* has preceded me by arguing the opposite. His Freud is culturally a German, not a Jew, who "offered the world but German wisdom." Gay is one of the most distinguished of cultural historians, but I read and teach Freud constantly, and I do not acknowledge that I read and teach "German wisdom." Every close reader of Freud learns that "they" are the gentiles and "we" are the Jews. Freud perhaps came to trust a handful of gentiles, of whom Ernest Jones was foremost, but I can think of no other modern Jewish intellectual so remorseless in dividing off, socially and spiritually, Jews from gentiles, and so rigorous in choosing only his own people as companions. Kafka, who had a far gentler spirit, also chose Jews as his ambiance. I do not think that I am citing a sociological element, an instance of defensive clannishness, or the simple reversal of Kafka's famous outburst in his 1914 diary: "What have I in common with Jews? I have hardly anything in common with myself and should stand very quietly in a corner, content that I can breathe." Seven years later, Kafka phrased this rather differently:

> In any case we Jews are not painters. We cannot depict things statical-
> ly. We see them always in transition, in movement, as change. We are
> story-tellers. . . A story-teller cannot talk about story-telling. He tells
> stories or is silent. That is all. His world begins to vibrate within him,
> or it sinks into silence. My world is dying away. I am burned out.

The *locus classicus* upon the vexation of what is Jewish in
Kafka can be found in Robert Alter's *After the Tradition* where Alter
confronts two antithetical truths. First: "No other Jew who has
contributed so significantly to European literature appears so
intensely, perhaps disturbingly, Jewish in the quality of his imagination as Kafka." But, second: "Kafka. . . addressed himself to the
broadest questions of human nature and spiritual existence, working with images, actions, and situations that were by design universal in character. . ." Following Alter I acknowledge the paradox and the mystery of Kafkan Jewishness as against Kafkan universality. But I have a curious suggestion as to the center of this
Kafkan antithesis, and I quote the following Kafkan parable as
proof-text:

> He is thirsty, and is cut off from a spring by a mere clump of bushes.
> But he is divided against himself: one part overlooks the whole, sees
> that he is standing here and that the spring is just beside him; but
> another part notices nothing, has at most a divination that the first
> part sees all. But as he notices nothing he cannot drink.

Is this a Jewish parable? It is called *The Spring* by its translator, which necessarily loses the German language overtone of
"source" or "origin" that also is involved in the work "Quelle." I
will assert that even if this was not a Jewish parable *when* Kafka
wrote it, it certainly is one now, precisely because *Kafka* wrote it.
In that assertion I am suggesting that Kafka, in at least some ways,
was a strong enough writer to modify or change our prior notions
of just what being Jewish meant. Since Freud, *in toto,* is an even
stronger writer than Kafka, I thus assert that Freud's Jewishness,
whatever it was or was not in relation to tradition, even more
strongly now alters our notions of Jewish identity. I would like not
to be too weakly misunderstood on this rather subtle point, and
so I will labor it for a space.

All origins or sources are arbitrary, yet if sufficient continuities issue forth from them, we learn to regard their teleologies as

being inescapable. I once wrote something like that and added that we knew this truth best from what we so oxymoronically called our love lives. I would think now that this difficult notion of the brute facticity of tradition is best known by meditating upon the indescribable history of the Jews. The continuities of that history are its scandal, and constitute the fine absurdity of this occasion. I stand here, just past fifty years in age, and worry out loud about the problematics of my identity, an identity inescapably determined for me by a continuity of ancestors stretched past at least thirty-five hundred years, or seventy times my age. Jewish mothers have given birth to Jewish daughters and sons for perhaps one hundred and fifty generations, a facticity so overwhelming as to dwarf every conceptualization as to what Jewish identity might mean, *unless* it is to mean precisely what the Talmud wanted it to mean.

The authority of so immense and so somber a history must compel awe and at least some recognition in every sensitive consciousness exposed to that tradition. This awe tends to obscure a curious truth about Jewish identity, or perhaps of any people's identity; always changing, such identity conceals its changes under the masks of the normative. The authority of identity is not constancy-in-change, but the *originality* that usurps tradition and becomes a fresh authority, strangely in the name of continuity. Freud and Kafka already have usurped much of the image of Jewishness, by which I mean precisely the cultural image. A Western secular intellectual, searching for the elitist image of Jewishness, these days is likelier to come up with the names of Freud or Kafka or even Gershom Scholem than with those of Maimonides or Rashi or Moses Mendelsohn. Originality in this usurping and elitist sense includes the notion of profound difficulty. Whoever J was, J here means the Yahwist or first crucial author of the Torah, J was more idiosyncratic and difficult to interpret even than Freud or Kafka. Indeed, he still is, perhaps more than ever. It may have been quite arbitrary that nearly every other Biblical writer took J as his point of origin. Once this had happened, J ceased to be arbitrary, and our relation to his work has been governed ever since by an inescapable contingency, however normative tradition may have misread it. We are imprisoned by a factuality that interpretations of J have imposed upon us, just as we are imprisoned by a Freudian factuality as well. In a high cultural sense, the Freudian images, and to a lesser extent the Kafkan ones, have invaded and by now contaminated the composite image of Jewish identity, at least for elitists. So the issue is no longer whether Freud or Kafka represent Jewish achievement. They have *become* Jewish high culture, in the sense that a writer like Philip Roth can only resort to them as icons when he seeks images of that culture.

If my admittedly curious argument is at all suggestive, then it is simple enough to say why we do not yet have an American Jewish culture. Our writers and speculators just have not been original enough until now, and probably will not be for some time to come. Freud and Kafka came late in German language Jewish culture. There had been Heine of course, long before, and American Jewish culture alas has not produced any Heine either. We have some good novelists of the second rank; there is not Faulkner among them, let alone a Hawthorne or Melville or Henry James. We have a few good poets, still young enough to undergo interesting development, but they do not include a Wallace Stevens or Hart Crane, let alone a Whitman or a Dickinson. We have various speculators, scholars and critics, but none among us will turn out to have been an Emerson. The absence of overwhelming cultural achievement compels us to rely upon the cultural identity of the last phases of *Galut,* yet we, as I have said before, scarcely feel that we are in Exile.

Kafka, in a letter to Max Brod, wrote that the despair over the Jewish question was the inspiration of the German Jewish writers, and he remarked that this was "an inspiration as respectable as any other but fraught. . . with distressing peculiarities." These peculiarities stemmed from the hideous distress that *their* problem was not a German one. We do not have despair over the Jewish question; it is not even clear that there *is* a Jewish question in the United States. America, like Hellenistic Alexandria and unlike Germany, is an eclectic culture, of which we are a part. The Jewish

writer's problem here and now does not differ from the
Hellenistic or American *belatedness,* from the anxiety that we may
all of us just be too late. Cultural belatedness makes the American
literary culture problematic precisely as is American Jewish culture; this problem, ours, is truly American. I think that is why
Nathanael West, who was something of a Jewish anti-Semite, is still
the most powerful writer that American Jewry has produced. His
masterwork, *Miss Lonelyhearts,* marvelously re-writes Milton's
Paradise Regained in American terms, though also in terms curiously less Jewish than Milton's own. West, like Heine, may have
arrived a touch too soon. A deeper awareness that American culture and Jewish culture in America could not differ much might
have saved West some self-hatred yet might also have weakened
him as a writer.

No one now can prophesy the appearance of cultural
genius, because we do have an oppressive sense of belatedness. I
want therefore to turn the rest of this speculation not to a messianic longing for an American Freud or Kafka, but to the other GALUT/ DIASPORA
paradox, which is the pragmatic ending in this country of the
trope or myth of *Galut* which remains essential evidently to and
for Israeli culture. I recall vividly from that Jerusalem dialogue of
a few years ago the troubled and hyperbolic eloquence of the
Israeli writer A. B. Yehoshua, proclaiming his conviction that
Israel had to break off all relations with American Jewry, in order
to compel the saving remnant of that Jewry to forsake Exile and
return geographically and nationally to Zion. My memories have
been stirred anew by reading the novelist's just-translated
polemic, *Between Right and Right.* Yehoshua is passionately sincere,
but he is so far from American Jewish realities as to sound more
ironic than he intended to be. He seems to offer only three alternatives: assimilate completely and thus forsake Jewish identity;
perish in another Holocaust; live in Israel. All of us here reject the
first two, and almost all of us reject the third as well. Yehoshua's
logic is appalling: *Galut* caused the Holocaust and will cause it
again. The Jew therefore must become either a gentile, or a
corpse, or an Israeli.

Yet I would praise Yehoshua for provoking us, because such provocation leads back to the central question of American Jewish culture. What is the identity of the secular American Jew? The question returns us to what always has been most problematic about us: a religion that became a people, rather than a people that became a religion. The religion of Akiba is not dead, in America, Israel, and elsewhere, but it no longer dominates the lives of the majority among us; here, Israel, wherever. And since we also are no longer a text-obsessed people, whether in America or Israel or anywhere, we are in truer danger of vanishing from lack of real literacy then from lack of religion or lack of defense against another Holocaust. If we lose our identity it will be because, as I have warned elsewhere, there is no longer a textual difference between ourselves and the gentiles.

To ask just what a textual difference can be is to confront the truest question of Jewish cultural identity. The difference is not so much in a choice of texts, our Bible and Talmud against their Old Testament and New Testament structure, as it is in the relationship of a people to a text or texts. I go back to my earlier formulation; we were a religion become a people, and not a people become a religion. The parodies of our process are all American, the most successful in contemporary terms being the Mormons, very much now a religion become a people. But of course the Yankees of New England, once a religion, are now a people also. Except for the Fundamentalists, this has been the American Protestant pattern, and so Jews, Quakers, Congregationalists, and doubtless someday Mormons, truly melt together. The authentic American majority is not Moral but whatever you want to call the peoplehood that survives a religious origin.

The cultural consequences of this analogy between Jews without Judaism and Protestants without Christianity are larger than any mode of study has yet chronicled. But at the least Jews become no more in Exile than Quakers are, or Calvinists of all varieties. If we are survivors of an Election Theology, why then so are they. A contemporary Jewish poet tends to have the same untroubled relationship, or lack of relationship, to Judaism that

Walt Whitman had to the Hicksite Quakerism of his boyhood. And, for similar reasons, poets as varied as Philip Levine, John Hollander, and Irving Feldman are no more in Exile in America than are say John Ashbery, James Merrill, and A. R. Ammons. The old formulae of *Galut* simply do not work in the diffuse cultural contexts of America.

I want now to draw together the two paradoxical arguments I have been exploring. When we speak of the relative failure of an American Jewish culture, what we mean pragmatically is our lack of strong figures like Freud and Kafka, becuase *their* achievement has now redefined Jewish culture, even though we could hardly say what was Jewish about them if we approached them apart from the facticity or contingency they have imposed upon us. That is to say, *they are Jewish cultural figures only when they are viewed retrospectively.* But now we come to the second paradox; they define for us the final Jewish cultural achievement of the *Galut,* yet we are not in Exile. They were cultural summits of a people, once a religion, in a hostile context. We are a people once a religion, in a diffuse context, in which hostility is less prevalent than is a variety of diffusenesses parallel to our own. What is culturally problematic about ourselves as a people is precisely what is culturally problematic about the other peoples of the American elite and establishment. But this too will only be seen clearly when it will be seen retrospectively.

Whatever the future American Jewish cultural achievement will be, it will become Jewish only *after* it has imposed itself as achievement. And because it will not bear the stigmata of *Galut,* it will be doubly hard for us to recognize it as Jewish, even after it has imposed itself. But by then it will be very difficult for us to recognize ourselves as Jewish anyway, unless an achievement will be there that revises us even as it imposes itself upon us.

II

What remains most problematic is the question of the normative Jewish religion. I cannot know what the religion of Moses was, let alone the religion of Abraham or of Jacob. It is clear to me when I read the first and greatest of Jewish writers, J or the Yahwist, that his religion (if he has one, in our sense) is not the religion of Akiba. The thousand years that intervened between the Yahwist and the *Pirke Aboth* were no more a continuity than the eighteen hundred years between *Aboth* and ourselves. What the masks of the normative conceal is the eclectic nature even of rabbinical Judaism. Philo obviously was more of a Platonist than Akiba, but even Akiba was more Platonist than (perhaps) he knew. Nothing, we think, could be more Jewish than the idea of achieving holiness through learning, but the idea was Plato's and was adopted by the rabbis to their own profound purposes.

Judaism has been Platonized several times since, and been brought closer to Aristotle by Maimonides, who is now another mask for the normative though widely denounced as heterodox by much of Jewry in his own time. The Judaism of the Lurianic Kabbalah, still with us as transmuted into belated Hasidism, is another version of the normative, despite its Gnostic kernel. We know what Jewish culture *was,* but we cannot know what it now is, let alone what it will be. Everything called Judaism today essentially is antiquarianism, insofar as its intellectual content exists at all. Of course, that same sentence would be as valid if the word "Christianity" were substituted for "Judaism," and as valid again if the names of many academic disciplines were the substituted words.

Can the Jews survive, *as a people,* the waning of rabbinical Judaism? Have they not begun to survive it already? Jewish spirituality, in our literary culture, is hardly identical with the normative religion. Kafka, Freud and Gershom Scholem already are larger figures in the ongoing tradition of Jewish spirituality than are say, Leo Baeck, Franz Rosenzweig and Martin Buber, and only because the former grouping far surpass the latter in *cultural* achievement. When I said precisely that, in the discussion after a talk, I gave

much offense, but the offense or injustice belongs to the nature
of a literary culture, and not merely to my opinions. A cultural
canon, in an era when religion and philosophy have died, and science is dying, creates itself by the fierce laws of literary strength. I
have written so many books and essays about the dialectics of literary usurpation, that I have no desire to resume an account of
those dialectics here. But I refer whoever is skeptical to either *A
Map of Misreading* or *Kabbalah and Criticism,* among my books, for
evidence and argument on such matters. My concern in the rest
of this essay is wholly pragmatic; what can we know about the elements in our culture that will help us to see, however retrospectively, that those elements indeed *were* somehow Jewish?

There is no Jewish aesthetic, and cannot be, because of the
deep and permanent warfare between Yahweh and all idolatry
whatsoever, and yet we cannot deny the aesthetic strength of the
Hebrew Bible, since its spiritual authority is inseparable from its
rhetorical power. Authority and power, in a literary sense, are
peculiarly the attributes of J or the Yahwist, a writer whose originality and difficulty alike surpass those qualities in all others, even
in Shakespeare. But we are in danger of losing all sense of the
Yahwist, because of the endless work of normative revisionists,
from Elohistic, Deuteronomistic and Priestly redactors down
through a long line of scholiasts, Jewish and Christian, of whom
the most recent is that great homogenizer of literature, Northrop
Frye, in his recent *The Great Code,* Emerson once observed that
the Originals were not Original. Yes, but the Normatives were not
Normative either, and the Yahwist is as close to an Original as ever
we will have. After all, the Yahwist has Yahweh staging an unmerit-
ed murderous attack upon none less than Moses himself, and
Akiba, as I have said, has his Platonic overtones. Gershom
Scholem fiercely kept insisting that Kabbalah was nothing but
Jewish, and indeed not so heretical as it might seem, yet Kabbalah
is wholly an uneasy compound of Gnosticism and neo-Platonism,
and all that these rival doctrines had in common was that each
was a misprision or strong misreading of aspects of Platonism.

I want to illustrate the problematic element in Jewish literary
culture, by briefly asking what is or is not Jewish about three mod-

ern texts: the Primal History Scene in Freud's *Totem and Taboo;*
some moments in Kafka's uncanny fragment, *The Hunter
Gracchus;* a few paragraphs in a celebrated essay by Scholem,
"Tradition and New Creation in the Ritual of the Kabbalists"
(reprinted in the collection, *On the Kabbalah and its Symbolism).* Of
these three brief passages or scatterings, I will venture to advance
observations that the first two – by Freud and Kafka – appear to
have no Jewish referentiality, and the third – by Scholem – implicitly appear to devalue the ritual of rabbinical Judaism. But Freud's
brutal fantasia of "that memorable and criminal deed" of patri-
cide and cannibalism is an early version of his even crazier fantasy
in *Moses and Monotheism,* where the murder of Moses the Egyptian,
by the Jews, becomes the founding event of Judaism. Kafka's dead
but undying hunter is no Wandering Jew, but his consciousness of
isolation and election is a paradigm for the mouse people and
Josephine, their prophetess and singer, in the last and, I think,
most Jewish of all Kafka's stories. Scholem's exaltation of Lurianic
ritual and its Gnostic creativity hints at a new sense of what we
may not be aware of in rabbinical ritual. What Kafka, Freud and
Scholem share is a kind of prolepsis of a still hidden form of
Judaism, one that necessarily is still unapparent to us. Somewhere
Scholem remarked that of all the Jewish writers who write in
German, only Freud, Kafka, Walter Benjamin and Scholem himself truly were Jewish rather than German writers. The remark was
extreme, but I think suggestive, and part of the suggestion is what
I intend to explore now.

Some years back Cynthia Ozick printed a lively essay, called
"Judaism and Harold Bloom," the very title of which placed me
under the ban. If I recall rightly, the essay insisted that: "In Jewish
thought there *are* no latecomers." The work of Leo Strauss
demonstrated that Maimonides, Jehudah Halevi in his *Kuzari,* and
Spinoza all shared a sense of belatedness, of needing to write
"between the lines," and in some clear sense Maimonides, the
Kuzari and even Spinoza *are* Jewish thought. It must seem disturbing to suggest that, centuries hence, *Beyond the Pleasure Principle,*
Kafka's *Letter to his Father,* and Scholem's memoir of Benjamin may

seem no less monuments of Jewish spirituality than the *Guide for the Perplexed* or the *Kuzari*. But nothing need be unexpected in the disturbing relation between Jewish memory and Jewish history, to employ the terms eloquently demonstrated by Yerushalmi to be in dialectical tension with one another. My reference is to his remarkable little book *Zakhor* (upon which I have written elsewhere). Yerushalmi emphasized how the Lurianic Kabbalah so flooded Jewish consciousness in the sixteenth century as to cancel what would have been the rebirth of Jewish historiography, dormant for the fifteen hundred years since Josephus. Yet who could have prophesied the extraordinary rapidity with which the palpable Gnosticism of Luria's Kabbalah captured nearly the whole of Jewry, only a generation or two after the Ari died in Safed of Gaililee? The stories of Kafka, the speculations of Freud, the revival of Jewish Gnosis in the scholarship of Scholem – will the generations ahead somehow so amalgamate and diffuse these as to formulate a new Jewish myth, rationalizing again a Dispersion that has lost its Messianic rationalization? The state of Israel exists and will go on existing, but three quarters of surviving Jewry will continue to prefer to live elsewhere. Normative Judaism will hold its remnants and, as ever, much of Jewry will vanish away into the nations. But there will also be a secular Jewry, culturally identifiable, by self and by others. What will constitute Jewish memory for the elite of this Jewry? What indeed already constitutes the recent phase of Jewish cultural memory for contemporary Jewish intellectuals who are unable to see the normative religion of Akiba as anything other than an anachronism or a pious antiquarianism?

I begin some tentative answers by turning to Freud's overt Jewish stance, immensely problematic as that was. What *is* most Jewish about Freud's work? I am not much impressed by the answers to this question that follow the pattern: from Oedipus to Moses, and thus center themselves upon Freud's own Oedipal relation to his father Jakob. Such answers only tell me that Freud had a Jewish father, and doubtless books and essays yet will be written hypothesizing Freud's relation to his indubitably Jewish mother. Nor am I persuaded by any attempts to relate Freud to esoteric Jewish traditions. As a speculator, Freud may be said to have founded a kind of Gnosis, but there are no Gnostic elements in the Freudian dualism. Nor am I convinced by any of the attempts to connect Freud's Dream Book to supposed Talmudic antecedents. And yet the center of Freud's work, his concept of repression, does seem to me profoundly Jewish, and in its patterns even normatively Jewish. Freudian memory and Freudian forgetting are a very Jewish memory and a very Jewish forgetting. It is their reliance upon a version of Jewish memory; a parody-version if you will, that makes Freud's writings profoundly and yet all too originally Jewish.

To be originally Jewish, and yet to be original, is a splendid paradox, as Freudian as it is Kafkan. Perhaps one has to be Freud or Kafka to embody such a paradox, and perhaps all that I am saying reduces to this and to this alone: the mystery or problem of originality, peculiarly difficult in the context of the oldest, more or less continuous tradition in the West. But Freudian repression, like that uncanny quality or idea we cannot name except by calling it "Kafkan," is culturally not so primal as it may seem. *Verdrängung* is now poorly translated by "repression," if only because "repression" has become a political and ideological term. Freud, as several Freudians have remarked, did not intend the trope of pushing down or under, but rather, the trope of flight, as befits the estrangement from representations, an estrangement resulting from an inner drive. To fly from or be estranged from memories, images, desires that are prohibited, and to be forced into flight by an inner drive, is to presuppose a universe in which all memories, images and desires are overwhelmingly meaningful unless and until the estrangement is enacted. What kind of a world is that, in which there is sense in everything? For there to be sense in everything, everything already must be in the past, and there can be nothing new. I am echoing the critique of Freud's theory of repression first made by the great Dutch phenomenoligical psychiatrist, J. H. Van den Berg, but I echo also the Jewish historian Yerushalmi, when in *Zakhor* he vividly describes the dialectic of Jewish memory and Jewish history that dominates the vision of the normative rabbis of the Second century, CE. They were master theoreticians of repression eighteen centuries before their descendant, Solomon (or Sigmund) Freud.

Rabbinical memory founded itself upon the insistence that all meanings, and indeed all permissible representations, whether images, memories, or desires, were already present in the Hebrew Bible and in its normative commentaries, or else in the oral low as embodied by the contemporary interpreters who stood fast in the chain of tradition. Conversely, everything in the Scripture, and in its written and spoken commentaries, was and had to be totally meaningful. There was a sense and overwhelming sense in every *yod*, indeed in every space between the letters. If you combine this conviction of total sense, with a rejection of all idolatry, of every mythology, and so of every irrationality, then you have arrived already at something very near to the authentic Freudian stance. I think that Freud consciously was aware of all this, and affirmed the inner Jewishness of his science upon just such a basis. Primal repression, which ensues before there is anything to be repressed, is Freud's version of the Second Commandment.

Yet even this, I suspect, was not the innermost center of Freudian Jewishness. Kafka once, in effect, called Freud the Rashi of contemporary Jewish anxieties, and though there is a sardonic element in the remark, Kafka generally was not merely sardonic, particularly where the Jews or his own Jewishness was concerned. Freud obsessively collected classical artifacts, and yet towards the Greeks and the Romans, as towards the Christians, Freud spiritually was not even ambivalent. As a speculator, Freud had come to replace all gentile anteriority whatsoever. But towards Jewish anteriority, Freud indeed was ambivalent. Yahweh, in Freudian terms, had to represent the universal longing for the father but Freud's own internalization of Yahweh issued at last in the most Jewish of his Psychic agencies, the super-ego. To argue against an old vulgarism with a new one, the ego may be the gentile but the id is not the Yid. As the "above-I," the super-ego has no transcendental element or function. It is not a reality-instructor for the hapless ego, but something much darker. In his late book that we know as *Civilization and its Discontents,* Freud writes a kind of tragicomedy or even apocalyptic farce, in which the super-ego compels the ego to abandon its aggressivities, but then goes on punishing the ego for supposedly manifesting precisely those aggressivities.

This sado-masochistic scenario is a parody of the role of the prophets and of their precursor, Moses, in regard to the ancient Israelites. But it is also an allegory, not so parodistic, of Freud's vision of his own function, as exemplary Jew, in regard to gentile culture, of which he belatedly regarded Jung as too true a representative. We are almost in the grotesque plot of Freud's "novel," *The Man Moses,* which we know as *Moses and Monotheism.* There, in a kind of absurdist revision of Freud's Primal History Scene from *Totem and Taboo,* the Jews murder Moses the Egyptian, who thenceforth becomes, in effect, their super-ego. Freud's account of St. Paul then internalizes this super-ego further through the concept of original sin, thus setting up Christianity as the religion of the son against Judaism as the religion of the father. In one of the most striking of Freudian leaps, Christian anti-Semitism, with its accusation of deicide, is exposed as a polytheistic rebellion against the triumph of the Mosaic and so Jewish super-ego:

> . . .under the thin veneer of Christianity they have remained what their ancestors were, barbarically polytheistic. They have not yet overcome their grudge against the new religion which was forced on them, and they have projected it onto the source from which Christianity came to them. The fact that the Gospels tell a story which is enacted among Jews, and in truth treats only of Jews has facilitated such a projection. The hatred for Judaism is at bottom hatred for Christianity. . .

Whether this is convincing is a matter quite apart from its ethos, which is positively Judaistic. After all, why should monotheism be considered an advance upon polytheism, in strictly Freudian terms? Is one really more rational, let alone scientistic, than the other? Manifestly, Freud thought so. But is "thought" really the right word in that sentence? Freud's obsession with Moses was complex, and the element of identification in it is therefore very difficult to interpret. Still, as I have written elsewhere, Freud's hidden model for the analytical transference was his own mythopoeic account of the taboo, and his even more hidden model for the analyst was his rather frightening vision of the totem-father. I venture now that the most surprising invention in the book *Totem and Taboo* is Freud's singular transference of the Hebraic trope of the fatherhood of Yahweh to the slain and so deified father of the Primal Horde. In Biblical terms, Baal or Moloch are anything but a father, and Freud's curious emphasis has the effect of somehow Judaising animism, almost as though the Yahwist were composing *The Origin of Species*. What turns out to be most Jewish in Freud is the Yahweh in whom Freud overtly did not care to believe.

Kafka's original mode of Jewishness is far more elusive and even evasive, as we would expect. Adorno, in his "Notes on Kafka," says that Kafka's "literalness," meaning the "fidelity to the letter" required of Kafka's reader, probably echoes Jewish exegesis of Torah. Adorno advises the reader to "dwell on the incommensurable, opaque details, the blind spots," which I would say is equally essential advice for the reader of the Yahwist. But Adorno went strangely astray when he interpreted "The Hunter Gracchus," which he saw as the transposition, into archetypes, of the end of the bourgeois.

Adorno perhaps forgot his own admonition, as to the authority of Kafka's uncanny literalism. The force of Adorno's allegory is undeniable, but what (even in death, or undeath) is bourgeois about the Hunter Gracchus, whom Adorno later rightly compares to the Biblical Hunter Nimrod? After all, the bourgeois world is well represented in Kafka's tale by the fussy seaport mayor, whose final dialogue with Gracchus juxtaposes bureaucratic inanity with Kafka's truly weird Sublime. Do you mean to linger with us in our beautiful town of Riva is the mundane query, and the more-than-courteous response of Gracchus is that he thinks not, since his ship has no rudder, and is driven by winds that come from the icy regions of death. This weird sublimity is no more Jewish than Kafka's subjectivity considered itself to be a Jewish instance of culture. But then, several critics have cited another moment in the Hunter's dialogue with the mayor as a fearful prolepsis of the fate of European Jewry. How are we to read this moment? The mayor asks: "whose is the guilt?," and here is the astonishing reply:

> 'The boatman's,' said the Hunter, 'Nobody will read what I say here, no one will come to help me; even if all the people were commanded to help me, every door and window would remain shut, everybody would take to bed and draw the bedclothes over his head, the whole earth would become an inn for the night. And there is sense in that, for nobody knows of me, and if anyone knew he would not know how to deal with me, he would not know how to help me. The thought of helping me is an illness that has to be cured by taking to one's bed.'

"Turn it and turn it, for everything is in it," said the sage Ben Bag Bag. By "it," he meant Torah, but we may say the same of Freud and of Kafka, or rather of Freud *and* Kafka, taken together. "There is sense in that," says the Hunter Gracchus, and he is more than justified, because of the terrifying Jewish principle, Freudian and Kafkan, that *there is sense in everything,* which indeed does mean that that everything is past already and that there never can be anything new again. That is precisely how Yerushalmi interprets what he calls "Jewish memory." The Hunter Gracchus is no Wandering Jew, but the Hunter too is a theoretician of what has become, more than ever, Jewish memory.

Kafka's final story and testament, "Josephine the Singer and the Mouse Folk," is now another monument of Jewish memory, though all we could say of it accurately is that the Mouse Folk are not *and* are the Jewish people, and that their singer Josephine is not *and* is their writer, Franz Kafka. But towards what principle of disavowal *and* affirmation does Kafka thus drive us? Well, perhaps towards *his* version of what Freud called "Verneinung" (in a profound, very brief paper of 1925). Freudian *Verneinung* is anything but an Hegelian dialectical negation. Rather, it is properly dualistic, as befits a High Freudian concept, and mingles simultaneously and so ambivalently a cognitive return of the repressed and an affective continuation of repression, or of flight away from prohibited and yet desired images, memories, desires. Call Hegelian

negation the most profound of gentile idealizations, and then say
of the Freudian and Kafkan mode of negation that always it was
fated to re-enact endless repetitions of the Second
Commandment.

I turn to Gershom Scholem as my coda, and this is a rever-
ent turn, since that great loss to Jewish culture is so agonizingly
fresh and recent. Scholem wrote so many remarkable books and
essays that a choice among them cannot be other then arbitrary,
but I myself always have been obsessed with, and most influenced
by, his essay "Tradition and New Creation in the Ritual of the
Kabbalists." This essay opposes the ritual of Rabbinical Judaism in
Galut to the ritual of Isaac Luria. Whereas the ritual of *Galut*
before Luria replaces the natural year by Jewish memory, the ritual of Lurianic Kabbalah is a theurgy, a mode of "representation
and excitation," as Scholem says. This theurgy, Scholem adds, is
expected to accomplish a fourfold change: harmony between
supernal judgment and mercy, sacred marriage of masculine and
feminine, redemption of the *Shekhina* from dark powers of "the
other side," and general defense against, or mastery over, the
powers of "the other side." Such a ritual desires triumph, rather
than mere negation, and compels awe and shock in us, as normative Jews. For it could not be more antithetical to the ritual of
Rabbinical Judaism which, as Scholem memorably remarks,
"makes nothing happen and transforms nothing." A ritual that
makes nothing happen and transforms nothing, call it the ritual
of the great Akiba, nevertheless has a quiet persistence and an
ongoing force that, as Scholem recognized, quite eclipses the
Lurianic extravagances. I recall, as all of us do, almost the most
memorable of all the grandly memorable apothegms in *Pirke
Aboth*, the Rabbi Tarphon's magnificent admonition: "It is not
required of you that you complete the work, but neither are you
free to desist from it." The work makes nothing happen and
indeed *transforms* nothing, yet perhaps the whole greatness of the
Jewish normative tradition is in such a conception of "the work."
If Yahweh's work *is* the work, then it is hardly for us to go against
the *Yahweh-dabar* that comes to us, and which does not bid us to

alter the balance between his judgment and his mercy, or to will those other Gnostic intentions of Lurianic ritual.

And yet, Scholem activates our imaginations now, and Tarphon does not. Scholem's versions or revisions of Kabbalah move us in ways that the normative tradition does not, and certainly Scholem seems closer to Kafka than either seems close to any part of the normative rabbinical heritage. Scholem's Gnosticism, masking as historical shcolarship, is somehow more available as an emergent Jewish theology than is *The Star of Redemption,* or Buber's curious softenings and idealizations of Hasidism. In a phantasmagoria that I believe to be already existent, many of us shape a still inchoate and perhaps heretical new Torah out of the writings of Freud, Kafka, and Scholem. I say "perhaps" because who can say, or ever could say, what is heretical in regard to our traditions? We call Elisha ben Abuya *Acher,* but was he truly "the other" for us, simply because like the Gnostics he believed in two Powers, rather than one?

Yerushalmi ends his *Zakhor* by observing that all of us must understand the degree to which we now are the products of rupture. As he adds, once we are aware of this rupture, we not only are bound to accept it, but we are free to use it. I think that we are using it already, not always with full awareness that we are doing so. We study the nostalgias, and wish we could persuade ourselves that we are in continuity with Hillel, Akiba and Tarphon, or at least with Maimonides, Jehudah Halevi and Spinoza (hardly even now an exemplar of the normative!). But, on some level, we are aware that our continuity must be with Freud, Kafka, Scholem. They are the Jewish culture that is now available to us, when we do not deceive ourselves, and in remembering and studying them we also join ourselves again to an ongoing version of Jewish memory.

21 Apocalypse Then

I

The Jews returned from Babylon in the year 539 before the
Common Era, or rather they began to do so then, since many
remained in Babylon, and those who came back to Jerusalem and
Judea did not arrive all at once. But they flourished, their num-
bers grew, and they were not much disturbed at first by the
Hellenistic kingdoms that were established all around them after
the death of Alexander the Great in 323 BCE. Their upper classes
were Hellenized, yet for more than a century most of them held
fast to their traditions. From 200 BCE on, they were ruled by a
Hellenized Syria, which sought total control over them. In 175
BCE, Antiochus Epiphanes, king of Syria, declaring that he was the
manifestation of Zeus, set up an altar to Zeus in the Temple at
Jerusalem. Confronted by this "abomination that desolates" (as it
is called in the Book of Daniel), the Jews inevitably rebelled.

From 167 BCE onward, Judas Maccabeus and his brothers
fought the series of wars that were to make the Jews independent
again until the Romans under Pompey invaded them in 63 BCE.
Until the year 66 of the Common Era, the Jews uneasily tolerated
Roman dominance, but the inevitable and catastrophic rebellion
then broke forth, culminating in the fall of Jerusalem and
destruction of the Temple in 70 CE. The ultimate catastrophe
came with the last Jewish war against Rome, led by Simeon bar
Kochba, who perhaps was proclaimed as the Messiah by the aged

Rabbi Akiba, the greatest spiritual leader in the long history of Judaism. With the second fall of Jerusalem to the Romans in 135 CE, the Jews became stateless again, and were not to repossess the site of the Temple until 1967, nearly two decades after the rebirth of Israel.

I sketch this familiar history as a prelude to reviewing the new edition of the Pseudepigrapha, or those Jewish writings (circa 200 BCE to 200 CE) falsely, but as a matter of convention, attributed by their authors to crucial personages in the Hebrew Bible. Necessarily, I choose to avoid the long but bad tradition that speaks of the "Old Testament," since truly it was and is the "Original Testament," while the "New Testament" more accurately was and is, shall we not say, the "Belated Testament." But that condition of belatedness, of an anxious sense that one lacks originality, is as much the peculiar mark of nearly all the Pseudepigrapha as it is of the supposedly New Testament. The four centuries of torment, first under Syria and then under Rome, with the troubled reigns of the Maccabeans in between, brought forth both the Pseudepigrapha and the Christian Testament, each scored by the political and religious disasters suffered by the Jews in that age.

This welcome new edition of the Jewish Pseudepigrapha, ably edited by James H. Charlesworth but abominably printed by Doubleday (try reading the footnotes without incurring eyestrain and headache), reopens endless questions about the precise relations between Judaism and the origins of Christianity. I shall evade those questions here in favor of analyzing two of the most important Pseudepigrapha, so as to venture some judgment about their spiritual and literary value (if any) in comparison with the Hebrew Bible and even with rabbinic writing, and also to speculate upon why they were rejected by the tradition that (following the Harvard scholar G. F. Moore) we have learned to call "normative Judaism," by which we mean religion prescribing for all Jews an ethical way of life based on sacred texts as they are interpreted by rabbinical authorities.

Normative Judaism is still the religion of the Jews, and presumably it always will be, but it came into existence quite late in

Jewish history, though it always has proclaimed itself as the religion of the patriarchs, and of Moses, and of David the King, and
of Ezra the Scribe who helped lead the Return, and of his followers down to the death of the High Priest Simeon the Just around
270 BCE. The actual origins of normative Judaism cannot be
traced precisely, but there was an undoubtable movement from
priest to rabbi long before the Maccabees rose against the
Hellenizers. Before the Temple was defiled, let alone destroyed,
the center of Judaism had been moved from priestly worship to
the study of the Bible. While the Temple could never have prevailed against Hellenism, Torah hardly could fail to win out,
whether one wishes to give the credit to God or to the absolute
devotion of the normatively religious. Perhaps the credit should
be given to Ezra, the sixth-century BCE scribe or interpreter,
whom nowadays we would call a critic rather than a historical
scholar. Ezra's followers – the scribes, called "the men of the
Great Synagogue" and "the men of the Book" – were the teachers
who developed his mode of interpretation, midrash, and who
strengthened the tradition so as to fight off Hellenism, an
achievement made possible by a later, ironic conversion to Jewish
purposes of the Platonic idea that a people could be made holy
through organized study.

For nearly a century after 270 BCE or so, we have no clear
information about the continuity of Ezra's tradition. In 196 BCE,
the Sanhedrin or rabbinical senate was instituted, and it probably
included a group strongly opposed to Hellenization. This group
may have had some link with the Hasidim, those zealous adher-
ents of Torah who joined the Maccabean revolt; and perhaps they
also were connected later on to the rise of the Pharisees under
the Hasmonean kings descended from the brothers of Judas
Maccabeus. The Pharisees, the "separated," became prominent
well before 100 BCE, and clearly were the precursors of the great
rabbis of the first two centuries of the Common Era with whom
we most centrally associate normative Judaism: Hillel, Shammai,
Gamaliel, Johanan ben Zakkai, Akiba, Ishmael, Tarphon, Meir,
Judah the Prince. My thumbnail sketch slights crucial distinctions,

since the Judaism of 200 BCE to 200 CE underwent enormous changes, had astonishing diversity, and perhaps displayed more discontinuity than any retrospective view as yet knows how to admit. What seems beyond dispute is that the rabbis of the second century CE, and Akiba in particular, represented the culmination of the processes that brought forth the normative Judaism that still exists today.

What we call the Pseudepigrapha was rejected by normative Judaism, just as the now better-known writings we call the Apocrypha were rejected. The Apocrypha or "hidden" books were regarded not necessarily as heretical but rather as inappropriate for group religious services. In an almost unique ancient act of translation, the Hebrew Bible was rendered into Greek for Alexandrian Jewry, and this version, the Septuagint, included what now is called the Apocrypha – a naming that follows the usage of St. Jerome in his great Latin Bible, the Vulgate. Among the Apocrypha are works far superior, in a literary sense, to any of the Pseudepigrapha. Especially remarkable are the books of Tobit and of Judith, the story of Susanna, the Wisdom of Solomon, and in particular Ecclesiasticus or the Wisdom of Jesus ben Sirach, which certainly should have found an appropriate place in the canon of the Bible. Indeed, it is a considerable puzzle why Jesus ben Sirach was not included by the rabbis since the book is eminently in the normative current, surpassingly eloquent, and profoundly within the chain of tradition passing from Ezra on through the Pharisees. The Apocrypha is of course not under review here, and I mention its exclusion because it raises sharply the issue of the canonical principles upon which the rabbis worked.

"Canon" is a Christian term, first used in the fourth century CE; the word itself appears to refer to a reed used as a measuring rod. The Hebrew notion of canonicity was far more vivid, being conveyed by the metaphor that sacred texts were those that "defiled the hands." This great rabbinical paradox, "defile" where we might expect "purify," presumably meant that the holiness of the book would defile hands not sufficiently sanctified. Since we have not lost the idea of canonicity, even in our secular academies, we can measure our estrangement from religious traditions by reflecting how odd the Hebraic metaphor would sound if we employed it now: "The poems of John Ashbery, unlike, say, those of _____ (fill in whom you will: the Imamu Baraka? Sylvia Plath? Allen Ginsberg?) truly defile the hands." Yet the curious power of the metaphor still abides, and it seems very clear why none among the Pseudepigrapha defiles the reader's hands. We cannot imagine Rabbi Akiba saying of the pseudepigrapha called 1 Enoch – with its frenzied vision of apocalypse and resurrection – or of the Sibylline Oracles what he beautifully said of the Song of Solomon, when he triumphantly fought for its entrance into the canon:

> God forbid that any men of Israel should deny that the Song of Songs defiles the hands; for all the ages are not worth the day on which the Song of Songs was given to Israel. For all the scriptures are holy: but the Song of Songs is holiest of all.

II

The subtitle of this new version of the Pseudepigrapha is "Apocalyptic Literature and Testaments." The promised second volume will be more miscellaneous, comprising wisdom literature, fragments of lost Judeo-Hellenic works, prayers, psalms, and expansions of books in the canon of the Hebrew Bible. Compared to that grouping, the volume under review is almost monotonously unified, since the "testaments" are more apocalyptic than not; nor would it be wholly unfair to say that when you have read one ancient apocalypse you have read them all. Apocalypse as a form has taken surprising turns in Romantic and modern literature, from Blake and Shelley to *Gravity's Rainbow,* but the form's early history, from the Book of Daniel on to the Revelation of John and the later Pseudepigrapha, shows relatively little development or variety. It is even something of a puzzle why the Book of Daniel got into the Hebrew canon, but that is a matter for speculation later.

The word "apocalypse" derives from the Greek *apocalypsis,* "uncovering," and represents a final unveiling or, to change the figure, a last taking-off of the lid. A traditional apothegm holds that failed prophecy becomes apocalyptic, while failed apocalyptic becomes Gnosticism – a permanent resigning of nature, time, and history to the powers of darkness. The middle place of apocalyptic in that saying positions it between prophetic hope and Gnostic despair, but however transcendent the apocalyptic hope, a despair over the here and now is always an apocalyptic stigma.

Beyond question, the most impressive of ancient apocalypses is the first, the canonical Book of Daniel – canonized by the rabbis of the second century, however, among "the Writings" rather than among "the Prophets," where it is to be found in the Christian Bible. Daniel, composed probably during the Maccabean revolt, is in a clear sense a work of patriotic purpose, a kind of war poem intended to inspire the Jews to the valor their difficult situation demanded. In the book's crucial seventh chapter, the author of Daniel has a vision in which four rough beasts rise out of the sea:

> Daniel spake and said, I saw in my vision by night, and, behold, the four winds of the heaven strove upon the great sea.
>
> And four great beasts came up from the sea, diverse one from another.
>
> The first was like a lion, and had eagle's wings: I beheld till the wings thereof were plucked, and it was lifted up from the earth, and made stand upon the feet as a man, and a man's heart was given to it.
>
> And behold another beast, a second, like to a bear, and it raised up itself on one side, and it had three ribs in the mouth of it between the teeth of it: and they said thus unto it, Arise, devour much flesh.
>
> After this I beheld, and lo another, like a leopard, which had upon the back of it four wings of a fowl: the beast had also four heads; and dominion was given to it.
>
> After this I saw in the night visions, and behold a fourth beast, dreadful and terrible, and strong exceedingly; and it had great iron teeth; it devoured and brake in pieces, and stamped the residue with the feet of it: and it was diverse from all the beasts that were before it; and it had ten horns.
>
> (Daniel 7: 2-7, King James Version.)

Tradition has it that the lion with eagle's wings was Babylonia, the bear was Media, the winged leopard was Persia, and the terrible horned beast Macedonia – Greece, particularly the Hellenized Syria against whom the Maccabeans rebelled. However arcane we find this symbolism, it probably was instantly clear to the Jews of the second century CE, and its effect upon them intense. How original would it have seemed to them?

I do not intend the secondary senses of originality by this question, but rather its primary sense, one akin to Plato's aphorism: "The beginning is like a god which as long as it lives among men saves all things" (*Laws* 775). There is a feeling of freedom in felt originality that perhaps allies all major cultural strands in our traditions, even the largely antithetical Hebraism and Hellenism. The Jews battling against Hellenism in the days of Judas Maccabeus must have heard echoes in the Book of Daniel, echoes of moments in the prophets Ezekiel and Zechariah in particular, and also in Joel and Isaiah 24-27. Yet the apocalyptic form and its promise to tell secrets was essentially new to them.

The Pharisees and the rabbis of the normative tradition after them rejected every other apocalypse, leaving them to the Pseudepigrapha, and yet they canonized Daniel among the Writings. Originality, odd as it seems, may have won Daniel its place. Patriotism perhaps was a motive, since the book might have reminded the rabbis of a heroic age in the life of their people. What seems likelier is that the Pharisees stressed right action above all, and Daniel is an apocalypse that has not yet despaired of the effects of right action among the living. It is with the movement from Daniel to Enoch that apocalypse forsakes all traces of what the normative rabbis considered the Way we ought to follow, and that a spirit moved among the Jews difficult to reconcile with what was most central in their traditions.

III

Reading through this new edition has sent me back to the earlier edition of R. H. Charles, *The Apocrypha and Pseudepigrapha of the Old Testament in English* (Oxford University Press, 1913), and to the same scholar's once standard study, *Eschatology* (1899; rpt. Schocken Books, 1963). Refreshingly missing in the new edition is the strong bias Charles manifests against rabbinic Judaism and in favor of the apocalyptic writers. Though this movement from Charles to Charlesworth is surely a scholarly advance, it perhaps obscures the crucial contrast between Talmud and Apocrypha, or between Pharisaism and apocalyptic, which had its own critical value. Charlesworth and his colleagues are responding not only to more general improvements in historical scholarship but to the highly specific discovery of the scrolls from the Dead Sea, which provide overwhelming evidence that Judaism before the first fall of Jerusalem was spiritually and intellectually more diverse than anyone had realized. Another factor working against too strict a distinction between early phases of the normative tradition in Judaism and the development of apocalyptic speculations is that our earlier information about the Judaic process of the formation of the canon has now been questioned by much recent scholarship.

Most scholars once believed that a rabbinical council meeting, with Roman permission, at Jamnia, Palestine, established the final canon of the Hebrew Bible in 90 CE. It appears now that the books of the Law had been established long before the second century BCE, and the Prophets perhaps just as the second century BCE began. After 90 CE, rabbinical debates continued on the canonical worthiness of the Book of Esther, Koheleth or Ecclesiastes, and Akiba's well-beloved Song of Solomon or Song of Songs. The apocalyptic pseudepigrapha were thus composed and disseminated during an era in which the canon was by no means fixed, whether for Jews or (from about 50 CE on) for Jewish or Gentile Christians. Indeed, for Christians the New Testament canon remained open until 367 CE. (The Revelation of St. John the Divine evidently was not accepted by the Greek Church until the tenth century, and Syrian Christians today still exclude it.)

Canonicity remains a troublesome category, both within the religions and in the literary culture of our secular universities and schools. Thus 1 Enoch and some other pseudepigrapha are still, I believe, canonical for the Falashas or Ethiopian Jews, who finally are being helped to come into the state of Israel, after long and shameful delays for which some elements in the normative rabbinate must be held partly responsible. Clearly, and sadly, the issue of canonicity, even among Jews, remains a matter of some pragmatic consequence, and of course it forever will divide Jews from Christians, since religious Jews would lose their authentic identity if they were to grant even a shred of canonical status to the belated or New Testament. There is, for believing Jews, simply no spiritually honest way to reconcile the Hebrew Bible with the Gospels, and each time I have attended an academic conference on Jewish-Christian "dialogue" I have witnessed a futile exercise in humane self-deception.

My earlier formula "from Charles to Charlesworth" therefore has a dialectical undersong to it, because though there is scholarly and social gain in the differences between editions of the Pseudepigrapha, there is also polemical and even spiritual loss. A scholar like Charles, once representative of Christian opinion, overvalued the apocalyptic literature because he believed it to be the true child of prophecy, in contrast to the rabbinic writings:

> It is now clear, I think, that from Nehemiah's time onward prophecy could not gain a hearing, whether the prophecy was genuine – that is, appeared under the name of its actual author – or was anonymous, unless it were acceptable in the eyes of the Law. From the class of genuine and anonymous works we pass on to the third division, the pseudonymous. . . . How are we to explain the pseudonymity of Daniel and the other apocalyptic works of the second century BC, such as Enoch, Jubilees, and the testaments of the XII Patriarchs? . . . These apocalyptists do not merely repeat the old truths, which in so many cases had become the mere shibboleths of a petrified orthodoxy, they not only challenged many of the orthodox views of the time and condemned them, but they also carried forward the revelation of God in the provinces of religion, ethics, and eschatology. Against the reception of such fresh faith and truth the Law stood in

the way, unless the books containing them came under the aegis of certain great names in the past.

This rather extraordinary view of "the Law" is merely a repetition of the parody of Pharisaism that dominates the New Testament, and is particularly virulent in the Gospel of John. But at least Charles, with all his prejudices, renewed the traditional polemic against normative Judaism, a polemic which is, after all, the essence of Christianity, inexpedient though it be to say so. The proper corrective to Charles was given by the English Unitarian Robert Travers Herford, in his splendid book *The Pharisees*. Herford's argument is admirably illuminated by Glatzer's observation that the Talmudic, Pharisaic, rabbinic "system" was "an ethical *discipline,* a guide to the application of ethics in active, private, and communal life, while the apocryphal books were books in the modern sense: expressions of the thinking of solitary individuals." This contrast touches upon something of the modern appeal of apocalyptic literature, quite aside from its affinities either to the Essene community of Qumran or to the early Christians. Against this appeal, Glatzer empathizes instead with Herford's preference for the Pharisees. Few moments in religious polemic seem to me as effective as Herford's cı ushing response to Charles:

> It is no doubt true that the "Law" did acquire a supreme place in the Judaism of the centuries since Ezra. But, if there had been, during those centuries, any real prophets who felt that they had a word of the Lord to declare, they would have declared it. Who would have prevented them? Certainly not the "Law," nor those who expounded it. Rather, who *could* have prevented them? Amos said what he had to say in spite of the priest and the king; and, if there had been an Amos in the centuries now in question, he would have spoken his word regardless of Pharisee or Scribe, in the very unlikely case of their wishing to prevent him.
>
> Also, if there had been a second-century Amos, there would have been some trace of him. But there is no trace. The Pharisees recognized the fact that prophecy had come to an end, and drew their own conclusion from that fact. And the Apocalyptic writings are a witness, not to "the tyranny of the Law," but to the feebleness of those who aspired to wear the mantle of Elijah. If their writings had

appeared under their own names, it is quite conceivable that no attention would have been paid to them; their device of introducing their works under the shelter of great names – Enoch, Moses, Solomon, Ezra – was one which men of original genius would not have needed nor condescended to use. Did John the Baptist fear "the tyranny of the Law," or let it prevent him from delivering his message? Yet he spoke without concealment of his own identity, and there was never any doubt about his gaining a hearing. The Apocryphal writers included neither an Amos nor a John the Baptist, else they would not have written anonymously. Their works bear out this opinion, for their want of original power is conspicuous. They are obviously based on the prophetic writings; and, what is more, the peculiar type of Apocalyptic writing is repeated in its main features over and over again.

Strong as this is, and wholly convincing to me, it is made still more severe by Herford's closing defense of the Pharisees against the visionaries: "Apocalyptic is full of promises, but it has never kept one of them." Even the great Akiba, leader of the Hillelite group among the Pharisees, was rightly reproved by another sage when the ninety-year-old scholar yielded to apocalyptic yearning and proclaimed Simeon bar Kochba the Messianic king: "Akiba, grass will grow out of your jaw and the Messiah will not yet have come!"

Herford, in the tradition of British Protestant dissent, which has roots in normative rabbinicism, was defending the Talmudic insistence upon right action and deep study. The defense was against the ancient apocalyptics' belief in salvation by faith alone, and so ultimately against the Essenes of Qumran (discovered only after Herford's death) and St. Paul, who put forth what, from the Jewish point of view, is an absurd but permanently influential parody of the Law in his Epistle to the Romans. The wilder texts of salvation by faith are precisely those the volume under review makes more available than ever before, and so I turn now to them, starting with Enoch, of whom Genesis 5:24 so mysteriously had said: "And Enoch walked with God: and he was not, for God took him."

IV

The oldest of the three Pseudepigrapha attributed to Enoch is the Ethiopic Apocalypse of Enoch, translated in this new edition by E. Isaac. Generally called 1 Enoch, this violent and gaudy book had an influence upon the New Testament that is out of all proportion with its intrinsic value. Indeed, it is a weird jumble, at least as we have it, having been composed by several different writers over a span extending throughout the last two centuries before the Common Era, and possibly well on into the first century CE.

Like Daniel, the original of the Ethiopic Enoch probably was a mixture of Hebrew and Aramaic. Fragments of 1 Enoch were found among the Dead Sea Scrolls, and the apocalyptic Qumran Covenanters may have included the book in their own esoteric canon. The reader coming to 1 Enoch now may be as receptive to apocalypses as the Essenes and early Christians were then, but it will be difficult for him to share in any of the ancient enthusiasm for this curious, composite vision of the end of all things. The authors, whoever they were, took as their starting point one laconic bit of the greatest of Biblical writers, the first major storyteller whom scholars call J or the Jahwist:

> And it came to pass, when men began to multiply on the face of the earth, and daughters were born unto them,
> That the sons of God saw the daughters of men that they were fair; and they took them wives of all which they chose.
> And the Lord said, My Spirit shall not always strive with man, for that he also is flesh: yet his days shall be a hundred and twenty years.
> There were giants in the earth in those days; and also after that, when the sons of God came in unto the daughters of men, and they bare children to them, the same became mighty men, which were of old men of renown.

The eloquence of the King James version here is worthy of the original. But something of the J writer's uncanny irony is lost: these mismatches between divine beings and earthly beauties brough forth the Nephilim, the giants who were the heroes of old, the men with a name. That is all the J writer cared to say about them; they did not interest him in comparison with his heroes, true men with a name, Abram who became Abraham, and Jacob who became Israel. But the apocalyptists who wrote Enoch were considerably more interested in this passage than J ever was. J lived probably during Solomon's reign or just after; they lived in a Judea always threatened by a Hellenized Syria. J's elliptical anecdote becomes in them a fall of the angels, and so the point of origin for an enormous demonology, appropriate to a time of troubles like their own, which was probably pre-Maccabean. The fallen angels presumably are the Macedonian princes of the Hellenistic world, and the vision of their punishment manifests the element of angry wish-fulfillment that is an unpleasant feature of all apocalypses whatsoever.

Yet 1 Enoch shows traces of the Hellenistic universe it opposes, so that the doom of the evil angels is associated also with an ascent of Enoch into the other world – almost as though only angelic sin yields a revelation to us. The heavens and hells Enoch describes are not very inventive, but all demonology, both ancient and modern, remains much indebted to them, since this book is our source for most of the demonic crew. More interesting, then and now, is the apocalyptic figure of the Son of Man, enigmatic in Enoch as he was in Daniel, where presumably he originated.

Chapter 7 of Daniel is a vivid fantasia in which the martyred Hasidim who died in the Maccabean revolt become associated with a younger demigod, the Son of Man, who is given dominion by an older deity, the Ancient of Days. In itself, this baffling mythopoeic projection presumably would not have so strongly affected Christians, except for its elaboration in 1 Enoch, where Enoch himself becomes the Son of Man and is celebrated as a divine redeemer. Though this part of 1 Enoch is still considered to be pre-Christian, and was not taken up by the Essenes, it has nothing left in it of the normative Judaism of the Pharisees. Talmudic rabbinicism was and is monistic, committed to an absolutely powerful God; a cosmos of fallen angels and a heavenly redeemer is already as dualistic as early Christianity was to be.

E. Isaac, introducing his translation of 1 Enoch in this volume, remarks upon its theological importance for clarifying "the rich complexities of both intertestamental Jewish thought and early Christian theology," but wisely makes no assertions about its intrinsic value. To a lay reader like myself, as opposed to a scholar of these matters, it is difficult to see how 1 Enoch could clarify anything. The book (or books) is not complex but merely complicated, and its authors lacked not only originality but also any theological coherence. Nearly all ancient apocalypses, the Revelation of St. John the Divine decidedly included, manifest a considerable incoherence that seems to belong to the nature of the genre, and perhaps also to the psychology of hysterical repression that informs it.

Apocalypse as a literary genre, I would grant, has to be distinguished from apocalypticism as a mode of feeling, thinking, acting – that is, as a system of belief. Yet the distinction, which is clearly valid for Blake and Shelley, or for the Yeats of "The Second Coming" or the later D. H. Lawrence, is difficult to justify for works like Daniel, Enoch, and the Revelation of John. The literary form of ancient apocalypse, as analyzed by an authority like P. D. Hanson in *The Dawn of the Apocalyptic* (1975), shows a fairly tight structure involving a divine revelation mediated by an angel or even a redeemer, and communicated to a visionary so as to foretell an inevitable future, catastrophic and yet at the last salvational. But apocalypticism transcends any pattern, and diffuses into a cosmos of torment that reflects a psychology of the tormented self. Jewish history from the Hellenic oppression under Antiochus Epiphanes through the Roman destructions of Jerusalem and on through the centuries would seem to be an inevitable spur to apocalypticism. The late Gershom Scholem magnificently researched and reconceived the later fortunes of Jewish apocalypticism, as part of his life's work of demonstrating that the counternormative tradition of the Jews and Judaism was as important a continuity as the rabbinical tradition, and indeed that the two frequently could not be distinguished from each other.

Scholem was fascinated by 3 Enoch, a Hebrew Apocalypse of Enoch which probably was composed as late as the fifth or sixth century CE, but which purports to be the work of the great rabbi

Ishmael, who was martyred by the Romans just before the rebellion of Bar Kochba and Akiba in 132 CE. The book is translated and introduced with great learning by P. Alexander in this new edition, and despite the prolixity and redundancy that marks this work, it seems to me that making it available is the largest single contribution of the volume under review. Though 3 Enoch is traditionally called "a Hebrew Apocalypse," its genre is not an apocalypse at all, but rather a vision of the Merkabah, the heavenly chariot that opens Ezekiel's prophecy, and that established not only a tradition of mysticism based on this vision but also one of Kabbalistic speculation that Scholem urges us to consider as "Jewish Gnosticism." This is a strange oxymoron, and one not acceptable to the normative tradition because it would deny that God is the author of this world.

Daniel, chapters 7-12; 1 Enoch, chapters 14-15; 3 Ezra, chapters 9-13; 2 Baruch: all these are as clearly apocalypses as are the Revelation of John or Night the Ninth of Blake's *The Four Zoas*, but 3 Enoch is something quite different, and for all its speculative wildness, it does not violate the fundamental ethos of the rabbinical tradition, at least not in Scholem's formidable judgment. This is also the informed conclusion of its current translator, Alexander, who observes that "The Merkabah texts concentrate overwhelmingly on the mysteries of heaven and on the description of God's throne: they show little interest in eschatological themes such as the last judgment, the resurrection of the dead, the messianic kingdom, and the world to come, all of which figure in classic apocalyptic."

With 3 Enoch the common reader, guided by Alexander's commentary and by his minutely careful translation, will have access for the very first time, in English, to a work absolutely central for the study of all Jewish esotericism. Mystical speculation was practiced in private by the Talmudic rabbis, was then handed on to medieval German-Jewish mystics, and culminated in the *Zohar*, the central text of late-thirteenth century Spanish-Jewish Kabbalah. In itself, 3 Enoch shows remarkable invention, though it is sometimes difficult to apprehend because of its heavily repetitive style. Nevertheless, the reader who persists will make an extraordinary journey into the heavenly regions, moving through seven heavens until she or he stands in God's own series of seven concentric palaces or temples.

At the center is the Merkabah, the chariot that carries the throne of glory, surrounded by vast orders of angels, who are shielded from the divine glory by a curtain, lest the terrible otherness or transcendence of the Jewish God destroy them. Visions of the Shekinah, the luminous cloud that is the divine presence, alternate with those of Metatron, chief of the angelic hosts, and probably an esoteric version of the archangel Michael as well as a transmogrified Enoch. There are detailed descriptions of the heavenly law court and of the fate of the righteous, the intermediate, and the wicked after death. The reader is thus enabled to approximate at least part of the fabled experience of the four sages who entered Pardes, the garden or park that is Paradise, as told in the Talmudic tractate Hagigah 14b:

> Four entered Pardes, and these are they: Ben Azzai, Ben Zoma, Acher, and Rabbi Akiba. Rabbi Akiba said to them: "When you reach the stones of pure marble, do not say 'Water! Water!' for it is written, 'He that speaks falsehood shall not be established before my eyes'" (Psalms 101:7). Ben Azzai looked and died: Scripture says of him, "Precious in the sight of the Lord is the death of his saints" (Psalms 116:5). Ben Zoma looked and went mad: Scripture says of him: "Have you found honey? Eat so much as is sufficient for you lest you be sated with it and vomit it up" (Proverbs 25:16). Acher cut down the young plants. Rabbi Akiba saw, and then went out of Pardes in peace.

Acher is the tragic apostate and Gnostic, the rabbi Elisha ben Abuyah, a scholar who was the jealous rival of Akiba. We have only hostile Talmudic reports of Elisha ben Abuyah's beliefs and career, but the angry Talmudic name for him, "Acher" – "the other" – indicates a fury that makes me doubt the tradition that reports him to have been a traitor, a quisling who became a Roman lackey and informer. Yet the Talmudic parable of the four sages who entered Pardes is sufficient indication of why Acher outraged the normative rabbis. Cutting down the young plants of

Paradise signifies the destructive effect of Gnostic dualism, of
Acher's belief in two principles – presumably principles of God
and of a demi-urge – rather than a monostic belief in the absolute
power of God. Today many readers, schooled by the insights of
Scholem, may reflect with some melancholy that they are more in
the mode of Acher than in that of the great Akiba.

V

The other texts in this new edition, though of immense interest to
scholars, will seem to most general readers largely bewildering
repetitions of the apocalyptic mode. Rather than comment on any
more of these texts, I will conclude with a general comparison of
the Pseudepigrapha and the normative tradition, by way of contrasting both 1 and 3 Enoch with the most moving and accessible
of the Talmudic tractates, the Pirke Aboth, the ethical sayings or
Wisdom of the Fathers.

Doubtless the pressures of Jewish history had to result in the
apocalyptic Pseudepigrapha, as they resulted also in the Essenes
and the Qumran Covenanters, and presumably in early
Christianity as well. But apocalypse then certainly is not apocalypse now, and despite all current slogans, the Age of Andropov
and Reagan is not yet the Age of Antiochus Epiphanes. I return to
Travers Herford's remark in *The Pharisees:* "Apocalyptic is full of
promises, but it has never kept one of them. Its immediate effect
may have been exhileration, but it has left despair behind it."
There are a number of ancient works to set against apocalyptic,
but the Sayings of the Fathers seems to me the inevitable
counterpoint to such yearnings for finality, such wish-fulfillments
carried to the outer edge of history.

Aboth begins with the maxim of the Men of the Great
Synagogue or Academy of Ezra: "These said three things; Be
deliberate in judging, and raise up many disciples, and make a
hedge for the Torah." Throughout the tractate, the great rabbis
speak their apothegms, each in the authority of his own name,
and not in the name of Daniel, or Enoch, or Ezra, or whoever.

Against the apocalyptics, though with all gratitude for this new edition, I wish to set two famous sayings, one of Akiba's, and one by Tarphon, his genial contemporary. Akiba said: "All is foreseen, and free will is given, and the world is judged by goodness; and all is according to the amount of work" (Aboth III, 19). That is immense and definitive, but I add the fine pathos of Rabbi Tarphon, which opposes all apocalyptic yearnings: "You are not required to complete the work, but neither are you free to desist from it" (Aboth II, 21).

22 "Before Moses Was, I Am": The Original and the Belated Testaments

"Your father Abraham rejoiced that he was to see my day; he saw it and was glad.' The Jews then said to him, 'You are not yet fifty years old, and have you seen Abraham?' Jesus said to them, 'Truly, truly, I say to you, before Abraham was, I am.'" (John 8:56-58)

This exchange from The Gospel According to St. John will be my text. In the Christian triumph over the Hebrew Bible, a triumph which produced that captive work, the Old Testament, there is no more heroic stroke than the transumptive trope of John's Jesus: "Before Abraham was, I am." Too much is carried by that figuration for any range of readings to convey, but one reading I shall give is the implied substitution: "Before Moses was, I am." To my reading, the author of the Gospel of John was and is a more dangerous enemy of the Hebrew Bible than even Paul, his nearest rival. But I can hardly go on until I explain what I intend to mean by "an enemy of the Hebrew Bible."

It is now altogether too late in Western history for pious or humane self-deceptions on the matter of the Christian appropriation of the Hebrew Bible. It is certainly much too late in Jewish history to be other than totally clear about the nature and effect of that Christian act of total usurpation. The best preliminary description I have found is by Jaroslav Pelikan:

> What the Christian tradition had done was to take over the Jewish Scriptures as its own, so that Justin could say to Trypho that the passages about Christ "are contained in your Scriptures, or rather not yours, but ours." As a matter of fact, some of the passages were contained only in "ours," that is, in the Christian Old Testament. So

> assured were Christian theologians in their possession of the
> Scriptures that they could accuse the Jews not merely of misunder-
> standing and misinterpreting them, but even of falsifying scriptural
> texts. When they were aware of differences between the Hebrew text
> of the Old Testament and the Septuagint, they capitalized on these
> to prove their accusation . . . The growing ease with which appropria-
> tions and accusations alike could be made was in proportion to the
> completeness of the Christian victory over Jewish thought.
> Yet that victory was achieved largely by default. Not the superior
> force of Christian exegesis or learning or logic but the movement of
> Jewish history seems to have been largely responsible for it.

Pelikan's dispassionate judgment on this matter is beyond disputation. Though the Christians were to "save" the Old Testament from those like Marcion who would cast it out completely, that is precisely what they saved – *their* Old Testament. The New Testament is to a considerable extent a reading of that Old Testament, and I would judge it a very mixed reading indeed. Some of it is a strong misreading, and much of it is a weak misreading, but I will concern myself here entirely with strong misreadings, because only strong misreadings work so as to establish lasting enmities between texts. The author of the Gospel of John is an even stronger misreader that St. Paul, and I want to compare John's and Paul's strengths of what I call poetic misprision before I center upon John. But before commencing, I had better declare my own stance.

"Who is the interpreter, and what power does he seek to gain over the text?" That Nietzschean question haunts me always. I am an enemy of the New Testament. My enmity is lifelong, and intensifies as I study its text more closely. But I have no right to assert that my own enmity carries the force of the normative Jewish tradition, because I am not a representative of that tradition. From a normative Jewish perspective, let us say from the stance of the great Akiba, I am one of the *minim*, the Jewish Gnostic heretics. My own reading of the Hebrew Bible, even if I develop it into a strong misreading, is as unacceptable in its way to the normative tradition as all Christian readings necessarily are. I state this not to posture, but to make clear that I do not pretend to the authority of the normative tradition. In my view, the

Judaism that moves in a continuous line from the Academy of Ezra through the Pharisees and on to the religion of my own parents is itself a very powerful misreading of the Hebrew Bible and so of the religion of the Yahwist, whatever we might take that religion to have been. But my subject here is not the text of the Yahwist.

What kind of authority can a literary critic, whose subject is the secular literature of the English language, bring to a reading of the New Testament, particularly to a reading that sees the New Testament as a text in conflict and confrontation with the Hebrew Bible? I cannot speak for other literary critics, as here too I am a sect or party of one, and have no authority other than whatever my ideas and my writings can assert for me. But the central concern of my own literary theory and *praxis,* for some fifteen years now, has been the crisis of confrontation and conflict between what I have called strong poems, or strong texts. I cannot say that my formulations in this area have met with a very amiable reception, even in the most secular of contexts, and so I do not expect an amiable response as I cross the line into the conflict of scriptures. Still, I have learned a great deal from the response to my work, a response that necessarily has become part of my subject. One lesson has been that there are no purely secular texts, because canonization of poems by the secular academies is not merely a displaced version of Jewish or Christian or Moslem canonization. It is precisely the thing itself, the investment of a text with unity, presence, form, and meaning, followed by the insistence that the canonized text possesses these attributes immutably, quite apart from the interpretive activities of the academies.

If so many partisans of Wordsworth or Whitman or Stevens find the offense of my work unbearable, then clearly I must expect a yet more pained response from the various custodians of the Hebrew Bible or the New Testament. I won't take more space here for unhappy anticipation or personal defense, yet I do want to make the modest observation that several years spent intensely in reading as widely as I can in Biblical scholarship have not left me with the impression that much authentic *literary* criticism of Biblical texts has been written. To make a clean sweep of it, little seems to me to have been added by recent overt intercessions by literary critics, culminating in Northrop Frye's *The Great Code*, a work in which the triumph of the New Testament over the Hebrew Bible is quite flatly complete. Frye's code, like Erich Auerbach's *figura,* which I have attacked elsewhere, is only another belated repetition of the Christian appropriation and usurpation of the Hebrew Bible.

But these matters I will argue elsewhere. I come back again to the grand proclamation of John's Jesus: "Before Abraham was, I am." What can an antithetical literary criticism (as I call my work) do with the sublime force of that assertion? Or how should that force be described? Is it not the New Testament's antithetical reply to the Yahwist's most sublime moment, when Moses agonizingly stammers: "If I come to the people of Israel and say to them, 'The God of your fathers has sent me to you,' and they ask me, 'What is his name?' what shall I say to them?" God said to Moses, "I AM WHO I AM." This is the Revised Standard Version, and like every other version, it cannot handle Yahweh's awesome, untranslatable play upon his own name: *ehyeh asher ehyeh.* I expand upon a suggestion of Martin Buber's when I render this as "I will be present wherever and whenever I will be present." For that is the Yahwist's vision of *olam* as "a time without boundaries," and of the relation of Yahweh to a dynamics of time that transcends spatial limitations.

The Yahwist's vision of his God certainly would seem to center with a peculiar intensity upon the text of Exodus 3:13-14. But the entire history of ancient Jewish exegesis hardly would lead anyone to believe that this crucial passage was of the slightest interest or importance to any of the great rabbinical commentators. The *Exodus Rabbah* offers mostly midrashim connecting the name of God to his potencies which would deliver Israel from Egypt. But *ehyeh asher ehyeh* as a phrase evidently did not have peculiar force for the great Pharisees. Indeed, Jewish tradition does very little with the majestic proclamation until Maimonides

gets to work upon it in *The Guide for the Perplexed.* One of my
favorite books, Marmorstein's fascinating *The Old Rabbinic
Doctrine of God,* has absolutely not a single reference to Exodus 3
in its exhaustive one-hundred-fifty-page section on "The Names of
God." Either we must conclude that *ehyeh asher ehyeh* has very little
significance for Akiba and his colleagues, which I think probably
was the case, or we must resort to dubious theories of taboo,
which have little to do with the strength of Akiba.

This puzzle becomes greater when the early rabbinical indifference to the striking *ehyeh asher ehyeh* text is contrasted to the
Christian obsession with Exodus 3, which begins in the New
Testament and becomes overwhelming in the Church Fathers,
culminating in Augustine's endless preoccupation with that passage, since for Augustine it was the deepest clue to the metaphysical essence of God. Brevard Childs, in his commentary on
Exodus, has outlined the history of this long episode in Christian
exegesis. Respectfully, I dissent from his judgment that the ontological aspects of Chirstian interpretation here really do have any
continuity whatsoever either with the biblical text or with rabbinical traditions. These "ontological overtones," as Childs himself
has to note, stem rather from the Septuagint's rendering of *ehyeh
asher ahyeh* as the very different egw eimi o wn and from Philo's
very Platonized paraphrase in his *Life of Moses:* "Tell them that I
am He Who is, that they may learn the difference between what is
and what is not." Though Childs insists that this cannot be dismissed as Greek thinking, it is nothing but that, and explains
again why Philo was so crucial for Christian theology and so totally irrelevant to the continuity of normative Judaism.

The continued puzzle, then, is the total lack of early rabbinical interest in the *ehyeh asher ehyeh* text. I labor this point because I
read John's greatest subversion of the Hebrew Bible as what I call
his transumption of Yahweh's words to Moses in the extraordinary
outburst of John's Jesus, "Before Abraham was, I am," which most
deeply proclaims: "Before Moses was, I am." To me, this is the
acutest manifestation of John's palpable ambivalence toward
Moses, an ambivalence whose most perceptive student has been

Wayne Meeks. John plays on and against the Yahwist's grand
word-play on Yahweh and *ehyeh*. However, when I assert even that,
I go against the authority of the leading current scholarly commentary upon the Fourth Gospel, and so I must deal with this
difficulty before I return to the Johannic ambivalence toward the
Moses traditions. And only after examining John's agon with
Moses will I feel free to speculate upon the early rabbinic indifference to God's substitution of *ehyeh asher ehyeh* for his proper name.

Both B. Lindars and C. K. Barrett in their standard commentaries on John insist that "Before Abraham was, I am" makes
no allusion whatsoever to "I am that I am." A literary critic must
begin by observing that New Testament scholarship manifests a
very impoverished notion as to just what literary allusion is or can
be. But then here is Barrett's flat reading of this assertion of Jesus:
"The meaning here is: Before Abraham came into being, I eternally was, as now I am, and ever continue to be." Perhaps I should
not chide devoted scholars like Lindars and Barrett for being
inadequate interpreters of so extraordinary a trope, because the
master modern interpreter of John, Rudolf Bultmann, seems to
me even less capable of handling trope. Here is his reading of
John 8:57-58:

> The Jews remain caught in the trammels of their own thought.
> How can Jesus, who is not yet 50 years old, have seen Abraham! Yet
> the world's conception of time and age is worthless, when it has to
> deal with God's revelation, as is its conception of life and death.
> "Before Abraham was, I am." The Revealer, unlike Abraham, does
> not belong to the ranks of historical personages. The egw which
> Jesus speaks as the Revealer is the "I" of the eternal Logos, which was
> in the beginning, the "I" of the eternal God himself. Yet the Jews can-
> not comprehend that the egw of eternity is to be heard in an histori-
> cal person, who is not yet 50 years old, who as a man is one of their
> equals, whose mother and father they knew. They cannot under-
> stand, because the notion of the Revealer's "pre-existence" can only
> be understood in faith.

In a note, Bultmann too denies any allusion to the "I am
that I am" declaration of Yahweh. I find it ironical, nearly two
thousand years after St. Paul accused the Jews of being literalizers,
that the leading scholars of Christianity are hopeless literalizers,

which of course the great rabbis never were. I cannot conceive of a weaker misreading of "Before Abraham was, I am" than Bultmann's sneering retreat into "faith," a "faith" in the "pre-existence" of Jesus. If that is all John meant, then John was a weak poet indeed. But John is at his best here, and at his best he is a strong misreader and thus a strong writer. As for Bultmann's polemical point, I am content to repeat a few amiable remarks made by Rabbi David Kimhi almost eight hundred years ago:

> Tell them that there can be no father and son in the Divinity, for the Divinity is indivisible and is one in every aspect of unity unlike matter which is divisible.
>
> Tell them further that a father precedes a son in time and a son is born through the agency of a father. Now even though each of the terms "father" and "son" implies the other . . . he who is called the father must undoubtedly be prior in time. Therefore, with reference to this God whom you call Father, Son and Holy Spirit, that part which you call Father must be prior to that which you call Son, for if they were always coexistent, they would have to be called twin brothers.

I have cited this partly because I enjoy it so much, but also because it raises the true issue between Moses and John, between Abraham and Jesus, which is the agonistic triple issue of priority, authority, and originality. As I read John's trope, it asserts not only the priority of Jesus over Abraham (and so necessarily over Moses), but also the priority, authority, and originality of John over Moses, or as we would say, of John as writer over the Yahwist as writer. That is where I am heading this account of the agon between the Yahwist and John, and so I turn now to some general observations upon the Fourth Gospel – observations by a literary critic, of course, and not by a qualified New Testament believer and/or scholar.

John does seem to me the most anxious in tone of all the gospels, and its anxiety is as much what I would call a literary anxiety as an existential or spiritual one. One sign of this anxiety is the palpable difference between the attitude of Jesus toward himself in the Fourth Gospel as compared to the other three. Scholarly consensus holds that John was written at the close of the first century, and so after the Synoptic Gospels. A century is certainly enough time for apocalyptic hope to have ebbed away, and for an acute sense of belatedness to have developed in its place. John's Jesus has a certain obsession with his own glory, and particularly with what that glory ought to be in a Jewish context. Rather like the Jesus of Gnosticism, John's Jesus is much given to saying "I am," and there are Gnostic touches throughout John, though their extent is disputable. Perhaps, as some scholars have surmised, there is an earlier, more Gnostic gospel buried in the Gospel of John. An interesting article by John Meagher of Toronto, back in 1969, even suggested that the original reading of John 1:14 was "And the Word became *pneuma* and dwelt among us," which is a Gnostic formulation, yet curiously more in the spirit and tone of much of the Fourth Gospel than is "And the Word became flesh."

The plain nastiness of the Gospel of John toward the Pharisees is in the end an anxiety as to the spiritual authority of the Pharisees, and it may be augmented by John's Gnostic overtones. A Jewish reader with even the slightest sense of Jewish history, feels threatened when reading John 18:28-19:16. I do not think that this feeling has anything to do with the supposed pathos or problematic literary power of the text. There is a peculiar wrongness about John's Jesus saying, "If my kingship were of this world, my servants would fight, that I might not be handed over to the Jews" (18:36); it implies that Jesus is no longer a Jew, but something else. This unhappy touch is another sign of the pervasive rhetoric of anxiety in the Fourth Gospel. John's vision seems to be of a small group – his own, presumably – which finds its analogue and asserted origin in the group around Jesus two generations before. In the general judgment of scholars, the original conclusion of the gospel was the parable of doubting Thomas, a manifest trope for a sect or coven undergoing a crisis of faith.

It is within that anxiety of frustrate expectations, perhaps even of recent expulsion from the Jewish world, that John's agon with Moses finds its context. Wayne Meeks has written very sensitively of the Fourth Gospel's ambivalence toward the Moses traditions, particularly those centered upon the image of Moses as prophet-king, a unique amalgam of the two roles that John seeks to extend and surpass in Jesus. My interest in John's handling of Moses is necessarily different in emphasis, for I am going to read a number of John's namings of Moses as being tropes more for the text than for the supposed substance of what the New Testament (following the Septuagint) insists upon calling the Law. I myself will call it not Torah but J or the Yahwist, because that is where I locate the agon. Not theology, not faith, not truth is the issue, but literary power, the scandalous power of J's text, which by synecdoche stands for the Hebrew Bible as the strongest poem that I have ever read in any language that I am able to read. John, and Paul before him, took on an impossible precursor and rival, and their apparent victory is merely an illusion. The aesthetic dignity of the Hebrew Bible, and of the Yahwist in particular as its uncanny original, is simply beyond the competitive range of the New Testament as a literary achievement, as it is beyond the range of the only surviving Gnostic texts that have any aesthetic value – a few fragments of Valentinus and the Gospel of Truth that Valentinus may have written. But I will return at the end of this discourse to the issue of rival aesthetic achievements. John's struggle with Moses is at last my direct concern.

There are so many contests with Moses throughout the New Testament that I cannot contrast John in this regard to all of the other texts, but I do want to compare him briefly with Paul, if only because I intend later to consider some aspects of Paul's own struggle with the Hebrew Bible. I think there is still nothing so pungent in all commentary upon Paul as the remarks made by Nietzsche in 1888, in *The Antichrist:*

> Paul is the incarnation of a type which is the reverse of that of the Savior; he is the genius in hatred, in the standpoint of hatred, and in the relentless logic of hatred. . . . What he wanted was power; with St. Paul the priest again aspired to power, – he could make use only of concepts, doctrines, symbols with which masses may be tyrannised over, and with which herds are formed.

Of course Nietzsche is extreme, but can he be refuted? Paul is so careless, hasty, and inattentive a reader of the Hebrew Bible that he very rarely gets any text right; and in so gifted a person this kind of weak misunderstanding can come only from the dialectics of the power drive, of the will to power over a text, even when the text is as formidable as Torah. There is little agonistic cunning in Paul's misreadings of Torah; many indeed are plain howlers. The most celebrated is his weird exegesis of Exodus 34:29-35, where the text has Moses descending from Sinai, tablets in hand, his face shining with God's glory – a glory so great that Moses must veil his countenance after speaking to the people, and then unveil only when he returns to speak to God. Normative Jewish interpretation, surely known to Paul, was that the shining was the Torah restoration of the *zelem*, the true image of God that Adam had lost, and that the shining prevailed until the death of Moses. But here is II Corinthians 3:12-13:

> Since we have such a hope, we are very bold, not like Moses, who put a veil over his face so that the Israelites might not see the end of the fading splendor.

There isn't any way to save this, even by gently calling it a "parody" of the Hebrew text, as Wayne Meeks does. It isn't a transumption or lie against time, which is the Johannine mode; it is just a plain lie against the text. Nor is it uncharacteristic of Paul. Meeks very movingly calls Paul "the Christian Proteus," and Paul is certainly beyond my understanding. Proteus is an apt model for many other roles, but perhaps not for an interpreter of Mosaic text. Paul's reading of what he thought was the Law increasingly seems to me oddly Freudian, in that Paul identifies the Law with the human drive that Freud wanted to call Thanatos. Paul's peculiar confounding of the Law and death presumably keeps him from seeing Jesus as a transcending fulfillment of Moses. Instead, Paul contrasts himself to Moses, hardly to his own disadvantage. Thus, Romans 9:3:

> For I could wish that I myself were accused and cut off from Christ for the sake of my breathren, my kinsmen by race.

It may seem at first an outburst of Jewish pride, of which I would grant the Protean Paul an authentic share, but the Mosaic allusion changes its nature. All exegetes point to Exodus 32:32 as the precursor text. Moses offers himself to Yahweh as atonement for the people after the orgy of the golden calf: "But now, if thou wilt forgive their sin – and if not, blot me, I pray thee, out of thy book which thou hast written." How do the two offers of interces-sion compare? After all, the people *have* sinned, and Moses would choose oblivion to save them from the consequences of their dis-loyalty. The allusive force of Paul's offer is turned against both his own Jewish contemporaries and even against Moses himself. Even the Pharisees (for whom Paul, unlike John, has a lingering regard) are worshippers of the golden calf of death, since the Law *is* death. And all Moses supposedly offered was the loss of his own prophetic greatness, his place in the salvation history. But Paul, out of supposed love for his fellow-Jews, offers to lose more than Moses did, because he insists he has more to lose. To be cut off from Christ is to die eternally, a greater sacrifice than the Mosaic offer to be as one who had never lived. This is what I would call the daemonic counter-Sublime of hyperbole, and its repressive force is enormous and very revelatory.

But I return again to John, whose revisionary warfare against Moses is subtler. Meeks has traced the general pattern, and so I follow him here, though of course he would dissent from the interpretation I am going to offer of this pattern of allusion. The allusions begin with John the Baptist chanting a typical Johannine metalepsis, in which the latecomer truly has priority ("John bore witness to him, and cried, 'This was he of whom I said: He who comes after me ranks before me, for he was before me'"), to which the author of the Fourth Gospel adds: "For the law was given through Moses; grace and truth came through Jesus Christ" (John 1:15, 17). Later, the first chapter proclaims: "We have found him of whom Moses in the law and also the prophets wrote, Jesus of Nazareth" (1:45). The third chapter daringly inverts a great Mosaic trope in a way still unnerving for any Jewish reader: "No one has ascended into heaven but he who descended from heaven, the Son of man. And as Moses lifted up the serpent in the wilderness, so must the Son of man be lifted up" (3:13-14). John's undoubted revisionary genius is very impressive here merely from a technical or rhetorical point of view. No heavenly revelations ever were made to Moses, whose function is reduced to a synecdoche, and indeed to its lesser half. To use one of my revisionary ratios, Jesus on the cross will be the *tessera* or antithetical completion of the Mosaic raising of the brazen serpent in the wilderness. Moses was only a part, but Jesus is the fulfilling whole. My avoidance of the language of typology, here and elsewhere, is quite deliberate, and will be defended in my conclusion, where I will say a few unkind words about the Christian and now Auerbachian trope of *figura*.

The same ratio of antithetical completion is invoked when Jesus announces himself as the fulfiller of the sign of manna, as would be expected of the Messiah. But here the gratuitous ambivalence toward Moses is sharper: "Truly, truly, I say to you, it was not Moses who gave you the bread from heaven; my father gives you the true bread from heaven. For the bread of God is that which comes down from heaven, and gives life to the world" (6:32-33). As the trope is developed, it becomes deliberately so shocking in a Jewish context that even the disciples are shocked; but I would point to one moment in the development as marking John's increasing violence against Moses and all the Jews: "Your fathers ate the manna in the wilderness, and they died. . . . I am the living bread . . . if any one eats of this bread, he will live for ever; and the bread which I shall give for the life of the world is my flesh" (6:49, 51). It is, after all, gratuitous to say that our fathers ate the manna and died; it is even misleading, since had they not eaten the manna, they would not have lived as long as they did. But John has modulated to a daemonic counter-Sublime, and his hyperbole helps to establish a new, Christian sublimity, in which Jews die and Christians live eternally.

Rather than multiply instances of John's revisionism, I want to conclude my specific remarks on the Fourth Gospel by examining in its full context the passage with which I began: "Before

Abraham was, I am." I am more than a little unhappy with the sequence I will expound, because I find in it John at nearly his most unpleasant and indeed anti-Jewish, but the remarkable rhetorical strength of "Before Abraham was, I am" largely depends upon its contextualization, as John undoes the Jewish pride in being descended from Abraham. The sequence, extending through most of the eighth chapter, begins with Jesus sitting in the temple, surrounded both by Pharisees and by Jews who are in the process of becoming his believers. To those he has begun to persuade, Jesus now says what is certain to turn them away:

> "If you continue in my word, you are truly my disciples, and you will know the truth, and the truth will make you free." They answered him, "We are descendants of Abraham, and have never been in bondage to anyone. How is it that you say, 'You will be made free'?" (8:31-32)

It seems rather rhetorically weak that Jesus should then become aggressive, with a leap into murderous insinuations:

> "I know that you are descendants of Abraham; yet you seek to kill me, because my word finds no place in you. I speak of what I have seen with my Father, and you do what you have heard from your father" (8:37-38).

As John's Jesus graciously is about to tell them, the Jews' father is the devil. They scarcely can be blamed for answering, "Abraham is our father," or for assuming that their accuser has a demon. I look at the foot of the page of the text I am using, *The New Oxford Annotated Bible, Revised Standard Version* (1977), and next to verse 48, on having a demon, the editors helpfully tell me, *"The Jews* turn to insult and calumny" (p. 1300). I reflect upon how wonderful a discipline such scholarship is, and I mildly rejoin that by any dispassionate reading John's Jesus has made the initial "turn to insult and calumny." What matter, since the Jews are falling neatly into John's rhetorical trap? Jesus has promised that his believers "will never see death" and the astonished children of Abraham (or is it children of the devil?) protest:

> "Abraham died, as did the prophets; and you say, 'If any one keeps my word, he will never taste death.' Are you greater than our father Abraham, who died?" (8:52-53)

Jesus responds by calling them liars, again surely rather gratu-
itously, and then by ensnaring them in John's subtlest tropological
entrapment, which will bring me full circle to where I began:

> "Your father Abraham rejoiced that he was to see my day; he saw it
> and was glad." The Jews then said to him, "You are not yet fifty years
> old, and have you seen Abraham?" Jesus said to them, "Truly, truly, I
> say to you, before Abraham was, I am" (8:57-58).

It is certainly the most remarkable transumption in the New
Testament, though I had better explain what I mean by transumption, which is a little exhausting for me, since I have been explain-
ing the term endlessly in eight books published over the last nine
years. Very briefly, transumption or metalepsis is the traditional
term in rhetoric for the trope that works to make the late seem
early, and the early seem late. It lies against time, so as to accomplish what Nietzsche called the will's revenge against time, and
against time's assertion, "It was." Uniquely among figures of
speech, transumption works to undo or reverse anterior tropes. It
is therefore the particular figure that governs what we might call
"interpretive allusion." Ultimately, it seeks to end-stop allusiveness
by presenting its own formulation as the last word, which insists
upon an ellipsis rather than a proliferation of further allusion.

When John's Jesus says, "Before Abraham was, I am," the
ultimate allusion is not to Abraham but to Moses, and to Yahweh's
declaration made to Moses, "I am that I am." The transumption
leaps over Abraham by saying also, "Before Moses was, I am," and
by hinting ultimately: "I am that I am" – because I am one with my
father Yahweh. The ambivalence and agonistic intensity of the
Fourth Gospel achieves an apotheosis with this sublime introjection of Yahweh, which simultaneously also is a projection or repudiation of Abraham and Moses. I am aware that I seem to be making John into a Gnostic Christian, but that is the transumptive
force of his rhetoric, as opposed perhaps to his more overt dialectic. His Gospel, as it develops, does seem to me to become as
Gnostic as it is Christian, and this is the kind of Gnosticism that
indeed was a kind of intellectual or spiritual anti-Semitism.
Obviously, I believe that there are Gnosticisms and Gnosticisms,

and some I find considerably more attractive than others. Just as obviously, the Gnostic elements in John, and even in St. Paul, seem to me very shadowed indeed.

Earlier in this discourse, I confessed my surprise at the normative rabbinical indifference, in ancient days, to Yahweh's sublime declaration, *ehyeh asher ehyeh.* If the great Rabbi Akiba ever speculated about that enigmatic phrase, he kept it to himself. I doubt that he made any such speculations, because I do not think that fearless sage was in the habit of hoarding them, and I am not enough of a Kabbalist to think that Akiba harbored forbidden or esoteric knowledge. To the normative mind of the Judaism roughly contemporary with Jesus, there was evidently nothing remarkable in Yahweh's declining to give his name, and instead almost playfully asserting: "Tell them that I who will be when and where I will be am the one who has sent you." That is how Yahweh talked, and how he was. But to the belated author of the Fourth Gospel, as to all our belated selves, "I am that I am" was and is a kind of *mysterium tremendum,* to use Rudolf Otto's language. That mystery John sought to transcend and transume with the formulation, "Before Abraham was, I am." Prior to the text of Exodus was the text that John was writing, in which the Jews were to be swept away into the universe of death, while Jesus led John on to the universe of life.

This transformation is an instance of just how the New Testament reduced the Hebrew Bible to that captive work, the Old Testament. Though the reduction is necessarily of great theological influence, it of course does not touch the Hebrew Bible. I have read the Hebrew Bible since I was a child, and the New Testament since I first took a course in New Testament Greek as an undergraduate. Clearly, I am not a dispassionate reader of the New Testament, though I do not read the Hebrew Bible as the normative Jewish tradition has read it, either. I come back to the issue of the interpreter's authority. When I read, I read as a literary critic, but my concerns have little in common with those of any other contemporary critic. Idealizations of any text, however canonical, or of the reading process itself are not much to my taste. Emerson said he read for the lustres. I follow him, but I emphasize even more that the lustres arise out of strife, competition, defense, anxiety, and the author's constant need for survival *as an author.* I don't see how any authentic literary critic could judge John as anything better than a very flawed revisionist of the Yahwist, and Paul as something less than that, despite the peculiar pathos of his protean personality. In the aesthetic warfare between the Hebrew Bible and the New Testament, there is just no contest, and if you think otherwise, then bless you.

But surely the issue is not aesthetic, I will be reminded. Well, we are all trapped in history, and the historical triumph of Christianity is brute fact. I am not moved to say anything about it. But I am moved to reject the idealized modes of interpretation it has stimulated, from early typology on to the revival of *figura* by Erich Auerbach and the Blakean Great Code of Northrop Frye. No text, secular or religious, fulfills another text, and all who insist otherwise merely homogenize literature. As for the relevance of the aesthetic to the issue of the conflict between sacred texts, I doubt finally that much else is relevant to a strong reader who is not dominated by extraliterary persuasions or convictions. Reading *The Book of Mormon,* for instance, is a difficult aesthetic experience, and I would grant that not much in the New Testament subjects me to rigors of quite that range. But then John and Paul do not ask to be read against *The Book of Mormon.*

Can the New Testament be read as less polemically and destructively revisionary of the Hebrew Bible than it actually is? Not by me, anyway. But don't be too quick to shrug off a reading informed by an awareness of the ways of the antithetical, of the revisionary strategies devised by those latecomers who seek strength, and who will sacrifice truth to get strength even as they proclaim the incarnation of the truth beyond death. Nietzsche is hardly the favorite sage of contemporary New Testament scholars, but perhaps he still has something vital to teach them.

What do Jews and Christians gain by refusing to see that the revisionary desperation of the New Testament has made it permanently impossible to identify the Hebrew Bible with the Christian

Old Testament? Doubtless there are social and political benefits in idealizations of "dialogue," but there is nothing more. It is not a contribution to the life of the spirit or the intellect to tell lies to one another or to oneself in order to bring about more affection or cooperation between Christians and Jews. Paul is hopelessly equivocal on nearly every subject, but to my reading he is clearly not a Jewish anti-Semite; yet his misrepresentation of Torah was absolute. John is evidently a Jewish anti-Semite, and the Fourth Gospel is pragmatically murderous as an anti-Jewish text. Yet it is theologically and emotionally central to Christianity. I give the last word to the sage called Radak in Jewish tradition, that David Kimhi whom I cited earlier. He quotes as proof-text Ezekiel 16:53: "I will turn their captivity, the captivity of Sodom and her daughters." And then Radak comments, rightly dismissing from his perspective all Christians as mere heretics from Judaism: "This verse is a reply to the Christian heretics who say that the future consolations have already been fulfilled. *Sodom is still overturned as it was and is still unsettled.*"

23 Criticism, Canon-Formation, and Prophecy: The Sorrows of Facticity

I begin with my search for a word, which I can't quite find, because the dictionaries don't have it, or else list it equivocally. What I need is a word that will describe our being so far inside a tradition, of inside a way of representing, or inside even a particular author, that only enormous effort can make us aware of how reluctant we are to know our incarceration. I need to say, here at the start, that I am not talking about a linguistic problematic, or any other development of Nietzsche's much misused trope of our being pent up in the prison-house of language. There is a textual aspect to my subject, obviously, but the containment I address is considerably larger than textuality, unless you conceive textuality so diffusely that all human action is textual. Manifestly, that trivializes human action, and increasingly I distrust any critical mode that so reduces us. But my subject does have to do with something inescapable that reduces us constantly, and which I believe the function of criticism must be to combat. There is a kind of brute contingency that compels us to misread figurative language as being literal; yet to call it "contingency" comes a little short of it. I could speak of "brute factuality" or even of "brute facticity," but I am aware that those words (or non-words) are slow to enter the dictionaries. "Factuality" would mean just the state or quality of being fact or factual, as in "I question the factuality of their account." But "facticity," if it becomes an acceptable English word, is better for my purposes. "Facticity" would mean the state of being a fact, as an inescapable and unalterable fact. To be caught in facticity is to be caught in the inescapable and unalterable. The stances or positions of freedom are not available, and the text or event reads us more fully and vividly than we can hope ever to read it.

Anyone who comes late into a story or a family or an institution is likely to have a sense that her or his status is forever uncertain. I do not identify this sense with what I call facticity, because uncertainty is something near to interpretive freedom, or can be converted into it. But belatedness has a peculiar relationship to facticity, and can be mistaken for it. Belatedness is a conscious anxiety, and results from a pervasive ambivalence. Facticity is a state or quality, not a mode of consciousness, and so pragmatically excludes any sense of ambivalence. And yet belatedness and facticity alike do follow from the assumption that everything has a meaning, or rather that there is sense in everything. If there is sense in everything, then all temporality is reduced to pastness, and invention becomes impossible. Dr. Johnson, the best literary critic in our language, insisted that the essence of poetry was invention. Belatedness threatens poetry, and yet can spur it; facticity, allowed a full sway over us, destroys poetry, by making trope irrelevant.

An easy but dangerous misunderstanding of what I am calling facticity is simply to see it as the negation of all irony. I think the negating force of facticity is larger, in that it destroys also every possibility of representation by synecdoche. As an instance I give Freud, the largest recent facticity that contains us. Freud depends upon the synecdoche that represents health by neurosis, which is to say that in his favorite trope, psychic health is completeness, and neurosis is a fragment, a broken symbol of health. Yet Freud is now so much himself a synecdoche for the facticity of our psychic containment that we must read *his* favorite synecdoche as a literalism. Indeed, facticity urges us to literalize all of Freud, so that we walk about now assuming that we are uneasy triads of id, ego, and superego, and mingled drives of Eros and Thanatos. It takes an effort to remember that the Freudian agencies and drives are tropes, and not actual entities or real instances of human life. This is the tribute we pay to Freud, and I mean "tribute" in more than one sense. We pay tribute to Freud involuntarily, as we do to all the powerful mythologies and idealisms that together constitute our historicized dungeon of facticity. Wittgenstein complained that Freud was a powerful mythologist. The complaint is useful, but even Wittgenstein was too enclosed by Schopenhauer's facticity to complain about that precedent mythology, of which Freud himself was never quite free. Philosophers, psychoanalysts, and those still involved with religion are all strikingly vulnerable to blindness about facticity, and to this grouping I would add literary critics who are enclosed by the facticity of Hegel and his tradition, down through Heidegger to Derrida. It is a charming irony that the conscious demystifiers of and by language themselves unknowingly are mystified by the larger entrapments of a containing facticity. Negation also has become a facticity, a literalizing of Hegel's prime trope, and this remystification is now the most squalid truth one can utter about contemporary advanced criticism.

What are the critical uses of a concept of facticity? Our culture in all of its most frozen aspects has been created by its literalization of anterior tropes. Indeed, our concept of culture itself is such a literalization. But I need to make clear that I hope not to be caught in the enclosure of merely literalizing the anterior trope of "facticity" that plays itself out in the early Heidegger. Heidegger's *Faktizität* is the modern equivalent of the *kenoma*, the emptiness into which we have been and are being thrown, according to the Gnosis of Valentinus. I follow Hans Jonas in so connecting Valentinus and Heidegger, and since I am a kind of belated Valentinian, I am all the more anxious to disengage my sense of "facticity" from Heidegger's. In the Heideggerian "hermeneutics of facticity," our understanding of the world and of ourselves is limited by our tradition and by our factual circumstance in history. Instead of the narcissistic ego of Freud, or the transcendental ego of Husserl, we have the factually existing ego, a thrown-clear fragment of Being. My own sense of "facticity" is a blend of the Freudian narcissistic and partly unconscious ego with a Gnostic or Kabbalistic *pneuma* or spark, which has been thrown all right, but not clear or into a possible clearing.

When a reader is limited by facticity, the limitation goes beyond the facts of tradition and of history. Foucault has tried to engage "notions of chance, discontinuity, and materiality" at the origins of historical ideas, but his mode of engagement is unknowingly tropological, as Hayden White shows. Heidegger is not much interested in the brute contingency of all origins as such, since he privileges Greece and Germany; thus the absolute arbitrariness of the engendering of every tradition whatsoever would not suggest itself to him as a facticity. I tend to cite the erotic analogue in regard to facticity, because almost all of us have immediate knowledge of the contrast between the chance start of our love affairs and the inescapable vicissitudes that ensue from initial haphazardness. The facticity of erotic suffering is shockingly disproportionate to the apparent blunder of erotic venturing, a disproportion that is a clue to many quieter versions of cultural facticity. But I need an example, and for that I turn to the one inevitable work in Western literary culture, the Bible, which is neither Greek nor German. What happens to us when we attempt to read the first great story of a mingled belatedness and earliness, the story of Adam, Eve, and the serpent in Eden?

The strongest writer in the Hebrew language, fully the rival of Homer and Dante, of Shakespeare and Milton, we know fittingly by the Kafkan name of the letter J, standing for the Jahvist. Fittingly, because J in one of his aspects is more Kafkan than Kafka, as in another he is more Tolstoyan than Tolstoy. J is a bewildering writer, uncanny beyond any other, and boundlessly difficult because wildly original, with an originality that perhaps three thousand years of commentary and revisionism have failed to subdue or even assimilate. This is originality in the strictest sense, for J is *our* original, as, say, *Gilgamesh* is not, precisely because J *was*. J was and is, and J has authority over us, whether we are Gentile or Jew, normative or heretic, concerned or indifferent. This is the authority of brute contingency, of our being imprisoned by what we might call J's facticity. J's stories are not merely just as familiar as Homer's. They are stories that were more than stories for most of our ancestors, and even if they are only stories for many or perhaps most of us, they are stories with a different aura than Homer's. Wrestling Jacob moves us more intimately than Odysseus confronting the Cyclops, and Yahweh walking down the road to Sodom is a touch more disturbing than Zeus swooping down as a swan. But why?

What I have called facticity or brute factuality is a truth about interpretation that we repress rather than neglect. These days we evade it also, by troping upon it, as the Franco-Heideggerians and their American *epheboi* trope, substituting the fashionable prison-house of language for the dank dungeon of historical contingency. Reflecting upon the difficulties of reading J can help remind us *why* rather than just *how* we tend to misread tropes as literalisms. J was an astonishing ironist, and yet nearly every mode of interpretation has read him as being anything but ironic. I am going to offer a belated (and brief) reading of J's story of Eve and the Serpent, a reading that will take into account some of the earlier interpretations, normative and Gnostic. But mostly I will attempt to take J's own irony into account, which means that I will try to escape the confinements of facticity, while acknowledging that it is quite impossible to do so. Still, I will try, while remembering that the irony of one age or language is not likely to be the irony of another, no matter what our current linguistifiers tell us to the contrary.

So I commence with J's irony, or rather his ironies. His minor modes of irony have something in common with Dante's or Milton's, but only because those poets are so much imprisoned by the contingency of his being the Word of God for them. J is even more massively self-confident a writer than Dante or Milton, fierce and primal in his approach to human personality, and totally daring in his apprehension of divine realities. It is when human personality and divine reality collide that J is almost invariably ironic, in a mode that Kafka catches best among all the descendants of J. This irony is neither classical nor romantic, Greek nor European. If irony is saying one thing while meaning another, or provoking an expectation that will not be fulfilled, then J is no ironist. But if irony ensues from the juxtaposition or clash of incommensurate levels of powerful realities, then J sets standards of irony that have not been met since. Consider Genesis 6:1-4. The sons of the Elohim look upon the daughters of men, find them beautiful, and take them. Yahweh says: Man is only flesh, and shall not be guarded by my spirit forever, so let him have just one hundred and twenty years. Why doesn't Yahweh say something about the sons of the Elohim, who certainly are showing that they are pretty fleshy also? The elliptical J makes no comment, except to observe that it was *then,* as well as later, that the Nephilim or titans appeared on earth, presumably as the children of Elohistic mismatches. And he adds, rather drily, perhaps even wryly: "Those were the ancient heroes, men with a name." Here is the late E. A. Speiser's quite normative weak misreading:

> It is evident, moreover, from the tenor of the Hebrew account that its author was highly critical of the subject matter. It makes little difference whether J took the contents at face value or, as is more likely (cf. vs. 5), viewed the whole as the product of man's morbid imagination. The mere popularity of the story would have been sufficient to fill him with horror at the depravity that it reflected. A world that could entertain such notions deserved to be wiped out.

Well, J's fifth verse says that Yahweh saw man's wickedness and evil schemes on earth, but *that* hardly seems a reference to the lustful antics of the sons of the Elohim. There is certainly sorrow in Yahweh's heart, but what J expresses is a kind of ironic apprehension and perhaps even appreciation. Men with a name – before the rather different ways in which Abram became Abraham, and Jacob became Israel, and Moses became the messenger of Yahweh – tended to spring from illicit marriages between earth and heaven. There is no horror and no morbidity in J's tone, but rather a high and sublime irony, which Speiser is too hemmed in by facticity to be able to hear.

But my example is the serpent in Eden, and not to hear J's irony is to be deaf to literature. First there is Yahweh's characteristic gesture, granting all yet ironically withdrawing that part of the grant which is incommensurate with the recipient. This is the problematic gift made to Adam, and more equivocal still is the

irony of Yahweh originally making the serpent more fully conscious than the man and the woman, yet not conscious enough to
know with certainty either their limits or his own. As befits a God
whose name is presence ("I will be when and where I will be"),
only Yahweh knows the limit of limits, the dialectics of infinite
human aspiration and finite human limitations. And the irony of
the serpent, much exploited by certain varieties of Gnosticism, is
that he is both human-all-too-human and more than human, even
if not of the Elohim. Any accurate reading of Genesis 3 begins
with the realization that Adam's wife (unnamed until under the
curse of Yahweh) is wholly unsurprised by the talking, standing,
clever serpent, whether in its proper person or in its message. J
clearly neither says nor implies that the serpent is bad or ill-moti-
vated, but only rather shrewd or crafty, an attribute which in the
Hebrew is connected to nakedness by a pun. Nor does J's serpent
lie; a half-truth is quite enough to engender our disaster. The
woman eats in order to gain wisdom; she gains instead the knowledge of death, and ultimately death itself, but only after Yahweh
takes action against her and her husband. But that, as I think J
implies, after all *is* a kind of widsom, though it comes first as the
previously nonexistent consciousness of sexuality – not, of course,
as sexuality itself. The new consciousness arrives through its sign
of nakedness, and so the serpent teaches that which it truly is:
consciousness or a sense of nakedness or a certain subtle mode of
quest, craftiness. J's God Yahweh marks that consciousness as one
limit, a limit that he presumably never intended us to touch. We
are expelled by God Yahweh lest we transgress further limits, and
we achieve that sense of time without boundaries that Abraham,
Isaac, Jacob, and their descendants are to achieve only through
an agonistic blessing, and then only within very clear individual
limits.

I turn now to some early interpretations of J's serpent
drama, and I will state my conclusion before I start. Both the normative and the Gnostic interpretations are strong misreadings of
J. I can scarcely decide which distorts or revises J more, and
because both the normative and the Gnostic interpretations have

enforced and maintained their own contingencies, I think we must call them equally strong misreadings. This is not to say that one cannot choose between them; I do not hesitate in finding the Gnostic misprision far more satisfying, morally and aesthetically and indeed spiritually, than the Jewish and Christian normative misprisions. The normative interpretation is perhaps too familiar for commentary, or rather the strongest commentary is available in *Paradise Lost*. What is central in that commentary is the identity of the serpent with Satan, which of course has not the slightest relation to J's story. Early Jewish legend invented the serpent's sexual envy of Adam, expressed most forcefully by the fine touch of the serpent pushing Eve against the tree, while urging independence of God upon the lady. This emblematic movement is reinforced by the detail of the serpent shaking the tree violently, bringing down its fruit. The interpretative strength of these physical details is that they do return to the implications of J's pun upon the serpent's slyness and human nakedness.

Gnostic interpretations antithetically began with the opposite principle, and so with a pragmatic exaltation of the serpent. Perhaps reacting to tropes of seduction, involving Eve and the serpent, in St. Paul and later Christian texts, the Gnostics emphasize the serpent's role in the liberation of human consciousness. The most sublimely outrageous of Gnostic texts in this regard is the book Baruch by Justin, where the serpent is identified with the tree of the knowledge of Good and Evil, and is a child of the Demiurge called Elohim and of the maternal figure called Eden, Eve being her later representative. Before Justin's rather tormented and grotesque story is over, the serpent has sexually violated *both* Adam and Eve, but in the interest of purging from both their souls all traces of the unfaithful Demiurge Elohim. The priapic function of the serpent is thus to purify consciousness by a kind of sexual scourging. As an interpretation of J, this is fantastic but exuberant. But as interpretations of J, all the normative accounts, Jewish and Christian, are fully as fantastic and very far, alas, from being exuberant. Rhetorically, the normative misreadings tend to literalize J's ironies, whereas the Gnostic misreadings hyperbolize

those ironies. Our inability still to read J as being primarily an ironist, of his own very strange and difficult kind, is a dark tribute to
his permanent originality.

Our inability adequately to read J extends to almost all of
the Bible. But I intend eventually to write a full-scale study of facticity as the blocking-agent that thwarts revisionism, and in such a
study the Bible necessarily would take a central place. Here I am
concerned with the function of criticism as an agonist wrestling
with facticity, and I want to emphasize particularly two aspects of
that function: canon-formation and prophecy, aspects that overlap but do not coincide. The greatest critics, such as Dr. Johnson,
Coleridge, Hazlitt, Ruskin, Emerson, and Pater, perfect and
extend the canon, while simultaneously prophesying changes in
the use and understanding of the canon, changes which are not
far in the unapparent, but rather extend the full awareness of
what truly is the contemporary. Coleridge and Hazlitt had violently different affective reactions to Wordsworth and his poetry, but
they shared absolutely the prophetic and canonical sense that
Wordsworth indeed was in the process of inventing modern poetry. Emerson, despite all his genteel later reservations, saw and said
instantly and precisely just what Whitman was doing in the first
edition of *Leaves of Grass*. If Wallace Stevens had displaced Eliot
and Pound, to some large degree, or if John Ashbery is in the process of displacing Robert Lowell and John Berryman, such dis-
placements are movements proper to criticism, which must protect and yet correct the canon while prophesying accurately the
kinds of discernment appropriate to the time, time as it is breaking over and through us.

I hear and read continually the complaint that criticism is
now too much concerned with itself, and too little devoted to the
clarification of work more primary than itself. I am moved to the
counter-complaint that criticism is still too little concerned with
itself, because it manifests too much anxiety over method. The
quest of contemporary criticism is for method, and the quest is
vain. *There is no method other than yourself.* All those who seek for a
method that is not themselves will find not a method, but some-

one else, whom they will ape and involuntarily mock. Poetry and
fiction share with criticism the mystery that post-Structuralist speculation seeks to deny: the spark we call personality or the idiosyncratic, which in metaphysics and theology once was called presence. Finally we read one critic rather than another for the same
reasons we have to read one poet or novelist rather than another.
He or she imposes upon us because there is something there that
we cannot forget, in a very intimate way. I have a kind of preternatural memory for what I read, yet I remember Wallace Stevens
or Nathanael West or G. Wilson Knight very differently than I
remember Robert Frost or Thomas Pynchon or Lionel Trilling.
This difference, unforgettable, I ascribe to the more successful
revisionist struggle against facticity in Stevens, West, and Wilson
Knight, a struggle against and yet *within* facticity. But to describe
just *how* any revisionist struggles against facticity from within, I
need to resort to the authentic precursors of so dialectical an
agon. These precursors were the line of Hebrew prophets, from
Elijah to the Jesus of the Gospels, which returns me to J, the
Yahwist, as the textual founder both of this facticity and the
prophets who emerged from it. There is a difficulty, always, in
relating prophecy to facticity in J's tradition, a difficulty that is
most saddening when we contemplate any idealization of that tradition. I cite here a great idealizer, Martin Buber, who impresses
me now as a much more problematic figure than he seemed in
my youth.

> The prophetic faith involves the faith in the *factual* character of
> human experience, as existence that factually meets transcendence.
> Prophecy has in its way declared that the unique being, man, is creat-
> ed to be a center of surprise in creation. Because and so long as man
> exists, factual change of direction can take place towards salvation as
> well as toward disaster, starting from the world in each hour, no mat-
> ter how late.

I would say that what Buber omits here is indeed brute factuality, the facticity of the prophetic faith as *literary* experience. Man
may be created to be a center of surprise in creation, but the writing prophet cannot hope to be a center of surprise in literary creation. Elijah *is* a center of surprise, but Isaiah and even Jeremiah

are hemmed in by facticity. Originality is again the stairway of surprise when Elijah enters the Biblical text, because only the accents
of breakthrough could allow the sudden violation of facticity that
Elijah represents and accomplishes. The rhetorical cost is an
abruptness that Biblical scholarship has been unable to assimilate:

> Now Elijah the Tishbite, of Tishbe in Gilead, said to Ahab: "As the
> Lord the God of Israel lives, before whom I stand, there shall be nei-
> ther dew nor rain these years, except by my word."

This is not the uncanny tone of J, which acknowledges no
possible antagonist, but rather a rhetoric of authority which pre-
supposes enemies, though they be only the priests of the empty
god Baal, who does not live. The chronicler of Elijah is like J only
insofar as J contains him. J's irony, as exemplified, say, in the story
of Eve and the serpent, is beyond the range of Elijah's narrator,
who knows only the simple and savage irony of the unequal match
between Yahweh and Baal. This decline in irony becomes sharper
in the writing prophets, until irony becomes wholly reduced to a
terrifying pathos with Jeremiah's sense of humiliation and
abandonment.

I am suggesting that the prophets, while they rely upon their
asserted belief that they are returning to the God of Abraham,
Jacob, and Moses, nevertheless are caught up in the facticity constituted for them by J's text. Or to employ the Gnostic trope that
Heidegger associates with *his* concept of facticity, the prophets'
relation to J's text is one of having been thrown. The uncanny
Yahweh of J is literalized by the prophets, though less literalized
than he was to be by later normative interpreters down to our own
time. When we reach the popular vision of an old white-bearded
sage up in the clouds, satirized by Blake as Urizen, we have at
once the final product of J's facticity and the weakest possible misreading of J.

The popular mind is so given to enclosure by facticity as to
be wholly innocent of any urge toward battling facticity. More of a
concern for criticism is the urge to idealize literature that too frequently results in the idealization of facticity. Most literary exalta-
tions of tradition, let alone *the* tradition, are concealed acts of wor-

ship directed toward literary facticity. I could cite here again the
Eliot of "Tradition and the Individual Talent," where facticity
masks as an atemporal "simultaneous order" of great works, but I
am compelled to look at those who have affected me more intimately, at two of my own heroic precursors, M. H. Abrams and
Northrop Frye. What appears in Abrams as the "Romantic heterocosm" and in Frye as the "verbal universe" are two more subtly
veiled and idealized versions of facticity. Since Abrams and Frye
are legitimate spokesmen for historical High Romanticism, it sad-
dens me to say that they expose Coleridge and Blake as grand
weavers of facticity, dangerous idealizers of harsh and unpleasant
literary realities.

Literature is a discursive as well as a linguistic mode, and no
discourse, alas, is autonomous. It is true that strong poems love
and hate other strong poems, as it were, far more than they react
to other modes of discourse. In the battle against facticity, against
the confining strength of prior poetry, a poem has no weapons
except the stances and positions of freedom, and for a poem
these must be tropes. This limitation compels the subject matter
of belated poetry, now dismissed by Deconstruction as the rejected referential aspect of an achieved text, to take on a curious col-
oration, one that I have not been able to explain to nearly anyone's satisfaction or understanding. When I've said that a person,
place, thing, or event, to get into a poem, has to be treated as
though it already were a poem, I have been judged to be declaring the autonomy of poetry. Yet I thought I was expressing a limitation of poetry, rather than celebrating one of its powers. The
self may not be what Nietzsche once called it, a rendezvous of persons, but even the strongest poem indeed *is* a rendezvous of
poems. This means that even the most organized and written-
through poem is necessarily fragmentary. Facticity reduces not
only originality and autonomy, but also unity and self-sufficiency,
the heterocosmic qualities that the spiritualizers and idealizers of
literature are likeliest to discover, early and late.

Since I chose the facticity of J as my instance of that literary
concept, I feel obliged to illustrate the idealizing refusal of factici-

ty by a critic of the Bible, and Northrop Frye is now very much to hand. Frye's book, *The Great Code: The Bible and Literature*, culminates his lifelong work upon his favorite literary form, the anatomy, and so Frye implicitly treats the Bible as a vast anatomy. Nothing could be more imaginatively liberating, but alas, nothing is got for nothing, and that liberation is achieved at the expense of the Hebrew Bible, which indeed is consumed in Frye's great Blakean Code of Art, a fiery furnace worthy of the authors of *The Four Zoas* and *Fearful Symmetry*. Even the uncanny originality of J is melted down in the visionary flames of Toronto. Frye rightly insists that "There is no way of distinguishing the voice of God from the voice of the Deuteronomic redactor," but he does not explain away our ability to distinguish the voice of J from the voices of all of his redactors. Presumably Frye's answer would be this:

> It is futile also to try to distinguish what is "original" in the Bible, the authentic voices of its great prophetic and poetic geniuses, from the later accretions and corruptions sometimes alleged to surround them. The editors are too much for us; they have pulverized the Bible until almost all sense of individuality has been stamped out of it . . . . We are so possessed by the modern notion that all the qualities we admire in literature come from the individuality of an author that it is hard to realize that this relentless smashing of individuality could produce greater vividness and originality rather than less. But so it seems to be.

Frye's position here is consistent with his critical theory, and utterly at variance with my reading of the Hebrew Bible. Frye is curiously free of J's facticity, but this freedom is purchased by bondage to another facticity, the typological traditions of the Christian religion, which imprisoned even William Blake. Frye's Bible, as he says, "is the Christian Bible, with its polemically named 'Old' and 'New' Testaments." I myself would prefer to name these, not unpolemically, as the "Original" and "Belated" Testaments, since I join my ancestors in declining to see the earlier Testament as somehow being "fulfilled" in the later. But I do not see this so much as a quarrel between religions; rather, it is a struggle between critical theories. Frye is interested in the totality of literature, but I am interested primarily in the work of individual poets, those strong enough to force their way against facticity into a canon that is complete without them, and must be compelled somehow to need them. Frye has formulated what he calls a "myth of concern," which excludes any negation from the understanding of literature. Linguistic and rhetorical modes of negation, modern versions of the Hegelian negative, interest me rather less than Frye does, but negation as a psychic defense against belatedness, whether in Shelley or in Freud, is necessary to explain the agonistic element in poetry, which Frye's idealism denies in the face of endless evidence. Ambivalence, to Frye, is only an episode that poetic desire surmounts, but the desire of any individual poet is to surpass the precursors who created *him* through the Scene of Instruction. Frye's St. Paul is a refinement upon the prophets; the Paul I read is a strong misreader, an ephebe struck down on the road to Damascus by the light of the Necessity of Misreading, which became the muse of his own originality. There are no types and no archetypes; there is facticity and there is revisionism, and they battle either to a standstill or to facticity's yielding up of a new name to the revisionist.

Let me contrast Frye and Bloom on a single text, J's account of the wrestling match between Jacob and a nameless one among the Elohim, in Genesis 32:36. I've written about this episode twice before, in *The Breaking of the Vessels* and in the introduction to a volume of Martin Buber's essays on the Bible, and so I want to be brief about it here. Indeed, I want to imitate Frye's pithiness as best I can, since whatever my ambivalence, I worship that great critic's stance and style. Here is the last sentence of the seventh chapter of Frye's *The Great Code:* "The inference for the reader seems to be that the angel of time that man clings to until daybreak is both an enemy and an ally, a power that both enlightens and cripples, and disappears only when all that can be experienced has been experienced." I would say instead: "The angel of death that man clings to until daybreak is an enemy, a power that cripples, and disappears only when an impending death has been averted and a new name for man's persistence as an agonist has been won." Frye's reading has the virtue of balance, which I would call in this context a triumph for the Bible's facticity over Frye, or more simply, Frye has balance but J doesn't. Frye omits the angel's terror of daybreak, and the real viciousness of the night-long struggle. The being who cries out desperately, "Let me go, for it is daybreak!," is no ally, and precisely what Jacob has refused to experience is literal death. Is it harsh for me to say that the idealizing or typological reading here, even when performed by a master, is by no means wholly adequate to the force of J's text?

Frye's ultimate idealization, always, is his moving faith that "imaginative literature" is *not* an "anxiety-structure." He concludes *The Great Code* by saying that man builds anxiety-structures around his religious and social institutions. What Frye cannot or will not see is that artistic institutions (including canons, and academies, and traditions) are necessarily anxiety-structures also. The Bible, like any real literary canon, is *an achieved anxiety,* and not a pro-gram to release us from anxiety. For what can a canon, or an academy, or a tradition be unless it has some residual authority over us? Such authority is now only rhetorical, but the Bible's rhetoric of authority, whether in J or in the prophets, is far more individual and personal than Frye, on principle, can allow it to be. How did Jeremiah, a prophet whom it would be kind to call "defeatist," ever manage to impose himself upon the canon? An acute individualizing of voice is almost certainly the only realistic answer. Jeremiah's sufferings became exemplary only because they are memorable, because they dramatize, with striking harsh-ness, the endless dilemma of Jeremiah's people: caught through-out history, as they are today, between rival empires; always threat-ened, as they are today, by a much more numerous surrounding and hostile people. Frye says, quite wonderfully, and I think accu-rately, that "The prophet may be right or wrong, reasonable or unreasonable: the thing he does not do is hedge." Prophecy, in the Hebraic sense, indeed is oratory without qualification. The *nabi* speaks his *davar* or word, which is also Yahweh's. What is old-est and farthest back in the *nabi* is brought forward and presented straight out as an act. It is for this that the *nabi* was born – consecrated, as Jeremiah says he was, from the womb until death. But who will listen to an impersonal and generalized voice? Frye, I think, misses something of the meaning of *davar* when Jeremiah or Amos or Isaiah proclaims "Thus Yahweh speaks." The paradoxical evidence for the voice's authority, for the word being sent from Yahweh, is that the figuration be wholly personal and magnificently individual. A writing prophet is received only because of his rhetorical power, and this power of troping always must make its anxious way against the facticity of Moses, which means against the facticity of J.

I am arguing now not only against Frye, but against Buber, indeed against all Biblical criticism that I know, whether normative or scholarly-historical. But the prophetic figurations are to a considerable degree a kind of deceptive rhetoric. Contrast Isaiah's call, in Chapter 6 of his book, to the call of Moses, upon whose authority supposedly it is founded. Moses attempts to evade the call, but Isaiah volunteers, saying: "Here am I; send me." Moses asks Yahweh to name Himself, that he, Moses, may declare Who sent him when he descends into Egypt to speak to his fellow-Jews. Isaiah does not even know what he is being called upon to do or to say. The legacy of J declares itself only in the frightening irony of Yahweh's injunctions to Isaiah:

> Go, and tell this people:
> Hear ye indeed, but understand not;
> And see ye indeed, but perceive not.
> Make the heart of this people fat,
> And make their ears heavy,
> And shut their eyes;
> Lest they, seeing with their eyes,
> And hearing with their ears,
> And understanding with their heart,
> Return, and be healed.

Isaiah's irony, like J's, involves the clash of incommensurate orders of reality, the clash of Yahweh and his people – always a clash, rhetorically speaking, despite the promise of every covenant. But Isaiah's irony swerves away from J's into an irony less uncanny to us. J is never bitter; indeed, like Homer, J is sublimely beyond bitterness. Isaiah, strong poet though he be, falls into bitterness *in order to get started.* His bitterness is the cost of his call, or as we would say, the sign of his originality. It *individualizes* Isaiah, by making him memorable at the very start of his prophetic mission. J's Moses is genuinely bewildered that he, a man anything but eloquent, should have been chosen. Isaiah is a knowing latecomer, and he tropes his own conscious eloquence through the image of the glowing stone with which one of the seraphim touches his, the prophet's, mouth. That glowing stone upon the lips is as much Isaiah's mark for his own originality as the transparent eyeball was Emerson's, or the Holy Spirit brooding over the vast abyss to make it pregnant was Milton's. J as narrator of the tales of Jacob or of the Exodus feels no need for self-dramatization, though I hear his personal sign in the extraordinary tribute he pays Wrestling Jacob: "The sun rose upon him as he passed Penuel, limping on his hip." But Isaiah, like all of the writing prophets, and like the Milton of the invocations, cannot get started without dramatizing himself.

As critics we can only confirm the self-canonization of the truly strong prophets and poets. What we cannot do is invent their canonization for them. Nothing, of course, is more pathetic in literature than the bathos of the false prophets and the weak poets. Pindar and Milton celebrate themselves, and we are happy to concur, but how embarrassed we are by the canonical gestures of those who cannot write their way out of a paper bag, let alone out of the facticity of giants. In a secular age, or more simply in a literary culture, why ought criticism to address itself to the almost undisplaced religious concept of prophecy, as well as to the clearly displaced notion of canon-formation? After all, no one thanks you for a canonical enterprise, and the academy certainly has no use for prophets. Were it not better done, as others use the discipline, to allow canonization to proceed as an implicit process, and to wait for consensus on all issues as to the nature and function of poetry and criticism? Professor Moldy Fig and Dame Gentility hold the field as they always have held it, and why should they not?

I would begin an answer mildly enough, by observing that poetry is not a criticism of life, but the criticism of poetry is or ought to be. It is very late in the West, and the academies increasingly serve as our sundials. In the evening land, you can see some things more clearly than before, or more clearly than elsewhere, and by our falling light poetry is seen for what it has become, a criticism of earlier poetry, an evasion of overwhelming facticities. A criticism that thinks itself through, in our situation, will prophesy unto us merely by being as and where it is. Our Elijah or Supreme Critic was Freud, who preferred to see himself as Moses, but the preference was misleading. Freud, like J, was an uncanny writer who created a new and enormous facticity for all of us, whether or not we are aware of it. We literalize Freud's tropes every day of our lives, and we have no way of freeing ourselves either of the tropes or of our literalizations. It is Freud who wrote the poems of our temporality, as opposed, say, to the poems of our climate.

I want to take as a closing text a few observations made by Freud in his last book, the unfinished but definitive work called, with a false modesty, *An Outline of Psychoanalysis*. Just before Freud breaks off his manuscript, he describes the relationship between the *I* and the *Over-I* or *Above-I* – the ego and the superego, as translation has taught us to call them:

> A portion of the external world has, at least partially, been given up as an object and instead, by means of identification, taken into the ego – that is, has become an integral part of the internal world. This new mental agency continues to carry on the functions which have hitherto been performed by the corresponding people in the external world: it observes the ego, gives it orders, corrects it and threatens it with punishments, exactly like the parents whose place it has taken. . . . The superego is in fact the heir to the Oedipus complex and only arises after that complex has been disposed of. For that reason its excessive severity does not follow a real prototype, but corresponds to the strength which is used in fending off the temptation of the Oedipus complex.

Freud is moving overtly toward a scene of recognition in which he himself can identify the id with the organic past and the

superego with the cultural past. This would be, I think, the
Freudian explanation of what I have described as a literary state
of facticity, and such an explanation apparently would be at variance with my own theory of facticity, which assigns to precursor
figures something more of the role of the id than of the superego.
But Freud is too subtle not to have anticipated this, as he anticipates all legitimate criticism. He goes on to doubt his own generalizations, and observes:

> Some of the cultural acquisitions have undoubtedly left a deposit
> behind in the id; much of what is contributed by the superego will
> awaken an echo in the id . . .

Even as superego and id begin to blend together a little *in
this specific context,* Freud manifests a realization of how he is affected by the facticity that Goethe's *Faust* constituted for him. He
quotes a famous aphorism from Part I: "What you have inherited
from your fathers, / Strive to make it your own." And to illustrate
this Goethean paradox, Freud ends this unended and unendable
last book with a remarkable declaration:

> Thus the superego takes up a kind of intermediate position between
> the id and the external world; it unites in itself the influences of the
> present and of the past. In the emergence of the superego we have
> before us, as it were, an example of the way in which the present is
> changed into the past . . . .

Why Freud breaks off just there we cannot know, but as our
master he has taught us how to surmise in something of his spirit.
The superego, being above the *I* (and above the *it* also) is, like the
Freudian trope of the drive, a frontier concept, neither internal
nor external, neither psychic nor societal, neither subjective nor
objective. Freud wants us to believe that the superego represents
all our abandoned object affections, as well as the revenge that
the abandoned take upon us. Literary facticity, as I seek to
describe it, assimilates the superego to the id and makes of the
most powerful texts – the Bible, Shakespeare, Freud – a kind of
drive within us as well as a partly internalized spirit of revenge.
When the present is altogether changed into the past in the agon
of reading, then facticity has triumphed over the reader's
Sublime, which is to say, it has voided the function of criticism. So

powerful is Freud's own facticity for us that it prevents us from seeing the extent to which his reductive authority has augmented our inability to be strong critics.

I would surmise, though, that Freud's belated invention of the superego marks the crisis in his own repressed sense of being hemmed in by cultural facticity – by the combined force of Hebraic and Classical culture, of Moses or the Jahvist and of Homer, but also of Shakespeare and Goethe, and of those great precursor speculators, Schopenhauer and Nietzsche. Freud's own Counter-Transference or cultural guilt, provoked by his own enormous usurpation of authority, results in what could be called the revenge of Yahweh or of the Yahwist, which is the belated, painful birth of the superego, or the spirit of revenge. As the strongest modern exemplification of the reader's Sublime, or the agon against facticity, Freud paradoxically fostered what has become the inevitable trope for facticity. Having been thrown, we are subject to the harshness of the superego, which religious rebels once enjoyed calling the Demiurge.

Criticism cannot teach us to be Freud, or even how to avoid imprisonment by Freud. The function of criticism at the present time, as I conceive it, cannot be to liberate us from the brute factuality of our dependent relation to culture, whether that culture be Biblical or Freudian. But criticism alone can teach us to stop literalizing our cultural dilemmas. Education, when it is most authentic, centers upon the precise project of showing the student just what degree of freedom is possible for her or him in relation to the presentness of the cultural past. The most critical of educations never will be capable of totally convincing us that the figurations of the past *are* figurations and not literal entities. Yahweh and the superego will go on haunting us, whether or not we are persuaded that they are ironies or synecdoches or whatever. The strong critic does not arrive to exorcise the colors of our involuntary imaginings, but she or he does stand at the threshold of culture's haunted mansion to admonish us to enter, not even as the most alert among spectators, but as agonists armed with the past's own weapons, the only weapons that will defend us honorably against the force of the past.

Agon: Towards a Theory of Revisionism, by Harold Bloom, Oxford
University Press.
The Breaking of the Vessels, by Harold Bloom, University of Chicago
Press.

The titles of these books represent their author's critical stance:
Longinian and Nietzschean in the image of agon, Kabbalistic in
the image of the breaking of the vessels. (Neither book urges criticism to be creative. Either it is or it isn't.) Emerson remarked: "It
is the praise of most critics that they have never failed, because
they have attempted nothing." Jarry's Dr. Faustroll proclaimed:
"*Pataphysics* is a science which we have only just invented, and for
which there is a crying need." These are among the treasured
insights appropriated by the mild and amiable Emersonian and
Pataphysician under review. Appropriation indeed is his method,
and seems to him the only *literary* method, and so also the only
critical method. He is fond of telling his students "There is no
method except yourself," while acknowledging Nietzsche's principle that the self at best is "a rendezvous of persons." (Note, however, that the rendezvous is of persons and not of phonemes. Poems
are written by women and men, and not by language; poems matter only if we matter.)

When the author began his present critical enterprise some
fifteen years ago, he showed an early draft of what was to become
The Anxiety of Influence to a worthy constituent, who deprecated it

with the observation that whatever it was, it was not literary theory. It seemed that literary theory had to be philosophical, in the Continental mode of German philosophy from Hegel through Heidegger, a mode already undergoing linguistic elaborations in France. The author retrospectively acknowledges that his cautioner was prophetic, at least in regard to the tides of fashion. But our author remains unphilosophical, believing as he does that Longinus began criticism's quarrel with philosophy, or rather advanced it, since the origins of the quarrel go back to Protagoras and Gorgias, true precursors of an antithetical criticism. The extraordinary prestige of philosophy among contemporary critics baffles our author, who knows that philosophy, like religion, is a stuffed bird upon the shelf and not a live bird beckoning like a playing card in one's hand. As a mode of literature, criticism has only one live rival: Freud.

The author values most in his own works the *deliberate* jokes, which, as a pious Gnostic, he blames upon history or upon time, into which we have been thrown. So the agonistic relation between criticism and psychoanalysis is seen as a historicizing joke. "Freudian literary criticism" becomes a phrase much like "the Holy Roman Empire," since it is not Freudian, not literary, not criticism. Our author then is *not* a Freudian, but is precisely contrary to critics of either the Lacanian *or* the American Freudian persuasions. The Freudian tropes, having been appropriated *from* literature, are taken back by criticism when they are seen clearly as being tropes only. The "unconscious" is structured not like *a* language, but like Freud's language, since it is Freud's language.

Rather then continue to describe what our critic is *not*, let us employ him to attack certain stubbornly false cloven fictions that prevail in critical journalism. Formalism and anti-Formalism constitute a meaningless distinction, as this critic continuously shows; and even more strikingly, he exposes the lack of a pragmatic difference between "objectivity" and "subjectivity" in criticism. Another of his favorite appropriations is Nietzsche's "Who is the interpreter and what power does he seek to gain over the text?"

The skeptics (deconstructors) and idolaters (moldy figs) alike manifest the will to power, as do the feminists, Marxists, Heideggerians, and all the other current covens and sects. Skepticism is cleaner than the various pieties, but is finally not a jot more disinterested.

The title essay of *Agon* carries on this Nietzschean polemic, while arguing that supposed changes in critical method are mostly changes in diction. What after all is memorable in criticism? I would rephrase that after asking: What after all is memorable in verse? There, the answer is *poetry*. Well, just as most verse is not poetry, most of what we call criticism is not criticism, and should be called journalism. Most of what is now called theory is a kind of journalism also. Nearly everything we call literary scholarship is journalism – poor journalism, since it is not news. Actual criticism, like actual poetry, is rare, and about as much of it comes out of courses in criticism as poetry comes out of poetry workshops. Criticism is a literary art, and courses are no likelier to produce a Hazlitt than they are to bring forth a Melville. A convention of some fifteen thousand critics is as sublimely absurd a gathering as would be a convention of fifteen thousand "poets."

Criticism, like poetry, is progressively more agonistic because both literary arts, as they become more belated, must strain increasingly to say what cannot be said. Stevens remarked that the imagination was always at the end of an era. Hazlitt wrote a superb fragment arguing that the arts were not progressive. *They* are not, but their shadow-side progresses, ambivalently and anxiously. Beyond the pleasure principle was Freud's vision of the death drive in the life of the individual. Longinus, and Shelley after him, defined the literary idea of the sublime in terms oddly prophetic of Freud's fantasia. How can we distinguish pragmatically between urging a reader to yield up easier pleasures for those more difficult, and urging a reader to see that even writing and reading necessarily turn aggressivity more against the self and less against others?

The sad undersong both of *Agon* and *The Breaking of the Vessels* is that we cannot make that distinction. Our author conse-

quently emphasizes critical personality, or *the reader's Sublime.*
Journalism is written by avatars of Hermes, criticism by minglings
of Narcissus and Prometheus. In yielding up easier for more
difficult pleasures, we risk yielding up pleasure itself, but though
every Stevensian rightly murmurs, "It must give pleasure," Hazlitt
is our authority for criticism's coming to see and say, "It must give
power," perhaps even in place of pleasure:

> We are as fond of indulging our violent passions as of reading a
> description of those of others. We are as prone to make a torment of
> our fears, as to luxuriate in our hopes of good. If it be asked, Why we
> do so? the best answer will be, Because we cannot help it. The sense
> of power is as strong a principle in the mind as the love of pleasure.
> . . . The imagination, by thus embodying and turning them to
> shape, gives an obvious relief to the indistinct and importunate crav-
> ings of the will.

It is in this sense that our author, following Hazlitt, attempts
to write a poetics of power. Power, to a skeptic or deconstructor, is
only pathos. To a feminist or Marxist critic, power is something
worse, perhaps everything worse. To our author, the powers of literature are inextricably tangled with the will's indistinct and
importunate cravings, and in particular with the will's cravings for
revenge against time. Time says "It was," and the will's best
revenge is a strong poem. Nietzsche perhaps hoped for something
better than revenge, even against time's "It was," but we come
later, and all that a strong critic pragmatically can hope now is to
become a master of the lie. The author of *Agon* and *The Breaking
of the Vessels* has returned obsessively, book after book, to certain
poems: Browning's "'Childe Roland to the Dark Tower Came',"
Stevens's "The Auroras of Autumn," Shelley's "Ode to the West
Wind," and Hart Crane's "The Broken Tower" among them. But
most frequently the obsessive return is to Stevens's meditative
lyric, "The Poems of Our Climate," with its marvelous closing
lines:

> Note that, in this bitterness, delight,
> Since the imperfect is so hot in us,
> Lies in flawed words and stubborn sounds.

That can be reduced to: Because the cravings of the incomplete are so importunate in us, pleasure and/or power, in this brokenness, tell us untruths and yet reside in the most memorable of our poems. But the apposition of bitterness and delight defies reduction, and matters most. The antithetical will, what the Gnostics called the *pneuma,* is at the center here, and by its rugged negativity defies mere belated skepticisms, such as deconstruction. Negative theology retains its priority over all philosophical versions of the Negative, and our author is most himself as a trudger upon the *via negativa.* Jaroslav Pelikan, expounding Pseudo-Dionysius, dryly remarks: "The dogma of the Incarnation constituted a special vexation for the *via negativa."* So much the worse then for the Incarnation, or for any dogma of positive religion, negative theology always hints. Transposed to poetry, that means: So much the worse for presence, unity, and all the other illusions of an idealizing criticism. Positive scholarship is merely positivism, and our author is happy to see the slow, patient labor of the Negative in contemporary deconstruction. But his sympathy with Gallic skepticism ends just there. "Nothing can be like an idea except another idea" does for him the work of its retranslation as "There is nothing outside of the text." Blessed and cursed by total recall, there is for him no text anyway, but only that one continuous poem that Shelley prophesied and Borges parodies. His obsession with the trope of transumption reflects his vision of all poetry as being one giant metalepsis, an endless substitution of images of earliness for those of belatedness.

As a reader obsessed by poetry for some forty years, our author is not much attracted by the moldy fig dogma of the critics' function. Literally hundreds of reviewers have expressed their outrage that any reader should forget his proper place in regard to the poem. The best summary of the moldy figs' position belongs not to our author, but to Edward Said, who said that they saw the critic as Howard Cosell and the poet as Muhammad Ali.

Criticism is a teachable art, but like any art it relies upon a gift. Certainly the early manifestation of that gift is a bewildering, excessive love of poetry. But such love need not be idealized.

Love, as Wittgenstein said, is not a feeling. Unlike pain, he added, love is put to the test: "One does not say that was not a true pain because it passed away so quickly." Journalistic love of poetry cannot be put to any test. Our author has not learned from his moldy fig reviewers to regard them as authentic defenders of poetry.

I confess, as I end, that I do not find these two books very reviewable. Their genre is unclear, and their rhetoric is sometimes rather hyperbolical. Hyperbole, according to the author, is the trope of the Sublime. *A Tale of a Tub* is hardly our author's favorite reading, yet he rereads it twice a year, as the truest reproach he has been able to find. The truest wisdom he has found is alluded to in the final sentence of *The Breaking of the Vessels,* and is anything but an antithetical or a Gnostic adage. It is the central apothegm of normative Judaism, as squarely set forth by Rabbi Tarphon in *Pirke Aboth:* "It is not required of you that you complete the work, but neither are you free to desist from it."

Index

WRIGHT, JAY · BLACK WRITER